IF I GET OUT ALIVE

IF I GET OUT ALIVE

World War II Letters & Diaries
of William H. McDougall Jr.

Edited and with an Introduction by
GARY TOPPING

THE UNIVERSITY OF UTAH PRESS
Salt Lake City

The Defiance House Man colophon is a registered trademark of the University of Utah Press. It is based upon a four-foot-tall, Ancient Puebloan pictograph (late PIII) near Glen Canyon, Utah.

11   10   09   08   07   1   2   3   4   5

Library of Congress Cataloging-in-Publication Data

McDougall, William H.
  If I get out alive : the World War II letters and diaries of William H. McDougall Jr. / edited and with an introduction by Gary Topping.
      p. cm.
  ISBN 978-0-87480-891-9 (cloth : alk. paper) 1. McDougall, William H. (William Henry), 1909-1988—Diaries. 2. McDougall, William H. (William Henry), 1909-1988—Correspondence. 3. World War, 1939-1945—Prisoners and prisons, Japanese. 4. World War, 1939-1945—Personal narratives, American. 5. Sino-Japanese War, 1937-1945—Personal narratives, American. 6. Prisoners of war—Indonesia—Correspondence. 7. Prisoners of war—United States—Correspondence. 8. Prisoners of war—Indonesia—Diaries. 9. Prisoners of war—United States—Correspondence. I. Topping, Gary, 1941- II. Title.
  D805.J3M324 2007
  940.53'175981092—dc22
  [B]

                                                      2007000238

All illustrations courtesy of the archives of the Roman Catholic Diocese of Salt Lake City.

CONTENTS

Illustrations follow page 150

Acknowledgments

It was Bernice Maher Mooney, my predecessor as archivist of the Roman Catholic Diocese, who introduced me to the papers of Msgr. William H. McDougall Jr., one of the largest and richest collections of personal papers in the archives. But it was not until I became archivist in the fall of 2001 that I had a chance to delve deeply into the collection and to realize what a treasure it is, particularly the World War II letters and diaries that appear here. During the years I transcribed these documents and prepared them for publication, I have received consistent and enthusiastic support from the staff at the Diocesan Pastoral Center, particularly my supervisors, Deacon Silvio Mayo of the chancery office, Msgr. J. Terrence Fitzgerald, vicar general of the diocese, and Bishop George H. Niederauer.

Several brief sections of the diary were written in Pitman shorthand, a system which McDougall learned from one of the British inmates at Palembang. It was a system that never caught on in the United States, where Gregg shorthand reigned supreme, and the difficulty of finding a Pitman expert threatened to doom the project. Eventually, however, Mr. Pierre Savoie, a Pitman expert in Toronto, came to my rescue, and I am most grateful for his generous labors in my behalf.

Finally, I offer my thanks to the University of Utah Press for making this book possible: Peter H. DeLafosse, acquisitions editor; Patricia Degges, copyeditor; Glenda Cotter, managing editor; and Jinni Fontana, production manager, who saw the project through the production process. Thanks also to Sarah Hoffman, marketing manager. I'm sure there were others unknown to me working behind the scenes, and I offer my thanks to them as well.

—Gary Topping

INTRODUCTION

THIS IS A FIRSTHAND NARRATIVE of the experiences of an American newspaper correspondent in Tokyo and Shanghai on the eve of World War II, of his narrow escape from death at sea, and his internment in four brutal prison camps in Indonesia. It is a story of an indomitable human spirit, but even more than that it is a story of faith and hope and their ultimate triumph over evil and suffering. Although the participant has told his story before in two memorable books, it has never been told in the intimate detail of his letters and diaries presented here. In fact, although there are many World War II memoirs, there are few if any Prisoner of War diaries as extensive, articulate, and insightful as McDougall's.

William Henry McDougall Jr. (1909–1988) was born in Salt Lake City as the eldest child of William H. and Frances Tormey McDougall. The McDougalls raised their family, which included two daughters, Gertrude J. (born 1911) and Dorothy Jean (born 1915) in a house that is at this writing still in use at 659 South 11th East. William Sr., a naturalized American of Canadian birth, traveled a great deal as a mining investor in the Gunnison Oil Company and salesman of correspondence courses for International Correspondence Schools, of which he himself was a graduate. Gertrude married immediately after high school and moved to California. The three who remained at home formed a tight family nucleus, a bond strengthened by the fact that the two remaining children never married and their mother was for brief but frequent periods a *de facto* widow.

The family home is located directly across the street from Our Lady of Lourdes Catholic church. This is a significant fact because, while William Sr. did not become a Catholic until 1952, Frances McDougall was a lifelong Catholic who took her faith very seriously and saw to it that her children were raised in the church. Although this book is not primarily about her,

Frances McDougall's diaries are fascinating documents that offer an intimate picture of the daily life of a Catholic housewife and mother in Salt Lake City in the middle years of the twentieth century. What they reveal is a seriously depressive personality struggling to mitigate the daily drudgery of domesticity by immersing herself in church participation (daily Mass, the Altar Society, and the Catholic Woman's League) and civic volunteerism. Although she was profoundly proud of her children's professional attainments—Bill as a locally renowned newspaper reporter, and Jean (as Dorothy Jean was known) as an official at Continental Bank—the glamor of their lives contrasted with the drudgery of hers and probably deepened her depression.

William H. McDougall Jr. was educated in public schools and Judge Memorial High School. After graduating from the University of Portland (Oregon), he went to work for the *Salt Lake Telegram*, where his reporting was distinguished by his use of pigeons to file up-to-the-minute stories from remote locations, particularly airplane crashes, which for some reason became a specialty of his.

On the eve of World War II, McDougall quit his job and sailed to Japan, where he worked on the Tokyo English language paper, the *Japan Times*. From there he moved to Shanghai, where he worked as a United Press correspondent. In that capacity he covered the fall of the Netherlands East Indies (Indonesia) to the Japanese. He escaped on a Dutch ship, but it was sunk by Japanese warplanes in the Indian Ocean and he barely survived by being picked up by a lifeboat after hours adrift in the water, an experience narrated in his *Six Bells Off Java*. Although the boat reached Sumatra, its occupants were captured and McDougall spent the next three years (1942–45) in Japanese prison camps, as told in his second book, *By Eastern Windows*.

Though both of McDougall's books are long since out of print, they enjoyed an extensive audience in their day, published by Scribner's and reprinted more than once for his local audience by Sam Weller's Western Epics in Salt Lake City. The present volume in no way supplants them, even though their narrative begins with his arrival in Shanghai and omits the observations given here in his letters from Tokyo during the early years of the war and during Japan's descent into conflict with the United States. Both books contain previously unrecorded material from McDougall's memory as well as his matured reflections on his experiences.

The letters from Japan and China during the early years of World War

II selected for this volume are mostly limited to those written to educate his family about the social, political, and military circumstances in those countries as the rest of the world pondered their likely roles in the developing maelstrom. Written by a prolific, articulate, and observant journalist, they offer a detailed and penetrating look at a collapsing world even though McDougall refused almost to the end to believe that the developments he was describing carried a serious threat to the United States.

When the Pearl Harbor attack at last did come, McDougall had been transferred to Japanese-occupied Shanghai, where obviously he and other Americans immediately came under jeopardy of capture. With the help of an emergency loan from a Catholic priest and aided by infiltrators from the free Chinese provinces held by Chiang Kai-shek, McDougall and two of his colleagues made a dramatic escape, memorably recounted in *Six Bells Off Java*, first to free China and then to Calcutta.

Although many people by that time may have had enough of staying one jump ahead of the Japanese, McDougall leaped back into harm's way. In the expansion of the Japanese through southeast Asia up to 1942, the rich oil fields of Borneo had already fallen into their hands, and they were close to taking Singapore. The next target would be the Indonesian islands with their tempting resources of petroleum, rubber, and metals. The island of Sumatra appeared doomed, but it looked as though the Allies had a chance of halting the Japanese advance in Java. McDougall caught the first plane to its capital city, Batavia.

It was a fateful move. The Allies found that their best hope of halting the Japanese was actually Singapore, and when it fell they could not hold Java. Although McDougall and five other correspondents who stayed to cover the battle filed some memorable stories, they quickly found themselves on the run again and this time what McDougall had once referred to as his "incredibly good luck" ran out. The last opportunity to leave the island was the Dutch passenger vessel *Poelau Bras*. With McDougall aboard, the ship sneaked out of Wijnkoops Bay, an obscure harbor on Java's southern coast, during the night of March 6, 1942, hoping to put enough open sea between it and the island that it would be out of reach of the limited range of Japanese bombers who would be searching for it the next morning. The ploy almost worked, but shortly after 11:00 a.m. on the following day, at the very outermost limit of their range, Japanese planes found and sank the ship.

McDougall's desperate hours of floating in the ocean, his improbable last-chance rescue by lifeboat, his arrival in Sumatra and eventual capture are all vividly narrated in *Six Bells Off Java* and in the diary entries in this volume. For the next three and one-half years Indonesia would be his place of residence. What kind of place was it?

Indonesia—known before its independence in 1949 as the Netherlands or Dutch East Indies—is a famously large, wealthy, beautiful, complex, and politically troubled nation. Consisting of some thirteen thousand islands in the south Pacific, fewer than half of which (about six thousand) are inhabited, Indonesia throughout its history has been profoundly shaped by a succession of invaders.

The first of those of whom we have record were immigrants from other southeastern Asia countries who implanted the Hindu and Buddhist religions among Indonesia's indigenous tribes around the beginning of the Christian era. Much more important were Arab mariners who began trading there during the Middle Ages and whose religion was so widely accepted that Indonesia, which in modern times has been almost 90 percent Muslim, is the world's largest Islamic nation.

The first Westerners to discover the islands were the Portuguese, who opened trading centers in the mid-sixteenth century. By the seventeenth century, though, they had been supplanted by the Dutch, who eventually consolidated the vast region into a colony. Dutch hegemony did not go unchallenged, for the British made significant inroads into Sumatra during the early nineteenth century. Although Dutch rule prevailed, the British presence continued in Sumatra in the form of individual plantations and corporate enterprises exploiting the island's resources. Thus there were both Dutch and British contingents in the prison population with McDougall, and it is not surprising that the testy prewar relations between them carried over into prison life.

The indigenous population was another story. European colonialization had bred ill will among native peoples everywhere, as they saw profits from exploitation of natural resources flow into European pockets, while western culture forcibly supplanted indigenous tradition and self-government gave way to political dominance by an alien elite. Thus when Japan began its expansion down the east coast of China, into southeast Asia, and out into the south Pacific in the late 1930s and 1940s, driving the western colonial powers before it, the exploited indigenous peoples sometimes welcomed the Japanese as fellow Asian liberators. It was an image the Japanese carefully cultivated as they welcomed new members into the empire they called the "Southeast Asia Co-Prosperity Sphere." In virtually every case, though, disillusionment with that image was not long in coming, especially when the promised "liberation" did not include prosperity. Thus during McDougall's Sumatran internment, he found the indigenous people arrayed across a considerable spectrum, from the "hi-hos," the Indonesian guards who found it expedient to collaborate with the Japanese soldiers, to the peasantry in the surrounding countryside who saw their best advantage in secretly trading with the prisoners.

Japan had good reason to covet Indonesia, which became one of its most productive possessions. Particularly after the United States embargo on metal and petroleum exports in 1940, the Japanese found Indonesia's vast oil deposits and groves of rubber trees essential to the infrastructure of their war machine. And rice, which then and now has been Indonesia's primary agricultural product, was essential for the sustenance of Japanese military personnel. Although the indigenous Indonesians as well as the Dutch and British colonists scuttled all the Indonesian industry they could in advance of the Japanese occupation, McDougall's diaries document the process by which the occupiers discovered those who knew how to get things functioning again and forced them to do so.

Only three Indonesian islands figure in this book's narrative. Java is the most populous and highly civilized island; its chief city, Batavia (now Jakarta), has been the capital of both the colony and the modern nation. Sumatra is the largest Indonesian island where McDougall was held in its largest city, Palembang, and in Belelau, an old rubber plantation from which he was liberated in 1945. Bangka is a small island a short distance northeast of Sumatra where he was held at Muntok in an old Dutch prison.

Sumatra is a long, narrow island oriented southeast to northwest at the western end of Indonesia almost touching Malaysia (Malaya in McDougall's day) along its eastern shore. A densely jungled mountain range runs longitudinally along Sumatra's western half, defying human habitation except for primitive jungle settlements. Thus most of Sumatran civilization is located along its eastern half, particularly throughout the complex drainage of the Moesi River in the southeast.

Palembang, a city of some 108,000 inhabitants in McDougall's day, built largely on pilings to protect it from flooding, sits astride the Moesi. The river is deep enough to admit large oceangoing vessels as far upstream as Palembang provided they were willing to wait for the flood tide to float them over the shallow bar at its mouth. Many were, for Palembang was the entrepôt for the agricultural and mineral wealth of the island's interior and for the produce of oil wells in the immediate vicinity of the city, refined in a Dutch facility there. Thus, with its oil derricks vying with its immense mosque for dominance of the skyline, Palembang was a tropical version of many oil-wealthy Islamic cities of the Middle East.

Once captured in Sumatra, McDougall all but completely vanished from the consciousness of everyone but his captors and fellow captives. Although he himself, following his reporter's instinct, devoured the rare and outdated news reports that filtered into the camps and even weighed the likelihood of the rumors that were much more common, virtually no news of him reached the outside world. But, to the immense benefit of our understanding of his experience, he communicated daily with the diaries that he secretly kept during the entire internment.

As the diaries document, McDougall's experience varied greatly among the four camps in which he was interned. The first two, in Palembang where he was kept from April 5, 1942, to September 1943, were country clubs in comparison to the other two. Food was adequate in quantity and varied, tobacco and even alcohol were available, and the prisoners' daily routine was largely of their own devising. Many of the prisoners were well educated Dutch or British colonial administrators or technocrats who offered classes or at least tutoring in languages or technical subjects, and McDougall helped organize a weekly series of formal lectures. Books were plentiful, and McDougall's diaries are full of his critical evaluations of his current reading. A few musical instruments were available, and the prisoners formed choirs and even staged musical variety shows on special occasions. McDougall plied his own specialty by producing a newspaper, the *Camp News,* in both English and Dutch editions and illustrated in color by a Dutch inmate.

To be sure, the prisoners were never tempted to forget that they were prisoners. Women and children were separated from husbands and fathers and communicated mostly through letters smuggled past the generally lackadaisical guards. There were regular morning roll calls and surprise musters at other times if the guards suspected someone had escaped. Prisoners were allowed outside the camp only for hospital visits or under tightly guarded work parties. Although the relationships between the prisoners and their Indonesian guards—as well as their Japanese superiors—were generally amicable, McDougall was suspicious enough of them that when he was transferred to the Muntok prison on Bangka Island, he hid his diaries and copies of *Camp News* under the floorboards of one of the buildings. (They were still in excellent condition when he picked them up after being liberated two years later.)

Muntok, by contrast, and only to a slightly lesser degree Belelau, were hellholes where some of humanity's greatest inhumanities were constant facts of life. Deaths from dysentery or from beri-beri (a consequence of malnutrition easily avoidable by a balanced diet or doses of vitamin B) were daily occurrences, and the total, carefully tallied in McDougall's diaries, built to hideous proportions. (It was McDougall's responsibility to type out the death certificates, so the mortality level was a vivid statistical fact to him.) Because McDougall worked as a hospital aide as long as his own strength held out, we have an intimate picture of Japanese prison camp life at its worst, and his diaries are the story of one man's struggle to retain his faith and optimism amidst unspeakable suffering.

Such demoralizing conditions eroded civility among the prisoners. A heightening of the congenital hostility between the British and Dutch colonists made self-government among the prisoners difficult, and individual personality quirks and flaws became magnified. It is in their dissection of those relationships that the diaries are especially valuable, for McDougall's books, written while most of the camp survivors were still alive and might be hurt if the ugliness of their behavior under stressful conditions was fully portrayed, understandably pull their punches.

A final word concerning editorial method: it has not been my intention to produce a scholarly edition with flawless transcription and full documentation of persons and events mentioned in the original manuscripts. Such an edition would far exceed my reservoir of energy and my historical expertise. The typescript letters have presented few transcription problems other than silent corrections of typographical and grammatical errors that inevitably crept in as McDougall pounded them out after a long day's work and a well deserved cocktail hour.

The diaries, on the other hand, offer immense transcription problems. Apparently unsure of the continued availability of the vest-pocket notebooks he used for his diaries, McDougall wrote in a tiny crabbed script with pens and pencils that often blurred words. It conserved paper, but at a high price of illegibility. I have done my best within a reasonable expenditure of labor and time to produce a complete and accurate transcript, revisiting each problematic passage at least once after the initial transcription. Gaps in legibility still remain, indicated by empty brackets—[ ]—or by bracketed question marks—[?]—where I have ventured a reasonable guess.

Scholars who have the time and energy to wrestle with the McDougall script at a deeper level than I will have ready access to the originals and my every encouragement.

Nor have I troubled myself to try to identify every bureaucratic functionary, military officer, or fellow prisoner McDougall mentions. McDougall himself supplies that information in most cases where it really matters, and where it does not, I have generally allowed that person to pass across the stage and identify himself only through the role he plays.

In the interest of smooth reading, I have silently expanded into standard English the journalistic shorthand McDougall often employed to save space and also no doubt out of long practice in taking rapid interview notes as a newspaperman. Thus "ex" becomes "from" or "out of," and "uppack" becomes "pack up."

Finally, parts of seventeen pages of his four-by-six-inch diary notebook in late 1943 are written in Pitman shorthand, which McDougall learned from one of the British inmates. Pitman was edged out in popularity in the United States by the Gregg system, but I have been fortunate in finding Mr. Pierre Savoie of Toronto, who generously transcribed those passages for me. They are marked in the text below by bracketed notes. I have taken the liberty of editing Mr. Savoie's text in the interest of readability, but I have preserved an unedited copy of his transcription in the McDougall papers for consultation by any interested reader.

If this is not a scholarly edition, I hope that it is not an *un*scholarly one. My goal has been a readers' edition for a general audience, and I have documented everything I thought essential to that audience's understanding and enjoyment. As Shakespeare reminds us, "the play's the thing," and I hope my readers will agree that the advantage of this light editorial hand is the timely appearance of these memorable documents.

IF I GET OUT ALIVE

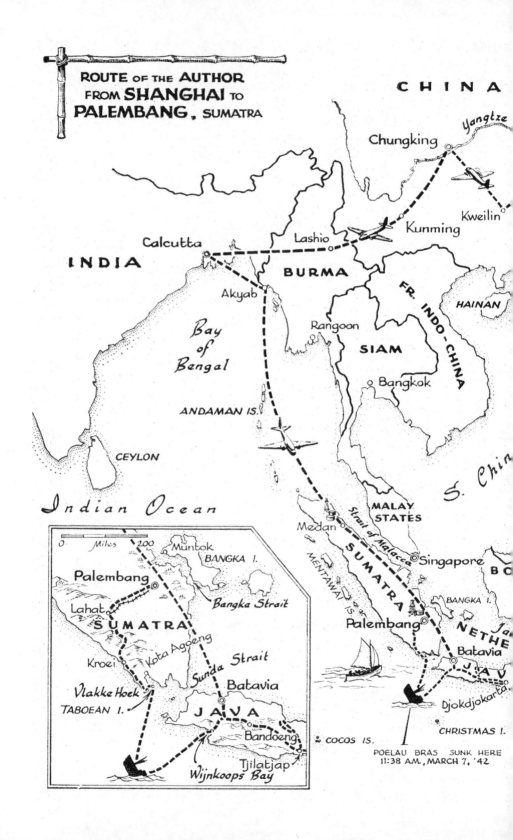

ROUTE OF THE AUTHOR
FROM SHANGHAI TO
PALEMBANG, SUMATRA

CHINA

Yangtze

Chungking

Kweilin

Kunming

Lashio

Calcutta

INDIA

Akyab

BURMA

Rangoon

HAINAN

FR. INDO-CHINA

*Bay
of
Bengal*

SIAM

Bangkok

ANDAMAN IS.

CEYLON

S. Chin

Indian Ocean

MALAY
STATES

Medan

Strait of Malacca

SUMATRA

MENTAWAI IS.

Singapore

BO

BANGKA I.

Palembang

NETHE

Ja

Batavia

JAV

Djokdjokarta

COCOS IS.

CHRISTMAS I.

POELAU BRAS SUNK HERE
11:38 A.M., MARCH 7, '42

Miles
0   200

Muntok

BANGKA I.

Palembang

Bangka Strait

Lahat

SUMATRA

Kota Agoeng

Strait

Kroei

Sunda Strait

Batavia

Vlakke Hoek

TABOEAN I.

JAVA

Bandoeng

Tjilatjap

Wijnkoops Bay

— LETTERS —

Might as well start from the beginning. The boat docked in Yokohama January 12. Tokyo hotels were full so we scattered and eventually found accommodations in Yokohama, which is about 30 minutes train ride from Tokyo. Four of us stayed at the Bund hotel in Yokohama and I finally got a room in the Dai-Iti hotel in Tokyo and moved up here. On the 15th I visited the *Japan Times* and landed a job immediately, starting to work the following day. Incidentally, Jim Tew, my cabin mate on the boat and a young New York newspaper man, today was promised a job on the *Advertiser*, beginning Friday, February 2.

I moved from the Dai-Iti, a depressing place, to the YMCA, even more depressing, and then to my present abode, the famed Imperial Hotel—single without bath for 150 yen a month. Intend to stay here quite a while.

Japan is a strange country to one who has never been here before. Everything is done absolutely opposite to American custom. It is a man's country, women are just necessities. Men don't give women seats on street cars, or anywhere else, women give men the seats. The wife walks behind her husband on the street. Speaking of seats however, children are supreme. The Japanese idolize their children, or anybody else's children. Time and again I have seen men and women get up and give their seats to children.

People do not shake hands on meeting, they bow deeply. Kissing is frowned upon, abhorred in fact. There is no such thing as "right of way." It is left of way, since all vehicular and foot travel is to the left. It's disconcerting to drive down the left side of the street. I still have a tough time looking right instead of left when stepping from the curbing into the street.

There are no raucous automobile horns, the horns are soft little toots. There are few automobiles, because of a gasoline shortage. The only vehicular traffic is taxi cabs, trucks and a few privately owned automobiles of the very rich or diplomatic corps.

There is no such thing as personal privacy. Men and women bathe in the same gigantic tubs at the same time. There are large public baths. The

Japanese love to bathe, they soak for hours in water hot enough to boil eggs. I lost two layers of skin the first time I innocently jumped into one, at least it felt that way. The whole thing is acutely embarrassing at first but you get over it. In a hotel like the Imperial, of course, it's different, but only superficially.

The thing that impressed me most, however, was the numbers of people. You get the impression of millions and millions of people swarming like ants over one another. Trains are jammed. Street cars are jammed. Theaters are jammed. You're wedged into something all the time. Space is at a terrific premium.

People stand for hours in lines to get theater seats. I went to a show one night with a young fellow, a student at the Imperial university. We stood up through one picture, with scores of other persons. When the film ended seats were vacated quite a distance from us, too far to get to ahead of other standees, but he solved the problem neatly. He had a small leather brief case which he sailed expertly through the air, about five seat rows in fact, and it landed right on one of the vacant seats. Then he sailed my hat into another one—all of which, according to custom here, clinched the seats for us and no one tried to take them, they let us through to them.

The Japanese are extremely polite and will go to great lengths to assist a stranger. I directed a taxi driver to take me to the Domei building where the press service offices are, that is I showed him the written address. He couldn't speak a word of English but he got the general idea. However, he couldn't figure out the exact spot—there are no street numbers in Tokyo—so he stopped his cab in the street, went into a building and came out with some people. They held a big conference and others on the sidewalk joined in. It must have been amusing to watch, me gesturing and drawing pictures and the whole crowd offering suggestions in Japanese. He finally got me there.

It is surprising, though, how many people speak English, or at least can read and write it if not pronounce it. And that's another thing. Somehow we expect the Japanese to understand us, especially hotel clerks and the like. Imagine what chance a Japanese with no knowledge of English would have of getting a hotel clerk in the United States to speak or understand Japanese. But plenty of Japanese here know English.

Tokyo is a strange mixture of ancient and modern times. Kimonos and old time, elaborate head dresses are worn by most of the women. But they also wear American style clothing. In a group of prosperous business men may be those garbed in latest cut suits or large sleeved kimonos, or whatever the male garments are called. Most Japanese wear sandals of various kinds with a strap dividing the big toes from the rest of the toes.

The city is full of tea houses and bars, all very small. Between the Imperial Hotel and the Ginza (main business sector) is a section of narrow streets with nothing but bars and tea houses, all full of girl hostesses.

You order a cup of tea or a glass of beer and a pretty little girl sits beside you to keep you company. She can't speak English, you can't speak Japanese, but she smiles and pours your beer and appears to be thoroughly enjoying herself.

As I mentioned before there are no street numbers, or at least very few. Your office isn't at 234 Blank street, it is in the vicinity of Joe Doakes corner, Fourth ward, Emigration Sector, 12th Precinct, Tokyo. The mailman must have a tough time.

Life is cheap, or at least its loss is played down. Yesterday, for example, there were numerous disasters in Japan. A gasoline powered railroad car overturned and 176 people were burned to death, and 68 seriously hurt. It got a two column head in the *Times*, a one column in the *Advertiser*. No banner line.

Remember the Southern Pacific streamliner in Nevada last fall?

Terrific snow storms and snow slides in northern Japan, only a few hundred miles from Tokyo, have taken 20 lives, tied up all traffic, etc., the last two days. Many more died last week from the same cause. It gets five paragraphs. Fires inflicted terrific losses in life and property in various places over the weekend. 8 paragraphs.

Asama Maru incident, when British stopped Japanese liner and took off 21 German seamen, is about 10 days old. Tonight's paper devoted four columns to it, smallest space yet, average has been six to 10 columns.

Although no airplane crashes, serious ones, have occurred since I've been here, I'm told they are buried in three or four paragraphs when they do occur.

It's all a matter of relative values, I guess. We look at things differently.

Human interest stories, in English language newspapers at least, are rare. Everything is politics, international affairs, government domestic policy. When I say rare, there just aren't any in our sense of the word. Occasionally something crops up that to an American is side splittingly funny but is very serious to the Japanese. The other day I handled a story, we do nothing but rewrite English translations of Japanese news papers, which detailed some brilliant police work.

It seems that a ring of high powered shoplifters were operating in Tokyo and Osaka—comparable to New York and Chicago—stealing goods in one city for sale in the other. In fact they opened their own retail shops in some instances. In the very last sentence of this long winded yarn was the revelation, tacked on as sort of an afterthought by the translator, that the thieves, in order to "improve their skill held contests on the one who could steal the most expensive articles and the one who stole the most expensive article was given the first prize which was 1000 yen and a girl." Wow!

A few more observations....

In some restaurants, instead of getting a finger bowl at the meal's end a hot towel is handed the customer so he can wipe his face and hands. Higher class, strictly Japanese places, also serve the towel before eating. Teeth are picked at the table, with much ceremony, but one must cover one's mouth with the free hand.

Overcoats and hats are worn while eating in most restaurants, probably because of the temperatures, which are plenty low right now.

Shoes are left at the door, you don special slippers or walk in stocking feet.

Department stores are open on Sunday and closed on Monday. Most shops remain open until 11 p.m. At 11 p.m. the town practically folds up, bars, restaurants, tea houses close, street cars stop running shortly after midnight as do commuter trains.

Geisha girls ride to work or home from work in closed rickshas. The rickshas are coal black and on the handle is a tiny horn which the ricksha pullers toot occasionally.

Japan is a colorful place and Tokyo is a city of gaily garbed women and twinkling, colored lights. Color plays an important part in people's lives. I'm looking forward to spring, when the blossoms are out in the country side.

Sunday Tew and I went to Kamakura, a sea side resort an hour's train ride from here, where we saw the largest bronze statue of Buddha in Japan, a gigantic figure, 46 feet tall, that has been squatting for countless centuries near the sea. At a great Shinto shrine in another portion of the city there were hundreds of doves, which perch on your shoulder and eat out of your hand. Small packages of grain are sold at the shrine especially for the doves.

This country is a strange contrast between the machine age and ancient manpower. When our ship entered Yokohama harbor it was surrounded by sampans, each with its square sail plus a sort of sculling oar on the rear, which the navigator pushed back and forth and churned his craft ahead.

This also is a country of bicycles, more so, I guess, because of the gasoline shortage, caused by war time needs. Often times it is an impossibility to get a taxicab and when you do get one, and intend going [for] a long ride, you must ask the driver if he has enough gasoline to get you there. Since the driver tries to coast most of the way it's pretty slow going sometimes.

Tokyo is an excellent place to be right now, Japan being the center of the Far Eastern theater. I'm anxious to know how much news space U.S. papers are giving the Orient, especially in view of the trade treat abrogation and the *Asama Maru* case. How about sending a few news papers to me?

I'm beginning to feel right at home here already. My only regret is I didn't come sooner, several years ago in fact, before the China Affair, in order to have seen Japan at its best.

My working hours are from 9 a.m. to 4:30 p.m. and on Saturday nights to about 10:30 p.m. getting out the Sunday morning paper. We get an hour off for lunch. There is one other American on the paper and two Japanese born in America. The rest are native Japanese. All our news is behind the Japanese language newspapers because most of it is a translation of them. but it's still news to the English reading "public.

⌐ "SIDELIGHTS ON THE PRESS IN JAPAN," McDOUGALL RADIO ADDRESS, MAY 18, 1940

The next time you pick up an English language book, magazine or newspaper which bears the label "Printed in Japan," stop a moment and think. In all probability the men who actually printed that publication, that is, the linotypers, pressmen and printers, did not know a word of English. To them English is just as much a jumble of sounds and symbols as Japanese is to the average American.

There are 236 English language publications in Japan and how they are printed, always, to me, was a major mystery. It still is, even though I see it done every day. I am an American newspaper man working on an English language newspaper in Tokyo.

Most of you listening in America are familiar with the American newspaper setup. How a story is gathered by a reporter, telephoned to the city desk and written by a rewrite man, who hands the finished yarn to the city editor. The city editor designates the "play" or position in the news it deserves and the headline it will bear. Then the story goes to the copy desk for copyreading and the headline is written. Both then go to the composing room for setting in type. It is a fast-moving, complicated process and every man on the job is an expert at his business and knows the English language thoroughly. He has to.

But it is not that way in Tokyo. Only a few men who handle the news can read or write English. Let's take a look at an English language newspaper in Japan.

First of all, there are no reporters. An American reporter cannot speak, read or write Japanese, so he would be useless as a reporter. At the present time there is only one exception to this rule. On my paper is a reporter who can speak a little Japanese, so he meets boats coming from America or other foreign countries and interviews prominent passengers who cannot speak Japanese.

Ninety-nine per cent of our news comes from two sources—wire news reports from abroad or local news translated from Japanese language newspapers.

We have a staff of translators, native Japanese who have learned enough English to translate the Japanese characters into English words. As soon as the translation is made, the story is given to an American newspaper man who rewrites it into a readable story and in a style to which American readers are accustomed. The reader gets nearly day old news, but then he is fortunate to get anything he can read at all.

Sometimes, as the deadline nears, and there is no time for rewriting, the translator's pure, unadulterated effort gets into print with ludicrous results.

The rewrite man also does something no rewrite man in the United States ever does, namely, he copyreads, edits and writes the headline on his own story.

Then comes the strangest part of all. The story goes to the composing room to be set in type. Not a man in the place knows a word of English. Letters and words are only pictures to the linotypers, printers and oftentimes to the proofreaders. But they have learned those pictures so well they seldom make a mistake in copying. Of course, if a serious "boner" already is in the story, having slipped by the editor, the linotyper blithely sets it without ever knowing the difference. And there again, some extremely strange appearing words or sentences get into print, for the proofreader also lets it go by, happy that the original copy checks with the galley proof.

If this all sounds strange to you, consider the plight of the Japanese language newspaper. There, every word of type must be set by hand because no linotype ever has been invented to accommodate the Japanese written language. There are only 26 letters in our alphabet, and every word is a combination of those letters, but to even skim the content of a Japanese language newspaper, one must know at least 3,000 characters!

Journalism plays a prominent part in Japanese life. Nearly every Japanese can read and write, the percentage of literacy in Japan being nearly the highest in the world. However, modern journalism here owes its start to America. The man who founded journalism in Japan was a native Japanese fisherman who was shipwrecked in 1850, rescued by an American vessel, brought to the United States and later became an American citizen.

His name was Joseph Heco. Heco was the first Japanese to become an American citizen. He had never learned to read or write his own language. So, when he returned to Japan years later as a naturalized American, he could speak but not write Japanese. He founded the first newspaper in Japan, dictating in Japanese American newspaper reports to a Japanese assistant who wrote them in Japanese. Heco then printed them on a home made press. Joseph Heco died in Tokyo in 1897 and is buried here in a cemetery reserved for foreigners.

From the time of Joseph Heco until today, great strides have been made in Japanese journalism. From a circulation standpoint two of the largest newspapers in the world are published in Tokyo, the *Asahi* and the *Nichi Nichi*; the daily circulation of each reportedly is over 3,000,000.

There are hundreds of smaller publications. As I mentioned previously there are 236 English language publications, seven of them daily newspapers and the remainder varying from weeklies to annuals. In addition to the English language publications there are periodicals in French, Italian, German, Spanish and other languages.

The current China hostilities and other international unrest have resulted in an acute shortage of pulp, which means a shortage of paper. The paper shortage, however, has resulted in one astounding phenomenon—

newspaper publishers dictate to advertisers instead of advertisers dictating to publishers. I am speaking now of Japanese language newspapers.

Thus, publishers in Japan have realized the great dream of every American publisher—to get advertising revenue without strings attached.

The reasons are that, despite the shortage of paper there have been sharp increases in circulation and decreases in space. To meet the demand, editions of fewer pages are printed and the number of editions per day is reduced, in order to stretch the limited amount of paper into more copies. This resulted in an acute space shortage. Merchants with goods to sell suddenly discovered they couldn't buy advertising space to tell about them. Advertising rates shot up, space is at a premium. Now it is the advertiser who fawns on the heretofore-kicked-around advertising solicitor instead of the solicitor fawning on the advertiser. To the journalists' joy the old order has been reversed.

The space the advertiser can have is limited. Full page ads for toilet goods, department and grocery store merchandise or doubtful patent medicine cure-alls are no more. No newspaper will accept them. Rates have risen and ads are accepted only from well established clients who faithfully will pay the contracted price.

With advertisers clamoring for more space and circulation skyrocketing, all daily newspapers would be amassing fortunes if only they could get more newsprint. There's the catch. More newsprint to print more papers, and bigger papers to carry more and bigger ads.

Present indications are that pulp will become even more scarce. All I hope is that it will not become so scarce I'll be out of a job.

⇀ To his mother, June 10, 1940

Don't get too wrought up over news from Tokyo. A lot of it is pure wind....

Your informant is wrong about no one being able to learn conversation in Japanese. There are many Americans here who speak good Japanese, old timers, and more recent comers who speak a fair amount of Japanese. Relman Morin of AP has been here three years and speaks it well enough to carry on a decent conversation. There is a German fellow on the *Times*, the music critic, who learned to read and write it, plus speaking it, in a year. He was a notable exception however, and still amazes the Japanese with his accomplishment.

Please don't worry about me. I'm as safe as a bug in a rug. Keeping more regular hours than for years. Am in fine health, and this country is more tranquil than you could possibly imagine without seeing it for yourself.

To the average man in the street, the war in China is an abstract thing, except when its economic consequences pinch him. The people's apathy is seriously alarming the powers that be, too. They are frantically trying to organize a mass political party with Prince Fumimaro Konoye, [the] only man the people trust, at its head. Their spiritual mobilization drive collapsed long ago, collapsed before it ever started because the people didn't give a hang about it. All they want are three squares a day and peace and quiet.

→ To Jean McDougall, June 10, 1940

Don't worry about me being stranded over here in case a war breaks out. If war should hit this part of the world it would be between U.S. and Japan over the East Indies, which is a remote possibility—extremely remote. There isn't anything else to fight over, unless U.S. should suddenly decide to take a hand in China, which is even more remote and the Philippines won't be a bone of contention until 1946. Anyway, if trouble should develop here it would be preceded by many rumblings or warning. Orientals work that way. They can seldom do anything on the spur of the moment, rather their actions are usually preceded by a lot of palavering. I would have ample time anyway, no matter what occurred.

I certainly feel like I'm isolated from what's going on in the world. Our principal news comes via Domei, which is highly unreliable, slow and incomplete. The other News Services we use, UP, Reuter, Havas, D.N.B. are unsatisfying. Our UP service is a mailer out of Shanghai, fine as far as it goes but not like getting it hot off the griddle.

Reuter (British), Havas (French) and D.N.B. (German) are nothing but pure propaganda of the rankest sort. In fact our D.N.B. copy comes straight from the German embassy. Once in a while we get some real news from the Embassies, since they are in touch by wireless with their home governments but most of the time it's just propaganda....

I haven't seen any evidence of war bitterness, except that of a repressed sort in the press conferences now and then and in the way the various nationalities avoid each other in the Imperial Hotel lobby or on the train. However, I am, to a certain extent, given the opportunity of *feeling* things you folks in the states don't get. It's hard to put it into words but it's there—

the tension beneath the polite faces and the hunch that a lot of them mask dark schemings.

Japan being at war, soldiers are always in evidence, marching in the streets, or lounging here and there. When I say marching, it's a different kind of march than you might think. Japan being a crowded country, the soldiers have to drill wherever they can find room. No one pays any attention to their marches, and little attention to their mock warfare conducted on the streets at times.

One afternoon I was walking beside the Imperial Hotel when all of a sudden, around the corner burst three soldiers with machine guns. They threw themselves flat on the pavement at my feet and industriously started pumping imaginary bullets at an imaginary enemy who must have been breathing down my neck the way the soldiers were concentrating.

I stepped to one side, the soldiers jumped up from their belly-flat positions on the pavement, raced a few steps and fell prone again. Pretty soon some more soldiers came up the street doing the same thing. By that time so many passersby were interested they cluttered up the street so much the soldiers must [have] had a difficult time aiming at the imaginary enemy. It got comical after a while.

Ordinarily, however, people pay no attention to them. In fact one can do almost anything on the street in Japan and no one will think any thing of it. School track teams are continually staging marathons in the streets. One is perfectly safe in practically any stage of dress or undress. In that way the Japanese have no inhibitions. Ever since being here I've harbored a secret desire to walk down the Ginza in a pair of long winter underwear and count the number of people who look at me twice. If I were Japanese I know they wouldn't even see me, but being a foreigner they would no doubt display a mild curiosity.

⟶ To his mother, July 11, 1940

Evidently you are receiving more alarming news about the Orient than we are here. It is hard for any one to understand, unless they actually experience it as I am, conditions here. Japan has been at war three years and there is hardly a sign of it in Japan, except for little annoying things like staple fiber shirts, no butter, matches on rations, and the like. The resounding, war-like developments you read about in the states, we take with several grains of salt here. You get that way after seeing how Orientals work and think and how much sound and fury there is without, actually, any action.

I'm sorry, but I still can't seem to explain it adequately. Anyway, don't let newspaper stories worry you. This is a pretty safe place. Japan has been at war with China for three years, going on four, yet Tokyo has thousands of Chinese living in it, unmolested, unharmed. In fact living without anyone paying any particular attention to them. Such a phenomenon wouldn't be possible in America or Europe, but it happens to be the way of life here.

Old timers tell me they are convinced the same treatment would apply to Americans if Japan and America were at war, because the Japanese are that way. I don't know. It's hard to believe.[1] But it works in one respect at least....

Goodnight, Mother, and as I said before—don't let the newspapers worry you. Things here are quite secure.

— To his mother, August 20, 1940

From the clippings Paul [Carrico, his brother-in-law] sent I can easily see why you may get worried about me. According to the stories, there is a vast wave of anti-American sentiment sweeping Japan. The stories, mostly from the *San Francisco Chronicle*, are based on the anti-espionage drive here, the arrest of Britishers and the incident in Shanghai between U.S. Marines and Japanese gendarmes.

Whatever the situation in Shanghai may be, there certainly is no reflection of it here. There hasn't been a whisper of anti-Americanism in Tokyo that I have heard. For a while, just after Cox's death, the Japanese language papers—inspired by the army obviously—were bellowing about the spy menace and warning all Japanese to beware of the foreign wolf in sheep's clothing, with heavy accent on the British menace. There wasn't a word, however, about Americans and every Japanese I talk to tells me that the Japs, for some unaccountable reason I can't fathom, have a deep liking for Americans as people in addition to American methods and mechanics.

There undoubtedly is a faction in Japan which hates all foreigners including Americans, with a deep, virulent hatred and this faction may be fanning, or trying to fan the flames, but there has not been a single reference, written, spoken, or otherwise against Americans that I know of. Jim has heard of none and neither have the few other people I've asked since receiving the clippings.

The Shanghai episode, I'm sure in my own mind, is a result of this particular faction I mentioned which is more in control in China than in

Japan. Japan's right hand, a good deal of the time, doesn't know what its left is doing. The amount of disunity and disorganization is astounding.

Did I mention in my letter of last week about the dinner the *Japan Times* gave a fellow, our best translator, who was fired after a scrap with the Managing Editor? Guess I didn't. It's the custom to always give anyone leaving the firm a farewell dinner. Sakakibara was no exception. After some bitter wrangling between opposing factions on the staff, the dinner proponents won and the dinner was arranged, but the guest of honor wasn't notified until two days previous, which he said was too short notice. So the dinner was canceled and after several weeks was rescheduled with adequate notice to the guest of honor.

It came off very pleasantly, with a pretty speech from the leader of the pro-Sakakibara faction and a return address by the man who was fired, capped by a toast to the victim from the managing editor who canned him. Such is life in Japan.

⁓ TO HIS MOTHER, AUGUST 15, 1940

The papers that come here from the states are certainly playing up news of Japan, especially the *New York Times*. Frankly, some of it is news to me, but in a way that isn't strange, the newspapermen here don't do much talking among themselves, in fact they seldom see one another outside of the thrice weekly press conferences. Every one has his own sources and keeps them secret from every one else, if possible.

Correspondents here gave a unanimous snort of anger, disgust and contempt the other day when Senator Shepherd, testifying on the conscription or national guard bill, I forget which, said he had information from undisputable sources that Japan is going to invade the United States via the Aleutian Islands, Alaska and the Pacific Coast.

It's talk like that which makes me see red. Japan has about as much intention of invading the U.S. as she has of conquering the Moon. Her hands are so full of China and other parts of East Asia she's on the thin edge now and by what wild dream she could gain anything by invading the U.S. or even having a ghost of a chance of starting it, is beyond comprehension. Shepherd should retire to the nearest mental hospital.

Iwado, our managing editor, had to write an apology to police today because in the lead of a story I wrote a few days ago I described an anti-British mass meeting as assailing Britain and fawning on the Axis Powers. They didn't like the word fawning. The *Advertiser* also had to apologize because they used the word "fawn" in a head, on the same story, the same day.

The cops came around midnight (we roll at 3 p.m.), and confiscated all the papers (16) that were left. They did the same thing at the *Advertiser*. The *Advertiser* story appear[ed] in the morning and remaining copies were picked up that afternoon, about the time we were going to press. We had some papers confiscated last week because of another story too, a little box about some arrested Britishers being released, which was put in the paper on orders of the Foreign Office but didn't met with approval of the Army. The papers were confiscated, what were left, a day later. Such is the thoroughness of Japanese bureaucracy.

Another screaming example:—Nothing is more secret than Japanese military or naval affairs, especially naval. Secretness is a sacred fetish. Several weeks ago we were taken to task because in the background of a photograph of the Emperor of Manchoukuo arriving in Japan for a visit, appeared the outlines of the warship which brought him here. There was a terrific rumpus raised about it. Penalty for such a dire offense, according [to] the Navy regulations, is *capital* punishment if they see fit.

Every morning on my way to work I pass a shop which sells nothing but picture postcards. Samples are displayed in glass cases on the street. One entire section of a case is taken up with photographs, in color and black and white, of Japanese navy ships. On the bottom of each post card is the tonnage of the vessel and the names of other ships of the same category. Wow!

From the postcards I counted 35 ships, battleships, cruisers, destroyers, airplane carriers, etc.

On such a haphazard, slipshod basis is this country run. The amazing thing is that Japan actually accomplishes anything at all. One fellow made a comparison which might be a partial answer, though. He said the Japanese nation reminds him of a colony of ants working on a big bug, or any other project. To look at them apparently there is no method but madness to their work, there are ants scurrying in all directions, pulling in opposite ways, quarreling among themselves, apparently getting nowhere, but eventually they all get the bug down the hold. And that's about the way Japan has been doing. She has been blundering along, in her determined way, for several thousand years and getting stronger all the time.

I went to a movie Sunday, it rained all day, and attempted to get some entertainment from pure Japanese fare. There were three pictures, all heavily moralizing, all with sad endings, to a westerner, but the proper endings to a Japanese. One picture told the story of two married couples. One wife was a "modern" girl. She liked to wear foreign clothes and smoke and gad about to moving picture shows and beauty parlors and wasn't at all polite. The other wife was a proper Japanese wife who didn't truckle to such new fangled ideas. Both husbands liked the old fashioned kind. Upshot of the "modern" wife was that she and her husband separated and she committed suicide. That's where the picture ended, with the suicide.

It was a very proper ending because the wife paid for her "sins" of being "modern" (foreign) and the other couple learned a heavy lesson in HOW TO LIVE.

One of the other pictures told of a girl's love to a guy but the gal had a sister and the father of the two gals wanted the one who was not in love to marry the guy, so the one who was not in love married him. Which pointed the moral that daughters should follow the dictates of their parents who arrange marriages. Love doesn't enter the picture.

You see, [in] the Japanese mode of living, though, psychology, everything is absolutely opposite to our ways and the two ways never can be reconciled. Neither side ever will understand the other and both will be happy if left alone without interference of the other.

The trouble is the foreigners, Americans, English, Germans, everyone, tried to force their culture, along with their business methods, onto the Japanese and now the Japs are revolting. The Japanese, of course were eager to learn and avidly lapped up everything we had, but when they reached the stage of satiation the foreigners weren't smart enough to see it and kept crowding them. Now Japan is going to the other extreme and earning the hatred of the world. I guess I should say democracies, because Germany and Italy are glad-handing Japan at every opportunity and Japan, the poor sappy copycat, is lapping it up and shouting totalitarianism from the house-tops and Down with Britain and America. When Germany and Italy get what they want from her they'll shuck Nippon like a hot potato.

It gets more interesting here constantly. I'm sure having the time of my life, just watching and taking things easy.

→ To his family, August 29, 1940

There is no correspondent in Tokyo, with whom I have talked, who thinks Japan and the United States will clash of themselves. If armed conflict ever occurs between them it will be as members of two camps—the Axis powers of Japan, Germany and Italy, against the Democracies of

United States and Great Britain. Such a clash, also, would not occur unless Britain is crushed by Germany in the present hostilities. Japan isn't going to jump into any fray before the British defeat.

There also is a strong school of thought which is of the opinion Japan couldn't do any real fighting with any one anyway, until she gets China cleaned up—which even from this sector looks like a distant dream.

Another thing—despite the loud clamoring for jumping into the totalitarian camp, and the avid aping—or attempted aping with ludicrous results—of things Nazi—a large segment of the people believe totalitarianism is not for Japan. There also is a very healthy distrust of Germany among thinking people in the government. Konoye himself, in his new structure statement yesterday, said Japan could not join the totalitarian camp because of Japan's peculiar concept of government, i.e., the mystical devotion to the Emperor.

One thing is certain, people and papers in the states are much more alarmed over affairs than people and journalists in Tokyo.

⚊ To his mother, September 5, 1940

Things are so opposite in the country to everything the westerner knows and understands that it also is easy to poke fun at everything without in the least understanding what is behind such screamingly funny things. In my clipping file I find myself [picking] out stuff I can write about in a satirical vein, with a barb every few paragraphs, instead of the other things which are so charming, alluring and loveable about Japan. I guess I don't see with the eyes of a Lafcadio Hearn.[2] Of course, working on a newspaper and handling so much stuff with a hollow ring to it, influences one's feelings toward everything he sees. You get sour on the wire pulling, hair pulling, chest thumping and grandiose air castles these bureaucratic officials are continually building.

Maybe this feeling is manifesting itself in my letters recently. A trip around Japan, a few weeks away from the newspaper, would freshen my viewpoint considerably, I'm sure.

One of Japan's keenest scholars told me last week that Oriental history, particularly Japanese history, is a series of cycles showing the battle between luxury and frugality. The average Japanese is happy-go-lucky, spontaneous, spendthrift. The military class, however, are all for regimentation and frugality for the benefit of the state. Wars help the military enforce their Spartan standards, but so great is the Japanese love of some fun in life, most of the decrees banning luxurious dresses, costly dinners, etc., collapse of their own unenforceability in time. Whether they will collapse this time or not remains to be seen. The Japanese are by nature so submissive to authority in most ways, that maybe they will. If so, the rulers of this strange nation will have won a great victory and will then be more able to win another one, to whip the people into backing more war than they already are standing.

I wonder just where the difference between the man in the street and the man in power lies. Are the rulers of a nation essentially any different from their subjects? They both spring from the same stock. Is it consistent therefore, to hold the one in contempt and love the other?

But I'm wandering too much, probably. I should confine these letters to factual events and not philosophizing. Or do you mind a bit of philosophizing?

⤙ To his mother, September 9, 1940

The blackout and air raid drills end tomorrow. It has been quite interesting to observe them but they also are a joke in many ways. People are instructed to dash from their dwellings when the alarm signals sound, and huddle under the eaves of houses for protection. What protection that affords I don't know. There is no such thing as an air raid shelter in the entire capital, or anywhere else in Japan for that matter, that I know of. But then, air raid shelters probably never will be needed. I don't know who would bomb this place, except possibl[y] Russia and that's a remote prospect.

At night the streets are dark as the inside of a cow. Street cars move slowly, with no lights except a dull glow from the head light, as do the few taxicabs permitted to operate. When the alarm sounds all traffic stops, except railroad trains. Today at 1 p.m. the *Japan Times* staff evacuated to a park across the street during a "raid." The catch was we on the desk continued working, so I didn't get to enjoy standing in the rain and listening to a speech given the assembled crowd.

Somehow or other all this rigamarole, I think, is much different from the practices they used to hold in Europe, before bombs really started dropping. I imagine the practice was more grim and realistic. Here it's all in fun and everyone seems to enjoy it, unless they have a date when the alarm sounds and have to stop dead still for an hour.

Last year, I'm told the drills were much more strenuous and detailed. A foreigner, a newcomer to Japan, was hurrying from a Yokohama hotel to the station to catch a train and meet someone in Tokyo. On his dash to a taxicab zone he was handed a blue ticket. He took it and kept going. (It so happened that [the] blue ticket meant he was "wounded" and was supposed to lie down in the street and be given first aid, but he didn't know that.) But he knew something was wrong very shortly. A policeman chased and caught him and tried to explain things, but it was all Greek, or Japanese to the disgruntled foreigner who shoved the cop aside and kept going. The next thing he knew he was flat on the ground with several industrious Japanese thoroughly bandaging him up for a broken leg, fracture[d] jaw, splintered ribs and other injuries.

Then he was tossed into an ambulance and rushed off to a "field hospital" and from there to a regular hospital. The little game ended several hours later. He never did make his Tokyo appointment.

I wish they were doing that this year. It would be fun to watch.

While eating dinner at Umikaze Friday night, it got dark before I had finished. Two Air Defense Corps volunteers appeared and politely explained to the Amah that I had better finish eating quick because the lights had to [be] put out or the windows covered tightly. Then they helped the Amah and me arrange things to make the house light proof and after much fussing, during which the living room was turned into practically an air tight chamber, they retired with bows and happy smiles.

I went out for a walk, groping my way through inky dark lanes, to see what other people's houses were like. Most of them were as black as my own and I met a lot of other people out for similar walks, to see what other people's houses were like.

According to what I hear, French Indo-China has sold out to Japan, allowing her to use Haiphong as a Naval base, to land troops, and do just about anything else she wants. To date, however, not a line has appeared about it here and the Foreign Office disclaims all knowledge of such a deal. They also deny stories, carried by Domei, of Chinese-French clashes on the Indo-China border.

— To his mother, September 11, 1940

When you receive this I'll probably be in Shanghai, working for United Press. The opportunity for which I came to Japan and China opened today. And now that I have a job on UP I'm not sure that I want it. I've been figuring more and more on a trip to the Dutch East Indies. In fact I talked it over with Mr. Go yesterday and he told me if I would stay until January 1 he would fix a free trip for me through Manchukuo and North China, free train fare that is. So I said I would. That would give me two wonderful trips.

Today Morris, Far Eastern Manager for UP who is in Tokyo, telephoned me that there is a job in Shanghai and he wants me to leave immediately. A fellow is quitting the 15th.

Because jobs on wire services don't happen like that frequently and since I came out here largely to connect in just such a way, I figure I had better take it. The pay is 870 Chinese dollars a month, which is a lot less, actually, than I'm getting here, based on living expenses. Shanghai prices are terrific.

The Shanghai job consists of expanding (rewriting) incoming cables for UP's Far Eastern service. The next job above that, which would be assistant bureau manager, pays in American dollars. If I am not getting American dollars in six months I'll quit and do some sight seeing.

Will be leaving Japan without seeing any of it except Tokyo, Yokohama, and Kamakura, unless I can get in some sight seeing on the way south. Boats are so crowded now passage may be difficult to obtain. In which case it would give me a week or so to visit Kyoto, Nara, Osaka and Nagasaki and maybe the inland sea.

— To his mother, September 16, 1940

Speaking of how Japan treats its guests, Randall Gould, editor of the *Shanghai Evening Post,* which has been bombed, etc., and who (Gould) was blacklisted by Wang Ching-wei as being anathema to Japan and who was ordered expelled along with 80 others from China, came to Tokyo this week to gather news. He also is a correspondent for *Christian Science Monitor.* Gould was one of the newspaper men who petitioned Roosevelt to enforce a total embargo against Japan. Despite all that he was allowed to come into Japan and is perfectly free to move around in Tokyo. I talked with him this afternoon in the UP office. Should a rabid anti-American who had been blasting the U.S. right and left from Germany suddenly appear in New York harbor and seek admission the the U.S., I'm afraid he would fare a lot worse than Gould is faring here.

— To his mother, September 30, 1940

Momentous events have occurred here which you have read about and worried about, undoubtedly. The French Indo-China affair and then Japan joining the Axis certainly changed the status of things, on the surface at least. The atmosphere here is in more a state of wondering uncertainty than anything else. Foreigners seem split about 50–50 on whether or not they will have to leave the country eventually. About half of them are optimistic and inclined to believe that now Japan has shown her teeth and demonstrated that she means business, the United States will come down from its high horse and talk business about settling the Pacific Problem. The other half think the U.S. will not change its attitude but will, eventually, put an embargo on oil, which will drive Japan into the Netherlands East Indies. If that comes the die will be cast and the U.S. will have to put up or shut up.

Personally, I am optimistic about the eventual outcome. I also am fed up with the U.S. foreign policy in the Far East. It has been a series of terrible blunders, deliberately antagonistic moves, since 1904 in my opinion. Now America is about to reap what she has so industriously sowed for so many years. That may sound unpatriotic but it is so. I hold no brief for those in the saddle here but they wouldn't be there if the U.S. had played its cards differently.

As things have turned out it is just as well that I am leaving for Shanghai and the United Press. However, I still regret I was unable to see more of this land of paradox.

⤙ To his mother, October 3, 1940

Mr. [Toshi] Go is giving a dinner for me tonight. He certainly has treated me swell. It is to be sort of a swank affair in a tea house. I've never eaten in a big tea house. They usually have geisha girls sing and dance at such affairs.

The weather has been miserable in Tokyo for weeks. Cold and rainy. The air raid drills are on this week but last night there were no raids, only the blackout, because weather grounded the "enemy" planes. To make things realistic dummy bombs are exploded with loud bangs in various parts of the city, the streets are roped off, traffic stops and pedestrians squat against walls or buildings.

⤙ To his mother, October 13, 1940 (from Nagasaki)

One of my many dream houses will be built in southern Japan.

My trip has been a delightful one & I regret it is almost over. Sail in the morning for Shanghai.

Didn't look at a paper all week, until this evening, & as far as the trip was concerned, it was like being in another world—no hints of strife or trouble—just a beautiful, peaceful country which few tourists see, in Kyushu district.

Just read in the paper, English edition of *Nichi Nichi*, that U.S. state dept. is advising Americans to leave China. I hope that doesn't put fresh worries in your mind about me.

The only time I ever feel concerned over conditions here, as related to myself, is when [I] worry over the fact you probably are worrying about me.

Actually, to me it's high adventure & only to be observed with interest, not fretted over.

⌐ To his mother, October 16, 1940 [from Shanghai]

Arrived here yesterday at 2 p.m., got a room in the Foreign Y.M.C.A., Bubbling Well Road. Because of the office being shorthanded I started to work early this morning. This is the first chance, 4:30 p.m., I've had to write.

Shanghai is as different from Tokyo as day is from night. It is a city of tension, excitement, suppressed emotion and the feeling of never knowing what is coming next. At least that is what impressed me first.

The Whangpoo wasn't swarming with junks as I have always read it is and things weren't as picturesque, generally, as I had anticipated. Maybe it's because under ordinary circumstances I would be looking with the eyes of a feature writer but now I'm looking with the eyes and thoughts of a news writer, with bigger things than color on the horizon.

With various ships rushing Orientwards to evacuate American nationals I know you are worried about me. I only wish that you weren't and that you could share my enthusiasm over being at the scene of things instead of worrying because I am there.

The Y is a magnificent building, 10 stories, first class hotel accommodations, gymnasium, swell swimming pool, excellent restaurant and all the good things I never looked for in a Y.M.C.A. They tell me this is the best Y in the world.

The room costs 121 Chinese dollars monthly and board, two meals a day, costs 240 Chinese dollars. So my salary will safely cover everything.

Incidentally, the press moves with the diplomatic corps in case evacuation of everybody really comes, so I'm safe there.

⏤ To his family, October 22, 1940

The chances of me being a war correspondent are remote. My job is strictly in the office, pounding a typewriter. I sure have gotten rusty on rewriting, not having done any to speak of on the *Times,* real fast work I mean.

In terms of Chinese dollars—17 and 16 to 1 American dollar, living is terrifically expensive. I break a $5 bill, Chinese, every time I turn around. Lunch is $3, dinner $5, a package of Spuds $2.40, a pair of good shoes $50, wow! It's a good thing I'm getting $870.

I'm glad I came to Shanghai, now that I'm here. I feel more in touch with what's going on in the world and more in the swing of things. Although it is pretty early for me to [be] venturing opinions I think Shanghai, in many ways, will not be as pleasant living as Japan was. There is no place to go on a week end. You have to stay put right in Shanghai.

Shanghai is like any big port city in many ways, only it is swarming with Chinese coolies and people of many lands. Never saw so many different nationalities before. Every language under the sun, practically, is heard in a 10 minute walk on the Bund. Our office is just off the Bund, which is a big street fronting on the Whangpoo river. The big ships, little ships, freighters, passenger liners, vessels of every description, are docked in the Whangpoo right opposite the main part of Shanghai.

⏤ To his mother, October 30, 1940

Several ships are due in here during the next few weeks to evacuate Americans from the Far East. I still look on the evacuation rather abstractly. It doesn't seem to have any connection with me. I'm still not convinced that things will become so bad in the next three or four months that evacuation is necessary.

London certainly is surprising the world with their resistance. Maybe the tide will turn. The tide out here is turning against the Japanese very forcefully, at least for the time being. Chinese have recaptured a number of cities in the interior and America's attitude of determination, which seems to be no longer bluff, is making them quite uneasy. There even are strong rumors of Japan easing out of the Axis pact. That sounds rather fantastic right now but things have become so complicated I wouldn't be too surprised no matter what happened.

— To his mother, November 30, 1940

I just learned that there is supposed to be a British boat sailing from here tomorrow for Vancouver and am going to try and get this into the post office before the 5 p.m. closing time for that particular mail. It's almost 5 p.m. now.

British boats move with great secrecy and we never know when they will arrive or depart. This may even be a false alarm but I hope it isn't. The next boat out of here for the states is December 8.

Today was a busy one. The Japan-Nanking treaty was signed, the Chinese police of the International Settlement[3] went on strike but called it off pending further negotiations, another Japanese gendarme was shot and news is rolling in from Indo-China and Thailand (Siam).

The appointment of Admiral Nomura to Washington as Japanese Ambassador seems to be a hopeful sign that the Japanese are backing down somewhat in their belligerency toward the U.S. However, it may be merely a straw in the wind. Nomura always has been rather friendly towards the U.S. however. He is a much better appointment than the other saber rattler who was being considered.

— To his mother, December 7, 1940

Finally got out to the Loretta school and saw Sister Mary Jane, Mrs. De Bouzek's sister.[4] She is a very interesting woman and we spent several hours talking about China. She has been out here nearly 20 years, having taught in the interior most of the time and in Shanghai about eight years. She is the Superior. The school has about 250 pupils, all girls, of 27 different nationalities. The Chinese are the most intelligent of all students, barring none, and the Japanese and the Russians the dullest, said Sister Mary Jane.

She showed me a composition written by a 16 year old Chinese girl who had studied English at the school for five years. She couldn't speak a word of English on entering. It was a masterpiece of beautiful writing, describing a threshing scene. And it was done in the class room during a regular lesson period. While the girl was an exceptionally good writer, Sister Mary Jane said the progress she made was typical of what the average intelligent Chinese can do in the way of acquiring knowledge when they really study.

Sister Mary Jane loves China and the Chinese. She has a very low opinion of the Japanese, as has every one else I've talked to in China.

For some strange reason the Japanese, who are so courteous and kind and likeable in their own country, are the nastiest examples of humanity you can imag[in]e when they get over here, at least their army is and the other representatives who bulldoze their way around. I'm glad I stayed in Japan long enough to know something of them and their country before coming here. I know they are swell people in their own bailiwick.

— To his mother, January 3, 1941

Tribune-Telegram used to give UP foreign news the play over AP because UP's foreign service [was] usually superior to AP's, although on domestic news *Tribune-Telegram* preferred AP. We received a letter from New York last month enclosing a copy of an ad from the *Telegram* which boasted of the *Telegram* being far ahead of competitors on several stories in the Far East because of UP coverage. They referred specifically to signing of the tripartite pact last September when UP beat all competitors by 48 hours that it would be signed, as well as a five day beat on Britain's decision to reopen the Burma road and were three hours ahead on U.S. warning Americans to evacuate the Orient.

I don't know how the volume of our outgoing cables to the states compares with AP but suspect AP sends out much more news since UP's policy is to send only major stories which will take front page play and not to send anything else. That would account in part for more AP stories appearing on the Far East than UP.

— To his mother, January 21, 1941

The Nanking puppet government opened its own bank in Shanghai Monday and is trying to force its currency on the city. Looks like a bitter currency battle between the Chungking dollar and the Nanking dollar. The Chungking dollar is weakening and yesterday was about $18.40 to one U.S. dollar, which means I could have gotten $188.40 instead of $177.77 for the US $10 you sent me, had I waited until this week to cash it. On the other hand, however, it might have dropped too and I'd have gotten less. Playing the exchange market is Shanghai's biggest financial game. Just like the stock market only worse, with fortunes made and lost over night.

The wildest rumor is sufficient to send the market soaring or falling.

The Russian Regiment is drilling in the race course grounds across the street. The strains of martial music shrill into my room as I'm writing.

The Russian Regiment was formed shortly after the great exodus of White Russians from Red Russia, to absorb some of the male refugees. It has become one of Shanghai's best policing units.

— TO HIS MOTHER, JANUARY 25, 1941

Monday is Chinese New Year's Day. They go by the Lunar calendar. All papers close down early and most do not publish Monday at all, so United Press also observes limited schedules.

I hope to obtain a glimpse of what a Chinese New Year's celebration is like, but am told that's a difficult proposition since most of the celebrating is in the home these days. The Municipal Council forbids firecrackers (they might be confused with gun-fire) and there will be no lifting of the curfew regulations. All Chinese must be off the streets by 12 midnight in the Shanghai Municipal Settlement.

Shanghai had quite a bit of excitement Thursday when the chairman of the Japanese Rate Payers Association shot the chairman of the Municipal Council during a rate payers meeting. Undoubtedly you read about it in the papers.

I was at the meeting but had to leave to get to work. The shooting happened five minutes after I left. When I arrived at the office the story was being telephoned in and they sent me right back to the race course to cover what was left. Just my luck.

An interesting sidelight on the shooting was that Hayashi, the would-be assassin, several years ago wrote a letter to the Municipal Council in his own blood demanding more Japanese representation on the Council. He may become a hero in Japan, but he certainly has wrecked what chances his countrymen here had for getting more representation on the council. As a matter of fact, Keswick, his victim, was in favor of giving the Japanese more representation, according to what I have been told.

— TO HIS FAMILY, JANUARY 30, 1941

You ask if I like my job. I'm not enthusiastic about it because I'm chained to a desk and I never liked that. However, it is the only way to learn how to file cables and differentiate between cableworthy news and that which is not, plus a lot of other things a correspondent must know. I am hoping that soon I may be able to get out on my own, be sent somewhere to dig up yarns in addition to just grinding out copy. It is invaluable experience, this job I have now, but not one that I would want to continue doing for any great length of time.

You ask also about my social life. It's nil. My recreation consists of reading or walking about the city, which is very interesting, or seeing an occasional show.

Unlike Tokyo, foreigners and Chinese here never mix, at least I've seen no sign of it. I've been wanting to get acquainted with some intelligent Chinese and knock around with them, but how to go about it is a puzzle. There seems to be an unwritten law here that it isn't done. You lose "face," I'm informed. Restrictions like that disgust me.

Japan pulled a diplomatic coup with her mediation of the Thailand French Indo-China dispute. Looks like she is going to be able to move into Saigon without resorting to force. Then she'll have an excellent jumping off place for the Netherlands East Indies and Singapore.

⤙ To his mother, February 9, 1941

The Rate Payers meeting interrupted by the shooting resumed yesterday, well guarded by 500 police and the Russian Regiment, the speakers and Municipal Council's stands surrounded by steel plates and every newspaperman in Shanghai present. Not a single Japanese voter showed up, however, and the Japanese amendment was defeated by a vote of 7,055 to 5. Four foreigners, one with a proxy, voted for it. There were only one thousand odd voters present but many had large proxy votes. Last the big companies here split up, on paper, into numerous small companies, so they could multiply their votes and defeat the Japanese at the Municipal Council election.

The meeting came off quietly and was exceedingly dull. I sat through it.

⤙ To his family, March 9, 1941

Matsuoka, Japanese Foreign Minister, is leaving for Berlin and Rome in the next few days, so I guess that means—at least it is my guess—nothing will happen in the Pacific, of Japan's making, while he is away.

Japan certainly has played a smart game in Indo-China and Thailand. She has used Hitler's blitz diplomacy and now has garnered herself some sweet territory. I think Japan will gain all she needs immediately by pressure and diplomacy and will not have to resort to armed force for some time, at least six months. If battle comes between Japan and the U.S. it will be over the Dutch East Indies. U.S. can't have any pretext to fight over anything else, unless it were a U.S. possession which Japan isn't likely to molest for quite a while yet. Maybe Uncle Sam will force the issue himself.

⤙ To his mother, April 18, 1941

Chinese newpaper men, pro-Chungking especially, are certainly having a tough time. At least 15 have been kidnapped in the past two weeks. One fellow, foreman of the stereotype [*sic*] room, stayed at the paper for two weeks, rather than risk going home. He finally took a chance yesterday and was shot.

War between the Chungking and Nanking terrorists on employees of the banks of the two regimes flared again this week with several Chinese slain on both sides and all Chungking government bank branches here closing yesterday. Exchange went to 19.40 but I was too busy getting the news to cash in on it. Dropped back to 18.50, where I bought my $15 worth today.

Here is a typical Shanghai incident. Colonel Lu Ying, Chief of the Special Municipal Government (Nanking controlled) police, travels with numerous bodyguards. About 2 a.m. this morning he was visiting in the French Concession,[5] his bodyguards, guns in hand, loitered outside in an alley. Along came a group of French Concession police, saw the bodyguards and the guns, thought they were kidnappers and opened fire, killing one, seriously wounding two, while others fled.

Body guards seem rather useless around Shanghai. Or maybe those who hire them are just poor pickers. Several times bodyguards proved to be the assassins. Yesterday, a Central Reserve bank employee (Nanking controlled) was being visited by his wife and daughter in a hospital where he was recovering from bullets of terrorists who didn't shoot straight enough last month. His bodyguard was standing outside the door. In burst three gunmen who shot him dead as the bodyguard ran away and hasn't been seen since.

That killing was avenged by the deaths of two pro-Chungking officials which in turn led to closing of the banks.

Al Capone was a sissy alongside the Shanghai boys.

⇀ To his mother, April 22, 1941

By this time maybe you are beginning to get the idea I'm fed up with the British of [the] Orient. I certainly am. Right now they are selling Shanghai to the Japanese. They already have made a deal whereby the Municipal Council setup was changed last week so the Axis representatives ultimately will have a voting majority. They tried to put over an even rawer deal during secret negotiations with the Japanese but the American councilors got wind of it and stopped it just in time. However, the British have the property and thereby the ultimate block of ratepayers votes and in ratepayers election can and do swing things the way they please. It is quite apparent that the British here are out for one thing only and that is the money and to hell with the British Empire or anything else. Would you believe that British tin and other materials are shipped out of British ports, Hongkong for instance, through Shanghai for transshipment to Germany via Dairen and Siberia? Well, it's so. The tycoons are after the dollar, or the pound or whatever other money they can lay their hands on and nothing else matters.

It certainly would do them good to spend a week in a London air raid shelter. The Canadians and the Australians and the New Zealanders, yes, and the Americans, will have to win their war for them or it won't be won. That's beginning to be quite obvious in Greece right now. Which about exhausts my nickel's worth.

P.S. I'm talking about the Far Eastern British tycoons, not about the rest of the Empire.

⟶ To his mother, May 3, 1941

Japan seems quite anxious now to make up with Uncle Sam. Tokyo is bubbling with suggestions for Matsuoka to visit Washington and secure a non-aggression pact. If that trend keeps up, it probably will be quite a while before Japan really strikes south in a big way and collides with the U.S. Navy. So don't worry about me becoming involved in any hostilities.

Shanghai is suffering an acute coal shortage which cuts down the power supply, so elevators in many buildings only run to upper floors. Occupants have to walk up the first three flights. There are penalty charges for electricity users using more than a certain percentage, 70 in most cases, of their former supply. The trouble is a shortage of bottoms (boats) to carry coal. Luckily this is a warm climate (allegedly) so maybe they can get enough boats by next autumn when the heat is needed.

The strangest request yet came from Goro. He asked me to buy him a side of bacon because it has been so long since he has eaten any. Some people I know are going to Tokyo next week and have promised to take it, along with a stock of other provisions. I was afraid for a while I wouldn't be able to find anyone willing to lug a side of bacon to Tokyo. I'll have quite a cablegram account to my credit in Tokyo if I continue acting as buying agent.

⌁ To his mother, May 19, 1941

The Far Eastern situation today looks more favorable for aversion of a U.S.-Japanese war than at any time in the past six months. There appears to be a growing school of thought in Japan that Japan can not conquer China by force and is now desperately seeking a way out, with U.S. mediation the only way. You are probably reading such stories now, so what I'm saying will be repetition.

However, today I'd be willing to bet even money, and might even give odds, that America and Japan won't come to grips for quite some time.

More peace feelers have emanated from Tokyo in the past few weeks than for more than a year. The trial balloons show which way the wind is blowing, to a certain extent. It remains to be seen which faction in Japan will gain the upper hand—those favoring a southern push no matter what the cost and those who are willing to concede that Japan can't whip China and are willing to come to terms through U.S. mediation—if the U.S. will step in.

Uncle Sam is getting tough and the Land of the Rising Sun is more than a little worried.

It all adds up that Shanghai will sail serenely—at least as serenely as it ever has—for a considerable period. Which is okay with yours truly.

⌁ To his mother, June 29, 1941

The Russo-German war has somewhat changed the complexion of things in the Far East. Opinion is divided. Business men are optimistic on the grounds that it means Japan and the U.S. won't clash. Military men, on the other hand, are more pessimistic, especially if the U.S. ships goods to Russia via Vladivostok. If Russia really starts cracking up, say the militariers, Japan will invade Siberia, whereupon the U.S. will attack Japan.

I am pessimistic about Russia's chances but at the same time believe the latest developments give the Far East an additional breathing spell.

The Russo-German war certainly has wrecked the business of hundreds of Axis agents in the Far East who were buying raw materials here and shipping to Germany via the Trans-Siberia railroad. Many were wiped out, allegedly.

An acquaintance of mine who lives in the Y had been dealing in metals, shipping via Trans-Siberia. He says he is washed up now, and will live on his savings and pray they don't run out before the war ends.

I'm glad I went to Peking for another reason. Since being in Shanghai my opinion of [the] Chinese had deteriorated a great deal. Old timers had told me that Shanghai Chinese were the worst in China and that my opinion would change if I ever went somewhere else. It did in Peking. Even the ricksha [*sic*] coolies there were gentlemen. Here it seems to be a case of dog eat dog. Foreign influence may have a lot to do with it. Shanghai was and is a get rich quick city. Foreigners came to make a pile and clear out, and so did many Chinese. Nobody wants to live here, but just make a fortune and get out, although more than 40 percent, I guess, stay.

The Japanese last Tuesday searched foreigners crossing bridges into Hongkew for the first time in two years or so. The Deputy Commissioner of Shanghai police, a Japanese, had been assassinated a few days before and that was his funeral day. Also, an unidentified Chinese was assassinated in Hongkew a few hours before the funeral procession was to get underway. All traffic was blocked along the entire route—from the Race Course through the International Settlement across the Garden Bridge to Hongkew.

Yesterday four Chinese members of the famed "Doomed Battalion" which was imprisoned in the Settlement since the '37 hostilities, were sentenced to death for murdering their commander last April 24. They did it from revenge for his disciplinary tactics in the prison camp, they said. But they may not be executed for years. More than 70 other condemned men are being held in the Shanghai Ward road jail—biggest in the world—because there is no proper authority to carry out executions since the '37 hostilities began. They are supposed to be done under jurisdiction of the Chinese National Government, which isn't functioning here just now. Incidentally, the battalion commander's funeral was the biggest ever seen here. Estimates were that about one million Chinese filed past his casket. His battalion held out against the Japanese in '37 then escaped into the International Settlement where they were interned for the duration.

— To his family, July 2, 1941

Japan today held the eighth Imperial conference in her history (modern history—since Meiji Restoration) which means a momentous decision has been reached regarding her policy anent the Russo-German War. Her last Imperial conference was held just prior to signing the Tripartite Alliance. No announcement has come yet as to what decision was reached, but our pipelines say she will adhere to both the Russian and German pacts by 1, not striking at Siberia and instead moving her fleet south which will please Russia and 2, also please Germany by immobilizing the U.S. Fleet in the Pacific. Japan is scheduled to move into Indo-China whole hog within two weeks, after which she will move into Thailand. That is what was decided, said our pipeline. There won't be any military invasion. She already has conquered Indo-China. Simply Japan will run the country absolutely. Then comes Thailand's turn.

What Japan will do if the U.S. moves aid to Russia through Vladivostok is still a moot question, but the consensus is she will do nothing, for the time being.

Here is the dope on Japanese Imperial conferences: Two imperial conferences were held during the Sino-Japanese war in 1894 to discuss plans of campaign; the third was held in 1904 when it was decided to declare war against Russia; the fourth in August, 1914, when Japan entered the World War on the side of the Allies; the fifth on January 12, 1938 when the Japanese Government concluded that it would no longer deal with Chiang Kai-shek and would support the establishment of a new regime in China; the sixth on November 30, 1938 was called to approve a "fundamental policy for the readjustment of relations with China." It preceded publication of Prince Fumimaro Konoye's (then Premier for the first time) statement of Japan's peace terms with China. The seventh was held July 20, 1940 when it was decided to adhere to the tripartite alliance.

Looks like the war of nerves in the Pacific is under way, if the dopesters are right for once. I personally think nothing is going to happen.

I've been thinking of taking a whirl at the consular service. I don't know whether I'd ever be satisfied at anything but newspaper work. But of late I've been wondering about the permanence of it. UP won't pay more than $150 a month unless you get a bureau, which takes about three years in the Far East. Shanghai bureau should pay between $250 and $300 a month. However, I have no desire to live in Shanghai that long.

There are opportunities to get into the consular service in minor posts out here, that do not present themselves in the states. Pay starts around $1,400 and goes up. That isn't much either, but in the long run it may be more, and have more permanency, than this kind of work. On the other hand it would always mean being outside the United States. I kind of like the United States.

The trouble with me is, I guess, I'm working for other people all the time and not for myself. I figured I might be able to do some writing on my own if I had a job that presented a little more leisure and to which no strings about writing for outside publications were attached.

What are your ideas on the subject?

— To his mother, July 27, 1941

The Far East seems in a turmoil now greater than any that have gone before. However, I think the United States is more alarmed than we are.

The majority of persons with whom I have talked, including Chinese bankers, American business men, Japanese diplomats, etc., think there will be no immediate show down between the United States and Japan. Chinese bankers, who are as hardboiled and realistic as anyone can be, insist the Anglo-Americans won't fight unless Japan moves into the Netherlands East Indies and maybe not then. Japan presently is too busy consolidating Indo-China to move elsewhere for a while.

I suppose you have been considerably worried the past few days by the Far Eastern news. Wish I could make you feel more at ease but by the time you receive this letter something else will have happened, or this crisis will have passed.

— To his mother, August 4, 1941

Did my bit for the British war fund the other night. Attended American night of the Moonlight Follies which the British radio station XCDN is staging here. The follies have had a difficult time of it. They are held in the huge garden of the wealthy Hayim estate here, a beautiful place. But it has rained so much only two nights have been held and one of them, Saturday night's which I attended, had been postponed two weeks. The entire foreign community turned out for American night, however (I should have said pro-British foreign community), in their long gowns and summer tuxes—black trousers, white mess jacket and stiff shirt. Floor show and dancing on an improvised floor. They also auctioned off a cheap 6.3 Kodak for, believe it or not, $22,000 Shanghai dollars. An American made the winning bid. Actually the winner does not pay $22,000 but in this case whatever amounts he bid above the last bid. For instance his last bid was 1,000 higher than next to last bidder, so he pays that plus any other bids he made. However, every person who bid has to do the same, so they actually collect $22,000.

The freezing orders certainly have turned Shanghai business upside down.[6] Gold can't be had here right now. We collect our accounts in gold and although clients can buy gold drafts they must be sent to New York for cashing. We can't collect our salaries in gold, either. It will work itself out somehow but in the meantime we are in a quandary. Fortunately there is no ban on Shanghai dollars so we can get plenty of those. You don't have a chance to get a few extra ones on the exchange market though when you have no gold to sell.

The Tutuila bombing must have cause[d] quite a momentary stir in the states, at least we got a lot of reaction out of Washington. We beat AP, INS and others by hours on the bombing. Got one of those lucky breaks, although I can't say how we got it.

Far East is the center of news now with one crisis seeming to pile on the next. I'm not worried however. It doesn't look like Britain or the U.S. is going to do anything but talk about Japan taking over southern Indo-China and pressuring Thailand. And they haven't applied any drastic freezing regulations yet. In fact the Americans out here are hit harder by the freezing than are the Japanese so far.

It now remains to be seen how stringently the oil ban will be enforced.

Yesterday Japan canceled all sailings to the United States and now Americans in Japan are stranded unless the State Department sends them a special ship. They can't book passage to Shanghai either for quite a while since the few boats from Kobe are booked months in advance, the Japanese allege, and foreigners aren't permitted to travel out of Nagasaki—Nagasaki, like the Great Wall of China, is now a military secret.

Things should be quite interesting out here during the next few months.

Now don't fret about me being way out here in the wilds of the Far East with a crisis brewing. I'm having a swell time.

— To his family, August 11, 1941

The enclosed UP story on Hongkong opium is a sidelight on the Far East. Since the smugglers, who are allegedly hunted down by the law, can't get any opium into Hongkong, the government kindly steps in and does it legally. Wow. Anything to make a few extra dollars.

Food prices, and prices of everything else, are soaring daily. It's getting more expensive to eat at home than in a restaurant. We are convinced our servants are squeezing us blind but we can't prove it or do anything about it. An old Chinese custom. The only way to get around it is to know all market prices yourself and spend a lot of time checking up. We can't do that.

One of Shanghai's biggest fires in recent months razed Wang Ching-wei's newspaper here, the *Central China Daily News*, Saturday night. An incendiary time bomb exploded in the place and when the fire finally was out it [was] just a hollow shell. The Japanese this week are celebrating the anniversary of the beginning of Sino-Japanese hostilities in 1937. All police and the Volunteer Corps are on duty, streets are barricaded, the French concession is blocked off and curfew is enforced at midnight, to prevent trouble. One would think the Japanese would have enough sense not to celebrate the beginning of a war in the country and city where war raged, and while it still is going on.

— To his family, September 5, 1941

The Japanese have instituted stricter control of access to the city of Shanghai. Barbed wire practically surrounds it and Chinese must possess passes to go in and out. Foreigners have no trouble yet, except inconvenience. At least I had no difficulty passing the barriers last Monday when I went bicycling in Hungjao [?]. It certainly is a nuisance crossing the creek into Hongkew, however. Everyone must show his or her cholera pass (showing you have been inoculated) and the Garden Bridge and other bridges are jammed continually. Hongkew is the Japanese controlled sector of the International Settlement and access to it is across Soochow Creek, as you probably already know.

Since a couple Japanese were assassinated there a few weeks ago, the Japanese have declared virtual martial law there between 7 p.m. and 6 a.m., when no Chinese is permitted to enter or leave. Foreigners, however, have no trouble getting in and out, and I hope it continues that way. Our twice weekly press conferences are held in the Broadway Mansions across the bridge. I cover the conferences. These are the only press conferences I've ever heard of where whiskey and soda is served. You can also have tea if you desire, or coffee, or cakes.

I was searched for the first time the other evening crossing Szechwan Road bridge returning from Hongkew. A Japanese sentry frisked me for deadly weapons. He felt a pen, pencil and notebook in my inside breast coat pocket, where a shoulder holster might be and I guess he thought it was a gun too, for he took no chances on me being able to draw it before he could investigate further.

— To his mother, September 13, 1941

All indications—and private reports from Tokyo—point to early announcement of Japanese-American rapprochement. We are all set up and even have the stories written, and are only awaiting the word to flash it.

Details of the deal we don't know, but no matter what kind of a deal I fail to see how it can be anything but a double cross to China, unless Chungking has decided to sell out to Nanking which is very unlikely. So it looks like a Far Eastern Munich—for which the U.S. will pay in years to come just as England is paying.

Anyway, temporary peace in the Far East from such rapprochement will calm things down out here and postpone a Japanese-American clash for quite awhile. And you will have less worrying to do about my safety too.

The Germans in Tokyo really did strongly protest because Japan was negotiating with the U.S. and not keeping Berlin informed. Japan is rapidly slipping from the Axis, unless the pro-Axis click [sic] is strong enough to pull the nation back into the groove.

➤ To his family, September 23, 1941

Lt. Matsuda telephoned me today and asked if I'd like to make a flying trip to the Hunan province drive on Changsha. If things can be arranged a couple of other newspapermen and I will be flown to Hankow, then to Yoyand (Yochow) and then go to the front by horseback or truck, or maybe tank. Will leave in a day or so, if at all. It will be the first time in several years that any newspaperman was permitted to go to the Japanese side of the front. The Japanese figure on capturing Changsha, which would be one of the biggest victories of the war, biggest since the fall of Hankow, and would open up all Hunan province and the way to Chungking. So they'd like to have a few newspapermen in on the kill. They must figure they have it in the bag or they wouldn't even think of a trip like this. Hunan province is one of the most beautiful areas of China. I sure hope the trip materializes. We would be gone a week or 10 days.

Incidentally, this Changsha drive probably won't take much play in the U.S. papers, which are having considerably more important war news than that to play. So don't wonder why you missed it, in case I do go and you didn't see anything about it. I should be back here within 10 days from tomorrow or the next day, if the trip materializes.

My latest bit of traveling contained several unexpected elements. About 20 miles from Shanghai, as the crow flies, is [a] famous shrine To Our Lady and also a Jesuit astronomical observatory which is connected with Zikawei. The place is called Zose. Buses run to a nearby village known as Tsingpu, and connect with a local line to Zose. The trip, ordinarily, can be made in a day.

Yesterday was my day off and I had made arrangements to go to Zose. Japanese officials here assured me passes were not necessary, that there would be no difficulties. Yesterday at 8 a.m. Mary Bell and I, with a lunch, caught the bus from Hongkew and started out.[7]

The Japanese control areas around Shanghai are cordoned into sections and all travelers must go through the barricades. The bus was jammed with Chinese, all of whom carried numerous bundles of all descriptions. The bus was stopped and every passenger searched, his bundles taken apart and examined, also his or her cholera and typhoid inoculation certificates and special passes the Chinese must possess to go through the barricades—all done five, repeat five, times in the first five or six miles. One hour after leaving we were still within the limits of Greater Shanghai.

Finally we passed Greater Shanghai's limits and were out in the open country on a frightful road over which the bus bounced merrily at full speed. Then came another inspection and we were notified that foreigners were allowed to go to Zose only on Sunday and then only with a special pass.

Fortunately I had in my billfold Matsuda's calling card on which he had written, in Japanese, an introduction to an official in Soochow. Matsuda's name was magic and we got past that barrier.

Two or three inspections later we landed outside the walled village of Tsingpu, only to learn we had missed the bus and the next one would be nearly two hours later. But we learned we could go by sampan. The trip would take about two hours and a half. We hired a sampan and were about to shove off, on the crystal clear waters of a meandering canal, when up dashed a Japanese sentry. He could speak no English but it was clear we weren't taking any sampan rides.

Matsuda's magic card (I never used it in Soochow) softened him somewhat but he suggested that we hire a taxi cab or wait for the bus. I played dumb. It was obvious the canal was a military secret or something. He also wanted to know if I had a camera. I still couldn't understand. Finally he posted a Chinese soldier (Wang Ching-wei puppet troops) at a respectful distance and went off to consult some higher authority.

When he came back the second time, he carefully searched the lunch basket, frisked me ([I] had concealed the camera in some blankets in the sampan) and insisted he must know if I had a camera. Then I realized some one on the bus had told him I had a camera. So it suddenly dawned on me (for his benefit[)], that I finally understood what he wanted and I jumped into the sampan and produced the camera. Which apparently convinced him I was honest, but he marched me off, through the village gate, to the army headquarters, where a big shot officer finally appeared, who also could not speak English, but who evidently thought a good deal of Matsuda's card. I also went through the motions of praying at Zose shrine and put over the idea of a personal, annual pilgrimage.

I previously had solemnly assured him we would return on the 3 p.m. bus from Zose to take the 4 p.m. bus from Tsingpu for Shanghai.

It was a long sampan ride. Much longer than two and a half hours, although it was enjoyable and the scenery was interesting. But it was slow going. An old man and his wife ran the sampan, he was 72 and she was 68 (Mary speaks Chinese fluently). He was too old and feeble to man the big oar sweep at the stern, so she did that, and boy it's hard work. He sat in the stern and paddled with a small oar. It was just before 4 p.m. when the sampan arrived at the foot of Zose hill.

Dick Meagher had given me a card to the director of the observatory. We visited the shrine and the big, new church and then the observatory. The director told us there were no more buses. Luckily, Zose has radio contact with Zikawei so I had them message Dick to relay word to the Bells & office that I would be late for work the next day. We also flagged down the sampan to take us back to Tsingpu, where we hoped we could find some place to stay. Mary's amah's aunt also lives in a neighboring village along the canal so that offered a haven also.

Darkness overtook the sampan before it was halfway to Tsingpu, however, and the old man and his wife tied up and said they were going to remain tied up for the night. They were afraid to move on the canal at night for fear of guerillas commandeering the sampan. So the four of us huddled in the sampan until dawn. The old man and his wife live on the boat so they had a couple quilts which helped keep off the chill, but boy, those boards got hard before morning. I'm still aching. The Chinese sleep on boards so it was natural for them. The mosquitoes were frightful. The only way to keep them off was to cover every possible inch of oneself with the quilt and then fan vigorously with a fan and create your own breeze to blow them off your face.

We started paddling again at dawn and landed back at Tsingpu at 8 a.m. just in time to catch a bus which the night before we had been told (in Zose) left at 9 a.m. Fortunately we were early. I got back to the office by 11 a.m., worked all day and now am certainly ready to hit [the] hay (7:30 p.m.). But we had a good time anyway. I've always wanted to travel in China by sampan.

⌐ To his parents, October 5, 1941

The trip [to Changsha] was swell and crowded with action every minute of it. But it was very short. We covered a lot of territory in a short time. On Sunday afternoon, the 28th, they notified us to be at Japanese army headquarters in Shanghai Monday at 7 a.m.

Clark Lee, of Associated Press; Fritz Oper, of *Christian Science Monitor* and editor of *Post Mercury*; Lavarent of D.N.B. and Kleineche of Transocean and myself were the correspondents. Lt. Col. Kunio Akiyama, military spokesman in Shanghai, Lt. Uno, a civilian employee of the army and a Nisei born in Salt Lake City on West First South, couple years younger than I, West High student; and an official army photographer made up the party, the objective of which was for the Japanese to prove to foreign correspondents that Japanese troops had captured Changsha and occupied it. Changsha is a vital city controlling northern Hunan Province and just south of it is Hengyan, junction of communications in all directions, including Chungking.

We covered the 600 miles or so to Kankow in 2 ½ hours but instead of continuing on stayed over in Hankow that day and night. It seems that although the Japanese had Changsha the airfield wasn't safe to land on yet. Full of land mines. Then followed a big tiffin given by Army officials and a conducted tour of the vicinity topped off that night by a banquet given by Foreign Office Consular officials, which lasted until the wee small hours.

At 4 a.m. we were called again and took off from the Hankow airport, where are based the bombers and fighters that bomb Chungking, and cover all the Central area for Yoyang (Yochow), Japanese field headquarters for the Hunan campaign. An hour's flight brought us to the airfield there, where are based between 80 and 100 planes of all types, fighters, bombers, transports, etc. There we were given the latest information and a picture of operations. Then we took off for Changsha.

The pilot overshot his mark and discovered he was over Chungking held territory way south of Changsha about an hour and a quarter later. So he hastily wheeled about & headed north again. We could see no signs of Chinese troops anywhere and didn't on the whole trip. I don't know where the 300,000 Chinese were. We did see Japanese troops marching south of Changsha and a few in the deserted city of Changsha. We saw plenty of bombing in one area, northeast of Changsha and two towns aflame, but Changsha itself did not appear to have been the scene of much fighting. At least from an elevation of about 500 feet. We practically scraped roof tops of the town for 10 or 15 minutes circling over it. The Japanese certainly looked like they were in control.

Yesterday the papers here carried a Reuters story from London describing how Japanese warplanes bombed Changsha continually Tuesday (while we were flying over it). Chungking never admitted the Japanese took Changsha and issued official communiques of bitter fighting going on there Tuesday (while we were flying over it).

The Chinese were smart all right. They figured the Japanese would repeat tactics of many similar campaigns and after breaking up Chinese troop concentrations would withdraw, which is exactly what happened two days later. Whereupon Chungking held a giant celebration of one of the "greatest victories of the war," in which the Japanese were "repulsed in the attack on Changsha and routed...."

We returned to the Yoyang airdrome then took a boat up the Yangtze to Yoyang itself which is across the river from the airdrome itself. What a river that Yangtze is. More than a mile wide way up there. Took us 2 1/2 hours to go upstream to Yoyang, against the current and one hour to return ... and about 1 or 2 minutes to fly across.

At Yoyang [we] were conducted into the presence of the commander of the Yoyang campaign. Whose name was kept so secret that Akyama didn't know who we were going to meet until we were introduced. He was Lt. Gen. Korichika Anami, former vice-minister of war and aide-de-camp to the Emperor. Drinks were poured and toasts drunk and Anami through an interpreter made a speech explaining the campaign and I replied in behalf of the correspondents, which was also interpreted.

Then we went back to the airdrome, after being conducted around the ruins of Yoyang to a beautiful temple which still stood intact. We landed at the Hankow airfield just after a big Russian built bomber which had been surrendered by its Chinese crew to the Japanese at Ichang, had landed. It was a wonderful break but for a time it looked like we wouldn't be able to do anything about it. Akiyama couldn't slice through the red tape required to allow us to inspect the plane and interview the crew. He finally did, however, but by the time we were conducted into the garden of Major-General Endo, commander of the Hankow area air force and the crew was also ushered in, it was dusk. However some pictures were obtained and interviewing started. Before it ended [we] were using candles and light of a full moon for illumination.

By that time we were two hours late for a big banquet at the Race Club, given by the General commanding the Hankow area (I can't recall his name at this moment) and at which the Chinese governor of Hupeh Province and the Chinese Mayor of Hankow (both puppets of course) were also guests of honor. We didn't even have time to wash.

(Our stories by the way were flown to Shanghai by special plane that morning as soon as we landed at Yoyang, but more of that later.)

The general made a speech and Gover[nor] Ho Pei-yung and Mayor Jen Li-chang extended greetings and I replied again, … my third speech of the trip. I lost track of the number of toasts drunk and the number of courses of food. It was a wonderful banquet.

The D.N.B. and Transocean men didn't get to attend though. The Race club is British and Germans are barred. The Japanese didn't know it until we were walking in the front door and the D.N.B. man suddenly remembered the Germans had been expelled long ago. There followed much talk but it wound up with them not entering. Both of them are very nice chaps, incidentally.

The main theme of all these speeches and greetings was that the Japanese hoped we would give truthful, factual accounts of what we saw and the theme of my replies [was] that we would but we weren't responsible for what censors might do to our dispatches or what interpretation the world at large would place on them.

The festivities ended around 2 or three a.m. and we were up again at 5 and took off at daylight for Shanghai. All during the trip we were photographed from all angles and doing everything—by both movies and still cameras. You would have thought we were diplomats on a great mission.

As a matter of fact we were given some rare privileges. Nothing is more guarded than Japanese military airfields and other military bases and we certainly saw plenty of them. Had we been military men we certainly could have obtained some good information on airplanes, and several other things. But I guess they had us sized up pretty well as just dumb newspapermen who wouldn't know a dive bomber from a pursuit plane. We didn't as a matter of fact. They had to point out the difference. They were swell to us.

On returning to Shanghai we were taken into the airport office and interviewed by the Japanese press and boy, did I and everybody else get a surprise. In rushed a Japanese reporter waving a *China Press* with a story under my byline and a headline saying "Newsman fails to ascertain Changsha fall." All the pro-Chungking Chinese vernacular press in Shanghai also had bannered the story and it caused quite a stir. The story itself didn't say what the headline did. The story didn't say whether I had or had not ascertained Japanese troops were in the city. What happened is that my original dispatch had said Japanese troops were south of Changsha, marching toward it after withdrawing from Chuchow and that I saw what appeared to be troops in the city but I didn't say Japanese, and the Shanghai desk thought I was trying to put across that maybe they weren't Japanese and thereby avoid censorship. So the story was a sort of [tongue]-in-the-cheek affair. The night rewrite man left out a few other vital things which, thank goodness however, were cabled to New York, so I was all right on that end, the most important one. At least we haven't had any queries.

The Japanese withdrew October 2. It's the old story of not being able to maintain communications lines and garrisoning all of China. That's why they'll never win the war, as far as a military victory is concerned, if China can still get outside aid.

Chungking is still celebrating the "great victory" and today, according to a message from our office, is going to fly some diplomats and newspapermen there. (We didn't land at Changsha because, the Japanese said, the airfield wasn't safe.) It will be interesting to see what stories come out of Chungking.

Incidentally, I regained the good graces of the Japanese by writing a few more stories, which were printed, saying Changsha looked to be in Japanese hands.

— To Jean, November 8, 1941

Everyone here seems to be pessimistic about future Japanese-American relations, except me, who believes and am willing to bet nothing will happen, of a war-like nature, for some time to come.

Following the pugnacious *Japan Times & Advertiser* editorial a few days ago, which you probably have already read about, plus other blasts from Tokyo's vernacular press and a few other events, things looked ominous. But Kurusu's departure for Washington lends strength to my belief Tokyo is trying everything to avoid war and Washington is getting tough enough to make them toe the mark but at the same time won't strike unless Japan strikes first. Which she is not likely to do yet. At any rate I'm not worried about the future.

⇀ To his mother, November 20, 1941

At 5:15 last Saturday morning the room boy awakened me saying there was a telephone call. I answered and it was Commander Jeffs, of the Navy.

"Well," he told me, "It finally has come."

I had a cold feeling in the pit of my stomach and mentally cussed myself for having been so darn optimistic all along. I thought he meant [the] United States and Japan had gone to war.

But he didn't. He meant the U.S. Marines had been ordered withdrawn. They are leaving on two President liners, the *Harrison* and *Madison*, due out of here the 22nd and 26th.

If the Kurusu mission fails, which will have been decided long before you get this letter, the bottom may drop out shortly thereafter, but I am still of the opinion America and Japan won't be fighting until at least April, if then. Very few others agree with me but I'm not worrying about that.

We are making necessary arrangements here, so no matter what happens, I will be okay. And covering the battle for U.P. should be plenty interesting. Headquarters for U.P. Far Eastern coverage will be Manila.

The Far Eastern crisis certainly blows hot and cold. Today very optimistic reports come from Washington, Tokyo and locally. Latest word is that Kurusu took definite commitment to Washington offering guarantee against southward attack—against Thailand—also to respect Siberia's integrity in return for U.S. restoring trade relations and using its good offices to mediate peace between China and Japan. According to these same sources, Japanese here, the bellicose Tojo and Togo speeches before the Diet this week were designed to prevent pro-Axis radicals in the Army and Government from kicking over the traces [altogether] on grounds that the present Cabinet isn't going far enough. Tojo, they say, is powerful enough to relegate radical army officers to remote posts where they can't make trouble, if the U.S. signifies willingness for Japanese-American rapprochement.

And so it goes. One day there's going to be a war and the next day there is not.

Anyway, war or no war, I am going to learn Chinese and have been taking lessons for several weeks. Am studying Mandarin—written and spoken. According to Dr. Erwin Reifler, the instructor, students will be able to begin taking up reading of vernacular newspapers in eight months. There are about 20 of us in the class.

Was fitted this morning, final, for my blue suit and ordered another brown one, basket weave with a stripe. Now I will be fixed up, sartorially, for some time to come. With my other suits, some of which are still wearable, plus some expert Chinese mending on the pants, will have more suits now than ever in my life before—seven fall, spring and winter ones & three whites. My tux is still good & can see a lot more service.

⬤ UP DISPATCH, JANUARY 7, 1942 BY ROBERT P. MARTIN AND McDOUGALL FROM TIENMUSHAN, WESTERN CHEKIANG PROVINCE

Rice riots, epidemics and terrorism accompanied Japanese occupation forces into captured Shanghai, disrupting the city's economic life and threatening widespread starvation.

We escaped from Shanghai after spending two weeks watching a disheartened population wage a losing fight against an acute food shortage, pestilence and severe cold.

The worst winter in Shanghai's history complicated the plight of thousands of helpless civilians. When we escaped, most of the city's industries had been closed, rice lines were growing longer daily and rice riots were increasing. Many Chinese along with Britons and Americans actually faced starvation unless the Red Cross can establish relief camps with American funds.

Japanese restrictions were changed frequently, ruining innumerable Anglo-American businesses and keeping the population in constant economic turmoil. It was obvious that the restrictions were amended because of continuous friction among Japanese army and naval officers, foreign diplomats and Shanghai authorities.

The first week Japanese forces occupied the city was uneventful. There was no bloodshed and very few arrests, undoubtedly because the Japanese had insufficient troops to patrol the metropolitan area. Occupation authorities constant[ly] sought cooperation of Chinese and foreign leaders, presumably with the hope of influencing favorable treatment of Japanese interned abroad.

Then came terroristic outbreaks. At least three Japanese soldiers were shot before Christmas, bringing reprisal threats from occupation authorities. A house-to-house search was promised if political terrorism continued.

Loyalist Chinese were unmolested, although severe restrictions were expected against them at any time. Supporters of acting president Wang Ching-wei predicted the Nanking regime soon would take over the French Concession, then seize the International Settlement.

Foreigners were handicapped financially because the Japanese seemed unable to establish a workable banking system, although most Anglo-American banks continued to function under Japanese control.

The starvation threat particularly affected foreigners receiving money from home, numerous Anglo-Americans employed as customs officials and those owning small businesses.

With the city facing economic collapse, Japanese authorities were urging Chinese to evacuate, a steady stream of refugees poured from the city, including thousands of Japanese civilians en route to the interior.

Lack of transportation facilities placed the city virtually under a 10 p.m. curfew. With only Axis diplomats allowed to use automobiles, Shanghai bankers and business men rode bicycles to work.

The pro-Japanese *Shanghai Times*, the *Evening Post* and most vernacular newspapers continued publishing under Japanese control, but only pro-Axis news was available.

— To his mother, from Chungking, China, January 29 [1942]

Arrived here by plane from Kweilin yesterday and immediately notified New York to notify you. I imagine you have been worried about me. Am sending you another message Saturday night via radio to a listening post in the states which picks up such messages and relays them to addresses by mail. This letter will go by airmail to you via India and Africa, I believe.

Pepper Martin, Francis Lee and I left Shanghai the morning of Dec. 26, after we had made contact with a Chinese who guided us to Chinese guerilla headquarters outside the city. We traveled by sampan though a maze of waterways to Lake Taihu, sailed across the lake at night and continued on foot and by boats still deeper into China's hinterland, eventually reaching railroads and bus lines.

The trip was long and cold but we suffered no undue hardships and were royally treated by the guerillas and Chinese army men. In fact our journey was sort of a triumphal march, with banquets at every village and town through which we passed. In some places mass meetings were called and we had to make speeches and sing songs. We had armed escorts all the way to the railroad.

I'm scheduled to leave here by plane February 7 for Calcutta from where I'll go to Batavia. So I'll get to see the Netherlands East Indies after all. Pepper is staying in Chungking and Lee probably also will remain here. He is not with UP now but used to be with us in Tientsin.

Our trip will make good telling when I get back home but there is no room here and the details can't be disclosed until after the war anyway. We left Shanghai with nothing but the clothes on our backs, passed through the Japanese barricades around the settlement with special passes we had secured and the guerillas sneaked us through three more Japanese lines, two of them in covered sampans and one on foot across a highway from where Jap patrols had been withdrawn to defend a guerilla attack a mile or so north of us.

We were sneaked under a Japanese held railroad bridge during the few minutes the Jap sentries were invited away from the bridge by Nanking puppet officers to drink a New Year's day toast. Guerillas brought pressure on the puppets to do it. We crossed the last Japanese held highway and stepped into Free China at 2:40 a.m. January 4. From then on we traveled openly. I'm certainly glad to have had the opportunity of crossing China the way we did. It was an education and I might never have been able to do it otherwise. And now I'll get to see a little of India and I hope much of the East Indies.

When the war broke out Pepper and I moved into the Metropole Hotel, where American consular officials were interned. We were able to move about the city freely. Despite the fact we had nothing to do, officially, in the way of work, since UP was closed, we were on the go all the time making preparations to escape. It took us quite a while to make the right contacts.

I managed to leave some of my clothes and other possessions with friends and may be able to recover them after the war but a lot of them, including two brand new suits which never have been worn, and were still at the tailors, may be lost for good.

Pepper and I had Christmas dinner at the Bells. At 4 a.m. the following morning we were awakened with news our guide was waiting and we lit out immediately. As far as we know only one other American escaped. Two British army officers and a British civilian also got out. We traveled part way with them. However, we sent word back to Shanghai by guerillas to some other people who might by this time have managed to get out.

Free China certainly is a different place from Shanghai. The people are different and a lot more friendly. I can see now, why Japan hasn't been able to conquer China and won't be able to.

Left my diary in Shanghai and so do not know the number of the last letter sent you, but it contained a clipping or two, I believe, and followed one written a week before in which was a picture of Mary Bell.

We heard in Shanghai that the boat on which Sam Titlebaum was being returned to the States was sunk. Some of my letters may have been on that boat.

Chungking is a city of hills, everything seems to be straight up and down. San Francisco is practically a flat plain compared to this place. We saw some beautiful mountain scenery on the trip. Kweilin is ringed with great stone pinnacles and cone shaped mountains which rise straight up from a flat plain. The mountains are full of natural caves and serve as air raid shelters during alarms. Two air raid alarms sounded while we were there, six days in all, but no planes appeared. Chungking is quiet now, too foggy for Jap bombers.

The trip certainly agreed with us. I believe I put on a few extra pounds. Don't worry about me. I'm being well taken care of and having the time of my life.

⏤ To his family, from Calcutta, February 13, 1942

I'm off for Batavia by plane tomorrow afternoon, Saturday. Arrived here from Chungking by plane Wednesday evening and have been busy as a bird dog since, running around on various errands.

U.P. has been moving heaven and earth to get me priority to Batavia, seats are in great demand, and their efforts were successful.

If Batavia falls I don't know just where I'll go. Probably try to make it to Australia or back here. In any event, don't worry about me no matter what happens. My incredibly good luck will see me through.

I'm sure glad I came to the Far East when I did, because it certainly puts me into the thick of things. Haven't had a chance to really see Calcutta but I probably will eventually. U.P. is opening up in India and this is a big field with a promising future.

Wish I could send you a letter full of details of my travels and experiences but that is impossible for several reasons. We will have plenty to talk about, however, when the war is over.

Dreams come true in the strangest fashion, don't they? Because of the war I'm seeing more country than I thought was possible a while back. And seeing it fast. The only trouble with traveling so fast is that you only get a few surface glimpses and have to guess the rest, about the people. I am more interested in people than politics and would rather find out how the people live than delve into political skullduggery. However, I have to concentrate on politics now.

No matter what happens, Mother and Dad, be sure that I'll come out all right eventually and that my Far Eastern junket was for the best.

― To his mother, from Djakarta, February 28, 1942

I'm giving this to Harold Guard to mail. He is going out in a few minutes on a big plane which was going to take both of us to Australia. But I elected to stay and see the war through.

I hope you don't think me foolish for not getting out when I had the perfect chance, but I think I will get out okay in the end and, for having covered the Battle of Java and done the good job I'm going to do, will be properly rewarded.

[John] Morris told both Harold and me to leave earlier this week, before he went to India. But I feel I would be letting U.P. and my own conscience down, if I didn't see this through to the end. So I'm sticking.

Have had some wonderful breaks so far and I have a feeling they will continue. This, I believe, is my opportunity of this war.

Java is a wonderful place. Hope it can be saved from the Japanese. Have never seen such a lush country, rich in every kind of resource.

― To his mother, from Palembang internment camp, Sumatra, November 19, 1942[8]

Today is your birthday. A little while ago I heard a Mass which was said especially for you. I hope that, across the thousands of miles of distance which separate us today, you feel the love in my heart for you and know, somehow, that my prayers are being offered for you.

I have tried many times to communicate with you through the Red Cross but we have not yet been put in touch with the Red Cross as far as I know. My one hope is that names of all prisoners have been sent to Tokyo and then been transmitted via the Red Cross.

We are treated all right, get sufficient food and are left to our own devices within the jail walls. It is better than I expected it to be. I wish you could know that I am well, and as lively as could be expected under the circumstances.

Many and poignant are the thoughts which well into my mind this morning—all thoughts of you and Papa and the family. One of my memories goes back a long way—to a summer night you and I sat on the porch and talked until late. It was during my high school days. I told you how I wanted to travel and see the world. You agreed that traveling was a good thing, but that sometimes it was hard on mothers whose sons were on the other side of the world. I said I didn't see what difference the distance made—whether they were only a few hundred miles apart or several thousand, that in either case the fact of separation was the same. But you told me some day I would understand. And now the day has come when I do.

My one wish today is that you are happy and well. And my one hope today is that when all this war is over we will sit on the front porch of a summer evening and talk. What stores of subjects will we have to discuss!

I love you, Mother, with all my heart. May God specially bless you on this, your birthday, and keep you safe and well until we meet again.

Love,

Son

Endnotes to Letters

1. Three and one-half years in a Japanese prison camp would disabuse McDougall of this notion of Japanese apathy toward citizens of nations with whom they were at war. The legacy of colonialism had built particular ill will among Asians toward Westerners.

2. Meaning with rose-colored glasses. Hearn (1850–1904) was an American writer who abandoned the United States for Japan and wrote about his adopted land before its corruption with Western ways as a place of serenity and cultural purity.

3. Beginning in the late 1890s when China was carved up into the infamous "spheres of influence" under the onslaught of European imperialism, the "International Settlements" were districts in Chinese cities where the foreign diplomats, business people, and missionaries lived.

4. The De Bouzeks were a Salt Lake City family who ran an engraving business on First South. Obviously they were friends of the McDougalls.

5. This was the area of the city controlled by the French under the "spheres of influence" mentioned in n. 3.

6. This was the United States' freezing of all Japanese assets in July 1941 which, as McDougall indicates and which was the intention of the measure, put a squeeze on the Japanese economy. Intended as a sanction to put pressure on Japan to stop their expansion into the Pacific, its effect instead was to provoke the Japanese retaliation at Pearl Harbor.

7. Never mentioned in his books about his wartime experience, Mary Bell had become, at least informally, McDougall's fiancée during his stay in Shanghai. As he introduced her shyly and in casual bits of information in letters to his family, she was a businesswoman living with her parents in Shanghai when he met her. During his internment in Sumatra, the Bells were also held in a prison camp in China for seven months, but then returned to the United States. On December 11, 1943, the McDougalls met Mary and her parents for

an hour and a half during a train stopover in Ogden. "Mary is a sweet lovable girl and very attractive," Mrs. McDougall recorded in her diary. After McDougall's return to Salt Lake City, Mary visited for a time, but the pull he felt to the priesthood doomed their marriage plans. Her letters to him during that period indicate a good deal of anguish, but she was a very serious Catholic who resigned herself to his vocation. She apparently never married.

8. This touching birthday letter never made it out of the prison camp, and it was delivered to Mrs. McDougall only when he brought his papers home with him after the war.

DIARIES

Book 1

Thursday New York telephoned me early & simultaneously call came through placed last night for Salt Lake. Talked 4 minutes with Mother, Dad & Jean—all of whom concerned lest I be trapped [in] Java. All said my stories taking big play. Mother said Gertrude got message thru to Mary Bell via Red Cross & would take month for reply. Mother's last words, "I love you, Son."

Hurried to R.P.D. where took N.Y. call, arranged [to] telephone them tomorrow morning 7 a.m. for morning ed. N.Y. said Hugh Baile, U.P. president congratulated me on my stories, which [are] taking smash play. (Previous N.Y. call Flory informed me Johnson said my salary doubled for this period & all expenses [ ] ed. London, N.Y. loudest in cheering my stuff.)

N.Y. said War & Navy Depts. contacted. War advises me use my "ingenuity" getting plane. Navy said powerless.

Informed N.Y. I hired W. J. Tichelman, 38, Burgemeester Ruhrweg 103, Dutchman 13 yrs newspaper experience as U.P. staffer (US $50 weekly). Rutman & Capt. (now Major) Zimmerman advised me to get out. Visited Gen. Van Oyen, chief N.E.I. air corps, who gave me note (for myself & D. W. Hancock) to Capt. of Dutch ship *Siber*, scheduled [to] sail from Wynkoop Bay dawn tomorrow for Ceylon. Packed, arranged Boumer pay hotel bill, got Hancock. Zimmerman gave me army car & driver as well [as] Lt. Allstroodt (?) young flier who with another pilot only ones left [of a] Dutch bomber squadron which fought [in] Malaya. Armed [with] rifle, tommy gun, pistol, we drove Paleau Ratoe on Wynkoop Bay, boarded *Siber* after dark. Along route passed U.S. artillery regiment which fell back either from Buitemgong or [ ]

Learned Batavia declared open city & undefended, that B.B.C. & Dutch radio said U.S. Navy destroyed a Japanese fleet off Manila. Passed many cars & convoys hurrying toward Bandoeng. End is near.

Hancock & I ate dinner from cans in warehouse at Bay.
Got cabin to ourselves on ship.

⌐ MARCH 6, 1942 FRIDAY

Awakened with ship's officers advice to transfer to *Poelau Bras*, a 10,000 ton Royal Dutch mail passenger freighter also in Bay. Because of *Siber* Captain's defeatist [?] capable only 13½ knots.

Talk me [?] at last minute switched & went ashore in boat with W. H. Van Oosten N.E.I. director Royal Dutch Shell Oil & Dr. A. H. Colijn, Major on General Staff & Manager of Terakan oil works & others who decided to change.

Malaya boy climbed coconut palm & got coconuts, which Oosten had him open for my first drink of coconut milk.

In life boat we went to *Poelau Bras*. During afternoon more people arrived, bedding down on deck. We slept in lounge on floor.

⌐ MARCH 7 SATURDAY

Coffee passed out on deck, then some food. About 9:15 a.m. Japanese reconnaissance plane circled boat, which fired ineffectively. We knew it would return with bombing planes so prayed for rain, but good weather held. 9 Jap dive bombers came instead shortly after 11 a.m. Meanwhile Hancock & I prepared for worst, filling thermos with tea, buying bottles [of] soda water, filling pockets with essentials. Passengers assigned lifeboats, we being placed [in] No. 1 on starboard side. When planes attacked we went below, machine guns chattered, 2½ inch antisubmarine stern gun boomed. First bombs, then submachine gun shattered starboard lifeboats. Direct hits [on] bridge, aft hatch, [and] engine room, with 1st direct hit disabling pumps, etc. 6 or 7 directs in all, mostly stern, which settled fast. 1st attack 11:03 & all bombing finished 11:17. Then machine gunning started. All starboard lifeboats wrecked & port boats lowered & pulled away while I remained on board, ducking into lounge every time planes zoomed over, machine gunning (planes originally attacked from 3 directions). When direct hits registered ship trembled, water heard gurgling in. Small daughter of Dutch woman cried when bridge hit & fixtures in lounge splintered. Her 16 day old baby in wicker basket thrown into boat from rail & man caught it. Commandant Mrs. J. A. Mueller, 9 yr. old daughter & 10 day old girl. (About 20 women included in 240 passengers & crew, of which 110 [were] crew & 130 passengers: ship's normal capacity

25 passengers, 55 crew.) First bomb killed one man on deck. Very few killed aboard by bombs or machine guns. Engine room crew escaped.

Bridge hit trapped, severely injured Capt. P. G. Crietee & Executive officer beneath debris concrete & steel reinfocements.

I didn't realize ship sinking rapidly until [I] went out on deck after a machine gunning & saw water rushing over stern main deck rail. Then I seized life buoy & tossed into No. 1 sloop which [was] half filled [with] water & alongside ship. In fact I banked on making that sloop & so stayed aboard so long.

Our basket of canned goods still on deck where I left it. Hancock appeared & asked "Can I help you with anything?" I replied "no." We both descended ladder to forward main deck. Hatch cover afire. I threw overcoat into sloop. Then flattened alongside rail as plane came over machine gunning. Hancock did likewise farther forward. A man jumped overboard near me. I waited for him to swim clear then jumped myself. Seemed long way down. Came to surface & swam to No. 1. A Malay pulled me aboard. A Dutch flying officer, R. L. Van Es in boat. Another Dutchman swam up & I pulled him aboard. I thought boat only awash & not holed so kept telling occupants to bail & push it away from ship's side. There was a moderate swell & we kept rising & falling, crashing against side. Water over knees.

Jap planes singly came back occasionally & Van Es screamed, "Get down, down, they're after you!" I crouched in water to neck. I thought it more important to keep working & get boat away, but ducked into water. Van Es said, "Impossible push it away." Ship under water amidships & sloop washed over rail & onto deck.

A woman stood on passenger deck rail & asked (in Dutch) Van Es to help her. He stood in boat & talked to her. I dove & swam hard away from ship. Another woman near me swimming & a man behind her. He called to her—apparently husband & wife—& she turned back to him & they seized each others hands, talking lovingly, desperately, hopelessly as tho said "We'll die together."

A life raft pulled away from starboard side, men paddling desperately. Sloop 4A, jammed with people, rowed away ahead.

I turned & looked at *Poelau Bras* (which means Island of Rice & is [the] name [of an] island north of Sumatra). Bridge awash, bow pointed skyward, number of people scrambling forward up steep deck. Hancock still wearing to[u]pee, stood leaning on rail, well forward, back to bow &

seemingly gazing at me swimming & watching water creep up. I wondered why he didn't jump. I [was] too far away to shout.

I thought, "I've always wanted to see a ship sink, now I am. Better keep watching." Although could feel no suction, kept swimming, occasionally looking back. Boat looked just like pictures of sinking ships. In fact everything I experienced in water seemed but repetition of my previous imaginings of such myself in such circumstances. I felt no fear or pain (incidentally no panic aboard ship at all—people calm). *Poelau Bras* bridge disappeared, bow pointed straight skyward, then disappeared in surge of water.

(Van Es told me later he went down with ship, was under water long time, then bobbed to surface & swam to sloop. He said suction not great. I wonder if stories of sinking ship's suction fables of sea or at least greatly exaggerated?) *Poelau Bras* sank 11:38 a.m., said 3rd officer Peter Pauw.

I swam for sloop 4A, which then [was a] long distance away. Had removed shoes in shattered sloop, & now kicked off socks. Couldn't remove pants because life belt tied under legs in crotch. As [I] neared sloop shout[ed] "Help. Please sir, Help. Help an American!" repeatedly, but they paid no attention. Swam desperately, finally reached sloop, begged them [to] take me aboard, but no one moved. A Dutchman in stern pointed behind me & said "There is another lifeboat over there." Two Malays stared at me poker faced. I extended my hands & begged them [to] pull me aboard. They never moved. I thought of seizing an oar but didn't for fear they would hit me on head & knock me out. Then I tried to swim around stern & seize rope trailing from starboard, but someone in boat yelled a command, the oars bit into sea & boat pulled away. I [was] too tired to make [a] final, desperate spurt, [and] grab rope.

I floated quietly awhile, resting as sloop pulled farther away. While first swimming, water filled [with] people crying for help. Now fewer cries. The man I pulled in swam behind me, using life buoy I'd thrown into boat. I noticed sloop halted some distance away & sail being put up.

"They won't, they can't refuse me a second time," I thought, & swam hard for it, the other man behind. But as I drew near, the sail went up, billowed, & the sloop pulled away northeast.

Nothing else was in sight. I rested a while, then started back in direction where *Poelau Bras* sunk, in hopes of finding wreckage to cling to.

"This is the end," I thought, regretting I hadn't followed Guard's advice & taken Flying Fortress to Australia. Staying wasn't worth it. No story worth dying for & breaking my mother's heart. I thought of her waiting for me in vain & of Mary Bell waiting in vain. I regretted several things & wondered how long I could swim before drowning. In a while, I said, "I will face & be judged by my Maker. I'm dying young, after all, as years ago I thought I would."

Strangely, [I] kept thinking of *Esquire* story of man drowning & wondered when, like in the story, I would forget which was sea & which sky & try breathing water for air. Stranger still, however, I can remember no feeling of fear or panic, only a feeling of finality & regret.

Then I asked God again to save me & promised I would never smoke or drink alcoholic liquors the rest of my life & would dedicate my life to Christ in whatever way he willed, if my life were spared & I reached an Allied port. I asked it in the name of the Blessed Virgin, St. Joseph, & St. Christopher for the sake of my mother. I firmly believed my prayers would be answered & that faith filled me with confidence that something, I didn't know what, but something would turn up to save me. I felt no more despair, only a calm confidence of rescue.

I sighted a piece of wreckage, a long piece of wood, & swam to it. But it was too light for security. Then a longer piece, sharp, broken point protruding, drifted by & I hung onto that a while. But it retarded progress, so I finally swam away. Then, while riding [on] top of [a] big swell, I spotted two masts of 2 life boats, far away. I prayed some more & swam for a point between them. Sails of one went up & I calculated its direction & angled to meet its course. By now the sea was silent. No more cries for help, except from the man behind me. Sloop with sails changed direction & went beyond my chance of catching it. So I headed for the other, to the left & prayed & swam & prayed & shouted. The sail went up & my hopes sank. "Oh God," I prayed, "Don't let that sail stay up." And it fell down. I drew nearer and shouted, "Help, help an American." Finally someone in boat shouted back and waved, but the boat made no move toward me. I kept going strong, & heard man behind [me] shout. Finally I pulled alongside & two men dragged me in. Weak as I was, I pulled out my watch. It was still running & said 2:20 p.m. I had been swimming about 3 hours. God's mercy & the life belt saved me.

I announced I had two compasses & handed them to Pauw, but water logged, they wouldn't work & he gave them back. I offered to row, but red-haired sailor told me to sit down & rest. I did, & then became violently ill & suddenly weak as a cat, fell across thwart & vomited into the sea. Then I became aware others were doing the same. (Later, people who had been swimming a long time said they experienced [the] same thing.) The nausea of exhaustion (similar to that I felt on the Mainliner plane crash hunt) plus swallowing salt water.

How happy I was to be in the boat. I stood up & thanked God. Every time I stood or sat up, though, nausea swept over me. Pauw shoved a can into my hand & told me to bail. "Your life depends on it," he said. So I bailed.

(Reverting back—first thing I did when pulled into boat was tell them "There's a man behind me, over there not far." But "red" ["(A. Samsen)" added later] replied, "We have to think of ourselves. It's our lives now, there's no room for more.")

About sundown a wind came up & we scooted along northeast at good clip. Still sick, I lay along the side, sleeping fitfully, soaked, & towards morning chilly.

There was one woman aboard, Helen Colijn, daughter of Dr. Colijn, 24 men & the ship's dog "Whiskey"—25 persons & 1 mascot in all. One man, Lt. Com. J. J. de Wolf, wounded in foot by machine gun bullet.

⌐ RANDOM NOTES

—Morning of 6th, in *Poelau Bras* lounge, Oosten announced to all that ship [was] short of water, food, & beer—so go easy. We had few cans [of] cold beer, also whiskey sodas.

—Hancock congenial traveling companion but obviously not physically strong enough for jungle trip of life boat life without his insulin injections.

—Gave Elsdroot bottle [of] whiskey when we arrived Wynkoop Bay.

—Wonder what became of men on raft. Weren't picked up by boats & must have died horribly of thirst.

—Survivors [of] No. 2 boat said many officers suicided in water with their pistols when it appeared hopeless to get life boat. Scheffer knew one officer, not 3 yards away—who [was] wounded by machine gun bullet while swimming. Col. Boynum said many shot selves on deck as well as in water. About 60 people jammed selves on deck amidships, men lying on top of women to protect them from machine gun bullets. A.D.C. to Major General de Fremery told B. look after Gen. Hour later in water B.P.C.—eyes like madman's—cried out for wife Annali, then unanswered, gave up to sea. 60 or so on deck like sheep, jammed together, but no panic. Went down with ship after Bridge life boat proved smashed—same one Van

Es & I looked up at & Van Es left sloop when washed amidships & tried to loosen, but found broken.

—I didn't hold it against No. 4 sloop people for turning me away, felt no resentment—just bitter disappointment & hopelessness. Obviously [the] sloop [was] jammed—later learned 55 people.

—Maj. Gen. de Fremery, saved, landed Kroe. Rear Admiral Van Staveren lost.

—No. 2 sloop, Oosten's, machine gunned, killing outright White Russian wife [of] Dutchman, believed name Kooy, husband not aboard. Seriously wounding 3rd Engineer Putnam, [and] Malay seaman; ugly wound [in the] left arm [of] Antoinetta Colijn, minorly wounding about 6 others. Many jumped in water to escape. When [name deleted] & Sheffer swam to No. 2 they first thought it empty, then, on reaching it, that all were dead, because they lay [on the] bottom, pretending [to be] killed [in] order [to] deceive planes. No. 2 badly leaking. B. let aboard only after shouting name, rank, & promising to fix leak. No. 2 started with 33 persons. Mrs. Kooy thrown into sea when discovered dead, about 1 hr. after shot.

—Lt. Jan Poorenbos, Capt. of 2nd life boat, & Van Es reunited for 2nd time under life-death circumstances. Poorenbos & 50 other men floated 95 hours on life rafts after Japs bombed [and] sank destroyer 150 miles off Biliton, Sumatra. Van Es in [ ] Flying Boat picked them up. Today Poorenbos picked Van Es from water.

—Bob Scheffer who [is] Singapore personnel man B.P.M. & bombed out aided woman aboard who wanted life belt as ship [was] sinking, so he went below & got one. Then she wouldn't jump, nor slide down rope, & people behind yelling hurry. So Scheffer told her to get on the rail; she did & he pushed her off into sea, losing balance & falling in himself. Once in water she [was] okay, instead [of] swimming for life boat, insisted [on] looking first for husband. Scheffer told her [to] get [into] lifeboat, then look, but she wouldn't. Then he [was] shot [in the] shoulder but managed [to] make life boat, pulled self in. 10 minutes later sloop sank. He saw No. 2 about 50 yards away, threw away life belt because [it] retarded speed, saying, "I'll make it or drown" & made it with one arm.

— MARCH 8 SUNDAY

Stiff, sick awakened [at] dawn & when full daylight came, had first drink of water, ½ beaker as rationed each man, & 2 biscuits, which I promptly vomited up, then lay down behind sail & stayed there 2 days. Wind continued 2 ½ days. By morning of March 9 my insides okay.

—Unable keep log voyage due lack [of] paper so 6 days here described in toto.

Each person rationed [to] ½ beaker water 2 times day. 2 biscuits morning; biscuit smeared with deviled ham (one day an asparagus tip), ½ can condensed milk, sometimes a second biscuit, at noon. At nite we got 1 mouthful wine, 2 biscuits, ½ beaker water.

Occasionally [a] can [of] something else opened, such as ketchup or tomato sauce. Best meal one noon—one gulp wine, 1 biscuit deviled ham; one biscuit & asparagus tip, ½ can milk, ½ beaker water.

Ship's cook R. Woltz did rationing.

Life boat salt water love developed between Peter Pauw & Helen Colijn.

One night terrific rain & thunderstorm. Rain so intense [we] reefed sail, spread it over sloop, threw out sea anchor, bailed furiously. Used [a] piece of canvas [to] catch water direct into empty cask. Each man also used his milk can [to] catch rain. Opened our mouths & turned faces skyward. Rain so hard [it] stung flesh, blinded eyes, continued [for] hours. Ceased before dawn & wind chilled us to the bone thru soaked clothing. At dawn opened bottle Cognac, sweetest drink ever tasted—1 gulp.

Rained nearly every nite & left us shivering till sun up. Days frightfully hot, literally frying us, blistering skins. Salt water wrinkled skin [on] hands [and] feet—we mostly barefoot—only few possessing shoes.

Doldrums last 3 days all daylight worst. Thought of R. W. Service's poem "On the Wire": "Oh God, take the sun from the sky. It's burning me, scorching me up. God can't you hear my cry? Water a poor little cup"!

Slept beneath awning in storm one night but soaked by water breaking over bow & pouring thru. Oar blades made fair bed but oar handles hell to sleep on. Most comfortable nite spent balanced on 4 inch board, just above water, in boat bottom, life belt under neck & piece [of] Pauw's & Helen's blanket over me. Another fairly comfortable nite in rear on side with canvas over me, the last nite in boat. Several afternoons we swam div[ided by] sex during doldrums.

Life boat rigged "Emmertuig" fashion: large rectangular sail & smaller one, ¼ size, both rigged same "ra" on crosspiece but smaller one, somewhat corresponding to spinnaker, is forwards & larger one behind.

Boat had 60 liters of water originally & on 4th day 30 liters. Since dog allotted same amount as 1 man each individual in boat averaged 1.15 liters during 4 days or .287 per day—slightly less than ½ pint.

W. Rooteveel, slender, sandy-haired, quiet, steered at helm practically 24 hours a day, sitting in stern with knees up, shoulders slightly hunched, eyes squinted, silent. And when heavy rowing came he rowed his share. Last night, crossing Semangka Bay, he rowed all [the] time & I pushed on oar all [the] time. He could be called a quiet Viking.

Food totaled—4 tins crackers, 4 cases milk (96 cans), miscellaneous tins deviled ham, tomato sauce, 4 qts. wine, 1 qt. cognac, ⅕ gin.

Never wear shorts & short sleeves in tropics unless certain of unforeseen circumstances. Will cast you into sun for long period. We all blistered painfully, faces, arms, legs.

Men—youngest 17, sang American songs, mostly modern swing & Stephen Foster, despite [the fact that the] others [were] all Dutch & many [were] able [to] speak only limited English. They all called me "Mr. American." Sailors talked much of good times [in] New Orleans, New York, other U.S. ports. Sloop's company good spirits, cheerful continually, despite some sick, one painfully wounded, all bitterly disappointed [to be] returning to be captured by Japs. However all thankful [to] be alive.

⟶ MARCH 11 WEDNESDAY

6:25 a.m. sighted first land which disappeared in haze, mt. peak piercing clouds & haze to northeast. Malay boy said it [was] Krakatoa. Others thought peak of Ingano Island. But we were becalmed all day, rowed all afternoon over blistering, glassy sea, swam about 4 p.m. No wind until midnight.

⟶ MARCH 12 THURSDAY

Wind died at dawn and again becalmed all day in great, glittering frying pan of the sea. We rowed all day. Thirst intense. Saw no sight of land. Haze cloaked horizon. However I am positive I sighted a peak directly east southeast of us. Others skeptical it land. Slept well on side beneath canvas, wind came about 10 p.m.

Awakened around 3 a.m. by news [of] land to port & surf heard. Kept sounding depths & finally ceased sailing [for] fear [of] disaster.

⟶ MARCH 13 FRIDAY

Dawn disclosed land on port & also straight ahead. Had good meal of many biscuits & one whole beaker of water. Rowed with [a] will for island. Figured we [were] in Samangka Bay of southern Sumatra opening into Sunda Straits.

Tried twice [to] land but rocky shore & surf prevented. Malay swam ashore with line, but shore too dangerous. Palm trees on shore promised coconuts & milk—"so near and yet so far" never sounded more true to me. Rowed northward & finally anchored [at] 10:30 a.m. off small indentation in coast. Malay swam ashore with long line, secured it to [a] tree & we all then jumped in, some swimming, some wearing life belts pulling [them]selves along [the] rope. Surf threw me onto coral rocks & I waded, on shaky legs, to dry land. Beach rough, rocky. Malay clambered up palms, tossing down coconuts, which we eagerly cut open, gulped milk, ate meat. Some too impatient [to] wait, smashed them open on rocks, losing most [of the] milk but sucking some from cracks. How wonderful it tasted! Drank my fill, gorged myself on meat, then slept a while in shade with banana leaves over bare legs & face to shield from sun. Awakened about [an] hour or more later to find [my]self in [the] sun & leaves awry & well burned in spots.

Men found [a] rivulet, fresh, clear water bubbling from jungle clad hillside. Dug it out, used long, stiff, thorn edged leaves for conduits & we drank & drank. I washed my face & head in fresh water for first time since leaving Bandoeng & drank my fill for first time. How good!

Island (Poeloe Laboean) natives visited us [in the] afternoon, bringing native tobacco, a coarse, blackish brown long fibered stuff, which they rolled in bamboo leaf papers. I tried one & found it rank & fairly strong.

Colijn contacted island Kampon head who for 300 guilders & life boat agreed to guide us across bay to mainland, where party would split, 11 of us heading for Blimbing lighthouse in attempt [to] reach northern Sumatra & freedom & remainder taking Wolfe in sloop to Roteragoen, a doctor & Japanese. We would cross [the] bay after dark & separate. Guide said 4 kilometers to Blimbing, so, barefooted, we started. I brought my lifebelt. In pitch darkness we hiked barefooted over lava rock, coral beach for the most agonizing hours of my life. Stumbling, falling, clambering over big rocks & trees, we staggered on, until exhausted we finally collapsed for nite on small cove of sand at 3:30 a.m., sleeping in our soaked clothing as sand fleas & mosquitos bit.

(written March 22)

Book 2

⚊ March 14, 1942 Saturday

Continued barefoot along jungle trail paralleling beach, then onto hot sands beach. After 2 have met natives who led us into Kampon of Tampan, male population 25 (females not counted) where Passara (mayor) took us in, gave us good rice meal—our first full meal since *Poelau Bras.* Even he gave us sarongs in which to bathe in creek. But we did it sarongless (Helen going elsewhere). Our first fresh water bath since Bandoeng.

Then we all lay on mats on floor & slept [a] few hours. When [we] awoke about 3 p.m., women who had kept [them]selves hidden in morning appeared on streets and on verandahs of native huts—which [are] built on stilts 5 to 6 feet off ground—some roofs thatched, others corrugated tin.

At 4:30 p.m. started hiking once more, with a guide & 3 porters & continued all night.

At dusk guides cooked us [a] meal of rice *sombal,* a reddish brown spice & brewed tea, also filled gourd jugs with water from shallow stream flowing into sea.

At midnite we rounded Vlaake Hooke (Flat Hook) southernmost point of Sumatra, a desolate waste of rock & sand rising to jungle. Surf beat loudly, wrathfully against it. [It] was this shore's surf we heard early Friday.

Natives found large circular spot high on shore of extremely soft sand & darker than rest, where turtles laid eggs. Turtle churns up sand for space perhaps 20 ft radius, lays about 50 eggs & buries them a foot or so deep. Natives probe with stick until "plink" feel one egg break, then carefully dig there & get remainder [of] eggs, which they keep to hatch turtles. Eggs *not,* repeat *not* eaten, I'm told. But when small turtles get big enough they are eaten.

⚊ March 15 Sunday

At dawn reached sluggish stream where guides cooked another meal of rice & I slept ½ hour. Continued walking 7:30 a.m. & sight[ed] lighthouse 15 minutes later, reaching it 8:35 a.m.

There learned *Poelau Bras* sloop No. 2 landed Thursday several miles up beach, with 30 persons including Dr. Colijn's other two daughters Anetta, 16; Antoinetta, 20, with badly injured arm from machine gun bullet. Oosten, Dr. Droop & one seriously injured 3rd engineer Putnam. We walked into lighthouse & onto Putnam's corpse staring at us from sightless eyes. He

[was] shot [in the] arm & lower back, probably dying (in lighthouse) of peritonitis.

Hancock not in boat. He must have drowned as I'm sure he didn't make other [boats]. Putnam suffered terribly, continually begging companions [to] shoot him. "Shoot me, please shoot me. Why should I live and suffer so," he cried continually.

Antoinetta, a bullet grazed her neck & her tongue & her esophagus paralyzed 2 days unable [to] speak, swallow, lay next [to] Putnam.

Doctor Droop, shell shocked, helpless & sick, unable to do anything. Oosten did all bandaging, etc. Droop stayed with Malay at lighthouse & others fled yesterday into jungle Kampon on news 14 Japanese (our party) approaching lighthouse.

Slept from 10:30 p.m. to 6 a.m. in *bed* in one lighthouse compound. Best & only restful, uninterrupted sleep since Bandoeng. Evening meal of rice, then with others slept [on] corrugated iron second floor lighthouse. Unable [to] sleep except fitfully, iron rivets ached so.

⌐ MARCH 16 MONDAY

7 a.m. left with Colijn, tall, blond, baby faced Sperdrink, red haired Pootjes, Javanese Manupassa for jungle camp, behind native guide who set terrific pace, nearly a run, along jungle trail & beach for 1st 2 hours. I had borrowed Koot's shoes (Royal Dutch Air Lines Major) & sand in them seriously galled feet. Stuffed leaves in shoes, which helped. Guide finally lent me [a] pair [of] socks. Trail into jungle began after wading wide, waist deep pond beside beach.

Then met men of No. 2 boat who had come after life belts & food left [in] sloop. Jungle trail nasty—filled with blood suckers, vicious little worms similar [to] measuring worms of U.S.A. which rise from ground or reach out from shrubbery & fasten [and] bury their heads in your flesh. You don't feel them until they're deep in, sometimes not at all. Wound mark bleeds profusely for some time, then difficult to dislodge. Bloodsuckers found only [in] clay & swampy ground, not in sand.

No. 2 sloop contained 12 naval men headed by Col. or Captain of Sea Bozuwa. No. 2 rationed to 3 biscuits, 3 cans milk & water per day.

We reached Kampon about noon, slightly farther upstream stayed 9 engineers who flew there after directing destruction of 4 oil fields [in the] vicinity [of] Palembang. They gave me [an] inner tube, 1 of 5 brought for use as life preserver on trip, from which I fashioned [a] pair [of] rubber sandals, with help of guide who refused tip, pointing skyward & saying "I did not for you but for Joean (Juan) up there."

Soaked feet [in] stream, watched natives snare shrimps using 2 small sticks—one baited with meat held under water beside rock under which shrimps hide. Other has fine gut loop on end, held near 1st stick. When shrimp goes for meat, sharp eyed, dextrous native throws loop around shrimp's protruding eye, twists & jerks him from water.

Slept top floor native hut, coverless. Cold & hard. Jungle is not always hot or even warm.

⇒ March 17 Tuesday

(St. Patrick's Day in other parts of world) Sailor Jack Haasnoot refashioned my sandals, sewing pair rubber soles. He also made 2 pair hide & skin shoes for Dr. C. & 1 girl. Doorenbos in charge [of] our camp. Various men talking of leaving. Had 2 meals today. Yesterday only 1.

⇒ March 18 Wednesday

7 men left in 2 groups for Koteragoen & Japs in hopes eventually reaching Java. Rained all last night & cold but my newly purchased sarong & roof [over] our new hut into which we moved last night because other threatened to collapse, kept me dry, fairly warm. Today a native Mohammedan feast day & all natives went to their kampons to feast. We had feast too—3 meals today, including chicken & tonight so much rice mixed with coconut we [were] unable to eat it all. Believe it or not—we had too much to eat. Never thought it possible again.

Bad news in camp—5 cases diahorea [*sic*] & 5 among Engineers. No more water for me.

⇒ March 19 Thursday

Left 9:30 a.m. with Colijn & 3 girls & Oosten for Kroe. Returned blood sucker jungle trail & hiked all day, still barefoot, along blistering beach. 5:30 p.m. found empty, battered, metal life boat of Jalarajan, Bombay. Opened, empty biscuit & sardine tins & empty water casks told mute story, shipwreck drifting open sea until death or rescue & setting boat [to] drift on alone. Met 2 grobucks (ox drawn carts) enroute [to] Blimbing with coconuts & bananas, which we eagerly dived into. About 6 p.m. reached Bandaralam Kampon, where Pasira dined us & we slept [on the] floor [of] his house. He served coconut milk ("Klappa"—Malay or "Klepper Mileu"—Dutch) & coffee.

⤚ March 20 Friday

9:30 a.m. started in 3 grobucks for Ngaras along beach & thru jungle. Progress slowest. Despite drivers assurances Ngaras reachable by nightfall, darkness found us far from [our] destination, so we slept in grobucks on shore of bay. During afternoon 2 grobucks Blimbing bound met us. Colijn & I bought rubber shoes from them. Rained hard all afternoon. 2 men in [ ] from Kroes said 4A sloop landed there 6 days ago & that Padang captured.

⤚ March 21 Saturday

Started before dawn. Crossing river, Colijn's cart overturned. Reached small Kampon 9:15 a.m. where [we] purchased rice & bananas. 3 field police from Kroe, dispatched to Col. Gerald Bozuwa, said Sloop 4A with 58 people including 2 women & 2 children, landed Kroe (dates vary from 15th to 17th). Police had medical equipment & bandaged our cuts & sores, then preceded us on bicycles to Ngara which we reached 9 p.m. after extremely rough riding. Natives have absolutely no conception of time or distance & majority we've met can not be trusted. Ate late dinner & drank much coffee. Slept bed with Col. B.

⤚ March 22 Sunday

Wearing our sarongs we bathed in river with other natives. It's custom sarong must be worn when bathing. Bought old flashlite, needle, thread, old coat in store. I found a place farther upstream this morning where I could bathe sarongless.

⤚ March 23 Monday

Messenger arrive[d] from Kroe with news. 30 Japs there from Palembang to supervise moving *Poelau Bras* survivors inland, after Dutch officials notified Japs boats arrived (one of survivors Major General A. S. P. Fremery. Rear Admiral J. A. Van Stavern lost).

Traders arrived with clothing. I bought 2 sports shirts (only kind available) pr. socks, toothbrush, 1 towel, 2 cakes Lux soap, 3 hankies for 8.40. Helen lost my newly acquired flashlite & I bought another old one, also last tube quinine in the store & some old caramels & peppermints.

Koot, Pootjes, Rootevelt passed thru en route to Kroe. Spending days sitting around Passabangaban, reading March, 1941 *L.A. Times* & *Oakland Tribunes*, obtained from store. Old papers shipped N.E.I. for wrapping, papering, other purposes. We found them pasted to hut walls everywhere for wallpaper.

➤ MARCH 24 TUESDAY

Followed usual routine, bathing [in] creek, bandaging sores, drinking coffee, eating bananas, drinking coconut milk, munching peanuts, eating 2 meals no string beans, Laboe (resembles squash) chicken, brushing away flies.

Bought Parang (large heavy curved knife) especially suitable for coconuts, cutting way thru jungle. Dr. C. has had infections [in] legs, Antoinette sick, infections seem to have spread instead of retarding. Navy men (only ones left in jungle camp) expected any time now.

➤ MARCH 25 WEDNESDAY

Spent all day transcribing notes. 3 police returned from Kroe with word Japs left, but Dutch officials expecting Bozuwa & rest of us & instructed where to send us. There's only one hope left.

➤ MARCH 26 THURSDAY

More bad news. Special policeman arrived from Kroe to escort party there. Finished transcribing notes. Took daily morning bath [in the] creek.

In Soko (store) today found letter dated Jan. 3, 1940 on stationery of New Lincoln Hotel, V. L. Reddicliffe, Prop. (Remodeled Throughout) 40 [ ] Rooms (Modernistic Tap Room) (Pix Lincoln letterhead) St. James, Minnesota, addressed to "Dear Gram" & signed "Love Grant." full news deaths & engagements—including Homer & his girl; Prof. Klaras & Germaine.

Began recital 30 days prayer.

➤ MARCH 27 FRIDAY

Started by grobuck & bicycle for Ngamboer, which I reached on bike about 1:30, ahead of others ½ hour or more. Field police came to Ngamboer with more messages. Road along beach but thru semi-jungle pleasant, fairly cool. Banana, papaya trees line road & coffee bushes frequent.

Bought 2 cans real Australian butter from native, in which eggs fried & rice flavored.

Privy hangs over creek & from same place in creek few yards down comes our water for washing, tea, etc.

Slept on floor beneath netting, as natives peeked through cracks in walls.

➤ MARCH 28, SATURDAY

Lay around house all day. Admired beautiful yellow, large but poisonous Alamanda flowers.

Col. G. Bozuwa & Pauw left for Kroe on bicycles, after 2nd message ordering B. report at once, however we can take our time. No bath this morning. Creek too crowded & dirty. Ate many papaya of which I prefer reddish one, Samangka, best. Tried suet treatment on Antoinetta's leg.

➤ MARCH 29 SUNDAY

Palm Sunday. Walked up the jungle road & read Passion gospel, then returned & took over first aid treatment—continuing with suet & boiling bandages & dishes—of people in party. Took 1/2 day.

Field policemen arrived in afternoon, bringing first aid material, *3 bottles beer*, tobacco, cigarette papers, candy. Colijn, Ooster & I drank one glass [of] beer each. Never thought I'd get any in jungle. Japs are back in Kroe. Sent car to end of road for Bozuwa. Stores here—4 in all, practically empty, but found coffee in one & some Kajopoeti oil for mosquito bites, & pieces Kajo (wood) Poetik (white) from white skinned tree.

Natives chant Koran, with or without drumbeats, day & night, or chant plaintive high pitch airs, said to be love calls, when moon is high. Tropic moon & star studded sky beautiful through high palms.

Tonight heavy tropic downpour known as "a Sumatran" beat on tin roof & drenched jungle. No mosquitoes this evening—wonder if [that] portended rain?

➤ MARCH 30 MONDAY

Spent all morning doing first aid work. Made mashed potatoes, using Klim, for dinner. No bath since hitting Ngamboer.

4 Japanese came on bicycles to look over, certify & dress our wounds & notify us to be at Kroe by April 3, Batoe Radga by April 5. However, be-

cause of our wounds & sickness necessitating slow travel, gave us permits beyond that time. They said after April 5 would come military army which would kill all Dutchmen not yet at Batoe Radja. One soldier spoke limited English. Another dressed wounds of Antoinetta & Dr. Colijn.

⇀ March 31 Tuesday

Japs arrived 8:30, took group picture, gave us permits & we left in 4 grobucks, crossing 3 rivers by canoe ferry (small prao) & arrived Tandjongstia midafternoon. Slept private house after excellent dinner of much variety—Terrong, a delicious tree grown fruit very close to a vegetable.

Tandjongstia on end of bay. Full moon lighted sandy, palm-fringed shore. Sky star-studded, waters quiet, gently lapping shore. Daytime view— beautiful sea, sand, jungle, low hills & lastly volcanic range rising to mountain whose top [was] blown off by some ancient volcano.

⇀ April 1 Wednesday

Left Tandjongstia 9:45 a.m., arrived Tenoembang few hours later on grobuck.

Here I had my first bath in creek since Ngamboer. Completed a deck of cards from cardboard, EverReady flashlight battery carton.

Bureau water (lead acetate) proving effective on wounds. Revinol (green tincture) also good. Need adhesive tape badly and we're out of shirt made gauzes I boiled.

⇀ April 2 Thursday

Continued by grobuck to Kroe, arriving about noon & eating at house of K.P.M. agent. Stayed Pasenangraban & had shirt & trousers made.

⇀ April 3 Friday

Japanese arrived & said we were being taken to Benkoelan. Loaded in trucks & a bus & started out, arriving [name crossed out] about 6 p.m. Stayed house of Dutch Controleur Molema, where I got some paper bound books. Had drink of rum, bought socks at village store.

⇀ April 4 Saturday

Traveled all day by truck & bus to Lahat, without food except what bananas [we] could get. Some rice [at] Lahat.

— APRIL 5 SUNDAY (EASTER)

Loaded onto freight car as native populace cheered Japanese. Everywhere we went natives cheered Japanese & seemed glad white man no longer supreme [in] their country.

Transferred to gondola behind engine. No food except what [we were] able to buy when train stopped. Nuns taken from Kroe & other place. All white men, women, as well as Indonesians gathered up. Arrived Palembang dusk, but didn't cross river, by ferry, until long after dark. Men taken to old prison. Women sent off separately.

— APRIL 6 MONDAY

Catholic bishop of Palembang & number of priests also in concentration camp. 207 men in camp, mostly Dutch & Indo's, but about 12 English, 3 Irish, 2 Australians, several Swiss & French & —lone American. All quarters shifted today & I ended up alone in [a] large room next [to the] hospital.

— APRIL 7 TUESDAY

Stood 2 hours in sun waiting for Colonel to inspect us. Good sleep last nite. Heard stories of escapes from Singapore in which boats without information ran gauntlet [of] destroyers, planes & submarines losing 43 ships, hundreds [of] people—women, children. 1 nurse in water 4½ days with lifebelt still alive when rescued.

— APRIL 8 WEDNESDAY

More Dutch prisoners came into camp, bringing news of heavy fighting off Australia & Timor & raids on Ceylon.

Came down with fever, possibly malaria.

— APRIL 9 THURSDAY

My room now the first aid center. Fever abated today. Englishman brought me swallow of coffee. Little comforts.

— APRIL 10 FRIDAY

Fever back & chills. Doctor says it's malaria. Japanese admitted first fruit to camp—bananas & pineapple. I had 2 bananas for breakfast & a slice of pineapple with my rice for lunch. They now permit 10 G[uilders] worth of stuff [to be] bought daily.

⇀ April 11 Saturday

Guard stopped fruit from coming in. Used what [was] left of butter I opened yesterday to mix today with rice, which for first time fried & spiced with sombal. Had a banana for breakfast. Ants getting worse, crawling over me & into everything continually. Fever down today. Not sure whether I have tropic or tertiana malaria. Former worst.

⇀ April 12 Sunday

Joyous Sunday—a banana for breakfast. Also doctor said I have malaria tertiana, mildest with no complications usually following. Other two types malaria quatriana—which has brain & heart complications & malaria tropica, worst kind—followed by serious kidney, spleen or bladder complications.

Three months after M. tertiana I must take 4 quinine tablets daily for 1 week, or will have another attack, said doctor.

4 old Dutchmen on pensions were brought in yesterday from Lahat. They asked for imprisonment because their pensions ceased & they [were] afraid of starving.

No malaria mosquitoes in Palembang, so no need of taking quinine as preventative.

Mass not allowed in camp. Nor is singing.

J. A. Gillbrook one of 300 or 400—mostly women & children who evacuated Singapore on *Mata Hari*. It surrendered to Jap destroyer to save lives. Believed only 1 of group not sunk. Survivors taken to Bangka (island) & imprisoned month & 3 weeks before coming here. Bangka 10 hours by boat from Palembang.

Began novena to Holy Name.

⇀ April 13 Monday

No fever today. Apparently am recovering.

⇀ April 14 Tuesday

2 bananas again today. No fever. Reduced to 3 quinines daily. 23 Indonesians let go today. Dutch official said he [was] informed by J[apanese] propaganda chief all whites will be driven out of Asia

25 Masses, Comm[unions], Ros[aries], Stations [of the Cross] if port reached.

Book 3

⟶ APRIL 15 WEDNESDAY

Japanese guards claim landings [in] California & Australia & attacks on Vladivostok. Other reports—Americans landed [in] Manila & Borneo. Russia & Japan at war. Tokyo bombed. 700 British planes [ ] Berlin.

Japanese guard said he fought at Hongkong, Singapore & here & that [h]is fate was to land with Japanese at San Francisco & die. "Then Japan will win, my ashes go back [to] Tokyo." His spirit will [be] enshrined forever.

Two Dutch commissioners of police said Palembang fell amid panic & very little fighting. About 500 J[apanese] parachutists attempted [to] land [at] oil field & airdrome but most [were] killed in [the] air & not more than 150 landed. 15,000 British & Australians—mostly without weapons, 15,000 well armed Dutch troops about ½ natives, fled panic stricken, when no orders came from Palembang headquarters because G.H.Q. fled. Japanese soldiers following day entered Palembang in little groups [of] 10 or 20 warily—expecting hail [of] bullets from houses—but all silence. They finally took all [of the] town & burst into laughter. [The] following day thousands [of] Japanese arrived from Singapore, rowing up river mostly in small commandeered craft such as Chinese junks.

10% of men in camp ill with various things including about 10 influenza cases. Minor wound treatments decreased from 29 to 13. I'm rapidly recovering. 52 more men due tomorrow—4 coming [to] my room.

About 5 p.m. 162 men came in, including 1 American. A number were carried in on stretchers. Tough looking bunch. Wonder if we looked like that? But they all seem to have plenty of clothes & suitcases.

⟶ APRIL 16 THURSDAY

American's name Eric Germann, a brewer caught when fleeing Singapore where he worked in Tiger brewery since November.

Camp so jammed—360—many sleeping outdoors on cement walks. Arrivals said they worked hard at Pladjoe unloading ships & carting oil pipes. 5 stretcher cases of dysentery among them. 2 died recently. Japanese doctor came yesterday & Oosten & 2 others sent outside to hospital.

⟶ APRIL 17 FRIDAY

Wrote letter to Mother, Dad & Jean. Wonder when if ever, it will reach them or when I can mail it? 336 persons in camp.

Bread today! Small individual loaves to [the] sick. [ ] washed my clothes. Also tobacco ration. I'm giving mine away. Spanish classes now held [in] this room.

— APRIL 18 SATURDAY

Bread & coffee for breakfast & remainder [of] my tin of butter! But diarrhoea hit me again later. Plenty of reading with 2 old *Times* & O. Henry's "The 4,000,000."

Discussed how Lux soap reached all native kampons. Also EverReady batteries, but most tokos [stores] out, supplanted by Hongkong made ones.

Curran Shaw teaching me Malayan. King Henry VIII bearded Allen teaching Spanish. Tall, lean Morgan teaching Japanese.

— APRIL 19 SUNDAY

First church services in camp;. Catholic bishop preached sermon in Dutch—no equipment for Mass—& Church of England minister led his followers in hymns & prayers.

3 men, one a priest, came to camp from hospital.

— APRIL 20 MONDAY

Black Monday in camp, 2 Britons died of dysentery. Robbins, 51, director of Malayan collieries; Atkin-Berry, Singapore architect, within 15 minutes of each other. J[apanese] officers & Dr. came immediately. Bodies placed [in] 2 wood coffins & buried. Van Fleet, camp director went out with bodies & en route bought chicken eggs for sick. Both men could have been saved by proper attention in time. Camp food immediately better as more rations allowed to come in.

Reports from outside say Sumatra only place Europeans interned because Dutch still resisting in north.

— APRIL 21 TUESDAY

Bread every day now. Our room houses W. Probyn Allen, 31, of Boats Pure Drug Co. with Henry VIII beard; Co-op Pres. George Holderness, Malayan planter [with] stomach ulcer; H. L. Mellor, 77, retired furrier, extreme hernia; and Henry Diakan, 37, Dutch planter, recovering from malaria.

Clinic now charging 5 cents per person per dressing & drug service in order to replenish stock.

↵ APRIL 22 WEDNESDAY

Diakan stricken with dys[entery] or dia[rrhoea] & transferred to hospital bay.

Toko—store—opened in camp today with cell buying. We got 1 can sardines, 1 can butter, 1 can corned beef, 4 pieces sugar for 2.56—terrific prices. Big cells [of] 30 men got 5 cans each! Much bickering.

↵ APRIL 23 THURSDAY

Another red letter food day. Breakfasted [on] bread & sardines. Got can cheese, another sardines, plenty tea, good lunch & dinner.

Bishop took critical turn & removed to sisters' hospital. Played bridge with Drs. Hollweg & Paddy West for 2nd nite with our new light & made grand slam clubs, also 5 clubs.

↵ APRIL 24 FRIDAY

Reports circulating British & Dutch separating. Van Fleet told me I'm on his list for inclusion with Dutch. Bad class of British in camp getting increasingly obnoxious & selfish, to detriment of handful [of] splendid Britons here.

Fish served to sick for first time. Epidemic of language studies in camp—Spanish, Dutch, German, Japanese, Malayan, English.

Singapore evacuees in bad way for money—those not flat broke have only Staats dollars. I changed 5 G. for $10 for Gillbrook & gave 5 to Germann.

Inoculated.

↵ APRIL 25 SATURDAY

First blackout in camp. J[apanese] colonel explained Flying Fortresses bombing Borneo & expected over here. Col. Gosenson, scarfaced from [ ] revolutionary days, Dutch commander holding out [in] northern Sumatra.

I'm now the doctor's assistant, swathing wounds, bandaging, etc. Rations improving daily, bread [and] coffee each morning.

Inoculated—cholera, Typhus A & B.

Roll calls becoming more frequent—6 a.m., 10 a.m., 3 p.m., 6 p.m.—Something is afoot outside.

⟶ APRIL 26 SUNDAY

Our daily routine: Up at first crack of daylight, since impossible to sleep with entire camp stirring. Wash, drink cup hot water flavored with coffee which Holderness manages to heat in kitchen [on] account [of] his ulcer. Then read my prayers. Kitchen coffee then—past few days—issued, after which bread issued &—also past few days—& we open 1 can of our treasures from newly opened store (toko).

By that time it's almost 8 a.m. Doctor's clinic hours from 8 to 10 a.m. & our room hums with first aid work. Then I go out in the sun with my Malayan lessons & study as much as possible—usually walking up & down.

Kitchen is busiest place in camp—4 a.m. to 7 or 8 p.m. every day. Smith—Palembang Hotel proprietor—in charge & doing marvelous job.

Van Fleet, camp director—doing best job of all—tall, cheerful Dutchman with ringing voice he overcame great obstacles & put camp on its feet & running order.

This would be a sorry place indeed without the Dutch who work like horses & carry bulk of load. They're always cheerful, singing, offering their help to others at every opportunity, sharing everything they have—in sharp contrast to the selfish, lazy, dirty riffraff of some other nationalities here. My hat will be forever off to the Dutch—they're tops.

Principal meal served about 12:30 p.m.—main course rice with a vegetable on the side & often garnished with something like *kedgeree*—a sort of fish chowder Pilau in India, Pilaff in Hungary. Sometimes a part which includes peanuts.

Our room usually busy all day with Spanish students, doctors, Brother Macarius who helps doctors & does yeoman service in hospital of 5 dysentery cases—one a big Dutch policeman who has been more or less delirious for days & continually tries to escape. He sees his wife outside, or motor cars, or threatens to fine attendants $25 for stopping him. Luckily he hasn't gotten violent.

Clinic reopens 4 to 5 then comes dinner—usually a cup of soup & small portion of rice.

We were without light in our room until a few days ago.

Chorus of lusty & good Dutch voices—accompanied by a banjo-uke—supplies song for some two hours after dark.

We usually are in bed by 9 p.m. Palembang time (11 p.m. Tokyo time). Haven't been able to get to sleep until 1 or 2 a.m. past few nights. Previously

I welcomed sleep—a surcease from prison & usually filled with pleasant dreams.

Got 1 can of Klim today for myself.

⟶ April 27 Monday

Frequent explosions heard at intervals day & night causing speculations.

Letters from interned wives delivered to husbands here today.

⟶ April 28 Tuesday

Finished hemstitching pair [of] shorts cut down from pair white pants of some former inmate of Palembang Jail.

Gordon Burt, New Zealander & engineer of R.P.C. (Asiatic Petroleum) gave lecture on Worsley's polar expedition of 1926.

Am now working few hours afternoon in dysentery ward—bed pans.

Dr. Bruin came from hospital & brought Mass essentials for priests.

⟶ April 29 Wednesday

Three Masses said this morning—first in jail—at 4:30, 5 & 5:30 a.m. I went to two & received communion.

Jiu Jitsu class had first real casualty today—which is Japanese Emperor's birthday.

⟶ April 30 Thursday

Birthday of Princess Juliana so Dutch had a lottery—good watch bought for 50 guilders as first prize & minor prizes—one a can opener which is valuable here, cigarette papers, bananas, few cans [of] food.

Brilliant full moon lit the night sky. Song fest afterward cut short by guard.

At tea time pisan kolak (boiled bananas, coconut milk, gula malaka & cinnamon) served—delicious.

Plenty of bed pans this afternoon.

Mass & communion this morning.

⟶ May 1 Friday

Mass & comm[union] 5 a.m. Began Novena B[lessed] V[irgin] M[ary] also 2nd 30 day prayer.

Rice saved from dinner goes good with Klim for breakfast—which is not served in camp.

Burt Smallwood passed out while I was doctoring his impetigo blisters.

⤚ May 2 Saturday

Making novenas & going [to] Mass each morning 5 a.m.

G[erman] doctor perfunctorily examining Blum—seriously ill [with] dysentery, malaria & other complications & just after he'd had shots, searched around in bag produced ampule anti-tetanus serum, filled needle & [was] about to inject when Hol[derness] noticed, stopped just [in] time, bawled him out. "They can shoot me or kill me or beat me," Hol said, "but they can't kill these patients."

⤚ May 3 Sunday

Mass in No. 3 bloc 6:30 a.m. large attendance. Fr. Elling sermoned in Dutch.

Smallwood, 220 pound, squat, mustachioed cockney of many past jobs one [of the] camp's best workers covered with impetigo blisters. I spend [at] least [an] hour or more each day going over him.

Morgan taken from camp 8:30 a.m., told to pack his barang (luggage) & leave.

Store issue today from which we got 1 jar peanut butter, 1 can sardines, 1 bottle lime juice, 1 tin Bully beef & some tobacco. Also put in new order.

⤚ May 4 Monday

3 taken to hospital, young Hobbs, 16, jockey's son, Park, & a Dutchman.

Pladjoe waterfront bombed—we heard explosions & ack-ack. (false report)

Story of 25 Australian nurses, Montok. Learned 13 men, including Wolfe from our lifeboat who went to Kotagoen, were clapped into jail 4 days, without aid, then sent to Palembang military camp & Wolfe now in hospital.

⤚ May 5 Tuesday

Harold Lawson, Remington representative Singapore, played uke & sang for me his own compositions, including one "Singapore Away"—

excellent. He said 12 or so years ago in London he wrote words & lyrics, submitted to publisher who later rejected but subsequently song under an American composer's name swept England—I remember it sweeping U.S.—"that I reveal exactly how I feel, etc.!"

Tomorrow, May 5, rumored [to] be "big change" in camp.

⟶ MAY 6 WEDNESDAY

R. H. Prior, 59, Rubber Regulations Officer, Kuala Kangsi, Malaya & now hospital hard worker, would make good copy. As would, to a certain extent, Brother Macarius. Airport heavily bombed today, ack-ack heavy. (false)

⟶ MAY 7 THURSDAY

Two months ago today *Poelau Bras* sank. This morning started calisthenics with Colijn. Strenuous course.

⟶ MAY 8 FRIDAY

Now 7 dysentery patients in hospital. Steak meat served dinner—first meat except miniscule pieces [of] pork since interned. Also special pisan, sweet potato & gula java sauce served for dessert.

More bombing reported. C[olijn]. said [he] saw [a] bomber disappear into cloud. Can't imagine where from unless seaplane base [on] lake [in] northern Sumatra.

Burt Smallwood's impetigo [pustules] very bad today. Washed him with potassium permanganate solution, soap & water, then broke scores [of] pustules, then pure solution & boric salve.

⟶ MAY 9 SATURDAY

Supplies issued from store from which we got Klim, Bully beef & little else of our large order.

Hospital rushed today. I on hop from dawn to dark.

MAY 10 SUNDAY

6:30 a.m. Mass & co[mmunion]. English. Parson Wardle—ran seaman's mission in Singapore, sick, Gillbrook conducting Church [of] England services.

⁓ MAY 11 MONDAY

Capt. McAllister nearly died in dysentery ward at noon.

Meat for supplies room.

Camp general fund so low there's talk of cutting out bread & other things & depending on Japanese supplies alone—which would be lean living. Store to be abolished entirely.

Van Brockeland, big, wild eyed Dutchman in dysentery ward who is able to get up & take bath still insists [on] messing bed [at] night.

Capt. McAllister, 59 four days ago, rushed [to] hospital ward [at] 8 p.m., died 15 minutes after arrival. Thus he got his wish, he has been wanting to die for weeks.

⁓ MAY 12 TUESDAY

Brown & Van Brockeland, dysentery cases, taken to hospital this morning. Then 4 more went before noon—Burt Smallwood, old man Meelor, Brother Iranius & a Belgian with ringworm.

Van Brockeland died one hour after entering hospital. Vander Fleet officiated [at] funeral because priests in camp & bishop ill in hospital.

Reports 5 May naval battle ending May 11. American & Australian fleet destroyed Japanese war fleet Australia–New Zealand bound—sinking 100,000 tons Jap shipping including 2 cruisers airplane carrier, number destroyers, 4 transports.

Russian general offensive smashing Germans back. Churchill speech said naval battle turning point Far Eastern war & said Allies gave 1,000 planes to Russia, therefore unable [to] send many [to the] Far East. Promised end [of] war this year.

4,000,000 German casualties against Russia—more than German losses [in] entire World War [I].

Japanese took Mandalay & drove 100 miles up Burma road but Chinese drove back & now storming Mandalay.

Hollweg returned from hospital & with twinkle [in his] eye, "I forgot & left Wenning at hospital with wife & newborn son. I wonder how he'll get back?"

Japanese becoming more lenient. Now will allow camp to send daily supplies to women's camp & fortnightly individual parcels.

Tailor made cigarettes, cigars, even whiskey & sherry reported in camp.

~ MAY 13 WEDNESDAY

Report—Chinese regular troops penetrated Shanghai, Hankow & Nanking!!! I don't believe that. Might be new riots, or guerrilla uprisings, including puppet troop defections.

Vyner Brook sunk off Bangka, Muntok Feb. 13—about 100 of 260 reached shore. 65 to 75 one group—Aus[tralian] nurses 15 or 35; 8 stretcher cases; 8 military, 4 ships officers. Men-women lined up separately. Mil first to nearby cove, then 15 more, including old man.

An American girl in her twenties on one, Ardalene Sutherland, address unknown, died Feb. 14 on life raft of bomb shrapnel wounds suffered on raft, 3rd day, on raft, whereupon pushed into sea. Others on raft 3 days more, reached Bangka. On other raft was American Chinese young woman, Mrs. Phyllis Ing Ng, Hongkong passport #302 % Mrs. Evelyn I. Tsui, 511 Calihi Street, Honolulu, who [were] given freedom & sent to Bangka's capital Pangkalping.

L. G. Jeffrey, 51, gnarled little Englishman who had charge [of] moving Hankow power plant to Chungking before Hankow's fall, is one [of] our camp members. He languished [in] Hankow jail 3 mos. after returning put their water works back in running order.

Dutch chorus tonight with harmonica leading. DeYoung's & Vander Fleet's tenors exceptionally good.

~ MAY 14 THURSDAY

Fr. Elling preached exceptionally good sermon in English—his first—& sang High Mass 6:30 a.m.—Ascension Thursday.

Last night I gave Vanden Fleet 25 guilders as a private donation, also 20 guilders to Eric Germann, making 25 in all so he will have something. Also gave 10 staats dollars to Women's Fund.

Read two sample American radio broadcasts to Scott's English class—one as I would describe Bandoeng's fall & the other as Winchell would.

3 civil service men captured Sunday came into camp saying 3 G patrols disappeared completely between Lahot and Benkoeler. Pasira's daughters.

~ MAY 15 FRIDAY

Enjoyed every free moment reading G. B. Harrison's anthology "A Book of English Poetry," which brought many thoughts of Jean to mind & the hope she someday markets the lovely poetry she writes—dear little sister.

Learned Cruikshank smuggled in the sherry wine. No bread today as [a] result [of an] altercation between G[uard] & breadman who [was] beaten up yesterday—allegedly result [of] G's activities.

Three men to hospital Sisters today—Stalin, a Maltese who lost eye in ship bombing & must have it removed, Rothies, a Dutch dysentery case & Junior [ ], ringworm Belgian kid whose father went May 12.

Vander Fleet ill in bed so Van Der Wettering, School Master, acts as camp leader.

⤙ May 16 Saturday

Palembang's flour supply gone so no more bread anyway. Rice also low.

All my bedding and clothes were airing in sun this morning while I bathed. A sudden shower sent me, covered with soap & water & nude, scuttling around camp rushing them inside. Shower also broke up various classes as men rescued their washing.

Dr. Holweg ill—diahorrea [*sic*], but refused hospital ward. Angry & excited when West tried [to] send him—he's afraid he wouldn't be able to return.

⤙ May 17 Sunday

To 5 a.m. & 5:30 masses instead of 6:30 because of early morning rush.
No bread today, but 2 bananas each.
Sinar Matahari—Japanese published native newspaper.

⤙ May 18 Monday

Paid 2 guilders Holderness for bread—1 guilder for Allen.
Small loaves of bread issued today—the last general rations. Holweg worse, needs hospitalization.

Yesterday Eric told off Cruikshank, short, swarthy chunky individual who claims he is Argentinian but of Scotch parentage, who is in solid with guards & acts as interpreter—also conducts camp business in getting things from outside & selling at huge profits. Cruik called a guard & said Eric & Jackson, an Australian, were malcontents & spreading dissatisfaction in camp.

Last night dreamed of Dad & Mother—first time he has figured in my dreams for years. The scene was home & a combination of 686 [?] J st. & 659 11th East. Strangely, every time I dream of going upstairs at home it is always the J st. stairs to the attic, & then, once up, becomes 659 11th East. Last night Dad was reclining on the bathroom floor, against the radiator, resting. He looked slightly ill but said he was okay. Mother was in my room doing something or other—apparently sewing. Dad had a blanket around him & smiled cheerfully.

⟶ MAY 19 TUESDAY

G[uard]s summoned out 3 Dutchmen. A.R.P., a chemist & a banker Rumor Morgan, a Singapore police force member, intelligence division, who has been out for several weeks is having rough go at P.D.

Prior still strongly predicting turns in Far Eastern war May 24. Based on 11 & 12 chapter of Book of Daniel—"Blessed is he that waiteth & cometh to the 1335th day." He dates it from Munich agreement, which he bases on Chapter 13 Revelation verse 5, "And power was given him (Hitler) (by England) to continue 40 & 2 months." "Him" is Hitler, Munich gave him power. Prior arbitrarily selects Hitler as the first beast in chapter 13 & Japan as the second.

Colijn points out all systems of contemporary government represented in camp by the way groups & individuals conduct their lives. I debate whether this camp is a comprehensive cross section of average human nature. Allen thinks no—says too many low class Englishmen to be representative of Britain.

M. L. Phillips, Malayan planter, says ship captain who [was] 14 months prisoner [in] Germany [during] World War I, told how on liberation large crowd went on feast orgy in Holland—they'd been existing on soup 14 months & all next day seriously ill—4 died. Let that be lesson to us. Altho we are not that badly off for food—I think we're doing fairly well [as] far as grub [is] concerned.

⟶ MAY 21 THURSDAY

Exceptionally fine tiffin today of rice, pork, thick vegetable soup, sambal, cucumbers.

To accompaniment of Gillbrook's concertina, Britishers had their first singsong last night. Pretty foul singing, in fact Dutch knew more *complete* songs than the Britons.

John Fonwa, Palembang assistant resident, reported how, last December, he received [a] letter from his two sons in Holland via Peking. They wrote as to a friend, "Dear John."

Natives in street in front of jail scoop from road any grain of rice which falls when rice carried in here—a thing strictly against Mohammedan custom—shows how dire food situation is outside.

I'm well tanned & healthy now—able to meet anything. Keeping my fingers crossed, though—because of much impetigo, athlete's foot, appapox (monkey pox) & other skin infections & diseases spreading.

Attitude of G's & H's being questioned is that of both allied against the natives.

Book 4

⚬ MAY 22, 1942 FRIDAY

Fried potatoes served for first time. This morning only 150 eggs came & since 330 men now in camp that was less than half an egg per man. We've been splitting hard boiled duck eggs—1/2 per man. So eggs scrambled & cooked with butter in potatoes—delicious.

No vegetables entered camp today.

Brown, a Mrs. Roberts, wife & mother of two men here, & a third person, not from here, died in sisters hospital last night 11 & 11:15 p.m. respectively. Brown & Mrs. Roberts of dysentery.

The Roberts were taken out this morning for funeral. As usual, following a death, Japanese allowed [a] few more of our patients to be taken to hospital. An Englishman, Johnston, & Miller—dysentery, Foulds, osteomyelitis, & a Dutchman, Sromp, dysentery. Total 21 patients removed to hospital since April 15, of whom 3 died there. Two others died here in camp.

⚬ MAY 23 SATURDAY

New G[uard]s imposed regulation allows only $200 weekly to be spent outside camp by camp, which eliminates toko & bread & limits purchases to kitchen essentials.

Camp rapidly running out of tobacco. I have enough for at least another week unless I give some of it away—which is inevitable.

⚬ MAY 24 SUNDAY

Prior's day of prophecy came & went with no news here of a turn in events of war. However if there was one, we might not hear of it for long time.

Minje indicated we might be shifted to airdrome—where quarters being prepared & where we would have to work. (Good chance of being bombed, too) Military prisoners [have] been working there [a] long time.

Crude oil refinery here—which allegedly so badly wrecked [it] would take [at] least 6 months to repair—now working again, G[uard]s assert.

Folkaringa, a Dutch Standard Oil man, acting as Dutch Protestant preacher on Sundays in hospital is all time worst patient. A diarrhoea case, he knows more than doctors & raises hell with everyone. "Inattention & self conceit of attendants has made of me, the most humble man in camp, a devil," he said this afternoon. Tonight, however, he apologized contritely.

⇀ May 25 Monday

Folk[aringa] & Prior went round & round today—Folk insisting it was raining & that his washing be brought in when it wasn't raining at all.

Women's camp elected two leaders—Mrs. Holweg for Dutch & Dr. Jean McDowall for British.

Women reportedly now getting ample supplies.

New variety of ants have invaded us now, tiny black ones which scuttle about like fleas.

Shortly after Palembang fell 60 Allied (British) soldiers dead buried *with* identification tags. City officials petitioned allow care for wounded—which refused, then only remove identification tags so names sendable [to] To[kyo], then Geneva. After long deliberation refused—with polite thanks, [on the] grounds [that] such tasks strictly job [of] G[erman] army. Civil officials could [not] tend wounded, bury dead, etc.

Camp this afternoon resembles Brig[ham] Young's back yard on wash day, with hundreds of articles of clothing hanging on every available inch of barbed wire, clotheslines & spread [on the] grass. [On] Account [of] overcast sky past two days long drying time required.

⇀ May 26 Tuesday

Llewellyn, English chief electrical engineer in Penang taken to hospital with T. B. Schrieff & Wenning & Brother Macarius also went—but the first two to see their wives. Wenning's with a new son & Schrieff's ill. Macarius for a brief respite from his arduous labors here.

Japanese collected new list of names, wherefore British & Dutch lined up, separated & names & dates of arrival re-registered. Roll call included names of camp dead & hospitalized. My name was included in Dutch list first and remains there, thank goodness.

Reports of Burma fighting indicate Japanese progressing in Yunnan & also practically reached Asams [?] border—British India.

Mexico has declared war on Axis, after Mex. ship sunk off Florida coast.

When roll call sounded today I thought we were being packed off to airport or elsewhere.

➤ MAY 27 WEDNESDAY

57 inoculations this morning for Typhoid 1 & 2, cholera & dysentery. Holweg brought serum from his last trip [to the] hospital.

R. H. Park, an English planter from Malaya who was removed to Sisters Hosp[ital] May 4 died yesterday of dysentery. He was a skeleton thin man while in sick bay here, but a good chap & a good patient. When I was answering a Jap questionnaire for him one day, under "Property" he instructed me to write "personal possessions of a sort." Camp death total now 6.

➤ MAY 28 THURSDAY

Three more to Sisters hosp[ital] today—Folkeringa, Josef & Von Rheeden. Oosten came back from hosp[ital] to camp, looking exceedingly fit. Said he lost 40 pounds.

Reports Japs landed 100,000 men on banks upper Sulween River & drove into Yunnan within 7 miles of Kunming.

Am now exchanging Malayan lessons for English lessons with Agerbrek.

G. plane gasoline analyzed highly leaded, 86 octane, & oil not optimum grade, not up to standard required by airplane designers & manufacturers—both meaning future maintenance high.

➤ MAY 29 FRIDAY

Kitchen rigged up meat scales, from which men hung by their hands for grand camp weighing in. I scaled 57 kilos, 125.4 pounds. Most men had lost much weight—as much as 40 pounds in some cases—but it was principally fat & all agreed they felt more fit—they certainly look fit for the most part.

All British Eurasians & Dutch Eurasians except civil service or police, taken out today by Japanese & told they could be released from camp & be strictly on their own—no food, money or lodging supplied by

Japanese. Cruikshank, who claims Argentinian citizenship, & 3 Czechoslovaks—2 Bata men & an engineer, included. Many wished to consult wives first before making choice. They're liable to face hard times outside on their own. Cannot leave Palembang. Only 3 neutrals who left here last month so far permitted to go to Java.

⚊ May 30 Saturday

Dutch Eurasians called out today—including police—& given choice of leave living outside. Colijn, Holdebrand, former burgomaster & others taken out for questioning regarding destruction in Palembang. R. H. Scott, British diplomatic official widely acquainted in China & F[ar] E[ast] had when Singapore fell taken out with his luggage (barang). I'm apprehensive about him. Scott one of best Britishers in camp. The heavy beard he's grown since the day he and another civilian volunteered to man a dinghy in rough Malacca Straits in effort to reach Japanese destroyer & inform them the ship *Giangbee* was filled with women, children & male civilians, probably will be shaved. He wanted to keep it—was a handsome one—until he met his wife & child in Australia. He's brother-in-law [of] Dewar Durie.

⚊ May 31 Sunday

Completed my month of special devotions to B.V.M. at two masses—5 & 5:30 a.m. & communion.

Two men taken to Sisters hospital today—Gilbrooke—to whom I gave 25 guilders to purchase Klim, flints, fluid, note books, exercise books, glue, pencil, & Gleroem, a Dutchman—both dysentery cases.

Told today on May 18 High Japan Naval officer passed through Palembang escorted by procession [of] 22 brand new autos, Fords, Chevs, Olds—Followed by day or two report fleet Adm[iral] recalled or [ ] dismissed.

Smallwood returned from hospital & promptly produced fresh pustules—looks like he'll break out again. Today started giving DeBout pot[assium] perman[ganate] bath.

⚊ June 1, 1942

Holweg said he heard bombing [at] 2:30 a.m., few minutes later heard plane motors. Brilliant full moon okay for night raids but I doubt it was one or that he heard it. Daylight raids more likely here as target—refinery—small.

Smallwood definitely breaking out again.

Bought small mosquito net from Curran-Sharp for 7½ guilders
I mentioned Oosten's supplies.
Began Novena to Sacred Heart.

⤙ JUNE 2, 1942 TUESDAY

Reports Japanese have surrounded Kinwa, Chekiang.
Schenk gave me sheaf of tobacco as birthday present. Holderness gave me *3 cigars* (Senators)! I traded him a sheaf of tobacco for 2 cigars (additional) to give Fr. Elling whose birthday is June 4.

⤙ JUNE 3, 1942 WEDNESDAY

My birthday—as usual—Fr. Elling wakened me 4:45 a.m. & I attended 2 Masses & received communion. Was pleasantly surprised at number of people who knew & congratulated me. Oosten gave me two sheafs tobacco & pkg cig. Papers Allen gave me 1 cigar & shortly thereafter Fr. Elling appeared & gave me 2 more—for a total of 6 cigars—phenomenal in this camp. I gave Elling 2 cigars—the Senators traded Holderness for tobacco.

At noon Allen & I dined with Colijn, Oosten & De Bruin—as a birthday dinner—they supplying sambal, doging goreng, Bully beef, soy sauce & for dessert—stewed stem ginger bottled in U.S.A. or Australia. Had 4 bananas today, too.

⤙ JUNE 4, 1942 THURSDAY

Finished Louis Bromfield's "Night in Bombay." Don't like this brand of story—too sordid.
Numerous explosions outside today—from direction of river—sounded like gun, but long intervals indicated blasting or demolition work.
Carruthers taken to hospital—mild dysentery.
Sold my big mosquito net for 7.50, same price I paid for Curran-Sharp for his smaller one.
Curran now giving Oosten conversational lessons.

⤙ JUNE 5, 1942 FRIDAY

Rice ration reduced to 400 grams per man—little less than a pound.
Cruikshank started raffle of tinned goods to get enough money to use if he is released. I imagine he already has a tidy stake from selling smuggled goods, unless he lost it gambling.

— JUNE 6 SATURDAY

C[olijn] rumor had Kitchen fighting still northern Sumatra—which amazed him because he thought everything would be over in 6 mo. (General who commanded capture Terakan told C. everything—including Australia's capture would be accomplished in 6 mos.) Gen. [ ] full Gen. & veteran of China but unfound name. May have gone down with transport.

Miri [?] British North Borneo reported producing again—normal capacity 40,000–50,000 tons monthly in result British policy [of] "denial" as compared [to] Dutch policy [of] total destruction. Denial is removal only of parts which [are] replaceable [after a] certain period—6 mos. [in] this instance—so quickly usable when recaptured but unusable to enemy. However, G. got it quickly [into] working order & crude now shipped here for refining.

Aviation gasoline supplies Java sufficient for 3 months when fell—unknown whether destroyed—were scattered at depots [throughout] Java.

C. invited into our house by G along with D[utch] C[ommander] in [Chief] to listen [to] long speech how all-powerful is J[apan]. At [the] end [of] which interpreter asked for reply—"NO" snapped D C in C & stuck to it.

Camp starved for news and I'm starved for intellectual stimulation. Would like to start a seminar for intelligent discussion [of a] given subject in order to spend profitable evening that was instead boring, idle chatter.

I appreciate American books & magazines now more than ever in my life, especially on seeing how far magazines overshadow British publications.

Late this evening unconfirmed report English landed Holland.

Dutchmen entertained one G[uard] in Block 7 with card tricks as part of campaign to procure a better light globe. Block 7 got it! The G seems decent sort of fellow.

— JUNE 7 SATURDAY

Another source this morning confirming Holland report. However I'll await better verification.

Attended 5:30 Mass & C & also High Mass 6:30 at which Fr. Bargka [?] parish priest at Muntok preached excellent, inspiring & thought-provoking sermon in English. Two months ago he could speak or understand very little English.

Dutchman named Praiswork, Palembang Water Board harbor employee, entered camp, gaunt, hungry. Said he'd been jailed since May 11, taken to Singapore because G[uard]s thought he was Scott! Then returned here when they discovered he was not! Morgan & Scott now both [in] Singapore.

Camp totally blacked out without warning for 1½ hour, not even smoking permitted.

— June 8 Monday

N. K. Faint, 21, Burton on Trent, Royal Marines ex-Repulse & Samuel Dalyrimple, 22, Greenock, Scotland, R.A.F. Outfitter entered camp from Jambe where hospitalized since Feb. 19 after their ships, *Quala* & *Tinpic* & 2 others sunk off Pompom islands. 4 other British, civilians, & 6 nurses, Matron Penary Hospital McKillin others from Singapore, including lady Dr. Thompson, who D. said G. Capt. struck over eye with flashlite, knocked to the ground, [and] kicked. When D. [was] discharged, same G kicked [his] leg wounds, knocked [him] down, [and] kicked [him] over [the] ground.

D. believes [at] least half aboard *Tinpic* (200 male airforcers & rest male civilians, many Chinese) perished. He [with] badly wounded legs clung with eight others to sides [of] crippled life raft whereon 1 Chinese girl drifted 2 days, [and was] finally pulled in by Malayan fisherman.

Faint on *Repulse* when sunk by aerial torpedoes—6 direct hits at once, [went] down in 5 minutes, after many successive waves [of] high bombers, low torpedo planes. Only 1 plane dived into ship & [could not] tell whether accidental or deliberate. A. A. [anti-aircraft] guns got many—said J. admitted 45. Planes came from field which warships had intended shelling. F[aint] picked up by [a] destroyer after 5 hours [in the] water, clinging to [a] keg. He [is] hospitalized here as convalescent.

— June 9 Tuesday

Completed Novena to Sacred Heart.

Report Allies landed northern France, Holland, Norway.

Managed to get bigger light globe for room by bit [of] skullduggery. Crui[kshank]'s tales get bigger daily—now he says Colijn offered him "big exploratory job in New Guinea" & another offer made to "do big planting job [in] Malaya."

"Star Spangled Banner" kept running through my mind today. "The land of the free and the home of the brave" really mean something now. A concentration camp is good for the patriotic sense as well as the soul. I am increasingly grateful to have had this experience. The hard part, though, is knowing how worried are the folks at home.

Informed today Int. Red + has inquired regarding *Poelau Bras* victims & survivors. Hope it is correct & our names have gone to Geneva. (false report)

Praisewerk saw only 1 European civilian & what appeared to be 2 European women in Singapore—except war prisoners—White & Black—working on damaged waterfront.

Sikhs appeared better treated than whites. One Sikh officer among workers allowed to walk about without guard. P. said he was well treated all [the] time [he was] in custody.

Scott taken [to] Singapore Friday morning. Trip takes 4 days to outer border, 1 day thru minefields—5 in all.

Mistaken identity caused by inadequately worded order from Lt Col Jap. Police Singapore "2 investigation cases"—Morgan one.

25 Korean women, camp followers brought to Palembang on launch which returned him. He was vaccinated & inoculated in Singapore Gen Hosp. library—now a laboratory—& given certificate before returning here. Tobacco, knife, pocketbook taken from him in Singapore but registered & returned when he left. Saw no damage except one store on streets he traveled. Native shops & Chinese, open for business.

⌐ JUNE 10 WEDNESDAY

A Japanese Major Gen. (Shoca) with Lt. Col. inspected camp & in German asked about food—whether getting bread "No." Potatoes? Rarely. 8 times since beginning. Meat "Extremely little."

Wardle & VanDam to dentist for extraction & Dumas & Faint to hospital—Dumas dysentery & Faint convalescing from wounds.

Fanoy (pronounced VONWAH) taking names all *Poelau Bras* survivors used my list for initials & checking.

⌐ JUNE 11 THURSDAY

Two palm oil planters, one a nephew [of] Colijn—same name, entered camp. They had been kept on estates since Sumatra fell by Japanese until factory producing satisfactorily—J's using it for lubricating oil—then sent here immediately. Wardle & VanDam not yet returned from dentist visit—which mystifies camp.

Rumor Allies captured all New Guinea & Japanese evacuating Borneo. And that Allied invasion of Northern France repulsed in one day.

The swell 34 watt globe we got yesterday burned out tonight.

↦ JUNE 12 FRIDAY

Feast of Sacred Heart. Priests & brothers sang 2 hymns in good 4 part harmony after second Mass.

Finished "First Case of Mr. Paul Savoy" by Jackson Gregory—not much but mystifying.

↦ JUNE 13 SATURDAY

Wardle & Van Dam returned. They'd just been left at [the] hospital & forgotten, in [the] belief they [were] hospital patients.

Read J. D. Beresford's "Camberwell Miracle" exceedingly good book—beautiful dialogue & much food for thought.

Report U.S. naval & air forces sunk or heavily damaged 15 J. warships in big battle off Midway which J's heading for—3 Ba[ttleships] 3 a.[ircraft carriers] 3 cruisers.

Kinwa [?] captured by J's also probably Kunming.

Palidrome [?] No. 2 said raided when we blacked out June 7.

Allied Euro. Invasion false rumor—also New G. & Borneo.

Got good, new globe.

↦ JUNE 14 SUNDAY

New globe burned out when switched on early this morning.

British king's birthday celebration today took [the] form [of] extra food. *Meat*, vegetable, rice, sambal tiffin Gula Java Pisan [?] at tea & rice, & excellent cabbage soup, followed by coffee [in the] evening. We ate by kerosene lamp. Holderness passed out sugar with the coffee. Fr. Elling added to occasion by blossoming out in white duck trousers Schmidt gave him

↦ MAY [*SIC*] 15

Four to hospital today, Sir John Campbell Baronet, Mgr. Perlis mine, 67, Commander Royal Scots World War, tall, imperial, striking man of lifetime adventure; phlebitis, Van Elode [?], diarrhoea & 2 dental cases. Hollweg also went, to stay a few days.

Read "Death at Breakfast" by John Rhodes.

⌐ JUNE 16 TUESDAY

Weighed 55 kilo—121 pounds, 2 kilo less than a few weeks ago.

Entire camp inspected for crabs (pediculae) & various skin diseases today. Took 3 hours. Of 286 examined, 26 ringworm, 21 impetigo, 6 pedic. All then weighed. Add men examined other times brought total around 300.

This evening we held [the] first of [a] series [of] weekly discussions [in] our room. West described leprosy. Present: West, de Bruine, Oosten, Colijn, Curran-Sharp, Fr. Elling, Drysdale, Schenk, Holderness, Allen, Prior, Harrison & I. Spending all spare time preparing lecture for Friday on "Job of Foreign Correspondent."

⌐ JUNE 17 WEDNESDAY

Had bread—similar [to] sourdough biscuit—this morning for second successive day. Cost 7 cents. Vander Vliet bought Chinese peddlers stock this morning, thus stopping daily morning fight to buy his limited stock & subsequent recriminations of various camp members.

Yesterday afternoon dreamed Philips drowned in sea after number of us from lifeboat had swum ashore. I went back to look for him but no use. Which reminds me, Mother, in a letter last summer, described how she saw me in water swimming from boat, that I needed help & kept calling out to her but she couldn't reach me. She awakened before dream ended. Was that foreboding?

Boddley discussed safety at sea this morning in another weekly seminar discussion in Tyjack's room.

⌐ JUNE 18 THURSDAY

Fourth day of my second novena to Sacred Heart. I've got appapox but not yet severe. Only 1 or 2 new spots each day. Treating them with Salicytic ointment, then applying piece of plastex. Also take sulfanilamide by mouth every 2 days.

Gillbrook, Carruthers, Rotier returned from hospital stays also last 2 dental patients. Gillbrook brought me can Klim, petrol & flints for lighter, gum arabic for glue, 19m notebooks & 6 tablets, 1 pencil. He also passed out bananas & bread to us. Spent day working on lecture. Total 19.25.

⌐ JUNE 19 FRIDAY

Spent all spare time on lecture.

⇀ JUNE 20 SATURDAY

Gave lecture 4:30 p.m., standing on well platform to an appreciative audience, which laughed heartily [at] my stories. I held their interest throughout. Lasted the planned 30 minutes on the nose. (Job of Foreign Correspondent)

⇀ JUNE 21 SUNDAY

Boddley asked me [to] give another lecture. Camp members saying yesterday's [was] one of [the] best yet. Read Eric Linklater's "Juan in China" exceedingly entertaining accurate picture [of] Shanghai life & full [of] colorful, infrequent & descriptive words. He coins a few too.

Fr. Elling's sermon in English extremely good & drew Holderness, Dr. West, & Harrison—all non-Catholics, to High Mass at 6:30 a.m. I also attended 5 & 5:30 a.m.

There is grousing among English in camp over clinic getting food first, Curran carrying it, etc.

Bread coming in regularly now for about ½ the camp; distributed in rotation ½ loaf a man for 10 cents.

Gula Java, butter, toothpaste, Lifebuoy soap issued today.

⇀ JUNE 22 MONDAY

Wrote 5 pages of letter to Mary. Last night Penryce lectured on kinds of cargo ships in Tiak's room.

⇀ JUNE 23 TUESDAY

Holderness suddenly & violently ill last night, vomiting flecks blood. This morning he [was] sent to hospital, also Brother Vincentines, the faithful kitchen worker, 2 dental patients also went but to their disappointment were brought back immediately after extractions instead of being allowed to stay.

Reports 57 J. ships sunk [in a] battle off Aleutians.

Natives here reportedly ordered off streets for 3 days. All flashlites [in] camp confiscated altho J's promised [to] return them.

Curran-Sharp lectured on Tamil coolies in Malaya during our Tuesday session.

⌐ JUNE 24 WEDNESDAY

J. announced at least 200 men this camp must work every day constructing road. Men over 50 exempt, also certain sick. (24 examined & excused of about 40 applicants) Guard doubled. Now patrol in two's—one behind [the] other. Presumably new military official has taken command.

Finished letter to Mary. Read H. G. Wells "The Invisible Man" by light of dysentery ward.

⌐ JUNE 25 THURSDAY

J. F. Jones, Mgr. Singapore Dock Repair Works, an Englishman, told me [an] amusing story: In 1936 he & wife booked airline passage Croydon to Calcutta. After several days [of] all kinds [of] persuasion by a United Press man he sold the seats & received 2 1st class boat tickets, money for new clothes he would need because others already shipped, etc. Deal closed Dorchester Hotel day after Unipresser visited him Portsmouth. Unipress made him all kinds [of] extravagant promises at first & Jones didn't trust him. Later, in Marseilles, Jones read fantastic yarn of "Who is Mr. X dashing across Europe ignoring frontier regulations, etc." My guess is that Jones seats [were] bought for Bud Ekins air fare around world for *World Telegram* against Mary Halloran & others.

⌐ JUNE 26 FRIDAY

Torrential rains caused cancellment [*sic*] of Mass this morning, so I missed for first time since masses began.

We haven't been called to work yet, although entire camp still buzzing with apprehension. Work assignment caused such a stir, classes were postponed or cancelled & even the singsong Saturday nite is matter of doubt.

Am starting to learn shorthand.

We finally got a globe for the room this morning.

Vander Bergh—Ran—dislocated knee, erysipelis taken to Cath. Hospital today.

New globes distributed tonight but burned out within 10 minutes. Voltage was 130 & globes 125.

Entire camp men thru clinic for physical exercises 7 hr. 30 min. Of 324 men, 237 fit, 73 unfit, 10 temporarily unfit, 4 children (under 16). Age groups—4 children, 16 to 40, 140; 41 to 45, 65; 46–50, 45; 51 to 55, 46; 56 to 60, 17; 61 to 65, 6; 66–3.

Book 5

— JUNE 27, SATURDAY

Successful camp concert staged by light [of] full moon with makeshift stage of doors & planks & south wall of water tank charcoaled with palms, wine goblets & "Men," "Women" surmounted by big letters "Cabaret."

D. T. Pratt, 34, British planter, acted as "compere" or master of ceremonies & unloaded some good stories. De Young, Dutch civil officer, block 4 leader & of good voice sang some beautiful Malayan songs & led two Boer songs—"Saint Maries" & another. Wardle, English person, recited comic poem, Gillhook played 2 Russian tunes on concertina. Curran-Sharpe sang two rollicking Cockney airs. I sang "God Bless America," "She Promised to Meet Me" & "Li'l Liza Jane," three verses of which I wrote myself, being unable to remember sufficient number. Got lots of laughter & applause. During 15 minute intermission coffee was served.

Report 4 J. ships sunk China Sea.

— JUNE 28 SUNDAY

To usual 5 & 5:30 Masses, then did some washing.

Curran-Sharpe lectured 2 hrs. on planting rubber in Malaya—during regular Sunday night session Tiak's room.

Obtained pair white tennis shoes, size 42, which [are] too large, thru toko.

— JUNE 29 MONDAY

Prince Bernard's birthday (Juliana's husband) so kitchen served extra good tiffin & brown bean & meat soup dinner, after which Dutch sang national songs beneath brilliant full moon.

Comparison between lists of Muntok & our physical exams showed about 10 Englishmen falsified their ages, adding 2 to 5 years in order to get over age limits for road working parties.

Camp News no. 3 issued, well typed but 60% inaccurate.

— JUNE 30 TUESDAY

Finished one month's communions to Sacred Heart.

Wrote short piece on significance of July 4 for *Camp News*.

Dr. Hollweg returned from hospital with news [that the] Red Cross transmitted our names to London, Washington, Tokyo.

All radios [in] Palembang confiscated.

Three men to hospital—Brother Loyola, dysentery, McKern, heart trouble & DeBond, impetigo.

Banker Schenk lectured on Netherlands history during our Tuesday seminar session.

⁓ July 1 Wednesday

Kitchen supplying clinic with coffee daily now 10 a.m.

Began July Mass and communion devotions.

Worked 8 to midnite shift in dysentery ward after "volunteers" squabbled among themselves over the job.

⁓ July 2 Thursday

Sinar Matahari of June 30 bannerlined Gandhi demanding U.S. & British troops leave India. 2 columned opening.

⁓ July 3

Palembang branch Yokohama Specie Bank, which article said world wide with offices now in "New York, Washington, London, Egypt, Iskandaring Singapore, Hongkong, Shanghai & 50 places in all in America, Europe & Asia." Said opening branches Sumatra—Javawide. Palembang manager will be a Mr. Wada of 20 years experience in Shanghai, London, Egypt; Mr. Hanedaka, assistant mgr. said although bank will work for glorious enrichment of N.E.I. people must await war's end for fulfillment [of] "glorious achievements."

Another article, from Singapore, said inflation impossible Malayawide because currency circulation [in] good condition. Another 2 columns said Javanese need not be alarmed over food situation because since Japan took over they showed natives how to work, consequently rice harvest, 397,000 hectares (1,985,000 acres) will be greater than ever in history. There will be no need to import, in fact a surplus can be exported! Dutch [have] been trying [to] achieve that happy goal [the] past 100 years.

Third article blamed food shortages on Dutch who allegedly stored food [on] purpose [to] destroy before Java's fall. Said food stocks could be brought from elsewhere, [but] now no ships so must wait but now can use native ships. Wherefore all [ ] owners must cooperate [in] shipping goods [to] needed places. However, all must [be] supervised by Js under a cooperative system.

Food article announced Japanese seized 70,000,000 kilograms coffee & 75,000 tons salt.

Sugar price now 30 guilders per 100 kilograms (33 cents per kilo). Prewar price 7 G. per 100 ks.

Natives ordered [to] bow [to] J. flag before [the] start [of] all sports games, etc.

Pastor Van Oort & 2 others called out about 1 p.m. with word Brother Loyola seriously ill.

⟶ July 3 Friday

Typed *Camp News* the fifth time, which included a long dissertation by me on significance of July 4.

Brother Loyola (H. J. Brecheisen), 34, died yesterday 11:15 a.m. we [were] informed today. Priests sent for yesterday [were] too late.

Japs offered exchange 10 Staats dollars for 9 guilders.

⟶ July 4 Saturday

In many ways the best Fourth I've ever spent. To 5 & 5:30 Mass. Then Everstibijn galloped in with two plates—one for Eric German & one for me. Two slices buttered toast, canned salmon & sardines garnished with chopped carrots, pickles & chile pepper. A small white note on each plate "With compliments of shop staff." Many people, Dutch & British, all day shook hands with me & congratulated on occasion of July 4. Everstein later appeared with butter for sale—just what we wanted for the evening banquet.

Attended 7 a.m. Mass, requiem for Brother Loyola. All blocks represented—many Protestants—biggest crowd yet at Mass.

Read Morgen Sharp's "The Nutmeg Tree" most [of the] day.

Fr. Elling had tiffin with us & we opened [a] can [of] corned beef & added bread & cheese for dessert.

Carruthers, M.B.C. announcer in Singapore, lectured on his job.

Allen & I spent an hour making three paper flags—I made France, U.S., he British & Dutch. Some job to get U.S. to proportion & put in the stars—for table decorations.

By 6:30 p.m. our long planned July 4 banquet got underway & Dr. Volney, bless his heart, appeared with a quart of Gordon's Dry Gin. He brought it early & I mixed it with lime juice & water in beer bottle. We poured out small amount in each cup & with amazed, then joyous looks on faces our guests were delightful. Using two borrowed homemade tables as one, my white sheet serving [as] table cloth. Green hedge leaves stuck in two medium glasses & the three flags upright on stiff wires were sprightly table decorations. Guests: Van der Vliet, Oosten, Colijn, Biesel, Hollweg, Curran-Sharp, German, West, + Allen & I.—10 in all. Biesel staggered in from kitchen with huge pan nagi goreng garnished with scrambled eggs & 2 tins [of] our hoarded Bully beef. Gin, lime juice, & coffee kept hot till end in big thermos of Edrickshaven, furnished sufficient beverage. Cheese, butter, bread & oranges for dessert. Naork for glorious enrighment of N.E.I. people must await war London, Egypt; Mr. Hanedaka, asstant mgr. said nagi goreng most excellent. Allen toasted "I give you the President of U.S.A, Queen Wilhelmina & King George of England." Then I spoke briefly.

A truly memorable evening. Memorable for what it meant—the first real patriotism I remember ever feeling [in] regard [to] July 4 & testimony of Dutch bigheartedness. I sat up in dark long after others [in] bed—watching moon rise, & finally retiring 1 a.m.

⁓ July 5 Sunday

To early Mass & began Novena to Precious Blood.

Sinar Matahari full [of] Axis successes [in the] Middle East & Sebastopol's fall. Alexandria surrounded. Tokyo radio said *Asama Maru* bearing diplomatic officials for exchange arrived & departed Hongkong. Hope Scott makes it out of Singapore.

Finished Nutmeg Tree by light [of the] first decent globe we've had 130 volts since others burned out.

White sugar sold [in] camp today [for the] first time, 10 cents for 250 grams. Tobacco 1.50 big sheaf.

Discovered 2 big field mice under Allen's bed & we nearly wrecked surgery during ensuing hunt. One got outside but we managed [to] kill it at wall of tent fellows & wrecked table Czechs just finished putting together.

⁓ July 6 Monday

Guard told Preswyck [of an] 18 day period truce [in the] Pacific while diplomatic exchange effected.

Sebastopol captured. Egypt gravely threatened, Alexandria & Cairo being evacuated, India revolting, Allied ships being bombed [in the] Caribbean, Gulf [of] Mexico, Churchill returns [to] London & angrily received, Japs capture Sikiang-Kianpi R.R.; Batavia-Souraboya R.R., & Semarang

R.R. repaired & running—says *Sinar Matahari*. Apparently Axis launched general offensive July 1.

Gasoline & oil permits required [in] Palembang. Gas price 36 cents liter—formerly 23 & 24.

Lt. Gen. Shogiro Idah commands Burma where 909 rice fields reported cultivated.

Nightly sessions in Malayan begun in clinic with Colijn, A. V. Poegemeier & P. Van Cjeuns, civil officers.

— JULY 7 TUESDAY

Sixth anniversary Sino-Japanese war. Van der Vliet said 1,100 J soldiers [were] exercise[d] & banzaied this morning.

Men from Batavia interned here today.

Oosten gave very interesting lecture on oil [in] our Tuesday night seminar session.

— JULY 8 WEDNESDAY

N. van Nifterik, garrulous Dutch tugboat captain, interned here yesterday after trip from Java gave me [a] picture [of] things there. Food situation good, R.R.s running, banks, schools closed, civil as well as military officials interned from Starkenburgh down, Batavia harbor blockage lifted sufficiently [to] permit 1500 tonners [to] enter. Most R.R., highway bridges restored. Harbors Batavia, Soungsboya [ ] totally destroyed, also B.P. no. 2, M.K.P.M. installations. Brit soldiers traveling trucks working parties unescorted. Food prices reasonable. Only autos J. field officers. Civilian male pass—150 G, women 80. Petrol collected house [to] house. All metal scrap, even lawn posts, automobiles dumped [in] boats for J yard. Oil arriving here from Borneo.

— JULY 9 THURSDAY

West gave me injection 5 ccs calcium, first since either Tokyo or early Shanghai. Felt no need of it, but didn't want to neglect opportunity.

Block G's campaign to get Kaptyn, a Dutchman with symptoms of dysentery out to hospital, approaching the ridiculous. Dutchmen constantly running to doctors with tales [of] Kaptyn's great sufferings, weakness, diagnosis [of] his ailment. Schenk seems to have appointed himself a self constituted physician in Kaptyn's behalf. Three days ago they announced, without consulting anybody, that Kaptyn was going to hospital. Tonight we brought him into [the] dysentery ward & probably will send him out tomorrow.

Although [we] sent [a] request out for removal [of] Johnson to hospital, Japs didn't appear today.

Reading "The Secret Battle" by A. P. Herbert. Story of World War trench warfare & psychology of one man.

➤ July 10 Friday

Finished "Secret Battle." After night dinner all men suddenly lined up by blocks in darkness of compound & Van der Vliet said guards had discovered [a] square hole through plaster of northeast wall but bricks untouched. Guard announced 6 a.m. tomorrow all food & water [will] cease & all men stand lined up until culprit confessed. Van der Vliet asked man who did it [to] come forward & explain. Consensus is that someone chipped off plaster for use as whitewash. All agree [it] would be insane [to] attempt [to] dig [a] hole [in the] wall for escape when [there are] so many more obvious easy ways, plus most [are] afraid to escape since [a] White man [is a] marked man. Guard Capt. screamed [at] Vliet [to] undo this insult [to the] Army, etc. Men dispersed apprehensive of what morning will bring.

➤ July 7

Sinar Matahari filled with 6th anniversary propaganda. Tokyo saw during Sino War, June 30, Japanese fleet [and] airforce destroyed 2,800 planes, 7 cruisers, 12 gunboats, 130 other ships, "several other ships." 24,300 guns, 2,700 R.R. cars, 607,000 war materials, several hundred motor cars.

Editorial signed by I. R. Ibraham, native burgomaster & R. A. Bakrie said all native men must salute & women bow to J. soldiers who [are] due honor for their sacrifices of lives & materials "highest as far humanly possible" made to rescue N.E.I. natives from the Dutch. Says J's suffered severe losses [of] men, materials freeing natives.

Military police ordered disbandment [of] religious political party Perhimpoeman Kaoen Moesliming.

➤ July 11, Saturday

6 a.m. lineup [did not] materialize & morning coffee [was] served on strength camp interested [in] investigation which resulted [in] guards interrogating 2 children, one of whom, Willy, said he'd seen John Close, 16, in vicinity of hole, whereupon Close [was] brought before guard captain,

whipped with belt strap on bare back & tied to metal post with hands wrenched up behind him. Miachi appeared 3 hours later, Close [was] released & [it was] announced [that] beginning Sunday no food could be brought in & none cooked [in the] kitchen until [the] real culprit [was] produced.

Reese, elderly English planter, who saw man chipping hole 8 days ago accompanied by Van der Vliet, Soki, Indo Police commissioner inspected all men [in] camp from rear as blocks lined up. 3 possible suspects picked although 1, a German, mentally unsound, really suspected. (Great, perfect ring around sun this afternoon) The three [were] then taken to [the] hole & made to reenact. Reese thinks Schmidt [was the] man but unable [to] swear to it. *I personally think it's teapot tempest & we'll miss no meals.* Guards erected barbed wire barrier [at] each entrance [and are] walking space between cells & outer wall—which ends our exercise strolls & much individual cooking on tiny, makeshift stoves & causes various classes to move their locale.

Our pleasant little guard had some more sores on legs dressed again & gave me 3 pirate cigarettes. Friday he gave me a package, after I told him I was from St. Luke's Hosp., Tokyo.

Holderness, Vliet, Hobbs, & Van Eerden returned from hosp. & Holder. put in Block 8. He brought few goods back. I got a bottle of ink.

Read Wodehouse's "Doctor Sally."

No Mass this morning because of threatened lineup.

Entire camp dejected & apprehensive. Surprising how easily men are cast down by threats of coming discomforts.

⟶ July 12 Sunday

To 5 & 5:30 & 6:30 Masses. No coffee or bread issued & kitchen locked. No food will be served & camp has until *Thursday* (?) presumably foodless meanwhile to produce [the] culprit.

All tools & other instruments such as scissors, which could be used for digging, called for by guard. Circumstantial evidence points more directly to Schmidt but no proof. All day [the] camp [was] subdued & [a] general air [of] melancholy. However, at noon [the] kitchen surreptitiously served brown beans; all men [received a] big cupful each, which with 2 slices bread we had saved was [an] ample meal.

Strangely, British Protestant services [were] first canceled, then held with no singing—that's how much camp affected. Dutch canceled entirely.

Altho I've now had considerable experience in fasting the depression & abrupt degeneration in morale of [the] camp majority surprises me.

Kitchen staff played bridge all day before kitchen closed doors as blind so [they] could secretly cook rice for sick, prepare beans, which [were] brought quietly to each block & make tea. Allen & I had one quarter [cup?] of beans for nite meal—conserving our hoarded bread supply just in case.

About 8 a.m. all camp told to "stand to" & in darkness Van der Vliet announced, due to [the] kindness [of the] Japanese army, camp punishment [was] ended. He said he had informed Lt. Ima (Aima?) he thought we knew [the] culprit but couldn't prove it & therefore did not wish to accuse or deliver him without absolute proof. Whereupon punishment [was] lifted, with [the] admonition [that] repetition [would] bring drastic results. As [the] men cheered, he said dinner would [be] served, whereupon kitchen workers fell to, cleaned & cooked rice & made sambul of coffee in record time—less than 2 hours. All were finished by 11:15 p.m.—So we did not really miss a meal after all & my hunch [was] correct. Wish someone had taken me up on offer to bet $1 we would not miss.

⏤ July 13 Monday

Read narrative version of John Fleming Wilson's play "The Man Who Came Back," & Claude Houghton's novelized version of Fox Film's "The Big Trail." Both pretty thin.

New wave [of] uneasiness swept camp when British, Aussie & Dutch technicians & shipping men called by name for individual interviews by J. officer. Followed report [several names], other military leaders & 50 civilian technicians would leave [for] Japan June [July] 16.

⏤ July 14 Tuesday

Ants have nearly disappeared from clinic for unknown reason. Maybe a new invasion [is] being planned by [a] larger variety.

K. G. Harrison, 38, Irish civil engineer, Malayan Railways gave interesting talk "Camponalogy"—art of bell change ringing.

German began making knapsack for me.

⏤ July 15 Wednesday

De Bonot & Brother Vincentius returned from hospital. Johnston & Kapsteyn went to hospital.

Thai-Indo-China border fixed. Koki Hirota, ambassador est. to Bangkok.

Rice now available to all Palembang, 12 cents kilo, formerly 7 cents. Permits *not* necessary.

Front page said Natives advised *not* [to] complain against restrictions because for their own good.

Proclamation [announc]ed natives no longer can get free water for bathing—only for cooking, drinking.

More editorials on saluting & bowing [to] J. soldiers.

Front pager "How Long the War?" it [is] impossible [to] predict but very longer account must continue 100 years if necessary—[in] order [to] oust whites from Asia. Holy war very beautiful for Japanese & only endable when all purposes fulfilled, wherefore J's gathering all war materials avaiable [from] conquered countries. "Asia Raya" Malay word equivalent "Greater East Asia."

Lt. Ima inquired if any Americans in camp whereupon German & I produced [ourselves]. He asked if we'd heard about Aleutians. No. Said all Aleutians [are] completely occupied, including Dutch Harbor. Midway captured 2 months ago. Middle & South China occupied also all Timor but P. Moresby still holding out. Kurusu & Nomura exchanged via Africa. *Hakone Maru* now exchanging diplomatic officials. Said war [would] last much longer maybe 5, 10 yrs.—30 or 100 if necessary until all Americans surrendered. U.S. has only 6 capital ships left.

Reading Jan Valtin's "Out of the Night" & Prof. R. A. Wilson's "The Miraculous Birth of Language."

⌐ July 16 Thursday

On strength [of a] rumor camp members compiled 12 word cables to their families via Red +. I address[ed] mine U.P., N.Y. "Advise Family Safe Well Palembang."

Long talk Poggemier attempting [to] salve his self doubts & problems he says [are] driving him [to the] verge [of] insanity. Think I'm on [the] right track. Read until 1 a.m.

⌐ July 17 Friday

Read all morning, slept all p.m. & read until 12:30 a.m.

⌐ July 18 Saturday

Finished "Out of the Night," powerful, stark tale of terror in Communism, Nazism.

Englishman arrived [in] camp after various sea adventures.

— JULY 19 SUNDAY

Pog's problem tough to solve.

Finished "Miraculous Birth Language." Interesting but not convincing concerning evolution or link between animal-man. In other words he leaves out the Divine Hand.

— JULY 20

Began Physical Training class 7 a.m.

Fr. Elling, Pog. & I discussed secular proof [of the] existence [of] God in evening.

Sinar Matahari 7/14 editorial extolled [the] regulated life [of the] Japanese in Japan, saying people's individual lives [are] government regulated from cradle to grave to [the] great benefit [of the] people. Examples—people not allowed [to] throw cigarette butts [in] street but place [them in] receptacles. They remove shoes [when] entering [a] public building & wear special shoes [to the] toilet. But when Dutch governed N.E.I. they made no attempt [to] interfere [in the] natives' private lives or religion—consequently natives [are] now backward & ill mannered & uneducated. Now, however, natives' personal lives should [be] regulated so [as to] acquire better manners in public. Example—no shouting, jeering or throwing things at players in Malay opera who give bad performances. We should be ashamed [of] our conduct & welcome Japanese criticism.

Moslem leader Hadji Kaharoedin said [it is the] religious duty [of] all Moslems [to] work body & soul with Japanese [in the] effort [to] drive [out] western powers. God only permits Moslems [to] fight people who [are] attacking their religion or country—which Japs [are not] doing.

Sinar said Dutch, Australian, English prisoners [ ] July 7 permitted [to] visit families in city or buy sweets at stores if no families.

— JULY 21 TUESDAY

Indonesian guards replaced Japanese guards after Lt. Nishimura [gave a] speech saying we had behaved well & he hoped we'd continue so. Czechs & few Indo-Europeans here notified they will be released tomorrow.

— JULY 22 WEDNESDAY

5 Indonesians, 4 Czechs & 2 boys & Cruickshank liberated.

I bought [a] pair [of] heavy leather shoes—Australian army issue—for F.4 from Czechs.

In camp fund lottery yesterday I won 1 tin Bully beef with no. 96 & 6 free lessons English! with no. 9. I traded the English lessons for 6 pancakes—rolled around pineapple jam—delicious.

West's room gave noon dinner for Allen, Hollweg and me of lottery winnings.

J's informed Van der Vliet [in the] presence [of] native guards he had sole charge [of] camp routine & guards only posted [to] prevent escapes.

⇀ JULY 23 THURSDAY

Worked all day typing up [ ] U.S. history for lecture Friday nite.

⇀ JULY 24 FRIDAY

Van der Vliet's birthday. His block—2—staged song fest & coffee [ ].
I lectured on American politics. Wright's room.
Poggemier again desperate. Elling helped him considerably.

⇀ JULY 25 SATURDAY

Missed Mass today, first time since began. Slept in.

West's room began amusing lottery on who in block would be first in line for food. Parson Wardle, Killich, Barnes are favorites. Wardle wins jostling techniques, Killich sizing up situation beforehand and getting first out of kitchen altho often 3rd or 4th in. But dark horse Stalini, one-eyed Maltese, won today.

Poggemier brought into dysentery ward as diahorrea case.

⇀ JULY 26 SUNDAY

English sermon this morning.
Finished "Only Yesterday" by F. L. Allen, history of 1920s in America.

⇀ JULY 27 MONDAY

2 Dutch, 2 British bridge teams played [a] match [in the] hospital under West's & Allen's supervision. Dutch won by 200 points.

⇀ JULY 28 TUESDAY

10 Dutchmen of Billeton Company—Bauxite mining concern, entered camp from Bintang in Rhio archipelago where [they were] taken

from Batavia in mid-April [to] work [the] mine. But they were business office people & knew nothing of [the] technical end. So, after 3 months [they were] taken here via Singapore.

Report Chinese drove ex-Changsha to Wenchow area.

"Shonan Times" publishing Singapore in English. Horse racing, native jockeys. Whitehouse Hotel. Chinese girls. No Europeans [in the] streets.

Concert tonight beclouded & once interrupted by rain. Clad in sheet for toga & crowned with hedge leaves, I recited "Daniel in Lions Den."

– JULY 29 WEDNESDAY

Report Allies occupied Timor, Amboen, possibly Mindanao & attacking Macassar.

Private telegrams from Sumatra to J. occ. China or Japan $1.15 word.

Ad in *Sinar* for oil drillers, electricians, mechanics work Tempino oil field between Palem.-Jambe.

Elling successfully lectured [on the] Pope's election [in] our room.

– JULY 30 SATURDAY

Spent all day composing letter to Red Cross & J's which Adolf Poggemeier translated.

– JULY 31 FRIDAY

Worked all evening on forthcoming lecture.

– AUG. 1 SATURDAY

Began month with Mass & Com[munion]
Gave letters to Van Der Vliet.
Completed lecture notes.

Book 6

– AUGUST 2 SUNDAY

Began Novena to Im[maculate] H[eart]t of Mary & 30 days P[rayer].
Won 1st game of Canfield Solitaire in months.
Lectured in Tiak's room on Modern Newspaper set.
British committee circularized petition voting for a change in British camp leader—ousting Penryce, & his committee & calling for new election.

⁓ AUGUST 3 MONDAY

British ring around rosie election today re-elected Penryce, whom they voted yesterday to oust. There is no accounting for British mind. Committee nominations contain some 40 names.

⁓ AUGUST 4 TUESDAY

British committee elected composed of Blake, Baddeley [ ] Gill, Philipps.

I won 2 games Canfield, now "up $751"

⁓ AUG. 5 WEDNESDAY

Block leaders meet set F16 plus F1.25 weekly subscription as limit per month per man allowed spent, in order [to] conserve camp funds over long period.

⁓ AUG. 6 THURSDAY

Lectured camp on workings [of] newspaper. Talked one hour, including 20 minutes on questions. Someone been [ ] bathroom several occasions so Allen, West, Earl, Hamson, Chambers & I took turns watching all nite to catch culprit.

⁓ AUG. 7 FRIDAY

Nite watch again. No [ ].

Move in Block 8 to oust Blake & make Curran-Sharp leader, by 24 votes to 4. Whereupon Blake for first time did some work as a leader & is reported to have threatened to stop letters to women's camp by his influence with Miachi. Blake a selfish, fat, lazy Briton who told Sharp & Gray he was out for himself & would "climb over anyone's shoulders in here to look after no. 1." He became block leader because of his previous acquaintance with Miachi in Singapore.

⁓ AUG. 8 SATURDAY

Began shorthand classes with Gilbrook, Thompson the dyspeptic young John Close.

⁓ AUG 9 SUNDAY

Drysdale lectured interestingly on plywood manufacture.

Batavia's new name "Djakarta," which was ancient Javanese name for it.

Asama Maru, Conte Verde arrive[d] Singapore with Kurusu, Nomura. New Governor South Sumatra, H. Kasai.

⚊ Aug. 10 Monday

Read condensation "This Above All" by Erik Night.

H. Hilling, 41, cultured sales manager Java Shell & one of the best Dutch speakers of English in camp. He thinks I'm depressed. Strange how even most level headed of Dutch are depressable & let emotions rule mind.

Another bridge tournament hospital but didn't use dysentery ward account [of] Van der Vliet's objections—excuse no visitors allowed Poggemeier. Probable real reason: disgruntled Block 2 Dutch who [were] not invited [to] participate. Intense personal likes, dislikes among Dutch now very evident.

⚊ Aug 11 Tuesday

Camp seething [with] politics as election [of] Dutch representative [to] camp committee nears. Dutch split two bitterly opposing factions—government & B.P.M (Shell) officials vs. antigovernmenters, private individuals & other companies. Some Dutch Protestant bigots also injecting religious issue—freemasons vs. Catholics.

Most of British planned "Info Please" quiz contest—4 Dutch vs 4 British even seized upon by Dutch camp officials to vent personal grievances against "unpopular" (to certain individuals) Dutch. Pratt, Carruthers, De Jong & I framing questions. V.D.F. for some reason dislikes Elling, de B, so he selected them & Fanoy & E de Rosdt, Indo-Europeans, for team, hoping they'll miss answers & can be jeered later. Bridge team play also aroused jealousy among Dutch.

I lectured on Mormonism during Tuesday nite session & listeners appeared pleased.

⚊ Aug 12 Wednesday

Fr. Elling lectured Boswell's room on sanctifying grace. B's room small shrine with [a] statue [of] Christ, crucifix, pix B.V.M. on shelf. L. Burns, English engineer & watchmaker by hobby, cleaned rust [out of] my watch but now too late [on account of] some parts rusted entirely away. Van Arhol said he [was] informed Japanese patrol killed entire battery at Terakan with jiu jitsu one nite, silently so as to conceal presence.

[ ] wanted to take 4,000 men, infilter & recapture Kalijati airdrome near Bandoeng, but superior refused. Later learned only 700 J. there.

─ AUG 13 THURSDAY

Double watch on Plant tonight. Dutch elected Indo-European Lub-link Weddig & F. S. Klaasen to camp committee, who with Britishers Penryce & M. Phillips will advise V. D. Vleit.

Searched P.'s clothes & luggage for knives, razors, etc. & removed.

Brief battle off Solomons & another north Pacific. Of[fensive] begun?

─ AUG. 14 FRIDAY

Double watch last nite. Pogg., Worthen, Hollweg to hospital.

Finished P. Buck's "Good Earth."

After Fanoy to me accused Elling of responsibility for Poggemier's mental upset, I arranged for F. to visit P., who flatly contradicted F., where-upon F. said Elling "clever man who already is known to have converted 2 or 3 in camp." Bigot & liar.

Read Dorothy Parker's "After Such Pleasures."

─ AUG. 15 SATURDAY

Feast of Assumption. I quit smoking today for good in accordance with my promises 3/24. Fixed schedule for my days' activities [in the] future.

─ AUG 16 SUNDAY

Elling preached English sermon 6:30 a.m. Mass & gave lecture in Dutch on Catholicity 4:45 p.m.

Several Dutch B.P.M. men got letters from wives in Japan. Stapples received one dated 6/14 informing him he had [a] son born in March.

Brady lectured on launching ships [in] Clyde yards—*Queen Mary.*

─ AUG 17 MONDAY

Dr. Hollweg returned from hosp.

Allen's birthday, 32, kitchen fixed nayi goreng dinner so in evening guests included Drs. West & Hollweg, resident A. Oranje, H. Helling, Curran-Sharp, Beissel von Gymnick.

─ AUG 18 TUESDAY

Col. Matsuki, retiring governor [of] J[apanese] occupied South Sumatra, visited camp officially, paid respects to H. Oranje, Palembang resident, whom he called Tuan Besar, informed him he [was] leaving & regretted [that the] necessities [of] war made civilian internment necessary.

Dr. Hollweg gave me 3 cigars—hosp[ital] tokens.

I gave Myazi my letters to Japanese authorities Palembang, Red Cross, Bandoeng & one note to himself requesting interview.

Beissel lectured [on] Dutch E[ast] I[ndies] civil service background, which provoked lively discussion. He said, & it seems so from my observation, that Eurasian problem here practically nonexistent. That is, Dutch Eurasian is regarded as a Dutchman & eligible [for] positions [in] government or army, navy, [the] way [any] other Dutchman is. Problem also not social inasmuch as Euras[ians] [are] admitted [to] practically all homes, clubs, etc.

Long poem, signed by all women in women's camp & bound in small book, passed around, thanking men for sending supplies there. Poem in Dutch & translated roughly into English, described adventures of an ant.

Hol[weg]'s wife 2 months ago cleaned [up the] mess there.

⇀ AUG 19 WEDNESDAY

First of my two special Masses said 5:30. Gave Elling F.5 for 2.

Elling lectured on Bible this evening. Gillbrook, supposedly at instance of anti-C[atholic] Dutch advertised [on the] kitchen door he's starting one tomorrow nite.

⇀ AUG 20 THURSDAY

A. N. Wooton, Australian Government Trade Commissioner in Malaya working office Australian Representative of Gov. Malaya, returned from hosp. with new glasses. He brought me 1 tin Klim F 11.50, 2 packs cards Poggemeier bought me. Also saw Myazi relative to exchange. Myazi said U.S. & Japan so far worked out exchange for Japan, Occ. China, Hongkong & Philippines—but not yet Malaya, Sumatra, Java, but 1800 [are] due [to] leave Briok Aug. 28.

Second Mass said for me 5:30 a.m.

⇀ AUG 21 FRIDAY

Worked all afternoon & evening on *Camp News*, which Agerbrek illustrated. Allen, de Jong, & I now issuing news, Dutch version of which [is] typed by Father Koendeman.

I invented a gossip character, Whispering Winifred, who lives in [the] well in column "Well Whispers."

Lt. Gen. H. Kasai, So[uth] Sum[atra] Gov[ernor], [said in a] speech [that] U.S. [and] Eng[land] must [be] defeated before Pacific troubles end & N[etherlands] E[ast] I[ndies] shortages relieved, whereupon natives must produce more rice, duck eggs, improve schools which [are of a] "very low standard." [He] said Americans & Eng[lish] must be driven out of N.E.I. *(No mention [of] Dutch, who J[apanese] seem no longer to consider.)*

⇀ Aug 22 Saturday

New So. Sum. Gov. Lt. Gen. H. Kasai made [a] surprise visit & inspected camp briefly. Then 2 Japanese officers called roll [in] camp & counted [the] number [of] various nationalities.

Read "The Verdict of You All" detective mystery thriller by Henry Wade, pen name Sir Henry Aubrey Fletcher.

⇀ Aug 23 Sunday

Myazi told me I had [a] chance of being exchanged had Japanese interned [in] India arrived [in] Singapore today or yesterday. Permitted letters [to be] sent [to] women's camp. Asked 100 men for work party [to] clear [the] site [for a] new camp for us. Finally agreed [to] accept 60 so volunteers asked. Response [was] heavy & [there were] more volunteers than places. I volunteered & [was] assigned [to] block 5.

⇀ Aug 24 Monday

60 of us hiked thru Palembang carrying parangs—grass cutters—to site contemplated [for] new internment camp about 1½ miles from the jail. Palembang [has] changed little, except [for] deserted houses [of] Europeans, unkempt lawns, etc. Hotels, office beds filled with J[apanese]. The site [is] in [an] open field near bungalows formerly occupied by married Britishers.

⇀ Aug 25 Tuesday

Dutchman Kremer, Block 4, hot headed, taken out of camp for writing in letter women's camp. Second working party went to camp site, including 2 priests & 2 brothers.

West lectured [on] malaria.

— Aug 26 Wednesday

Scheduled moonlight concert tonight cancelled [on] account [of] Kremer's detention. Dutch very gloomy over it.

— Aug 27 Thursday

Working party coming & going cheered from afar by women's camp members, who, some 200 yds., yelled, shrieked, waved [as] long as we [were] in view along road near our new campsite. Worked leisurely cutting grass, frequently resting. About 9 a.m. big bomber closely resembling Flying Fort[ress] flew eastward from the direction [of the] airport at about 10,000 [ft.]. 30 minutes later 6 fighters zoomed after it.

Camp News name contest ended [in a] tie [between] "The Terompak Echo" & "Hot'n Lesshot News." J. C. Brodie, Scotch engineer submitted Hot'n Lesshot, while Terompak jointly submitted by J. F. Jones, H. T. [?] Hammond, & C. M. Jenkins of Block 1.

2 Jap officers inspected camp today.

— Aug 28 Friday

Worked [on] *Camp News* all day. Ronkers Agerbeek illustrated it splendidly.

— Aug. 29 Saturday

Counted F882—my total capital. Women again cheered working party. We're leveling field now with shovels & mattocks. Bought 20 small papaya for 20 cents, exorbitant price.

Distributed *Camp News* during evening meal.

— Aug. 30 Sunday

Monday Aug. 31 is Queen Wilhelmina's birthday but Dutch [are] celebrating it today. Te Deum sung at 6:30 Mass which Oranje attended. Dutch & British Protestant services well attended.

Read W. Stanley Sykes, "The Missing Money Lender," good mystery thriller, insulin used to kill victim.

Rev. B. Bakker conducted choir in 3 songs this afternoon, one of them his own composition dedicated to Queen. Choir excellent, loudly encored.

Then horse race action staged. 6 [ ] horses heads "ridden" by Australian jockeys from Malaya advanced around square track of 28 spaces on dice throws. Betting tickets 25 cents each. Horses auctioned in middle of race.

I bid F.35 & bought "Sea Biscuit," No. 2 in 1st race. Incidentally, my bid [was the] highest of entire meet. Hildebrand, Palembang Burgomaster, bid against me. I had bets on Sea Biscuit & Bahram, No. 5. Bahram, owned by "Uncle Pete" Cranenburgh for $20 won & paid F1.10 for 25 cents. In both races I [was the] only non-Dutch to buy [a] horse or even bid higher than F.5. Next highest bid [was] $25 on Blue Peter. Horses #1, Blue Peter, 2 Sea Biscuit, 3 Whirlaway, 4 Phar Lap, 5 Bahram, 6, Gloaming, which second in 1st race & alone bought by Pete. 2nd race Blue Peter, bought by Hildebrand for F.8. won. Sea Biscuit, bought by DeRuyter for F.22, [was] second. Of total profits $103.60 split between hospital & kitchen. Pete donated his winnings of 60 to war prisoners in hospital.

⁃ Aug 31 Monday

Congratulated Oranje & Hildebrand on Queen's birthday & Oranje made brief but hearty speech to me.

Loaned Gillbrook 10 G.

Today Queen's birthday. Britishers volunteered, I among them, to take places [of the] Dutch on working party today so they had holiday. When gang approached site in sight [of] women's camp, women & children as usual wildly cheering but today they waved Dutch colors on separate pennants & on 2 standards hoisted large Dutch flag—all for our benefit. However, I think it was foolhardy thing to do.

Women probably had big feast as did we today. Dutch put themselves out to produce at tiffin—large steaks, new potatoes, rice, plenty [of] gravy, spinach, fruit salad which [was] delicious, & cigar. Meal late & eating finished after 3 p.m., tea followed & about 7 p.m. dinner of rice & meat sauce, bringle, followed by sweet omelette with goelad java & ginger sauce.

Choir sang [a] number [of] songs 5 p.m. & did [a] splendid job.

Dr. Hollweg & Harley Clark, Singapore dentist, taken away today to work in clinic for Japs or natives, uncertain which.

Native quarter [of] Palembang featured ramshackle low wooden buildings on stilts, tidal creeks sluggish & dirty, houses close together, tiny shops, general air [of] somnolence, naked children.

⁃ Sept 1 Tuesday

Began novena to Holy Cross. Quinn lectured on language & phonetics at our regular Tues. session. Dental, eye & hospital patients taken out quickly now, since visit [of] J[apanese] doctor.

⇀ Sept 2 Wednesday

Went out on working party.
Read Edgar Wallace thriller "Red Acres."
Diahorrea [*sic*] & dysentery epidemic has struck camp.
Elling lectured [on] 1st 3 chapters [of] Genesis.

⇀ Sept 3 Thursday

Kremer returned to camp, also 2 hospital operation cases.
Worked all p.m. [on] *Camp News*.

⇀ Sept 4 Friday

Wrote all afternoon on *Camp News* & expunged [the] most humorous
story—of R. N. Hobbs, 42, round-shouldered jockey, who said [a] rat [as]
"fat as loaf of bread & a yard long," attacked him about 4 a.m. enroute [in
the] rear. I [wrote the] headline "Rat Attacks Hobbs Senior; Waylays Night
Walker, Enroute Rear Stall; Former Jockey Saddles marauder, Wrathfully
Rides Rodent Until Bucked Off." On asking Hobbs if he'd be offended he
said yes—that he [is] supersensitive [on] account [of] his back & might get
mad if his leg [were] pulled.

⇀ Sept 5 Saturday

J. Van Mourik attacked Fawin, Belgian, when F. objected [to] Mourik
moving into his cell, [calling him] a filthy [ ] dried fish, stinking [of] stale
urine, etc. Fight occurred Thursday [in] front [of] hospital. Was 3rd battle
in camp. Previous encounters—Jockey J. Martin & A. Jackson over working party & kitchen duty, & German P. J. Schmidt (suspect in hole in
wall) & white-haired whiskered Dutch Eurasian pensioner soldier Dumas.
Cause unknown. Dumas held Schmidt's hands but Schmidt butted him
beneath chin with head.

Read Nancy J. Johnstone's "Hotel in Spain." Interesting narrative how
she & [her] husband built, ran hotel at Tussa Gerona, Spain. Also gives me
heart to write my own narrative.

Work party this morning [with] no tools, 15 men, so I sat around all
morning on job doing nothing. Family gave Fr. Elling coconut cake which
he distributed [at a party].

⇀ Sept 6 Sunday

Read "White Man Brown Woman," by T. L. Richards with Stuart
Gurr.

New *Camp News* with cardboard cover designed [and] drawn by H. J. A. Ronkers Agerbeek issued. It is very attractive, combining outside new jail [on] top page with two pix illustrating "Terompak Echo" & "Hot'n Less Hot News." 1st page shorts clad bespectacled man [with] huge feet & wooden clogs rushing [toward a] bog. 2nd, rear view G. A. Deerens, 3rd, tremendously fat Indo-European ladling out sambal.

Last week's *Camp News* issued [with news of] Block 11 missing.

⟶ SEPT 7 MONDAY

Hollweg visited camp few minutes, reportedly announced list [of] names gone [to] Tokyo, Singapore, Geneva, Bandoeng. Red + office opened Singapore. Servicemen can send messages [to] relatives but not civilians.

R. St. G. Johnson, Brit Malayan businessman, returned from hospital reporting much anti-Dutch feeling among British & hospital discrimination against Brit.

⟶ SEPT 8 TUESDAY

Wrote to International Red Cross representative Singapore & also note to Myagi asking permission [to] communicate [with] Tomohazu Hori spokesman [in] Tokyo. Letters given Hollweg.

Reading R. H. Mottram's "The Spanish Farm."

A. N. Wooton, Australian trade commissioner to Singapore, presided [at] Tuesday night lecture period answering questions on Australia.

More English dictionaries will become more important & necessary in future in order to know more not only about our enemy but about our own selves. 3 Webster's Unabridged.

Pix girl student who said all interned women released [on] parole [were] kindly treated. 24 journalists treated with diplomats.

⟶ SEPT 9 WEDNESDAY

Guard asked permission [for] *Sinar Matahari* [to be] brought in & Myagi granted. Obviously it [was] never asked before. Dutch reported [to be] opposed to camp taking any steps toward release or repatriation for fear guards misinterpret it as plans for escape! Ridiculous.

⟶ SEPT 10 THURSDAY

Dr. Hollweg pays flying visit to camp. Throng [of] Dutchmen run round him, peer thru bars of ground room, shout, [and] try & get him to run errands. Myagi received my last letter.

Telegrams now sendable Singapore possibly London, Geneva, says Fanoy.

Dutch-English bridge tournament played [in] our room & kitchen from 8 to 11 p.m., British taking 886 up. 24 hands played 4 tables.

— SEPT 11 FRIDAY

Gave two telegrams to Fanoy: "McDougall United Press London Inform Mother Jalex safe Palembang W. H. McDougall Jr." "Int. Red Cross Geneva Inform W. H. McDougall Salt Lake City Son Safe Palembang."

Fanoy already quibbling over sending list [of] telegrams on [the] grounds [that] Hollweg has [no] time [to] copy individually.

Natives now leveling camp site by contract with grobacks, sapis & by hand baskets.

Ramadan—Mohammedan fasting month—begins sunset tonight. Good Moham[medans] can eat or drink nothing—even can't swallow [their] own saliva between sunrise-sunset [during] Ramadan—but make up for it by feasting [at] night time.

— SEPT 12 SATURDAY

Camp's one & only Mohammedan—C. G. Rebel, 44, Holland born Dutchman—is observing Ramadan fast. So native guard wakens him 2 a.m. to eat.

Subscribed to *Sinar Matahari*, 10 issues 30 cents. *Shanghai Times* saying Americans mistreated interned Japanese. Article [was] worded [in] such [a] way [it] indicated Americans [are] interned [in] Shanghai.

— SEPT. 13 SUNDAY

5:30 & 6:30 Mass. Fr. Bakker preached sermon.

During afternoon nap dreamed for first time of *Poelau Bras* sinking. Dreamed I rushed below, rescued ship's cat, tied life belt to her & tossed [her] overboard. Also that submarines picked up swimmers unable to get [to] life boats.

British camp canvassed for money, set up system whereby each man pays 6 mos. subscription 1.25 weekly to kitchen fund, same as Dutch are doing. Individuals with money then are asked to subscribe additional amounts, same as Dutch system.

⤙ Sept 14 Monday

W. F. Roberts, 60, whitehaired Britisher & jack of all trades in Malaya died yesterday of dysentery in Cath. Hospital. He went to hospital Sept. 6, same time as P. W. de Bayer, 43. Both seriously hit by particularly virulent form of dysentery. H. Hammett, 36, Malayan civil officer, went to hosp. today suffering same kind [of] dysentery.

West warned working party against buying, eating anything outside except what could be cooked or prepared in camp.

Curran-Sharpe & Rev. Wardle went to funeral.

P. H. van Gisbergen, 36, went out to conduct funeral for a Chinese. First time such a thing permitted since internment.

⤙ Sept. 15 Tuesday

Curran-Sharpe returned from hospital with word Roberts died Sunday night & Mrs. Mellor, wife of Mr. H. L. Mellor died Monday morning. Said Mellor [is] completely senile, curses sisters when forced to bathe, & [a] general nuisance.

On working party today stripped to jockey shorts & von Geuns told me several camp members thought such scanty attire would shock natives.

Sinar Matahari said Americans landed [in] French Africa. Also on 9/4 landed [in] Congo—both places with intention [of] driving for Dakar. *Syonan Times* for early August or late July said American or British [were in] African Gold Coast. But British attacking Madagascar (we understood it [was] captured [at] least [a] month ago).

Latuta Maru due Syonan Sept 16 with 396 Japanese who formerly worked [in] Malaya as planters, teachers, etc. *Latuta* left Syonan Aug. 14 en route [to] Laurencio Marques with British diplomats who boarded [ ] Tokyo & Shanghai 8/7. (276 Brit & Allied nationals boarded *Latuta* [at] Shanghai.)

⤙ Sept 16 Wednesday

Camp committee decided not to forbid carrying letters by hospital & dental patients on grounds it could not be enforced among Dutch. British leaders favor force among themselves but no use applying it [to the] British if [not] applied [to the] Dutch. D. A. Buitenhuis, 32, Block 5 leader & P. M. Preiswerk, 44, quarreled [with] native guard who asked them not [to] play bridge on job.

⁓ Sept. 17 Thursday

Wrote all *Camp News* & typed it, including financial story & report which Van Der Vliet cut out of [the] Dutch version. Elling lectured [on] angels & devils.

⁓ Sept. 18 Friday

Went on working party. Framework bldg. already up. No one working now except few like myself who'd rather swing [ ] than sit around. V.D.V. issued notice forbidding letters via hospital patients after Oranje [was] bawled out [on] account [of] one.

⁓ Sept. 19 Saturday

Issued *Camp News* but withheld it from Block 11 because of one previous issue missing there. *Sinar Matahari* said Jap plane sending bombs in [to] some city [in] Oregon. Masayuki Tami, new foreign minister 8/17.

⁓ Sept. 20 Sunday

Read Pearl Buck's "East Wind: West Wind." Wish I had read some [of] her books before coming to Orient.

To 5 & 6:30 Masses.

Because of outside purchasing the F 16 monthly spending limit per person exploded. Camp leaders exercise little control over camp members.

⁓ Sept 21 Monday

Because of beefs, Curran-Sharpe today stopped bringing our food. Camp full of chronic complainers who [are] jealous because hospital staff goes first for food each day.

Block 11 kicking against my withholding *Camp News* from them but I left them only one [which anyone] who wishes can read in hospital.

⁓ Sept. 22 Tuesday

Javanese coolies seem [to] enjoy my efforts [at] merrymaking & adopt [the] same attitude toward whites working alongside themselves & most others do—something temporarily beyond control & which will not last. Field now entirely cleared & almost leveled. Javanese & Malays working under Chinese contractor doing it. Most of the morning white men [are] merely in sight. Native guards keep telling men, "Please make an appearance of working" in case J's appear, but few men pay attention. Their selfishness

[is] spoiling a good thing. I work morning with Malays & practice conversation. De Bruin also does. Von Geungs works part time. Various groups [of] men, hidden [in the] bushes, play chess, cards, read, sleep or gossip.

Schenk lectured describing—uninterestingly—a trip thru [the] Near East.

— SEPT. 23 WEDNESDAY

Rev. Wardle [was] called out to conduct funeral services for British naval reservist & expatriate, Leggett, of Service Camp.

D[utch] strongly against censoring [on the] grounds [that] native reads letters.

— SEPT. 24 THURSDAY

Best camp concert yet staged tonite, using kitchen porch as stage, lighted & with sarongs for backdrops. Rotund G. E. Magnay, 26, master [of] ceremonies. Scotch J. C. (Jock) Brodie stole [the] show with [a] Scotch number after [the] manner [of] Harry Lauder. Kilted (red sarong) sporan of half coconut shell, bagpipe red covered pillow, a stick (with Gilbrook's concertina supply[ing] pipe-like music) & tam o'shanter red covered Malay hat. He joked, wisecracked & sang rollicking Scotch songs. Completely surprised [the] camp, who never dreamed he had such ability.

Full moon rode [a] cloud mottled sky. Andrew Carruthers of M.B.C. Singapore & Magnay staged show. Block 1 Eurasians, augmented by H. A. Gilbrook, E. F. Kennard, 32, several Boswell brothers, Magnay, Carruthers clattering clogs, Eurasian 1 guitar, 6 ukuleles & 1 mouth trumpeter, comprised orchestra.

E. Boswell, 27, brought down [the] house in final number when he appeared [in a] grass skirt leis & brassiere & hulaed [in the] best tradition. Curran-Sharpe's topical song "Palembang, So Early in the Morning," in which he versified humorously various camp members [was] also hilariously received. Encores also brought back Norman Boswell garbed as Modern Malay, dark glasses, white coat, sarong & Eurasian [ ] Van der Meulen in shorts & looped sarong hung over shoulders singing Terang Boelan 3 Eurasians V. P. Meulen, Stout, Breuer sang Malay song "The Fisherman" with gestures [that] also brought down [the] house. Other numbers, Phillips jokes & card tricks, De Jong singing.

Fr. Bakker's choir did splendid job.

⭑ SEPT. 25 FRIDAY

On working party bought 2 cans Libby's Spaghetti & 1 can corn beef hash. Obviously there [is] no serious shortage [of] food stocks, otherwise such things wouldn't be sold. Pd. 60 cents a can. Native grocery stores all seem [to] have plenty [of] fruit on display. Hawkers also sell various pastries & bread, evidence [that it is] still possible for natives [to] get flour & rice. Prices high but commodities still available.

Workmen today seemed unwilling [to] indulge [in] conversation with me. Evidently they [are] afraid.

⭑ SEPT. 26 SATURDAY

Camp News delayed by having translation review twice. V.D.V. displeased with de Jong.

⭑ SEPT. 27 SUNDAY

5, 5:30 & 6:30 Masses & Communion. All day read Upton Sinclair's "Oil!"

Issued *Camp News* day late because of Dutch translation difficulties & typing trouble.

⭑ SEPT. 29 TUESDAY

Went to Catholic hospital known as "Charitas," run by Dutch Sisters. A large hospice surrounded by lawn & trees. Originally rich Chinese home, then sisters hospital, then in 1937 new hospital completed & brothers took over this as school for boys. Airy, clean, pleasant place, but packed [with] beds. My bed in chapel.

Met Dutch flying officer who [was] in my lifeboat. He has charge [of] war prisoners [in] hospital.

⭑ SEPT. 30 WEDNESDAY

Camp News numbers welcomed. Bishop thinks not much use prohibiting [letters] entirely since [communication can] divert [to] other channels but people extremely imprudent.

Hospital stands on corner, roads flanking it [on] two sides. Hospital one story large wing, high ceilinged, crucifixes [on] walls [in] every form. Every room jammed [with] beds—about 110 people in now. Staffed by Dr. Peter Tekelenburg, Dr. J. H. Ziesel & 15 Sisters.

‒ OcT. 1 THURSDAY

Womens camp leader Rev. Mother Lorenki [?]. Typical day, rise 7:30 a.m.. Common washroom, shower, toilets & wash taps shared by both men & women. Breakfast soft rice "Boeroer" ordinary rice & soya sauce, with vegetable. Noon meal rice, vegetable, meat, also rice soup. Persons with money supplement by outside ordering such as saute-barbecued meat and lamb or steak, brown beans, Mei Mei (Chinese noodles) curried egg, bananas, sugar. Sisters arrange buying or native. Dinner rice, vegetable. Anything can be bought.

‒ OcT. 2 FRIDAY

Sent note Myazi asking [for] reply concerning exchange & he returned it with notation "You must await instructions from Syonan Gunseiboe." Showering this morning beneath trickle [of] water when well soaped, water ceased entirely. Scurried out & got bucket [of] water to sluice off. Informed water works can pump only 200 tons hourly, whereas sometimes 800 hourly used.

Sister Paula, midwife, competent, white-garbed figure, close fitting bonnet & veil stiffly starched, averages 1 birth daily, before war, least 3 daily personally. Rises 4:30 a.m., prays 1 hour, washes & dresses men [in] chapel ward, pedals around city on bicycle morning & afternoon & frequently during night, as stork's visits [are] untimely. Sews clothes & washes in spare moments, performs all duties [of an] ordinary nurse plus janitor, midwife, seamstress, spiritual consoler. Prays ½ hour right after supper, then sisters bath or shower.

‒ OcT. 3 SATURDAY

Attended Mass 5:45 a.m. [in the] Bishop's narrow room, 6 nuns, 4 Malay & 1 Chinese girl, 1 serviceman, filled small space where altar set up on wash stand cupboard & table. Sisters made responses.

Bishop stays [in his] room all day with leg propped up—has thrombosis.

Am stuffing myself with fruit. Ate whole big papaya last nite. 10 or 15 bananas daily & 3 eggs daily.

‒ OcT. 4 SUNDAY

5:45 a.m. Mass, all nuns attending, read "Land of Last Chance" by G. W. Ogden, story somewhat similar to Cimarron.

➤ Oct. 5 Monday

Reading E. Snow's "Battle for Asia."

Big Dutch woman, red hair, silly, disjoint[ed], crying brokenheartedly to Sister. Young Australian nurses paintless, powderless, wearing hospital sarong & hair unkempt, look much older than their years.

3 duck eggs daily make good meal. I'll try & get duck eggs in [ ]—much larger.

➤ Oct. 7 Wednesday

Myazi came to hosp[ital] today on business. He assured me "Everybody's name has gone to Tokyo." Said [he was] unable [to] answer whether I [would be] permitted [to] cable Hori.

Sinar Matahari said 420 Japanese arrived [in] Yokohama from Australia, Indonesia, Borneo—other places—exchanged.

Geishas & Sing Song girls from Hongkong evacuated out of Palembang. Geishas rode autos but Sing Songers had [to] walk [to the] pier, angering Sino [Chinese] men.

➤ Oct. 8 Thursday

Hearing Mass, receiving communion daily 5:45 a.m. [in the] Bishop's room. Finished "Battle for Asia." [ ] of operation N.E.I. natives unite if left independent [on] account [of] disparity [of] races. Nationalist spirit only evident [to] intellectuals. Great masses unaware [of] what's going on. "Palembang Mind"—clever tradesmen superior [to] Javanese, already trying [to] oust Javanese cops. Great bulk [of] Java's seething 60,000,000 living [on the] verge [of] hunger, eking out precarious existence. Land not self sufficient but no matter how hungry they never ask or think of looking for help because of "Maloe," untranslatable indefinable quality somewhat approximating Sino "Face." Javanese [are] easy going & spendthrift, impractical, always borrowing.

When 60,000 colonists returned [to] Java from Sumatra, [it] was thought trouble over food might ensue but they simply disappeared, absorbed, Palembang natives easy time. Plenty money, little work, food easy matters.

➤ Oct. 9 Friday

Read Wodehouse's "Bill the Conqueror." Bustle of departures & arrivals including Mrs. Curran-Sharp.

⌐ Oct. 10 Saturday

Dr. Mildern vigorously condemned Chiang & Sinclair. Read Buck & 55 others resolution Sino-Am. Med. Ind. He displays same contempt, dislike most [of] Britons [in the] Far East for Indians, Malays, which more & more convinces me that if such are typical sentiments of [the] British Government, Indian problem will never [be] solved by British, but only American ultimatum [and] Sino-pressure will force English [to] give India a break.

⌐ Oct. 11 Sunday

Reading Amely Rihani's "Arabian Peaks & Desert."

⌐ Oct. 12 Monday

Finished Rihani.

⌐ Oct 13 Tuesday

Playing bridge nightly with Sir John Campbell, Mountain, Dutchman.

Oct. 14 Wednesday

Read Ida Treat's "Pearls, Arms & Hashish" Pages from the life of a Red Sea Navigator Henri de Manfred [ ] as Abu El Vai.

Curran-Sharpe entered hospital.

Sir John Campbell born Loch Gilpheid, Scotland Jan 3, 1876. Ran away to sea, then joined Second Life Guards at 17. Left Guards in 1895 to [go to] Australia & mined gold, then slated for Klondike but Boer War [broke out] so sent [to] Australian Mounted Infantry as enlisted man, wounded [returned] to Australia, back to mining, then pearl fishing. Then tin mining Malaya, Gen Mgr. Trona Mines Limited, Peru, biggest tin mine [in the] world. Made world production record, 47,000 [ ] 6 months. Then planted rubber 1908 Sant Pirak estate his own. Later sold it then prospecting in Siam for tin, using elephant transport.

Home in 1914 joined King Edwards Horse, then Royal Scots. Commanded 11th Battalion from 1916 to war's end. D.S.O. & Bar for Battle Arras, Battle of Somme, cited for crashing battery of guns [more biography].

⌐ Oct. 15 Thursday

Returned to camp to learn Fanoy spread tale of my sudden visit to hospital because my mind was affected, despondent, & associated with Poggemeir—just as Allen & I thought he would & predicted so before I left. Allen had planned to have some fun with him & went at it, but [that] wasn't necessary. He spread it without provocation.

Camp News of week I left carried Agerbeek's caricature of me in goggles.

⚊ Oct. 16 Friday

S.T. had article on American fliers in China which quoted Pepper Martin at length describing visit he made to them Aug. 5.

⚊ Oct. 17 Saturday

Read Hakon Michaels's "Journey to the End of the World" trip to Tierra del Fuego.

Block 11 beat Block 2 in quizzing contest by lopsided score—10 to 6.

⚊ Oct. 18 Sunday

Read "The Swathlying Count Murder" by J. J. Cottington (J. C. Stewart)

Plagued by acute attack restlessness, maybe "nerves." I got up a poker game—Prior, Christie & Germann & I, whereof I came out winner—stakes only matches—it proved good soother & by [the] time [the] game [was] half over the nerves [were] gone.

Our roof leaks considerably now. Good thing I got camp cot which [is] easily moveable.

⚊ Oct. 19 Monday

Spent most [of the] day making supports for my camp cot which [has] weak legs.

⚊ Oct. 20 Tuesday

I told about ghost camps & narrated my ghost story at Tuesday nite session.

Fr. Elling & Brother Macarius to hospital.

Rumored nitely excursions.

⚊ Oct. 21 Wednesday

Spent day writing *Camp News*.

Belgian Taow now gets [ ] drunk, only gay, on "arak," a native beverage made from rice which his Chinese wife brings him. He starts early morning & sings loudly. Poor guy, he deserves something like that, he's so far gone physically, just a hulk of a once big, powerful man. Locomotor ataxia.

― Oct. 22 Thursday

Wrote letters addressed to Synonan officials: Swiss Consul W. Arbenz & Delegate International Red Cross Malaya Hans Schwezer, also a letter to Marishita, Palembang Assistant Resident & telegram to T. Hori. Probably Marashita will do nothing with any of them. He has taken Myazi's place in charge of civilians.

― Oct. 23 Friday

Began series [of] descriptive letters to Jean.
Camp News completely finished by noon, a new record.
54 men examined for teeth fillings of which about 20 might be suitable for temporary fillings.

― Oct. 24 Saturday

Cabaret concert held kitchen veranda with Edgar Magnon as woman. Carruthers directed show. Full moon illuminated scene. Not as good as last month's show, however.

― Oct. 25 Sunday

Feast of Christ the King. Did not smoke all day & intend making this definite date for quitting, having relapsed for a month, starting while in hospital.

― Oct. 26 Monday

Meeting with Oranje, Oosten, Hilling on letter question after threats [of] B[ritish] to expose Dutch.

― Oct. 27 Tuesday

After D[utch] gave words they would not carry letters, all came back loaded. Obviously they can't be trusted.
My shoes returned repaired.
Dr. West lectured on V.D.

➤ Oct. 28 Wednesday

To working party first time since Hosp[ital]. Framework of all building up. Our barracks floor is sea of mud & water. Poor drainage will be a menace.

Reading Douglas Reed, "Insanity Fair."

Jockey W. S. Bagby, little Australian, has slung a hammock just below roof of veranda. He clambers up nails driven [in the] wall into bed, like monkey.

➤ Oct. 29 Thursday

U.D.T took letter matters in own hands, said W. talking nonsense about possible trouble & H.O. will inform women go ahead. He is an absolutely irresponsible double crosser.

Worked *Camp News* all day.

British Malaya policeman H. B. Sims wrote honey of report on missing ladder.

➤ Oct. 30 Friday

Camp Leader announced in *News* [that the] July culprits are not punished in camp "because it would mean interference from the outside into internal running of camp" & advocated "boycott of the offender by decent camp members." Gets more absurd & dangerous daily.

Many Dutch advocate smuggling because it's "brave" & puts one over [on] the enemy.

➤ Oct. 31 Saturday

Issued *Camp News*.

Block 7 won 15½ to 14 from Block 5 in quiz contest. Curran-Sharp returned from hosp[ital]. Note from R. Waltz of *Poelau Bras* lifeboat.

➤ Nov. 1 Sunday

Reading Paul de Kruif, "The Microbe Hunters." Read Rufus King's "Crime of Violence" which cheats the reader, authors like King a[re] unfair to readers when their mystery stories, supposedly solvable by acute reader-detective, prove completely at variance with clues supplied.

➤ Nov. 2 Monday

Reported British officers released from camp & now living [in] houses near Mailoe school.

Am once more on a non-smoking basis, after succumbing at Charitas Hosp. Not a single cigarette today.

━ Nov. 3 Tuesday

British committee by 4 to 3 vote against excluded Dr. West from deputation interviewing Japanese after Penrise, among other things, said West [is] an Irishman & therefore not a Britisher! Later Australian constituents of F. W. Gill, big miner, rebelled against his con vote so he reversed it, notified Penrise & informed him committee must meet tomorrow morning & vote again. Since large portion of camp trusts neither V.D.I. nor Pen., they want someone present whom they trust to give honest, accurate report of proceedings.

W. Van Arkel, fat Dutchman with [a] sense [of] humor visited hospital, saw Fr. Elling, returned & encountered J. Fanoy, ginger bearded little conspirator of Block 2, who spread stories [that] Elling & I [are] going insane, when we went [into the] hospital. "I've talked with Elling & he's not mad," Arkel answered [in a] loud voice.

G. St. J. Johnston related anecdotes of Irish rebellion 1916 at our Tues. lecture. Johnston [is] an Ulsterman who fought rebels.

Nov. 4 Wednesday

Van der Vliet & J. Penrise interviewed Marishita, Chief [of] Palembang Police who altho[ugh] refusing requests for furnishing additional food, clothing, bedding, visits to women's camp & camp purchasing directly at market, did say our names were in Tokyo, we can write to Red Cross Tokyo; he will investigate whether we can write Malaya & Java; mail can go to & from women's camp every 14 days; occasional interviews in future may be had: "serious friendly disposed toward Japanese may be released later on. Each case will be examined individually." Dr. West can see chief medical officer here.

━ Nov. 5 Thursday

Guy Fawkes day in England & we wish we could pull a fast one on our ginger whiskered, droopy drawered little conspirator, but couldn't think up a good one. Wrote *Camp News*.

A. H. Sellenraad, 53, Block 3, died heart disease a.m. stricken suddenly.

⌐ Nov. 6 Sunday

V.D.F. censored letter to Editor, decrying parcels to women's camp when they prohibited by Js. However I got one in ridiculing his last week's article saying [it is] impossible [to] punish rules violations because [it] would mean outside influence in camp.

⌐ Nov. 7 Saturday

Practicing nightly for forthcoming concert. *Camp News* issued 6 pages. Priests came back after night out in hospital due to mistake—[by] Js—Pole died [in] Pladjoe [was] thought to be Catholic death but he wasn't.

⌐ Nov. 8 Sunday

To 6:30 a.m. Mass & C[ommunion]. Wrote brief story to tell with song about Roundup at concert.

⌐ Nov. 9 Monday

Belgian Taow tangled with Van Eerde, his cellmate & they [were] separated [by] New Zealander M. F. Enright.

⌐ Nov. 10, Tuesday

S[inar] M[atahari] said U.S.-British landed north Africa. Rain stopped concert after first number.

E. W. Crocker, 32, London, British ship officer, seriously burned when *Madeira* bombed near Singapore Sept. 4, came to camp from Charitas Hospital where he has been [ ] since being landed here.

⌐ Nov. 11, Wednesday

Armistice Day began with Requiem High Mass at 10:30 a.m. Rev. A. V. Wardle conducted Protestant Memorial service. Concert which was interrupted last night held tonight & best yet produced. Indian Troup numbers by Wm. Attenborough, Victor van Geyzel, Elder Boswell, Frank Kennard & Gillbrook hysterically funny. I sang "Bury Me Not" & "Last Roundup," building up latter with story of an execution as Roundup sung. I also recited "In Flanders Fields," after which taps played.

⌐ Nov. 12 Thursday

Wrote *Camp News*. *Sinar Matahari*, now called *Nippon Palembang Shimbun*, full of American-English attack [on] North Africa.

Syonan-Times says Shenton Thomas, Ge[n]. Wainwright, Sumatran Governor Spit in Formosa. Also named 4 American aviators [taken] prisoner during raid [on] Japan [in] April, one of whom a Nielsen from Hyrum, Utah.

Editorial decried Malay attitude [of] apathy & indifference, also keeps stressing need [to] grow foodstuffs.

— Nov. 13, Friday

Third Friday 13th this year. First—Feb. 13 I [was] in Calcutta & luckily got ticket for Batavia. Second Friday 13—March—my lifeboat landed on island [in] Semanka Bay.

Nippon Palembang Shimbun full [of] North Africa, saying American-English occupied Algiers; Italy occupied Corsica from which bombing. German planes based [in] southern France. First American-German clashes scheduled [in] Tunis desert.

— Sat. Nov. 14

Block 6 defeated Block 3 by 2 ½ to 18 in quiz contest. Had a busy week preparing for concert putting out *Camp News* & preparing quiz.

Dr. West's birthday today, 37th. We gave him a pineapple & can [of] sardines. Biesel & de Graaf staged big dinner—nasi yoren & delicious steak—in kitchen after night meal. Resident Oranje, Oosten & West spoke. 23 men present in all.

— Nov. 15 Sunday

Every day reading bits from Thomas a Kempis, "Imitation of Christ." Despite all my resolves not to smoke I still take a cigarette after meals. Wrote last will & testament of Herbert Smallwood, big, fat, redfaced hammer toed, bald, spike moustached kitchen porter, ex lumberjack. His entire estate consists of 10 pounds in a Liverpool bank & wages due him since Oct. from Canadian Pacific Steamship Co.

Lost 7.6 cents at poker session with German, Christie & Curran.

— Nov. 16 Monday

Yesterday J. Drysdale & A. Curran-Sharp resigned from British Committee, [as a] result [of a] long series [of] incidents between them arising over Drysdale's sponsoring [an] active policy & Penrise a passive one. Endeavoring to have both sides explained in *Camp News*, I approached

Penrise who flatly refused [to] have anything in *Camp News*, said nothing on subject was to appear in it. I am determined that it will.

3 new men came to camp today who have been at liberty all the time on tobacco, rubber, coffee plantations, getting them in order so Japs could take over.

⟶ Nov. 17

Yesternite output news summary A's taken N[ew] G[uinea] but possess only Henderson field on Guadalcanal island, Sol[omon]s. Report Talang Betoets [?] bombed.

⟶ Nov. 18 Wednesday

Administration outside undergone some change resulting only New Zealander, Enright, 62, going Charitas Hospital with severe carbuncle on neck. New doctor who appeared [not to] know even [that] there was such a hospital, but he seemed a good, thoughtful man, examined all prospective patients & succeeded in getting Enright out.

Curran-Sharp posted letter publicly on board giving reasons for resigning & accusing Pen[rise] of dilatoriness regarding R +. Caused quite a stir.

Many postcards from Java arrived mailed fron Oct. 6 to 18, also some letters from Hospital, all bro[ugh]t by J. officers.

Rumors Timor occupied, all N[ew] G[uinea] & part [of] Celebes.

⟶ Nov. 19 Thursday

Mother's birthday. Fr. Bakker said 2nd Mass for her & I received Com[munion] for her. After Mass I wrote her a letter, which cannot be mailed until the war is over. I feel she & Dad are alive & well & that by this time they know I'm alive & a prisoner.

Wrote *Camp News*.

⟶ Nov. 20 Friday

Camp News passed the censor including 2 controversial letters on Brit[ish] Com[mittee] & Curran-Sharp's letter & one bit of blank verse castigating Killick for filching bananas each morning. He drops loose handkerchief on loose bananas on ground when they arrive, picks up both & slides furtively into pocket. Altho at least $1/2$ of camp knows he does it & watch & jeer at him, he seems oblivious & [thinks] that he is getting away with it.

Penrice (full name Walter Penrice) suggested Dr. West, hospital staff better empty stall buckets now.

⇀ Nov 21 Saturday

Full moon monthly concert had good weather but was too long for me—3½ hours. I "broadcast" a farce wrestling match between W. D. Christie, 23, Canadian, "Lothario the Lithuanian Loon," & E. W. German, 25, American, "Basha Bazook, bearded burly Bulgarian." Pure slapstick, it went over all right. A. Wrigley, 21, British made up as formal gowned woman—excellent characterization. J. P. Quinn, 23, Australian diplomatist, directed first scene, a pub in England. Andrew Carruthers, 24, Malayan B.C. announcer, directed 2nd scene, Amsterdam cabaret & G. E. Magnay, 26, rotund Brit., directed 3rd scene [ ] too long.

⇀ Nov. 22 Sunday

Eric Germann, Christie, Curran-Sharp & I playing Sunday night poker sessions regularly now. I won tonight taking two big pots, one with 4 queens.

⇀ Nov 23 Monday

Indonesian policeman, J. van Mourik, 43, attempted suicide by slashing left wrist with new Gillette razor blade. He did it quietly & bled for probably 10 minutes—cut vein but not artery—and was discovered by neighbor at 3:38 p.m. West fixed him up & he went to Charitas Hosp. after Jap. Doctors came & saw him. Mourik [had] long been a problem to camp, unable to get along with anyone & continually trying to get out to hospital. He's been bad nervous case with no one seemingly able to help him.

I'm conducting [a] poll of camp endeavoring [to] discover what members want for New Years Eve concert.

⇀ Nov. 24 Tuesday

Shimbun unmentions Solomons where last Saturday's first time mentioned J. losses in attack on Guadalcanal.

⇀ Nov. 25 Wednesday

Brit[ish] Com[mittee] wrote to Red+ enclosing list [of] names asking for financial assistance.

I completed camp poll on New Years show. Voting favored a compere, slapstick, lots [of] music, sketches, Magray as compere & was against recitations 94 to 61. Choir favorite entertainment, with Malcolm Boswell, 2nd, Indian troop, Coons, myself, Parsons Puddle, Lawson & De Jong, in that order.

— Nov 26, Thursday

Shimbun said Brit & Aust. Troops massed in Burma between Chittagong & Akjab [?] suffering from quinine shortage! First direct word [of] Allies in Burma. [ ] said breach between U.S. & Britain over who shall command Africa for Free French, Darlan or De Gaulle, with U.S. favoring Darlan.

Went on working party. H. P. Kendall, white haired red faced barrel chested Malayan planter who has taken over Prior's job while Prior in hospital, went out also, first time. Every day now a few men over 45 are included in the working party.

In afternoon Kendall at well told story of shooting a tiger in Malaya— as the first of a series of *Camp News* sponsored lectures.

Am reading "Fame is the Spur" by Howard Spring, a story of the British labor movement. Interesting reading.

— Nov. 27 Friday

Began John Gunther's "Inside Asia." Lots [of] good reading in camp now.

Wrote *Camp News*. Only one page this week.

White pated F. G. Ritchie, 56, Scot senior marine consulting engineer & one [of the] wealthiest men [in] Malaya, has sewn blue shorts with white initials for all hospital staff.

— Nov. 28 Saturday

Issued *Camp News* 6 a.m., earliest yet.

All day yesterday & until night without smoking. It's a tough battle quitting now, much harder than in ordinary life—probably because we have so few comforts or luxuries & the food lacks so much nourishment our systems are used to.

Block 1 won quiz 30 1/2 to 24 1/2, from combined team Block 8 & hospital. Quizzes more & more popular.

⤙ Nov. 29 Sunday

High ranking officer from Singapore, reportedly a General but [ ] a Col. or Major Gen visited camp with 3 other J. cursorily inspected kitchen & Block 1 & 2 section camp. Ignored V.D.P.'s question regarding communication [with] relatives.

⤙ Nov. 30 Monday

Finished Inside Asia. St. Andrews Day (see Dec. 1).

⤙ Dec. 1 Tuesday

Syonan Times for 11/16 said rice rations [in] Malaya reduced to 17 [ ] per person per month.

Ashes of General Margius Toshinasi Maeda C.I.N.C. Borneo who [was] killed there in incident in Sept. arrive Tokyo.

Domei's Lisbon quotes Pepper Martin is [in] Chungking after month's tour [of] India as Indians hate British.

Papers claim smashing victories [in] Solomons, claiming 3 battles [in] Solomons—the last beginning Nov. 12 & 1 battle of South Pacific off Sunta Cray [?]. Says U.S. fleet now hopelessly crippled. However does not claim capturing Guadalcanal or Henderson Field.

Boiled our mosquito nets to kill bedbugs which infested room from wicker chair.

Last night Scotch of camp celebrated St. Andrew's Day. Heavy rain halted outdoor ceremony & speeches but kitchen served a fruit salad spiked with "arak" & coffee, for dessert. Scots then gathered [in] Brodie's room [in] Block 8, sang & joked. Evening ended with singing "Auld Lang Syne" as we all locked hands in crowded cell & shook arms up & down during last verse.

⤙ Dec. 2 Wednesday

Finished Howard Spring's "Fame is the Spur," which deeply impressed me. In Spring's portrait of Hames Shawcross, I see so well reflected the many leaders who rose from the streets of poverty to great heights then denied, or tried to, their beginnings & fellow workers. But also, for the first time I saw a logical reason why in some cases that was so. In the Shawcross case his keen vision saw that coalition was necessary, a union of all factions—in order [to] save [the] empire—but nevertheless he betrayed those who supported him & believed in him.

⌐ Dec. 3 Thursday

Wildest rumors—including one that J.s threatened dire penalty to anyone spreading a rumor concerning Dec. 10 [sic] report [of] Gandhi [issuing a] proclamation supporting allies against J., also that U.S. & Brit. jointly guaranteed Dominion status for India.

Guard being treated for sores said Allied Recon plane flew over Pladjoe, but no bombs, as previously reported.

Report radio broadcast list [of] N.E.I. towns scheduled for bombing, with Palembang [the] name at top.

Camp notified postcards can be sent to Java, Malaya.

⌐ Dec. 4 Friday

Mailed two cards, one to Mary in Shanghai, one to J. H. Rutman, former Chief R.P.D. Bandoen—Batavia. Address of jail is Raadhuis Weg 4.

Rumor J.s tied [to] trees [in] Pladjoe [on] account [of] refusing [to] go [to] Singapore.

Big rat hunt after dinner in surgery wherein Allen, West, Earl, Kendall & I practically tore place to pieces but finally got rat, which originally appeared from under Allen's bed, when wounded, he hid in rolled up mat & I stamped him to death.

⌐ Dec. 5 Saturday

Yesterday Japanese issued black stringed sacks for every light in camp. Looks like we'll have permanent blackout henceforth.

Birthday of banker J. Schenck, 40, Block 6, cigars, cigarettes, coconut sweets & coffee served assembled throng. Dutch birthday song sung.

L. R. Blake, 46, Block 8 leader who once bootlegged in New York when stranded there [in] 1930, distilled a fermented rice liquor some[what] similar [to] Chinese beigar I drank [in] Peking. Still consisted [of] big coffee tins—one a steam boiler, & another a condenser with coil made from electric light conduit pilfered from house near new dump site. Big fire built [in] his cell & mixture—2½ bottles liquid dynamite, sampled [as] soon as cooled.

⌐ Dec. 6 Sunday

Reading Margaret Halsen's "With Malice Toward Some," which Jean told me to read years ago.

One reason I like the book, in addition to its droll humor, is because so much of it is like Jean's witty observations on things.

Spent a good deal of day getting things line[d] up for New Year's show.

Bomb shelter trenches being dug around town, or rather re-dug. Nightly curfew, reinstallation all A.R.D. system, indicates something more than practice only.

⚊ DEC. 7 MONDAY

Report Andamans & Nicobara recaptured. Pasar Malam celebration scheduled [to] begin tonight for 1 week as past Dec. 8 celebration canceled account [of] air raid "practice."

Persons interested [in the] concert elected me [to] produce [the] show New Year's Eve, however, Quinn, Carruthers, Magnay, Attenborough voted against & later held big powwow with me. They obviously wish no one but themselves to produce [the] show. Anyway, I've urged holding another meeting tomorrow & putting their objections forward & having a vote.

⚊ DEC. 8 TUESDAY

At today's meeting I withdrew from concert, then put [the] question of producer to vote & big majority favored 1 man [instead of a committee]. Carruthers [was] subsequently elected, & he rejected octet which Fr. Bakker consented to organize & train.

J. sponsored celebration included long parade [of] glum Malays [and] Chinese who stared in at us between the barred gates. They had no looks of joy on their faces.

My thoughts went back a year to U.P. office & Mary.

⚊ DEC. 9 WEDNESDAY

I went on working party today. Big posters & an effigy at gates of Padang to stir anti-Allied hatred. Poster showed "Dr. Churchill," altho labeled "Inggers" stethoscoping patient marked Indonesia. But Dr.'s shadow on wall proved him a wolf with slavering jaws about to bite off Indonesia's head.

Best, though, was effigy of a soldier labeled "Australia" crucified to red stripe of British Union Jack, a Japanese soldier (effigy) gallantly is cutting the wrist bonds which tie Australia to the Union Jack. Australia is being freed by Nippon!

Read Conan Doyle's first Sherlock Holmes story, "A Study in Scarlet."

— Dec. 10 Thursday

Worked from 5:43 a.m. to 7 p.m. helping Kendall. We are taking turns helping him, so that Curran-Sharp, Hamson, Earl & I alternate taking a day each. Cooking soft rice for dyspeptics & keeping water hot for septic feet bathers plus other odd jobs keeps one on feet all [the] time.

— Dec. 11 Friday

Composed *Camp News*. DeYoung too tired to continue, proposed drop [ ] & *Camp News* & when we demurred gave work to Van Geuns who will continue & which is a good thing both ways.

Finished memorizing Poe's "Raven."

— Dec. 12 Saturday

Reading Agnes Newton Keith's "Land Below the Wind." Description [of] her life in North Borneo.

Syonan Times in Tokyo communique lists U.S. Navy losses in vicinity Solomons from Aug. 9 to Nov. 30 in Battleships, 4 sunk, 3 heavily damaged; Air Carrier 4 & 4, Cruisers 31 & 5, Dest. 21 & 15, Submarines 9 & 1, Transports 17 & 6. In all 119 ships sunk or damaged & 850 planes shot down or damaged. Listed 1st Battle Solomons Aug. 7 to 9, 2nd Aug. 24. Battle Santa Cruz Oct. 24, 3rd Battle Solo. Nov. 12 to 14. Night Battle off Lunga, Guadalcanal, Nov. 30.

[That would] mean practically all battleships, cruisers, [and] carriers U.S. possessed when war began now lost & she [is] fighting with newly built ships.

Newspaper men [in] Manila brought [to] Shanghai including Carl Myolans.

Cigarettes available after Dec. 8 [in] Malaya at fixed prices 50 cents for 20 [other prices given]

— Dec. 13 Sunday

Finished "Land Below the Wind."

Lost 7.6 cents at poker.

— Dec. 14 Monday

Read S. S. Van Dine's "Canary Murder Case."

Fr. Elling returned from hospital.

No hope.

→ Dec. 15 Tuesday

On working party today. Native cop said 2 meter wooden fence will be built around camp, which will require 2 months because [of the] wood shortage.

→ Dec. 16 Wednesday

Earl lectured on explosive mines at sea.

G. have refused [to] accept our postcards for mailing. However service men last week given cards on backs of which [are] G. characters for writing home.

→ Dec. 17 Thursday

Dutchman C. Simons, 32, sawing boards he explained were splints for Mrs. Kuni's Womens Camp who fell off wall 4 days ago while waving to working party & broke leg.

About 9 p.m. as jail inmates strolled beneath a half moon & Statius Muller tried out his new accordion, accompanied by guitar, uke & harmonica, a nanny goat appeared at the front gate. She was promptly whipped in by Nemers & added to our animal population of two dogs, an expectant tabby cat who birthed one stillborn kitten, & numerous roosters, hens & chicks.

→ Dec. 18 Friday

J. guard played chess today with Rebel, Mohammedan Dutchman. He likes to hang around the men & try to joke, altho[ugh] seems not [to] understand [a] word [of] English or Dutch.

Oosten & Hilling treated us to a fish & fried potato dinner, topped with fruit salad. Delicious.

Sy[onan] T[imes] said Wash[ington] published Pearl Harbor losses, story named only 8 battleships. (I understand 8 B[attleships], 3 C[ruisers], 3 Dest[royers], 5 other ships.)

Patients like my soft rice cooking.

→ Dec. 19 Saturday

Fr. Bakker helped black bearded Morgan, Norman Boswell, De Young & me with cowboy songs for concert.

Dutch choir gave short concert tonight—Christmas preview. A nearly full moon brightened things up. Afterwards camp had one of its best impromptu sing-songs, which developed into a competition between two groups, Dutch & English.

I described it in another letter to Jean.

⟶ DEC. 20 SUNDAY

Learned there is a group of spiritualists in camp, about 10 men, who meet secretly at night & with probably a ouija board or other indicator [to] learn [the] progress of the war from the "spirits." Believe Sturrman is one.

⟶ DEC. 21 MONDAY

Five Dutch Caucasian prisoners brought in, kept incommunicado in Guard room. [Not] allowed [to] speak [to] anyone, escorted [to] toilet, bathroom, etc.

Working *Camp News* Christmas number.

⟶ DEC. 22 TUESDAY

Oosten lectured on art & Jewish problem, Middle East, Palestine.

Prisoners named Van Houten, middle age & known as a hunter & jungle man; Buchanan, whose father Canadian, mother possibly Chinese. Both oil workers Loengi Gerong living Pladjoe. Arrested [on] account [of] maps in [their] possession.

⟶ DEC. 23 WEDNESDAY

Finished *Camp News* typing Allen during past 3 months composing general knowledge questionnaire based [on] English literature, history. Dec. issue 5 sheets, single spaced, illustrated—16 copies.

⟶ DEC. 24 THURSDAY

Horrible, blood chilling screams awakened camp 2:15 a.m. First thought [it was] someone's nightmare but continuance brought us out as they dwindled [into the] distance. Best screams I ever heard. Proved to be Malay guard, bleeding from head wound. Van Houten escaped: guard took him to toilet. Went out back, walking side by side [in] front [of] Block 8. V. H. seized guard's short sword, struck him [a] heavy blow [on the] head— from wound probably while sword sheathed, bolted across yard & out gate. Stories henceforward vary—generally saying he struck 3 more Malays who tried [to] stop him, stabbed Jap. soldier & took his bicycle. Reached Moesi River. At dawn he was seen swimming [the] river by search launches. Soldiers about to fire on him but ordered [to] desist & swim after, capturing him alive, but he disappeared. West dressed guard's 2 inch head wound.

When working party started back from new campsite at noon, about 100 women gathered [on the] highest point [of the] women's camp, led by one conductor, sang 3 Christmas carols to men of working party. Clear voices floated across the some 150 yards of fields & houses, bringing mist & choked throats to many eyes.

Despite my feeling to the contrary, my editorial, first in *Camp News*, was well received & [a] number [of] favorable comments. Allen wrote extremely good poem "To My Wife at Christmas."

Gordon Burt lectured on motor trip Suez to England.

After dinner Rev. Wardle, Church [of] England parson, led some carol singing & Allen did [a] splendid job condensing Dickens "Christmas Carol" with appropriate quotations to 38 minute reading.

Full moon brightens camp these nights & makes for late going to bed.

Despite circumstances, cheerful Christmas atmosphere pervades camp.

⮥ DEC. 25 FRIDAY

Attended Mass 5, 5:30 & 6:30 a.m. High Mass in Block 3. Altar decorated [with] orchids, gardenias, palm leaves sent by Chinese woman florist. Behind & above [the] altar [was a] mural [depicting] Bethlehem's barren hills with 2 shepherds & two angels painted by Fr. Bakker. 6 tall candles in conical cardboard sticks which underneath were ketchup bottles. Fr. Elling preached [the] sermon [in] Dutch which he preached as his first sermon of priesthood Christmas 1926 [in] Utrecht with parents, 3 brothers, 3 sisters in church. English & Dutch Prot[estant] Services with Wardle & Colijn preaching 8:30 & 9:30 a.m.

Then little jockey Donnelly, smallest man [in] camp, dressed as Santa Claus & trailed by Reans, Gill Cotton, Van Mealen & Allen—biggest men—distributed presents from women's camp & taffy to all. I received a red Christmas wrapped present of a cloth-bound notebook monogrammed "McD," which Colijn girls must have sent since their father & Oosten got same, but no card or name enclosed.

Impromptu orchestra [of] accordion, guitars & [a] few singers sat in front of kitchen & serenaded kitchen workers (conveyors) preparing big dinner which proved to be plenty[:] steak (700 pieces), fried potatoes, vegetables, rice, etc.

Dutch choir gave impressive cantata of sacred music beneath velvet cloud flecked sky, sprinkled here and there with stardust. Cantata Christmas story from Bible read in Dutch & English by Biesel & Allen—short readings followed by songs—from Annunciation to Nativity & ended by Silent Night. For [the] first time since camp began utter silence reigned during 2nd half of concert.

All in all, it was happy, cheerful Christmas—despite the circumstances—with a beautiful ending.

— DEC. 26 SATURDAY

Choir marched in working party & sang three songs to women's camp in answer to carols they sang Thursday.

Block 7 defeated Block 6 13½ to 18 in quiz.

Scheduled community sing cancelled because guard said we'd have to stop at 8 p.m.

Buchanan taken to see body found floating in Moesi River which he identified as Van Houten's who apparently drowned. B. then allowed [to] come inside jail & live among us as regular internee.

Boxing Day community sing canceled because guard said [we] had [to] stop by 8 p.m.

— DEC. 27 SUNDAY

Copied "Whispering Winifred's Christmas Card" in letter to Jean.

— DEC. 28 MONDAY

My day on hospital duty. Rehearsed [in the] evening for cowboy number.

— DEC. 29 TUESDAY

On working party & rehearsed for concert.

— DEC. 30 WEDNESDAY

Worked all day hospital & all evening to midnight on *Camp News*.

— DEC. 31 THURSDAY

Issued 8 paged *Camp News* which began with message by Resident A.

Oranje expressing positive confidence [in] Allied victory. Van der Vliet's message thanking camp for cooperation, etc. Review of year & "Whispering Winnifred's Christmas Carol." Agerbeek's front piece showed jail mug (enamel ware cup) lifted [in] toast [to] 1943 with planes against sky above. Red, white & blue motif.

4:30 p.m. Allen at well asked crowd questions appearing [in the] Christmas number. People [were] able [to] answer most of them. One Dutchman, a banker, Rothier, surprisingly able [to] answer most of questionnaire based largely on British literature & history.

7:30 p.m. Dutch Protestants held religious service.

8:30 p.m. Concert sponsored by *Camp News* began. I started it with introduction [of] participants, based on poll of camp. Also participated later in the cowboy number. Was disappointed in concert as [a] whole—lacked punch & Magrey's compering poor—he did not seem to get into his stride.

Concert ended 10:45 p.m. after which there was [a] period in which Dutch & British Protestants held separate religious observances. At 11:43 camp gathered at kitchen again while Magrey named various people about camp & thanked them for good work during year. He then called Vliet, Penrice, West, myself, & Biessel for special thanks. 4 of us held big card each with Chinese character one side, together meaning "Happy New Year." Attenborough, in his Chinese garb, explained [the] cards, then we turned them around & audience saw "1942" instead of Chinese characters. I held the "2." Attenborough placed silk handkerchief over my card as I flipped it down. Vliet whisked off handkerchief & "3" appeared in "1943" & soon kitchen tong [*sic*] gonged in midnight & New Year! Everybody shook hands [with] everybody else. Guitarists played in Block 1 until 1:30 a.m., then camp quieted & men slept.

I smoked my last cigarette of 1942 & I hoped of my life. Am definitely stopping in conformity with my vow in the sea last March 7.

—And what of 1942 & me?—

On debit side my decision at Djokdjakarta to remain in Java [a] while longer & not fly [to] Australia—although [it] gave me temporary front page splash in U.S. & London because of exclusive stories—resulted in me boarding *Poelau Bras* which sank, landing me here. As a prisoner I'm a total loss to U.P. & cause of great sorrow to my family, if they think me dead, especially. Further—waste of precious time in here by unsystematic

& inconsistent efforts at Malay & shorthand, total lack of attempt [to] learn Dutch or *write*, except diary & few letters to Jean.

Also, failure to keep my promise of never smoking or drinking again. Drank beer on the jungle trek & some spirits at Jiwa when prisoner enroute here, also some gin which Holweg produced July 4. Stopped smoking [a] few times but started again.

—•—

On credit side:

This year probably my greatest spiritual adventure—from Shanghai to Palembang showed me that my thirst for adventure was genuine and so far insatiable—because I want more. It sounds like *daring*—but I can now recall no moment when I was conscious of *daring* or courage. Nor was I conscious of any defined plan as such—except the goals—Chungking, then Java—which I made & *escape* to India of Australia which I didn't.

I am & will be I hope eternally grateful for the opportunity of coming closer to God. My near death at sea—when I had a long time to think—proved to me that *nothing* can compensate for [that] since nothing is more important than my own soul.

Since being in jail I have had the wonderful opportunity of attending Mass each morning & of receiving Communion. I have had more opportunity, too, of assessing myself—my spiritual, mental & physical worth & to gain a few lessons in *patience*.

Have had time to read, to write, to study & have done some reading, some studying, but little writing. In 1943 I *must* 1. write; 2. not smoke; 3. humbly & cheerfully accept whatever fate God has in store for me.

As for smoking this year, despite my vow, I say only that during [my] early days of jail life I was so terribly hungry all the time I smoked to relieve the hunger. It did. Incidentally, Fathers said it was alright under the circumstances. Now that hunger has passed.

Book 7

— JANUARY 1, 1943 FRIDAY

Attended 6:30 a.m. Mass (High). Read Sr. Rider Haggard's "Finished." Learned some Dutch, while not condemning, do not approve such acts as concert Cannibal number & Lawson's skit. Say actors should not appear scantily clothed, such as cannibals—a thing we Americans & British find hard to understand. However [it] must be remembered Dutch culture & Luther & Calvin religions somber, dark, hide-bound & ultra conservative. Recall all Dutch acts contain no nudes—all subjects fully clothed.

After dinner Dutch—Van Arkel & Maal—put on old traditional Dutch skit of Thomas Vaer & Peter Nell—latter part always taken by woman, but since no women [are in] camp, name changed to Peter Man, a review—usually sarcastic—of the year.

First New Year's Eve or Day in many years I didn't drink at least one toast with some spirit beverage. Last year Pepper, Lee & I drank some Chinese wine in a farmhouse. But [this] year—nothing—unless last nite's fruit punch can be counted. 3 bottles arak went into mixture [with] bananas, papaya, pineapple & others—giving juice a slight kick. Blake said his brew [was] all given to kitchen.

Community singing followed Dutch skit with Dutch & British groups alternating song—led by Vander Wetering & De Young, Carruthers & Magray, with guitars & uke accompanying. Rain ended it at 9:30 & I went to bed.

⇀ JAN. 2, 1943 SATURDAY

My day on hospital fire duty. Wood wet; many baths for those with septic feet or bottoms—on hop all day.

⇀ JAN. 3, SUNDAY, 1943

Three Masses & Communion.

Played poker with young John Close, Eric Germann & Christie, lost 2 cents.

⇀ JAN. 4, MONDAY—1943

Javanese pedlar at field had *Syonan Times* August 29 which detailed with 3 col[umns under] Head[line] "British Woman Owes Life to Our Great Commander" & pix General Yamasita who permitted Lady Catherine Heath, wife [of] Lt. Gen. Sir Lewis Heath, 2nd in command Singapore, [to] be taken [to] General Hosp[ital] from internment camp to give birth [to] stillborn child. Her husband permitted [to] visit her. Therefore she owes her life to Yamasita, say *Times*.

New camp completed, even to mats on hospital beds. Only workmen there today cutting new grass & pounding out laterite walks.

Mandalay also destroyed.

⟶ Jan. 5 Tuesday '43

Hospital work day begins [at] 5:45 a.m. [with] emptying night soil bucket, then build[ing] fire—half [the] time with wet wood—made easier by getting coals from kitchen. Our hospital consists [of] two room cell block separate from other buildings & fronted by barbed wire & high hedge. Our fireplace a small thing of tin, brick & iron rod bottom, used to heat hot water for soaking septic sores; cooking soft rice for dyspeptics, brewing tea for patients & at night we make our own coffee. After heating water in 5 gal. coffee tin, I cook rice, stirring it over fire & getting blistered by splashes of boiling stuff. Hospital rush requires plenty [of] hot water for boils, septic feet, hands & bottoms. Wood chopping takes much time. Must saw up logs, then split into pieces small enough for crude fireplace about 9 X 14 inches. Takes *at least* 30 minutes [to] boil 5 gals water, usually longer, depending on wood. Brew tea 10 a.m. & 3:30 p.m. Soft rice 7:15 a.m., 12:30 & 6 p.m. Also must keep hauling cold water for big wooden tong, washing & tempering [?] boiling fluid. Hard day's work ends when dinner dishes washed after dark—usually about 7 p.m. or so.

Wootton lectured describing Shanghai.

⟶ Jan. 6, 1943—Wednesday

Gertrude's birthday. Hope she, Paul & Jean Francis are okay.

Dreamed last night of heroism displayed by men in camp who had chance [of] escaping by burning [their] way out of big room. Men drew for position & started fire, which burned so hot no smoke & slowly crept toward door from opposite end [of] room. Silence was necessary & not one man even whimpered as flames devour[ed] them, some threw themselves face down in coals to choke off possible cries. I can remember only 1 face in dream—Malaya policeman Livingston, who sat & watched with interest as flames approached him..

Burma captured, fighting approaching Akyab.

Write letter to Gertrude.

⟶ Jan 7, 1943 Thursday

Mrs. Curran-Sharp entering Charitas Hosp[ital] was searched & 62 letters found in handbag, causing much trouble—closing down on reports & letters.

Gilbrook lectured U.P. work Tientsin.

⟶ Jan. 8 Friday

Harley-Clarke, dentist, hasn't been in since before Christmas. Unknown why.

Worked at day hospital which now [is a] 14 hour job.

Working party men did too much shouting to women, so noise now forbidden entirely.

⟶ Jan. 9 Saturday

New camp now completely enclosed by barbed wire topped board fence joining buildings plus outside ring [of] barbed wire encircling all. Working party members, however, freely wander in adjacent shrubbery & visit Malay coffee shop in bushes for coffee, ten-teng (a peanut brittle) or rice flour cakes, fried coconut oil with jam inside. Pedlars sell fruit, tobacco, canned goods, at outrageous prices. No more books sold. Evidently all looted books now disposed of to us, military or hospital. Pedlar said G.s used to trade English or Dutch books to pedlar for tobacco, candy, etc. I got several bargains—volume of Keats for 60 cents & big illustrated volume "As You Like It" for Guilder. Pedlar also took orders, then meet working party in mid-town, when we're halfway home, run beside us & thrust our orders to us. Saves us long carry. Pedlars honest & always are there—even though their prices are robbery. Occasionally G. or Indo. Guards beat them up & drive [them] away from camp site, but next day they are back again. They know the good & bad guards by now. Coffee shop woman was beaten the other day but shop still running. Indo. Guards, bad actors, do it. Most guards friendly fellows who like gossip.

⟶ Jan 10 Sunday

Mangostine & Ramboetin season beginning—both tasty fruits, which with Doekaro, bananas & pineapple (ananas), plus limes (djeroeka) help our diet. However fruit [is] expensive. Mangostines (thick, brick red, bitter skin with 6 segmented, sweet white fruit inside) cost 2 cents each. Doekans, [the] size [of] our plums, thin skinned white meat, juicy, bitter pit, 50 for 10 cents; limes 1 cent each; Doerian—a large fruit, thick green, rough

skin, inside mushy, creamy substance tastes similar boiled spanish onion—
strong smell.

⟶ JAN 11 MONDAY

On hospital duty, made first goela java—sago with coconut milk for
sick men of kitchen—Brothers Vincentius & de Grager.

⟶ JAN 12 TUESDAY

Nippon Pal[embang] Sh[imbun] 2 column Editorial message by Lt. Gen.
N. Kaspi, Gov. So. Sumatra, saying natives filled with propaganda Allies
would arrive here & destroy Japanese forces. Kaspi termed such reports
false, ridiculous, said Allied forces long ago destroyed completely, however
concluded by warning that although Allies [will] never [be] able [to] resur-
rect their strength sufficiently [to] land troops in force here, they probably
would air raid Palembang & could land small group of men by submarine.
Therefore warned Palembangers to expect anything. But have confidence
[in] Nippon strength & once again hit at false propaganda from enemy
spread by radio or other means.

Paper also carried announcements all radios must be reported & li-
censed for medium wave (natives say reported radios all confiscated).

Banner said Nanking declared war on England & America, also that
English troops withdrawing from Burma-India borders.

Then, suddenly strange coincidence—cornet sounded loudly, clearly
outside on highway playing, of all things, "Whispering." Men rushed to
gate but player, riding bedja (bicycle ricksha) passed too quickly to be
seen. He blared "Whispering" right in front here as though for a purpose.
I wonder.

First run-in with Dr. West & Kendall over bucket emptying, which I
hope established [the] point [that] I won't be imposed upon longer & also
that matter will not kindle into anything more serious.

⟶ JAN 13 WEDNESDAY

R. Wilson, slender, quiet New Zealand surveyor, joined hospital staff in
place of Curran-Sharp, who is more or less invalided & Prior, who returned
yesterday to Charitas Hospital [on] account [of] septic hands & tempera-
ture after being back only short time from operation [for] hernia. Prior
aged considerably during 6 weeks [in] Charitas & now is really petulant old
lady. Strangely, Curran is getting petulant & aging too after few weeks [in]

our own hospital. In fact I've noticed the ones who stay a long time either here or there—but more markedly here, develop "hospitalitis," eventually becoming hypochondriacs & reluctant to leave our dingy confines.

Working party today—probably my last since we are rumoredly moving [into] new camp permanently 15th or 16th.

4 Dutchmen arrive[d] from coal mine near Moera Enim where [they have] been all [the] time running mine.

— JAN. 14 THURSDAY

Notified we [are] moving Saturday.
Read Wodehouse "Right Ho, Jeeves."
Shimbun 4 column Editorial entitled "We Can Win & We Must Win." They're protesting too much.

— JAN 15 FRIDAY

Members working party carried sticks & firewood to new camp. Those who left sans wood booed by onlookers. Those who carried 2 or more sticks cheered. When they arrived [in] new camp [they] found [a] big load [of] wood there. We [are] busy packing things up to move. Despite fact [that] most of us arrived here with nothing, we sure have accumulated plenty. The surgery, 13 ft. square is full of barang of patients here in Charitas. We're taking everything moveable, even bricks embedded [in the] ground [in] front [of] dysentery ward, wire, boards, bottles, sacks, cans, makeshift tables, chairs, etc.

Germs of sing song planted when guitarists & accordion began last musical in jail, but spirit lacking & never really got underway.

— JAN. 16 SATURDAY

Piles [of] luggage, furniture—barang consisting [of] every conceivable object from black kitchen fire boxes to hospital stretchers. Cells stripped of everything—G's said cell doors mustn't be taken away but they went in the shape of bed frames, fire grills, etc. 7 a.m. Vliet called out [by] Gunseibu[,] informed 126 men from Pladjoe today would [be] added [to] our new camp, plus 40 more later, while wiped out our plans [for] allocating places. Truck & motor bus appeared 8 a.m. & moving began. Kitchen first, then hospital luggage, then hospital patients, then rest [of] camp. Men didn't have to carry barang after all. Rush unloading stowing barang—ours included firewood,—2 gunny sacks, 2 cans filled bricks, wooden toilet buckets, old iron, tin, rope, string, cans, etc. We just got hospital barang off the road when Pladjoe truck arrived loaded [to the] gunwales [with] men & equipment for their own—they thought—new camp, including 53 ducks, and 100 chickens, several dogs, 126 men, making our total population 456 men, 6 dogs, 53 ducks, 100 chickens.

When Pladjoers—all oil workers of Shell & Standard—learned we [are] here & running camp they gave us [a] great deal [of] material, including several stoves, many dishes, pots, kettles, buckets, etc.

Kitchen staff served regular Saturday noon meal at 2:30 of beans, rice & gravy, peanuts—an excellent meal & real accomplishment. Men squeezed into 8 sections averaging 54 each & which Japanese allotted 60 [to] each; leveling off process will begin soon. Pandemonium in sections as men squeezed in with barang but for most part everyone philosophical. 8 Indonesian guards & 1 Jap on duty, Indo in each sentry box. All Europeans & J civilians evacuated from Pladjoe & new soldiers arrived. A[nti]A[ircraft] & searchlight batteries installed & practicing. Rain late afternoon turned grounds into mud sea.

— JAN 17 SUNDAY

Mass is celebrated [in] dark interior unoccupied front block, altar consisting [of] planks laid across passage between shelf bunks.

3 Pladjoe Dutchmen built us good 2 place stove & began constructing hot water boiler. Flattened sheet corrugated iron turned it into tube with earth roller, lined with bricks & metal tank in center.

I washed dishes & cut wood all day. Between jobs snatching reads [in] Thorne Smith's "Did She Fall?"

Hammering, sawing, pounding, scrounging sounds all day as men dig in, natives complete shelf building.

— JAN 18 MONDAY

Boiler completed & after all morning session of washing & woodchopping, finished up cleaning all donated dishes, pots, jars, etc.

Episode:—J. guard displayed stump of rotten, loose tooth which West extracted. When evening came, J. presented us with bean stuffed tea cakes & West gave him phoney sleeping tablet. We've also managed [to] wrangle several light globes.

Guards in good spirits. Hospital staff no longer stands [to] attention for roll call, as does rest of camp.

Water shortage bad for camp bathing & washing & two bathrooms. Hospital o.k. however, plenty [of] water because altho only small flow in pipe, our demand less.

Pix:—J. guard exercising by sawing plank, imitating native carpenters, who sit on plank & saw backwards, away from themselves.

⌐ JAN. 19 TUESDAY

Rain continued, beginning in morning for third successive day. Rarely rains here in morning.

⌐ JAN. 20 WEDNESDAY

Rains continue. Ducks thinning out several nipped each day for duck dinners. Spirited chases as ducks flee & pursuers slither wildly after them through mud.

Eurasian Dutch guitarists start No. 2 Block kitchen to undersell No. 1 & give poor men of camp chance to buy. Designed [to] run sans profit. Putting out my last *Camp News*, as I have too many duties [in the] hospital, where [I] go from 6 a.m. to 8 p.m.

⌐ JAN 21 THURSDAY

Britisher Elston says he's rolled about 20,000 cigarettes since internment. He charges 30 cents a hundred for rolling. Smokers supply paper & tobacco. It keeps him & his pal in spending money for necessities. He averages between 100 & 150 per day. If he buys a towel for 1.90 he figures it cost him 600 cigarettes.

Camp is almost a mud lake now.

Septic tanks overflowing & stench bad.

⌐ JAN. 22 FRIDAY

Air raid precaution practice includes shutting off water supply, which seriously hits our already scanty water flow. By late afternoon there is practically no pressure & consequently bathrooms [are] waterless.

Buildings are gloomy, crowded, damp, sweaty.

⌐ JAN 23 SATURDAY

Issued my last *Camp News*—3 sheets both sides, 2 pictures—one of a line of ducks following a drake & entitled "Reinforcements from Pladjoe."

Fr. Elling conducting special prayers for International Week of Prayer.

⤙ Jan 24 Sunday

Read C. S. Forester's "Flying Colours" in which I was introduced to Captain Hornblower.

Mass held in vacant section of main building reserved for future arrivals. Altar consisted [of] board across aisle between shelves which run entire length [of] each building I serve for bunks. Altar linen, etc. disguises planks. We either sit on edges of shelves or drop sandals & squat or sit on shelf mats. Mass held every morning here also, much better accommodation than in jail.

⤙ Jan. 25 Monday

Reading Pearl Buck's "The Exile."

Because of water shortage water regulations enforced—7 dippers per man for bath, no dishwashing except from tub, one bath a day, no clothes washing water from tank but must take from tap, also automatic flushing system for W.C. bucket fills & tilts every 10 minutes. One man on duty constantly 5 a.m.–8 p.m. enforce[s] rules. Has resulted in everyone being able to bathe at least once a day, where previously workers not finished until late [were] unable [to] obtain water for bath.

⤙ Jan 26 Tuesday

We now have 15 patients in hospital & clinic averaging 60 to 70 treatments daily.

Men line up outside barracks for roll call, counting beginning at Block 8 & ending with hospital. On rainy days guard sometimes allows it to be inside. Hospital staff does not have to line up.

Curran-Sharp lectured on last years [of the] Victorian era. Thus resuming our Tuesday night sessions.

⤙ Jan 27 Wednesday

Pladjoe Eurasian, slender, fuzzy moustache, mentally unbalanced, has hallucinations of strong lights, spirits & other things, sometimes stamps heavily up & down—rousing ire of guard—& also stands stiffly at attention, bowing—Jap fashion—or saluting Boy Scout fashion—imagining people.

Australian Manning & couple Pladjoe Dutch built me a saw horse, good & solid for my woodsawing which I do each day with assistance [of] Banker Schenk for hospital fires.

Mary Bell, 1986.

McDougall with diaries at Palembang, 1945.

McDougall recovering diaries at Palembang, 1945.

Belelau Camp, unidentified inmate.

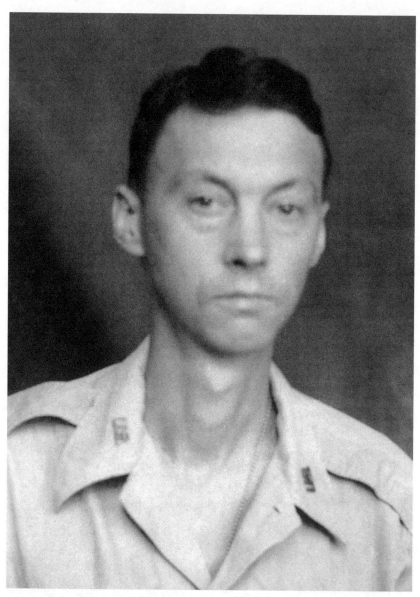

McDougall in Calcutta after liberation, 1945.

McDougall disembarking in San Francisco, 1945.

Belelau Camp, women and children.

Belelau Camp, unidentified inmate.

Belelau Camp.

Palembang Camp drawing, exterior.

Palembang Camp drawing, living quarters.

Palembang Camp drawing, exterior.

Palembang Camp drawing, living quarters.

Embarking on Lake Tai during escape from China. McDougall second from left.

Escapees at Lake Tai. Left to right: Pepper Martin, Francis Lee, McDougall, with Colonel Lin, January 1942.

TEROMPAK ECHO

CAMP NEWS

Incorporating
Publishing

HOT AND LESS HOT NEWS

Vol. 2 No. 2.

Jan. 9th, 1943.

WHISPERING WINNIFRED NURSES NEW YEAR HANGOVER

Winnifred found Beissel's fruit punch bowl more attractive than the
Concert New Year's Eve. Consequently, she spent more time in the kitchen
than in the audience, and although it was fun while it lasted, not all Dr
West's bottles, nor all Dr West's pills could put Winnie back into shape
again for a full-sized Camp News this Saturday. For that matter, Winnie
believes Campmembers have also not yet fully recovered from their Christmas
and New Year festivities, and super-super Camp News issues. So they will
probably welcome something short and light; to wit:-

Left Hook Lawson Dazzles Ring Fans..... When Man Mountain van Arkel playfully
pulled Librarian Lawson's beard the other night, the book-worm turned, and
tatooed Van's chin with some left hooks and right crosses which warmed the
cockles of Winnies heart. She is thinking of signing up the new fistic
discovery, now known as Left Hook Lawson, for a match next Michaelmas.

OPINION SPLIT ON CAMP NEW YEAR'S SHOW

Camp opinion was split sharply concerning the New Year's Eve
show, Winnie learnt. One school of thought said that the Concert was the
best yet, and the other said that the show was among the worst ——because
it did not come up to expectations. Camp News, which sponsored the show

was disappointed in it.
To us it seemed that
the show lacked that
spark necessary to
lift it from mediocrity
to a hit — from just
another concert to a
bangup New Year's Eve
production.

It is difficult to
place the finger on any
one thing wrong with
the concert, except that
Compere Magnay couldn't
seem to get into his
usual stride. For
the rest, it was a matter
of that indefinable "it"
of showmanship. At least
that is what Camp News
Editors think. Many
other Camp Members disagree
with us, and declare it
was not only a fine show,
but the best yet.

Director Carruthers ran things smoothly, there were no time lags, and acts
were snappy. Most popular numbers, judging by Camp comment, were the
Dutch Choir's rendering of "Old Black Joe", Anderson, Starkey and Morgan
in the Hospital Satire, and the new guitarists, Wener and Breuer. Bill
Attenborough's characterization of a Chinese dentist was in a class by
itself, and our hats are off to him also   for his idea of ---

Camp News.

in the New Year with the 1942-1943 placard trick at midnight.
Other performers, selected as a result of last month's balloting,
were Tenor Malcolm Boswell, Comics Gillbrook and Kennard, Camp Leader van
der Vliet, Hero, Villain, Damsel — Quinn, Lawson, Wrigley; Cowboy Tunester
McDougall; Baritone de Jong, and the Rhythm Masters Max Breuer, Stout, van
der Meulen, van Maaren, this time in the role of Cannibals.

FOR SALE One blue sports shirt, as new. F. 3.50 Apply Morgan, Block 11.

COMMUNITY SONGSTERS.... in spite of our large and sumptuous lunch,
brightened the night January 1, under the leadership of van der Watering
and de Jong heading the Dutch, and Carruthers and Magnay British warblers,
while Breuer and Wener hotted up their guitars for both groups. Singing
followed presentation of typical Dutch New Year's Day feature — Thomas Vaer
and Peter Man (in this case) done by Maal and van Arkel.

COME AND CLAIM THEM..... The Toko holds the halves of four one-guilder
notes, numbers 42805, 96719, 156122, and 171248. Possessors of the other
halves are requested to present them at the Toko for exchange.

KITCHEN FUND ACCOUNT DECEMBER 1942

		Expenses	
Total available	1500	Brown Beans, peas, butter, meat, eggs etc.	1384.80
Total expended		Fruit (free Distribution)	84.98
1199.07		Free supplies to kitchen staff	26.65
		Debit bt. fwd. from previous mths	2.64
		Credit c.fwd. to Jan. 1943	0.93
	1500		1500.00

The Kitchen stock on Dec. 31st, 1942 was worth F. 216.80, including
Brown Beans F 50, Peanuts F 28, and Green Peas F 35.

Account of money for the Woman's Camp

Cash in Hand	1.90	To Charitas Hosp.	75.00
Received from Blocks	144.50		
" " Horseracing	25.00	100 kgs potatoes, 2 tins fat,	
" " Collecting Box	32.11	25 kgs onions	66.00
₤₤ 9.30 exchanged at 0.85	7.90	60 kgs meat	66.00
	211.41	Gratuity to Carter	2.00
		Balance in hand	2.41
			211.41

Camp News.

CAMP NEWS
Incorporating
Terompak Echo   (publishing)   Hot'n Lens   Hot News
Vol. 1 No. 25   Nov. 14, 1942

CONCERT HITS NEW HIGH IN CAMP HILARITY

Camp concerts hit a new high in hilarity Wednesday when Attenborough, van Geysel & Company convulsed spectators with Indian musical high jinks. And when Bosun Brodie slid down the hemp to climax the Indian rope trick, the audience practically rolled in the aisles. Consensus of camp comment was that the show was the funniest yet.

Because the announcer's thoughts were dallying in fields where nautch dancer Fatima dwells, he forgot about the collection box for the Womens' Camp Christmas Fund. It should have been beside the coffee urn at intermission. As result, Block Leaders will be asked to gather the cash from their constituents.

Since you all saw the show there is little need to describe it. Undisputed hit of the evening was the Indian troupe, with Bill Attenborough as Hamed Din doing his magic and card tricks; Elder Boswell as Fatima the nautch girl, Victor van Geysel as moustachioed Gunga Din with his drum, snaky fingers, flashing eyes and India rubber knee; Frank Kennard the gullible sailor lad, redoubtable Jock Brodie was Barnacle Bill the bosun and J. A. Gillbrook as Hussain Din, the silent stooge.

Jock Brodie, doubling in kilts and later as a crusty salt with designs on Fatima, more than lived up to his previous reputation for humor.

Black faced Gillbrook and Kennard, with their dice and drinking act, and later with N. Boswell in the darkies' southern plantation number supplied many laughs and were well received.

(over)

Camp News.

Malcolm Boswell, singing, "Rainbow on the River," was another hit. The stringed instrumentalists, Max Breuer, E. Dobrichy, A. van der Meulen, supplemented by Case Steur on the harmonica, did yeoman's service. P. Stout sang two numbers, a Malay Kronchong and "Schooier." In the later he appeared as a hobo.

The cowboy songs "Bury Me Not on the Lone Prairie," and "The Last Roundup," sung by W. M. McDougall Jr. as well as his recitation of "In Flanders Fields," which opened the concert with an Armistice Day note, also were well received.

The concert began where it was interrupted by rain Tuesday night, just after F. Boswell sang "Bill Bailey" and "Maggie." Stage hands Wally Bagby and E. Hasselhuhn are due plenty of kudos for their lighting effects and decorations.

As was expected, Elder Boswell brought down the house with his hulah hula in "Hawaiian Night" and later as Fatima in the Indian number. Enthusiastic admirers presented him a bouquet, plucked during a recent working party.

To the regret of producers and spectators, one scheduled number was canceled. Illness prevented Bert Smallwood from singing and trumpeting.

———

The regular full moon concert will be held as scheduled, Impresarios Carruthers and Magnay said as Camp News went to press.

———

Camp News editors are planning a New Year's Eve revue, wherein it is hoped the best numbers of previous concerts will be reproduced together with some new, surprise turns.

Camp members are invited to submit suggestions and propose personnel for the Revue. Let us know what numbers were your favorites.

BIRTHDAY GREETINGS

Camp members today extended many happy returns to Dr. G. F. West, whose birthday it is. He is keeping his age secret but Winnie has noticed twinges now and then, suggestive of lumbago, creaking joints and other manifestations of advancing years.

Dr. West denies the lumbago accusation and terms it Palembang Stoop, brought on by much stooping over Palembang feet and peering up Palembang Bottoms. Be that as it may, we all are glad he is here to do the stooping, peering and probing which has done so much toward keeping most of us fit and in good health.

LETTERS TO THE EDITOR

In last week's Camp News appeared a letter signed "Skeptic," criticizing a letter on punishment, written by Mr. van der Vliet which appeared the week before. Mr. van der Vliet, in last week's Camp News, said he would reply this week to "Skeptic," however, Mr. van der Vliet informed Camp News editors he had changed his mind, explaining, "the gap between my opinion and that of 'Skeptic' is too great to bridge and can not be done by letters."

Another letter on the punishment subject has been received and follows:

(next page)

(more)

Camp News.

— Jan 28 Thursday

Resumed Thursday public lectures—Gordon Burt describing 1939 Grand Prix auto race Berlin.

Another addition to our staff: Carpenter L. D. Thompson, British ships purser, making 9 on staff.

— Jan 29 Friday

Read Pearl Buck's "The Mother."

— Jan. 30 Saturday

Reading another Buck, "Sons." Also read Noel Monk's "Flying Squadron."

— Jan. 31 Sunday

Gunseibu indignant because of "V" for Victory sign carved on tree near entrance. Been there [a] long time, also word "Johnnie" both probably working party doings.

— Feb. 1, Monday

Gunseibu man again inspected tree and "V" sign.

Elder Boswell & helpers finished rolling badminton court & first games played. Also first full fledged game Dutch basketball, which has 12 players per side & in Holland usually half are girls. Basket is on high pole (12 feet or more & no backboard). Court divided into sections & players assigned [to] one section cannot play in another.

Agerbeek giving me Malay lessons now.

— Feb. 2 Tuesday

J. doctor inspected camp with West before taking patients to Charitas for regular Tuesday treatments. Said our conditions better than internees [in] Singapore, worse than Java. Admitted crowding but said much less crowded than J. troops barracks, however said we'd get more because more people being rounded up & all being sent here account [of] wireless transmitting station discovered north coast. "When we [are] going forward—winning—must take prisoners & intern them & if lose & go back, must take more (with us?)." He also gently warned V. Vliet one man's indiscretion can get whole camp difficulty.

Dr. wants [to] buy wrist watch because lost his & all his possessions in fighting Malaya. He followed entire campaign from Singora (just inside Thailand) to Singapore. However he won't buy gold wrist watch because "looks too Jewish!"

Admitted food insufficient but said only 25 to 30 cents per man per day allowed, admitted we lacked vitamins & said J. soldiers supplied Vt. B tablets wells [?] butter, etc.

Dutch ex flyer said Navy 0's same as Heinkel 109.

⏤ FEB. 3 WEDNESDAY

J's still after watches but paying for them now. J. guard paid G. 55 for a waterproof non-magnetic, etc. wrist watch tonight. Beissel handled deal for Dutchman Wiesfuss.

Young papaya trees in Chinese yard across road from our window bearing fully. Papaya grows rapidly. Seeds planted in early jail days became trees & were bearing small fruit long before we left.

View from our window (only window in camp) an expanse of tropical greenery beyond barbed wire fence & road of red laterite earth. On the opposite road edge is an attap hut with high, sloping roof in which lives a Chinese gardening family whose small fields were wiped out by our camp & field. In the middle distance is another farm hut beside a small patch of papaya trees probably 70 feet long. Usual bloekar growth obscures view for any distance, but a group [of] tall, slender trees higher than [the] rest marks boundary of what I presume is native cemetery as one or two patches of white resemble tombstones.

⏤ FEB 4, THURSDAY

During debate whether [to] change Tuesday night lecture to another night in order to accommodate Fr. Elling who gives 3 lectures a week, West & Allen revealed openly their opposition, which had long been obvious from West's cracks & inferred from Allen's remarks. They refused [to] change date, or rather West did & Allen followed. Others said nothing.

⏤ FEB. 5 FRIDAY

Dentist Harley Clark returned to us after about 6 months outside working in Dr. Gani's hospital with Holweg for natives & Jap civilians. Said [he was] brought back without warning of any kind. Holweg & wife still there, also few Dutch & Australian nurses.

Burmese woman who married British [man in] Singapore [the] day they evacuated & who [was] on *Giang Be* floated ashore clinging to chair, A British airman clinging [to the] same chair, felt himself going, so he pulled something from pocket & asked her to give it to his wife, but she demurred, telling him she'd probably die too, since [she] couldn't hang on much longer. He let go. She hung on, was eventually taken to an internment camp somewhere north of here & fairly close where there are 800 British & Aussie men & women survivors of Malacca Straits. Some Aussie & British nurses also there.

Mrs. F. L. Jones, women's camp, notified by J.'s that her husband, F. L. Jones, editor *Malay Mail*, safe in Singapore. About 40 women were so notified concerning their husbands, thus proving some survivors [of] Malacca Straits [were] taken back to Singapore at that time.

All B[ritish] & A[ustralian] troops removed from Malaya where food shortage [is] severe & vicious black market. Many B[ritish] planters, technicians sent back to work estates, etc.

Thousands [of] Sinos executed shortly after S[ingapore] fell. All rounded up & slain, especially Communist Volunteer Corps.

Local natives sentiments now turning toward us. Reports all native spears, swords, etc. being confiscated, which if true [is] an insult to natives, who keep them in families for generations.

Food still plentiful & shops well stocked.

5 ducks hatched out [a] few days ago by old hen are now gaily swimming in their "pond," a deep dish sunk in the ground & following their foster mother around camp.

— FEB 6 SATURDAY

Japanese brought papers to sign wherein each internee takes [an] oath in name of God "Tuan" he will not escape nor attempt to escape & if he does either accepts any punishment whatever befalls him. Spineless camp committee signed without question, not even asking what the alternative would be. Pladjoe leader & an Asbeck objected to taking an oath & so far he & others who wished alterations allowed whereby wording changed to "promise" to Japanese Government. I signed on later, but wrote under my name "Signed Under Protest, Civilian Internee." On another form each man wrote his name, age, occupation, & date of internment, a space marked "Welfare" was left blank by everyone.

Lahat Postmaster (Indo-European) entered camp today—just picked up sans warning. Said *all* radios confiscated [a] month ago—even sealed sets.

In first full fledged Dutch basketball game oilmen defeated others 3–1. Few baskets are made in this game.

⤙ FEB. 7 SUNDAY

All promises signed today.
One Dutch Pladjoer removed to Workers Camp.
Bakker preached sermon 6:30 Mass.

⤙ FEB. 8 MONDAY

Began Nov. to S[acred] H[eart] for Jean.
Buchanan, Indo-Europ. whose companion Van Houten escaped from jail & drowned in Moesi, taken back to jail today to serve 5 days without food for attempting to escape. In Pladjoe he drew a map of this region because he wished to get away to Java where his father died. Notes issued in Malay by J's dated Feb 2, but a check can be postdated.

⤙ FEB. 9 TUESDAY

Missed first Tuesday lecture of our group because Fr. Elling gave his own & I elected [to] go [to] Elling's. Looks like first break.

⤙ FEB. 9 TUESDAY

Well diggers have hole down about 2 meters between main buildings & outside barbed wire fence near gate.

Because of shortage of wood coming in a party of choppers is allowed to go outside & cut it. Because of water shortage we are also allowed to cross road & haul water in buckets from Chinese farmer's well.

⤙ FEB. 10 WEDNESDAY

Finished Booker T. Washington's autobiography, "Up From Slavery."

⤙ FEB. 11 THURSDAY

Dokos gave camp lecture on trip to Japan.

⤙ FEB. 12 FRIDAY

Year ago—Friday Feb. 13, Allen rescued from water in Bangka Straits, hauled into tiny dingy wherein huge Kendall [had] already been hauled.

Allen now weighs 95 kilos & has cut about 40 kilos. Kendall weighed about the same. Allen had swum in darkness for an hour when picked up by dingy manned by Scott & another man, both who volunteered attempt reach J. cruiser & persuade it not sink *Giang Bee*, but never reached cruiser, which shelled & sunk vessel.

→ Feb. 13 Saturday

A year ago Feb. 13 was Friday & the Singapore debacle was in its climax, hundreds of refugees were dying in Malacca Straits. I myself was in Calcutta.

In camp today's events included a clash between a Dutch congeries of Block 1 & British Australians of Block 5. Dutch tried to erect a kitchen in the area in front of Block 5 near the kitchen where all British kitchens are. Aussies drove them off with bitter hot words. The Block 5 corner dotted with small fireplaces whereon much cooking [is] done & one still operated by Blake & Messenger—brewing a foul smelling alcoholic potion reminiscent of biegar & peking.

Official camp crier is baldpated, white-fringed, horn rimmed spectacled bony bass voiced Dutchman, Schroder, whose deep voice, so Aussies says, shiver the attapo like aspens in a sirocco.

Pladjoers donated 61 garments (18 shorts, 16 shirts or coats, 15 pr. Socks, 4 prs hats [?]) to needy Britons.

Camp News contained verse comment on the word "bloody" as used by many Britons & especially by Aussies:-

> *"Yes, if you bloody really mean*
> *To talk about your bloody blood,*
> *Or if you're really bloody cross*
> *To criticize the bloody mud*
> *But otherwise, ye bloody men*
> *Please leave the bloody word alone*
> *Because, by bloody gentlemen*
> *It bloody simply isn't done."*

Feb. 14 Sunday

Informed native officials & others who betrayed Dutch to J. therefore given high & responsible posts when J's took over—were pumped dry & then kicked out by J's who told them "you were disloyal to the Dutch government & therefore you will be disloyal to us." Natives who worked loyally & well for Dutch are now in key posts for J's. Traitors [are] now interned [in] political camps whereof one reportedly here, or given minor jobs & watched.

Younger generation very pro-Nip.—they see J's treating Malays as equals, paying native officials higher salaries than [they] receive themselves, see all children compelled [to] go [to] school & learn Japanese. Previously only moneyed natives could send kids to school where Dutch [was] taught. All persons [are] compelled [to] study Japanese.

Eric Germann & W. D. Christie milling rice flour with coffee grinder for 35 cents kilo. Sell hot cakes 4 cents each and also experimenting with coconut candy. Takes one hour & 20 minutes steady grinding with good rice to turn out 1 kilo.

Men busily hauling water from the well as all taps campwide—except ours—dry. Ritchie & Jimmy Martin policing lower bathroom—restricting 1 dipper per man—had trouble with few men who insisted [on] using more.

Today is Valentines Day. I would not have realized it had not Allen reminded me. He now (8:30 p.m.) is lying inside his mosquito net perusing Hamlet for apt quotations to "send" to camp members as Valentines. He chose "He waxes desperate with imagination" for Fanoy.

— Feb. 15 Monday

This date 1942, which was Sunday, Palembang & Singapore fell & I land[ed] Batavia from Calcutta.

Began another Nov. to S[acred]H[eart] for Jean, having missed Sat. Com[munion] when not awakened for 5 a.m.

My badminton game poor one. I play about twice weekly.

Resident Oranje described Palembang's fall over after dinner coffee well, factually & amusingly. His story of Myashi & 70 pros. Sidesplitting.

— Feb. 16 Tuesday

Anniversary Eric's Muntok adventure.

Twice recently Pladjoe oil workers have been called to gate & paid back salaries.

Presided [over] first of Tuesday night lecture series for camp. Talk on London's A[nti] A[ircraft] defense given by planter D. F. Pratt, 34, who served briefly before discharged [for] ill health. I no longer attend our group lectures in hospital because West declined [to] change date previously.

⟶ FEB. 17 WEDNESDAY

Inoculated with typhus A & B vaccine. Second time since captivity.

During heavy rain this p.m. several men stood in downpour & bathed, soaping themselves down & having for first time since camp began here ample water for rinsing.

3 Eurasian soccer enthusiastists also played around in the downpour. They do it regularly.

Young man named Van der Meulen, Dutch Eurasian, entered camp. Been free since brief internment last March in Badang where he was in army when collapse came. Been staying [in] Palembang with Dr. Ziesel since June.

⟶ FEB. 18 THURSDAY

V. d. Meulen said approximately 2000 women interned Padang, of whom 300 odd Eurasians [were] released early. Remainder Dutch refugees from Medan, other places, & few British from Malaya. Internees' conditions there & in Benkoelen more lenient than here. Dutch Resident of Pedang & old British resident & probably honorary consul, Levinson, not interned.

⟶ FEB. 19 FRIDAY

Barber Pratt cut my hair short, practically only a stubble on top now. I decided it would save combing & keep it out of my eyes, since it won't lie down without grease or oil. I'm tired of smelling like a Kampon dandy from using the highly scented grease I've been employing since internment.

Block 4 cast out a member because he thrashes around so much in his sleep & last night blacked the eye of a neighbor. So now he is building a lean-to against the fence behind hospital bathroom. (He does not sleep there [arrow pointing to hospital]—only joke)

⟶ FEB. 20 SATURDAY

Continual rain every afternoon or evening has washed out concert nightly.

Reading Joseph Conrad's "The Arrow of Gold."

⇀ Feb. 21 Sunday

Pancakes of rice flour self made yeast manufactured by Germann & Christie getting better. Had some this morning. Lost 5 cents at poker in session with Germann, Christie & dentist Harley Clark.

⇀ Feb. 22 Monday

First concert in new camp finally held tonight. Cloud raked sky blacked out stars & resultant blackness seems even darker than normal. Concert stage constructed of latrine doors draped with sheets & sarongs. New orchestra a hot one with 3 guitars & sometimes 4 who doubles on "saxophone" (a reed in small mouthpiece of a megaphone), two other "saxes" or "clarinets" (Morgan & Carruthers) on combs & "snare drummer" Dutchman with various boxes & tins & reed broom. Morgan & Law dueted on "Sympathy," "Drifting & Dreaming" & another hotter. Whole thing excellent. Preponderance of Dutch in first half—only orchestral songs being English. Even De Jong fooled us & sang 2 [songs in] Dutch & no English. Second half considerably brighter, however, & Attenborough's Sultan number a side splitter. Germann & Bryant, be-turbanned as eunuchs with trumpets towering over Jockey Donnelly—like the little king—beating a tub (drum), herald Sultan Van Arkel as a paunchy, lascivious Esquire Sultan who announces he's very happy because Queen sent away for the weekend. Whereupon Hawaiian guitarist in sarongs & leis & hula-hula dancer (Dahlen of Pladjoe) come on. Sultan's eyes pop, [he] makes passes at Hula & exclaims "After a whole year" Someone in audience shouted "Awas! Perawan!" ("Look out: that's a woman!") & audience roared. Then Sultan (Attenboro) unexpectedly returns & faints, is revived by "Blake's Brew," gets gun & tries [to] shoot Sultan, but holding gun backwards. He excitedly gets her to reverse it & suddenly realizes it's pointing at him. Pandemonium follows. Good slapstick, short & snappy.

DeJong ended show singing "Nina Roblo" parody which wowed us at first jail concert.

Today Jean's birthday. Tomorrow novena for her completed. Dear little Jean. God bless her.

⇀ Feb. 23 Tuesday

Natives continued emptying hosp. septic tank, began yesterday. A large tank on wheels is placed next to septic outlet & a pipe run from tank into muck below. Metal trap door on tank closed & gasoline poured in & ignited. Resulting explosion blows out air through trap door when it explodes up then clangs shut again exerting vacuum in tank & gases in septic blow coupled with siphon effect of explosion force septic contents up into tank. Dutch Stearman jolly spiritualist who continually picks a date in future & flatly predicts our freedom on that date—simultaneously agreeing to give up certain amount of tenteng if prediction fails, failed again today. When freedom did not materialize Nov. 28 he gave me four cold banana fritters. I'm going to censure him severely.

Dutch Van Diman, whose uncle runs potato chip factory in Salt Lake City, gave lecture in Dutch—first since camp began—beginning series alternating Tuesdays. He will give it in English next Tuesday. Aerodynamics.

⟶ Feb. 24 Wednesday

Reports more & more optimistic with big things hinted May or June.

⟶ Feb. 25 Thursday

Elderly Dutchman, pale ill health entered camp first time interned. He operated brick factory in swamp 15 kilometers from Palembang & had not seen white man since March, when his radio [was] taken. He had not visited Palembang since Japanese capture. No news.

Began taking notes on oil from Oosten.

⟶ Feb. 26 Friday

Men began digging well inside camp near upper bathroom.

I've been washing dishes alone past few days as Wilson down with asthma, from which he suffers severely.

Finished A. J. Cronin's "The Citadel."

Van der Vliet fell in darkness & dislocated left elbow.

⟶ Feb. 27 Saturday

Dutch de Beyer, studious tin miner & Dutch Werkman, pugnacious Civil Service man tangled. Werkman backhanded B. who wears glasses & whose left arm [is] in sling & right hand bandaged, breaking glasses & cutting over eye. Seems Beyer, who sleeps on cot during night unconsciously flung out arm or leg on Werkman below who sleeps on mat. Words led to blow—first damage of any consequence resulting from quarrel since internment.

⟶ Feb. 28 Sunday

Read selection Damon Runyon's short stories. Won 7 cents at poker.

⟶ March 1 Monday

Began Daphne du Maurier's "Rebecca."

Saturday [it was] announced because [of] a shortage of "obats" (puri-fiers) for city water filter, water henceforth shut off 9 p.m.–5 a.m. Morning bathing prohibited—even for officials—also flushing W.C.s

Wilson's asthma still keeping him down.

⟶ March 2 Tuesday

Japs limited Soeria to selling F.50 worth weekly fruit, etc., which panic[k]ed Block kitchens. Will put them out of business if continues & drastically reduce our fruit consumption. However I think it another flash in the pan which [will] blow over.

⟶ March 3 Wednesday

N.P.S. first time mention real fighting [in] Burma. Says Allies at-tempted [to] reoccupy Burma beginning February but [are] now driven back to India-Burma borders. Dispatch datelined Rangoon 2/28.

March 4 Thursday

Because Allen's hands spotted up, Harley Clark, Wilson both sick, I abandoned wood cutting & dishwashing jobs to work once more in sur-gery where we're swamped for 2½ to 3 hours mornings daily with Palem-bang bottoms, feet & hands. I prefer woodchopping, which [is] cleaner, more exercise.

Debating again whether [to] take [up] study [of] Dutch. This camp perfect opportunity but I dislike dividing further my already full & pre-cious time & also dividing my energy. Malay & shorthand take about all my spare time, except after dinner at night when I read. Also my progress extremely slow at both because of lack of study time. I know that sometime I'll regret not learning it.

⟶ March 5 Friday

Altho new regulations strictly limit amount of food brot [sic] into camp—barring brown beans—beans brought in today with rice in brown reed pack & no attention paid it. Year ago today I telephoned home & a few hours later left Bandoeng for Wynecoop Bay.

⟶ MARCH 6 SATURDAY

Camp News announced new rations imposed from Js per man per day—rice 500 grams, meat 50 grams, vegetables 100 coconut oil, salt sugar, tea 5 grams each.

⟶ MARCH 7 SUNDAY

Been using all spare moments 5th, 6th & today writing letter describing year ago. March 7, 1942 was a Saturday—the Saturday the *Poelau Bras* went down & I swam for my life—3 hours before rescue.

Offered two Masses & Communion for thanksgiving this morning. But for God's grace & mercy I would have died one year ago today.

⟶ MARCH 8 MONDAY

Resident Oranje stirred up because Penrice, whose policy has always been peace at any price, suddenly and to me unaccountably, informed Lublik Weddick he, Penrice, when [the] war [is] over would report to British government the Dutch treated interned Britons scurrilously in financial matters and that entire British community fed up. Meeting held today to discuss his charges, with Penrice & Ritchie representing [the] British. I think Penrice off on wrong foot. His words do *not* represent entire British community but only a segment of it—a segment that always has been anti-Dutch. Although there have been individual instances of Dutch profiteering on exchange, some returned the profits or sent them to women's camp—there have been more instances of British lead swinging—men swearing poverty but patronizing block kitchens & buying extra food to cook themselves.

The British have a legitimate grouse, however, concerning Dutch reluctance to lend Brit. community a fund to pay its own way & give down & step a small amount per month as the Dutch do themselves—F.5 per man first month & 2.50 subsequently.

When Pladjoe men arrived & surveyed situation they vigorously condemned this attitude & pointed out the now existing Dutch government is in London subsisting on British charity & good will. They also donated garments to broke Britons.

➳ MARCH 9 TUESDAY

Guards at hospital very sticky. Minutely searching patients going in. Indian troop guards wearing complete British equipment.

Today I traded jobs with Harrison, he coming into clinic as dresser & also woodchopper; I took over kitchen.

Heavy rain & thunderstorm tonight reminiscent of bad night in life-boat 1 yr. ago tonight or tomorrow night.

Block kitchen workers held protest meeting against Committee's tentative setting of F.1.50 per man per month limit spending money. Conveyors also protesting possible ending of allowing them [to] get food first at noon.

➳ MARCH 10 WEDNESDAY

5 ducklings rapidly growing but still mothered by old white hen whose life [has] been made miserable by a rapacious red rooster who chases her top speed around yard, sometimes catching & pecking her severely—all while ducklings quacking with alarm.

➳ MARCH 11 THURSDAY

Drysdale sits in chair some every day grinding burned bones in a mortar & pestle making "sinatigen" or calcium to powder on rice for patients. He also makes toothpaste which hospital sells [for] 30 cents a portion. The ground bone, it is hoped, will supply diet deficiencies of skin cases.

➳ MARCH 12 FRIDAY

Spending all spare moments writing account of *Poelau Bras* in letter to Jean.

➳ MARCH 13 SATURDAY

Year ago today our lifeboat made Poeloe Laboean in Semanka Bay, [ ] opening into Sunda Straits from South Sumatra.

➳ MARCH 14 SUNDAY

Camp members issued postcards "Services des Prisonniers de Guerre" & told we could send them three times a year anywhere in world. Mine addressed home said, "Dear Mother, Dad & Jean, I am in good health eating sufficiently and treated all right. Time passes quickly doing camp duties plus studying shorthand & Malay. You'll be glad to know, Mother, I'm attending Mass here daily. The climate is pleasant, nights cool. We can live & work in shorts & sandals. Greetings to Getrude & Paul. Tell my office I'm okay but Hancock missing since shipwreck last March. God bless you all. Love, Son. W. H. McDougall Jr."

⟶ March 15 Monday

Reading moving story, Richard Llewellyn, "How Green Was My Valley."

⟶ March 16 Tuesday

Report 2000 uniplanes destroyed attack Australia by 200 ships, whereof over 100 sank.

⟶ March 17 Wednesday

St. Patrick's Day. Harrison celebrated by cooking pancakes for hospital with rice flour ground up during past week. Big day in our kitchen and cooked [ ] boiled eggs, soft rice & kept many hot baths plus tea & coffee going.

⟶ March 18 Thursday

⟶ March 19 Friday

Second well being sunk inside camp by oil diggers. First one, near upper bathroom, is about 20 feet deep & fills with muddy water which [is] okay for washing clothes.

Block leaders this week decided to poll camp on whether or not dogs should remain. West strongly against them (citing two cases of round worm in camp). Anyway, camp vote was 245 against, 176 for, 26 indifferent. Now remains to be seen if dogs will be ejected. Some swear they'll fight to keep them. V.F. in quandary & hinting anti-vote was result [of] solid British vote against & most Dutch favoring retention.

⟶ March 20 Saturday

Began Lin Yu Tang's "Importance of Living." Duck eggs now coming in for hospital. Patients, as well as everyone in camp, badly need vitamins & protein which [are] lacking in our food. Men's sight failing through lack of A & B. Skin sores thought a result [of the] lack [of] vitamins.

➤ MARCH 21 SUNDAY

Four tins of crude palm oil brought to camp. West been trying to get it for 9 months in order to use [it] medicinally. Palm oil rich in A & D.

➤ MARCH 22 MONDAY

Biesel lectured on Bali, narrating how overridden, by tens [of] thousands [of] dogs. An American woman decided [to] donate large sum & an expert to Bali for ridding it of dogs. He arrived complete with gas chamber. Government cooperated fully, glad of chance of getting rid of dogs. American expert surveyed situation in despair said only way he could use his equipment would be if 99% of all dogs first slaughtered by other means. He began by wholesale shooting—with government supply unlimited ammunition. One morning Biesel saw him kill 1,100 dogs in one camp especially rounded up. After an 8 months losing battle he quit, without any appreciable diminution of canine population.

➤ MARCH 23 TUESDAY

Guess it's impossible to eliminate bedbugs. Found some more in my cot today after long spell without them. Lice also appearing in ward but haven't reached our room yet.

Today Allen's mother's birthday & he celebrated by passing out some tengteng—first we've had for a long time.

Dr. Ashingawa made his Tuesday visit alone today & when [he] took patients to Charitas allowed them to visit others there. He's a good guy, alone. Also demonstrated his sword, pointing to stains near handle & saying it cut off 2 heads in Malaya.

➤ MARCH 24 WEDNESDAY

I'm too busy lighting fires, cooking eggs & soft rice & getting underway in the kitchen to enjoy the best hours of the day—early morning from 6 to 8 a.m. The Moerai, or Straits Robin, sings in nearby trees & I am trying to hear a Baraou Baraou, also known as bull-bull in Malaya & Tjotjoe—Rawa in Java, but there are few here. Moerai a black bird with white plumage—resembling magpie, but smaller & more graceful in flight.

➤ MARCH 25 THURSDAY

Insufficient wood being furnished us, necessitating regular wood cutting party going out daily & cutting down trees. One species yellow wood produces an ash which irritates skin, making kitchen workers unpleasantly itchy.

Our vegetable rations doubled, from 60 grams to 120 or 130 per man, which improves meals remarkably.

— MARCH 26 FRIDAY

Attended my first session of debating society comprising about 50 men & presided over by Lawson. Tonight Blum defended proposal that [the] cinema [is] detrimental to mankind, which [was] opposed by Husband. Vote afterward overwhelmingly favored Blum. Next week Malay Civil Service officer K. G. A. Dohov proposes "That the privately owned newspaper is an evil which should be eliminated from the state." I will oppose.

— MARCH 27 SATURDAY

Entertaining, amusing, well executed concert directed by Gilbrook staged tonight. Stringed orchestra playing better classical music every time, [as] background [for a] Russian number. Second act parodied Shanghai courtroom wherein various characters appeared on charges. Wrigley successfully impersonated female tightrope walker, in street clothes, of flowered dress. Wrigley shaved off his beard & makes a good impersonator.

— MARCH 28 SUNDAY

Mike Treurniete gave me a Lucky Strike cigarette. The first American cigarette I've seen since Biesel gave a Camel last summer. Haven't touched tobacco since Dec. 31. I lit the Lucky & breathed a few ceremonial puffs. Mike handed me the cigarette through the window, as I lay on my cot reading & drinking coffee after morning surgery rush. Just right circumstances. And ah, how delicious the cigarette tasted. Deeply I breathed the smoke right down to the innermost crevices of wherever Lady Nicotine's incense goes. What relaxing, blissful pleasure, to blow out the smoke, watching it float away, mingling with the thin spiral rising from the ashes between the fingers. Then I put it out. Crushed the glowing end gently, so as to preserve it. For I am going to save it and surprise Eric & Christie tonight at our poker session, by lighting it & passing it around. Only a quarter is gone, ample left to sample this evening.

Just those few puffs registered, the heart speeded up—making itself known & the brain lightened, onto the fringe of giddiness. Obvious evidence that tobacco does no good to some sections of man, even though it may relax, or otherwise soothe or please others.

Tonight German & Christie brought three "lemon pies" to poker session. They used one egg, rice flour for dough & got batter rising rapidly. Filler flavored with limes. They baked all on the ting fire place. During evening poker game Curran-Sharp made record clean-up, winning 27 cents.

⇀ MARCH 29 MONDAY

Bucket brigade now filling bathroom tanks from wells. Men line up across yard & pass filled buckets along.

⇀ MARCH 30 TUESDAY

Guards [are] tough [at] Charitas, beating up two Dutch—one for talking with wife, [the] other for entering kitchen. Men & women patients [are] forbidden [to] speak [to] each other for [a] long time now, probably [in the] aftermath [of] letters being discovered on women.

⇀ MARCH 31 WEDNESDAY

Syonan Sinbun for 1/26/43 Shanghai dispatch says war prisoners [in] that area [are] now allowed [to] publish [their] own newspaper. *Shinbuns* for 1/18 & 1/26 first Syonan papers seen here since new camp began.

⇀ APRIL 1, 1943 THURSDAY

Allen's report of hospital activities since it began a year ago showed 12,690 out-patient attendancies by the camp hospital staff; 138 in hospital as patients. One year ago today Dutch & Europeans in Palembang were interned in the jail. We of lifeboat were south of Kroe, traveling by grobak north toward capture.

Sending of fruit as well as packages to women's camp stopped because a Dutchman contrary to his written pledge, wrote note on a label of a package addressed to the camp. Several days ago all men sending packages to W[omen's] C[amp] signed a pledge they would enclose no notes, messages, or any writing except address on packages. Whereupon Japanese let packages go. But one man immediately broke [his] word & was caught.

⇀ APRIL 2, 1943 FRIDAY

Tonight debated with K. C. A. Dohov on his resolution which I opposed. Won debate by score 29 to 11. However, before debate poll showed

15 to 9 [ ] with number not voting, so I [was] given 14 & D. 2 votes. He presented his resolution well, eloquently & without notes. I [was] personally dissatisfied with my presentation. I discover I have lost the ability of thinking clearly & quickly with the long view, on my feet. I can write more eloquently & persuasively than I can talk.

⁓ APRIL 3, 1943

Doctor West's medical report concludes that generally we are well off from general health & food standpoint but financial boys objected to its publication because they were given no credit for spending camp money to buy with! Self-centered, short sighted men. It was published with indirect salaam to money interests by saying we were fortunately able to buy extra food supplied (thereby giving us more nourishment).

⁓ APRIL 4 SUNDAY

One year ago Sunday was April 5 & Easter Sunday when we arrived in Palembang Jail after dark, lined up on the grass of the front yard, looked apprehensively at the barbed wire from behind which earlier arrivals stared out at us.

Most disastrous poker session yet for me—lost 17 cents, a phenomenal sum to lose at our games.

⁓ APRIL 5 MONDAY

Camp orchestra proudly boasts huge homemade bass viol about 6½ feet high, square, heavy wood, copper wire (electric light wire) strings.

⁓ APRIL 6 TUESDAY

Lin Yu Tang's philosophy of life as expressed in "The Importance of Living" extremely shallow & concerned with superficialities. His conception of real Christianity false & based on erroneous hypotheses. He judges Christianity by studying unchristian acts & persons. However, his observations on Chinese thought & custom interesting, informative.

⁓ APRIL 6 [*SIC*] WEDNESDAY

Fr. Elling in camp hospital after he fainted last evening at roll call's end. Suffering from flux, in my opinion, nervous strain. But he is right in assertion that for him & other priests here, this internment [is] the opportunity of a lifetime for sound missionary work & every moment of it should be utilized. I think he should relax more, however, if he can, to not burn himself out before his work is done—if such work can ever be called done.

Lin Yo Tang frequently & flatly states he is a pagan, there is no immortality & no God & yet in every other breath he refers to God as the omnipotent creator of the universe. But, says Lin, God is too busy & too big (& we too infinitesimal) to bother with us & our problems. He continually contradicts himself & cites trivialities as the great things which led him to forsake Christianity & become a pagan. Lin studied in a western theological seminary & was discouraged by differences of opinions & doctrinal teachings of various Protestant [?] theologians—all disagreeing. I can understand his bewilderment & disgust, but he appears not to have inquired further. He makes false, flat statements as : "...from pursuing literary studies I feel, like all modern Americans, no consciousness of sin & simply do not believe in it...All I know is that if God loves me only half as much as my mother does, he will not send me to Hell." (p. 407)

Lin later says he & every pagan believes in God: "A pagan always believes in God but would not like to say so, for fear of being misunderstood. All Chinese pagans believe in God, the most commonly met with designation in Chinese literature being the term 'chaowu,' or the Creator of Things."

Why then [do] Chinese [practice] ancestor worship & such belief in life after death—if Chinese do not believe in immortality?

Lin says life & philosophy is reasonableness & that "the best thing that China has to offer the West" is the "Spirit of Reasonableness." His own philosophy seems to be this & my observation of Chinese agrees—they are, by & large, reasonable people. I wish I could find, in all this philosophizing, however, some philosophical reason for their "squeeze."

⸺ APRIL 8 THURSDAY

Report Dr. Holweg jailed & wife returned to women's camp for violation [of] blackout regulations, also that Charitas Hospital being taken over by Japanese.

Bass viol manufactured (2 Eurasians) used a house for their sounding box in Pladtjoe. Discovering walls of one house reverberated when struck. They constructed bridge & neck protruding from walls, painted outline of sound box on wall & Van Dorp, who plays viol here pounded away on it.

I'm still using the cheap $1 fountain pen "Varsity" brought from home when I left. We never used it around the house.

→ APRIL 9 FRIDAY

Colton, supporting "Man, by nature, is predominantly good," & Jackson opposing in tonight's debate. Although pre-vote favored motion, final vote after against—Jackson & supporters winning.

→ APRIL 10 SATURDAY

Dutch Schyff allowed go [to] women's camp yesterday [to] collect effects of wife who died last spring, but he [was not] allowed [to] enter camp & strictly supervised during collection.

Guards getting stricter continually on possible communications.

Wide rumors German government collapsed, Von Keitel overtaken & asked [for] armistice.

R. W. Emerson's analogy interesting of "Great Spirit" as expressed in Eastern writings from his essay on Plato: "As one diffusive air, passing through the perforations of a flute, is distinguished as the notes of a scale, so the nature of the Great Spirit is single, though its forms be manifold, arising from the consequences of acts."

→ APRIL 11 SUNDAY

Camp handicraft exhibit revealed suprising number of variety of objects, utilitarian & artistic, made by camp members. Metal work—ornamental hinges, candlesticks, cigarette boxes, ash trays & a clock face; wood work—containers of all descriptions, clock frames, terompaks (sandals); bookbinding; musical instruments—all stringed & some [of] which being played by orchestra, but most suprising—wooden *organ* pipes for organ being made Oom Peter Cranenbogh & Kunis—a crude xylophone (wood) by ex-soldier Dumas also shown. Cranenbogh's drawings of jail showed excellent perspective & detail. Agerbeke's caricatures in *Camp News*, Grixom's sketches & Statius Muller's portraits also well done. Young Roberts architectural plans & Brodier's ship & other plans also exhibited. Miscellaneous:—carven pipes, Scotch sporan [?] bonnet, small Indian musical instruments.

Orchestra played continually during exhibit, which continued most of day, with men queuing up to file past exhibits.

I've been interned a few days over a year. Taking stock of myself, I realize:—That I have lost the art of *thinking* logically to a conclusion. For years I have [been] acting automatically or on intuitive "hunches" or following the dictates of my emotions. This loss of thinking intelligently is accompanied by diminution of my power of mental *concentration* (as distinguished from daydreaming) and weakening memory. My second most important object therefore, is to recover this art by mental drill & discipline. (First importance of course my spiritual salvation.)

2. My sense of values has changed considerably. Journalistic success is no longer so important, except in so far as it may aid me in admiring the cause of the Church—the mind of God.

Nothing is more perishable—nor more fascinating—than news. But little of it is of any permanent worth & much of the modern newspaper's contents are definitely harmful morally.

3. I am slowly, extremely slowly & with effort, learning to stop & think. Learning the art of doing nothing physically but concentrating mentally.

4. Crystallizing my intentions for the future, or rather, comprehending what for me will be the only satisfactory (spiritually) vocation.

Book 8

[No entries for April 12–May 15, 1943]

⌁ Cont—May 16, 1943

But I'm still behind the game.

Kato—Ginseibu chief over us—returned yesterday from Singapore. He said he would give our rations his immediate attention, also that family internment will be a certainty as soon as camp is ready.

Traubel, who rumoredly entered camp with 16,000 guilders, has standing order that he'll pay any price for tinned food. However, he said he was getting too low financially to continue aiding Crocker or do exchange business. He is paying as much as F.5 for a tin of cheese. Today 4 fowls were killed & sold to unknown purchaser for F. 20.

⌁ May 17 Monday

Helping Fr. Elling translate Dutch Boy Scout prayer book (the Mass) into English for youngster who will make first communion soon. Brother Edward, in addition to organizing classes for boys, spends much time directing them in games. However, one Dutch lad, named Van Zijl, never participates or mingles with other children. His father—a tremendously fat Dutch school teacher, keeps boy constantly by his side & never lets youngster play or converse with other boys.

⤳ May 18 Tuesday

Three men attempted [to] get medicine from Charitas in West's name. Befting at Charitas procuring eggs, meat, etc. for private customers here but refusing [to] do anything for camp hospital. Reason unknown.

⤳ May 19 Wednesday

White bearded Armenian Arathoon several months ago gave two watches to a Malay guard for sale at F.225. G. & watches disappeared. After warning Indonesian fellows he would act if not reimbursed, Arathoon today informed Japanese guard who notified Gunseibu which acted promptly, producing Malay guard who produced one of the watches but said [the] other had been sold & he agreed to pay F.10 a month for 9 months. He also being put on trial for theft. This is another instance where Japanese acted in behalf of white prisoners.

⤳ May 20 Thursday

Germann & Christie have switched their manufacturing activities from flour milling (because no more rice to mill) to tobacco curing & have succeeded in transforming raw, bitter tobacco we get here into pleasantly smokeable product.

Fr. Elling gave excellent factual lecture on the Inquisition, which considerably surprised listeners.

⤳ May 21 Friday

Gardens surrounding camp buildings on 3 sides now well filled with growing things. Maize is very high. Gardeners even have extended their activities to space between hospital & administration block's front door & strolling path crossing yard & founding basketball ground.

⤳ May 22 Saturday

Heavy rainstorm tonight flooded Block 8, turning it into a dirty mess & inundated hospital kitchen.

Soya bean addition to our diet, plus other changes—notably gaplek soya bean porridge for breakfast—a gluey, flavorless mixtur—has upset many stomachs but none seriously.

⤳ May 23 Sunday

Block 8 leaders battling with Camp Committee over flood conditions

& how to remedy. Committee holding out for peace [at] any price & arbitrary they determine remedy without consulting Block & Block insisting on going directly to Japanese.

⟶ MAY 24 MONDAY

British Empire Day: in honor of which Thompson cooked another of his tasty puddings of tapioca flour—this time garnished with coconut milk & goela Java sauce. Tasted finer, especially since [it has] been months since we tasted anything sweet to eat.

Schmidt & Dumas staged an altercation this evening about 7 p.m. Schmidt's terror-stricken yells aroused camp. We thought [it was] another episode such as last December when Van Houten escaped after slugging native guard.

⟶ MAY 25 TUESDAY

I lectured on Mormons to camp in evening. About 130 men in audience and lecture apparently a success. Public lectures are given from main entrance of Committee Block, the building being on an embankment about 18 inches higher than adjacent ground. Same site also used as stage for concerts.

Agerbeke caricatured me in blue shorts and eyeshade spurning a cocktail being offered by a stunning damsel as the advertising poster for the lecture.

⟶ MAY 26 WEDNESDAY

Camp P.W.D. building dyke completely around blocks 7 & 8 to keep out rush of rain water which floods them out every heavy storm.

Finished translating prayer book (helping Fr. Elling translate from Dutch to English) for Armstrong boy who makes first Communion next Sunday. Also rewrote Elling's English sermon for Sunday on Sacred Heart of Jesus. Very few changes necessary but inserted a few original paragraphs [of] my own thought.

⟶ MAY 27 THURSDAY

Elling lectured [on] Eastern schism.

I'm bathroom cleaner this week & it takes a good hour of scraping & sloshing to do it. After which difference is discouragingly small.

⭢ MAY 28 FRIDAY

Allen debated J. P. Quinn, Australian diplomatic neophyte on motion "Poetry is Bunk," which Allen proposed and supported with brilliant shafts of wit. Quinn's defense was sophomoric, & as he said at its beginning, wandered with beautiful but empty words in a Celtic twilight. I began to speak on Allen's side as last speaker of general discussion, when Malay guard stopped us with word Nippon guard ordered us cease because he wished to sleep—at 9:15 p.m. So debate ended without a final vote, original vote 7 to 17 against, would have reversed original odds & given win to Allen, I think. Crowd—about 50—wished to be amused & Allen certainly did it.

⭢ MAY 29 SATURDAY

First quiz in considerable time held tonight & rather tedious. Novelty has worn off, questions not entertaining & badly staged.

⭢ MAY 30 SUNDAY

Hospital fees reduced from 5 to 3 cents per treatment. Persons receiving loans allowance will not be charged more than 25 cents one month.

Shimbun said newspaper Malay is becoming Indonesian language & has won battle for precedence against Javanese in Java.

Mohammedan Japanese V. M. Abdul Muniam Inada speaking Ma'aland festival said question will surely [be] asked why, if Japanese aims [are] so exalted, Indonesians have not become wealthy since Japanese came. Answers 1—because we [are] still at war; 2—that they wish to become rich immediately without working, merely because Japanese army has come, means that one is only self seeking—a totally wrong attitude.

Quinn's description of dyking operations around Blocks 7 & 8 to keep out rain floods: "a cross between a Zuyder Zee reclamation project & a medieval walled city in course of construction."

From *Camp News*: "Tidings of the land of Joseph Smith & Brigham Young were brought to us by McDougall on Tuesday evening last, when he gave what he would call in his native tongue an 'angle' on the Mormons & their conjugal affairs. The bachelors among us bewailed the absence of a heavenly telephone book in which they could look up the numbers of Thais, Cleopatra & Helen of Troy. The men of the world expressed grave doubts regarding the ability of these ladies to make the grade with St. Peter & suggested that the discomfort attendant upon meeting them elsewhere might outweigh the advantages of their company; those who kept their gaze most steadfastly on things of this world were the men concerned with the proposed move to a family internment camp. Speaking from their vast store of experience as family men, they expressed the conviction that the theory of Mormonism might be a good thing, but that its practice must entail serious difficulties for internees."

⭢ May 31 Monday

Completed month's devotion to B[lessed] V[irgin] M[ary] petitioning for voc[ation].

⭢ June 1 Tuesday

Most camp members seem resigned to spending [at] least [the] remainder [of the] year here. This time last year most members classed me as [the] rankest pessimist when I said [we] would be at least another year & at minimum probably two years—which opinion I still hold—will be another year unless or at least until next March or April, unless Germany collapses much sooner than expected. I have hunch I won't spend Christmas here myself but no logical reason for so thinking.

⭢ June 2 Wednesday

Von Asbek, Deputy Camp Leader & anti R[oman] C[atholic] short-circuited Elling's Thursday nite talk by organizing lecture group to hear Dutch history from Van der Wetering. He claimed right to the night on grounds English lectures occupied it other nights. He's a smooth article, or as the Dutch say, "a soft egg."

Rice distribution Palembang limited to *3 kilos* per person per time & available only one place but no restrictions on number of times buyer may purchase—all he has to do is wait in queue for hours.

Gardener who tends plot in front of hospital was fertilizing his plants with effluvia run off from septic tank, causing extremely unpleasant stench.

⭢ June 3 Thursday (Ascension Thursday)

My birthday passed uneventfully. It was remembered by Elling, who remembered me at Mass & whose own birthday is tomorrow, when he too will be 34. Eric Germann learned of it this evening & presented me a dish of sweet potatoes, flavored with cinnamon. So I received a present after all. Attended three Masses, 4:45, 5:15 & high at 6:30.

Van der Wetering started final of series Dutch lectures on Hollander history, which Van Asbeck organized in opposition to Fr. Elling's English lectures.

⌐ June 4 Friday

Finished letter to Jean begun yesterday, analyzing myself during past 10 years. Lots of things which I think of now should have been put down, but they didn't occur to me while writing. One thing—obviously I haven't the same fluency of language or store of ideas as 10 years ago. That's evident in my letters.

⌐ June 5 Saturday

Read H. C. Armstrong's "Grey Wolf"—biography of Mustafa Kemal, Turkey's modern iron man. Would that I had spent all my spare time of the past 10 years reading worthwhile informative books such as this one, instead of frittering away that precious time reading magazine & newspaper trash & doing other things. Now that I should have time to read there are few such books, but even at that I don't read enough because all my time is spent working in hospital or studying shorthand, Dutch & Malay, in none of which do I seem to make much progress. Harold Guard was right when he told me I try to do too many things at once.

⌐ June 6 Sunday

Story going the rounds that Tanker Fauble & Miner Doristien, who seem to be in [an] eating partnership—buy anything tinned available at any price—today had a tin of Bully beef for breakfast, a chicken for tiffin, plus another tin of something & opened a tin of *caviar* to top off the evening repast. Fortunately for them camp is getting fairly good meals now & hence their fellows in Block 5 only growl & sneer. If circumstances were really lean they might lose their tins. Although, in my opinion, it's their own business if they want to spend such sums of money in such ways, it's anti-social in so far as others have nothing the contrast is acute. Also it is an example of how money is flowing from camp when it should be conserved against lean days ahead. Rather inconsistent of finance committee to ask contributions to personal loans fund when men with large sums of money are allowed to keep [it] all and spend like profligates on themselves.

⌐ June 7 Monday

Allen & I on dishwashing this week, which takes about 2½ hours of our time each day.

⌐ June 8 Tuesday

Few mornings ago Dog Face slapped Von Asbek's face after latter refused [to] call out several men lying in [on] account [of] alleged illness. He said it was [the] doctor's business, not his. After slapping, he wrote letter of protest to Gunseibu. Today letters given to officials who came for Charitas Hospital patients.

⌐ June 9 Wednesday

We [are] now limited [to] certain hours of day, 7–8, 12–1, 4–5 for getting water from well across road.

High finance here has reached point where [ ] hospital "insures" for bad eggs. Now that we can buy eggs an extra cent is added to each egg to pay for bad ones. Jokingly Harrison & I decided to form a "holding" corporation, candle eggs, bribe Goleng to furnish us only good ones, but since we would continue insurance tax, it would be clear profit. Thus we would have an income of 30 to 40 cents a day to spend on such luxuries as peanuts, bananas, tengteng, even canned goods.

Chicken raisers here now torn between two desires—whether to sell eggs daily or kill chickens & sell for F.5 each. One man is rearing & selling fowl, which takes a great diligence as they must be guarded against marauders—men, dogs & rats—bed examined before liberating to determine if an egg is about to be hatched & if not, watched carefully in order to get egg if & when hen lays it while at liberty in camp. Everyone is on lookout to steal the egg if one is laid at "random."

A hen made sad mistake of wandering into Australian section of Block 5 one evening & was quickly & silently strangled, plucked & cooked next day.

⌐ June 10 Thursday

Odd believe it or nots—Here, only 3 degrees below the equator and in a swampy sea level country, mornings are so cool one can see one's breath.

Reading Robert Sencourt's "Winston Churchill." Interesting but so eulogistic it reminds me of a funeral oration.

⤙ June 11 Friday

Our heavy soya bean diet is giving the boys a run for their appetites. Seems as effective as castor oil. I understand soya beans normally are not eaten like ordinary beans, as we are doing.

⤙ June 12 Saturday

Some high officials inspected camp today & after they had gone, guard complained to V[an] V[liet] that we had not stood to attention & bowed sufficiently—that entire camp should have stood as to a roll call. This is second time such has happened—entirely due to language barriers. Our captors speak not even Malay & we can not understand each other half the time.

⤙ June 13 Sunday

Fr. Elling wakened me 4:45 a.m. as usual. As I hurried thru the dark ward noticed Ward "Matron" Kendall fussing with E. F. Hunter, 52, Cable & Wireless Limited. Several others also there. "He's been making funny noises and now we can't wake him up," said Kendall, shaking him again; "Hunter."

I felt Hunter's leg, shook it once, called him, determined there was no sign of pulse—it felt dead to me—& hurried off to rouse Doc. West. I was sure Hunter was dead. He was. West jumped from his top bunk, over Harrison in their room, at my summons, snatched his flashlight & we hurried back. I told West "I think he's dead." Raising the small mosquito net which covered Hunter's upper torso & head, West flashed the light in Hunter's white face. Half opened, blank eyes & open mouth—that "dead look" so familiar to those who have seen it.

"He looks dead, alright," said West & confirmed his words with stethoscope. Probably an aneurism. Last night Hunter complained to Doc of pain high in the chest and running down the arms. West thought it muscular.

Later during night I noticed Hunter sitting up on [the] end of his bed when I passed enroute to bathroom.

We picked him off the bed, laid him in a stretcher and carried him into the surgery, where West examined him further, & as I sat him up so West could look at his back & be sure he had died lying down & not fallen, one of his plates fell out. I picked it up and West removed the other dental plate. Harley Clarke is going to boil them up & use them for needy patients here.

The episode began & ended in 15 minutes or so. I arrived at the first Mass just before Communion, shortly after 5, before dawn had begun to lighten the darkness. The double row of mosquito nets seemed scarcely disturbed, but many patients must have been wakened by the stir and especially shocked must have [been] Fraser, a tall, gaunt Briton sleeping next to Hunter. For Fraser is living on borrowed time. He is one of those men, rare in medical annals, who survived a coronary thrombosis caused by an embolism. Five years ago he was stricken. In this camp he has seen 4 men die of heart attacks, & this morning one of them in the next bed.

Ernest Freeman Hunter was a white haired, pale skinned pleasant man of 52, possessed of a dry wit. We used to rag each other over his spots which I treated for a long time. He was back from Charitas only a few weeks after a hernia operation. Hunter spent all of World War I in France, mostly at the front, in the signal corps. He went unscathed through that war and saw much of this one, having evacuated [from] Greece, then Crete & finally Singapore & always among the last to leave. He was sent to Singapore to train operators. He long was in the traffic side of Cable & Wireless & knew many journalists. I regret that I let all this time go by without really talking to him concerning his experiences.

Just before roll call Hunter's corpse was laid in the committee block. At 11 a.m. Rev. Wardle conducted a short memorial service. The plank coffin resting on the bunk shelf. At 4 p.m. an open truck pulled up, the same one which brings our rations. Six barefoot Malay coolies, wearing black trousers, coats & songkas [?] (Mohammedan hats). After a last inspection by Javanese officer to confirm it was [the] same corpse, coffin was nailed shut & six camp members bore it on their shoulders to the truck. Wardle, V.F., Fermaugh, Banks, Penrice & Tisham rode on the open truck with the coffin & coolies. He was buried in the cemetery behind Charitas Hospital where other British & Dutch internees & military prisoners lie.

When the coffin was being carried out, Japanese & Malay guards bowed their heads & stood at attention. But a certain Briton kept working in his garden plot near the fence, paying no attention, & his disrespect incensed the J. guard, who threw rocks at him, but did not shout, as all else was silent.

Right now I think I will remember for a long time Hunter's face when Doc raised the mosquito net & shone his flashlight rays on it. The white face of death doubly pale in its natural whiteness, the slack mouth and jaws half opened, blank eyes, the white hair—all nestled in the small space within the net.

When Hunter was in the morning surgery line while I treated him for various sores, I told him that once I got him in the hospital his goose was cooked, because he would go out only in a wooden overcoat—*Words spoken in jest!*

— JUNE 14 MONDAY

Finished Robert Sencourt's "Winston Churchill" which proved superb study of the man. The eulogistic tone of the introduction, which described W.C.'s ancestry, was changed to analytical narrative when Churchill himself was discussed. Sencourt is critical of W.C. on several counts, especially his presumably deliberately ignoring the voice of the Vatican when it warned of trouble pending in Europe (1914–1918), ignored or refused its peace efforts when negotiated peace possible. Sencourt concludes that historical study proves [the] only permanent peace possible in Europe is one based on Christian principles of social justice as enunciated repeatedly by Rome.

— JUNE 15 TUESDAY

Afflicted with tummy trouble I've spent yesterday & today lying up with a hot water bottle on the belly. Read "Reader's Digest" for July '38.

Realize more & more what I missed since college days in neglecting serious reading. Until college I was an avid reader, devouring books continually. During college I slacked off on all but necessary reading after confined myself almost exclusively to light stuff—mostly magazines. Consequently my knowledge did not deepen, my mind spread itself in width but not depth & missed much of the best thought of contemporary times. How much more deep is Jean's mind than mine! I used to pity her loneliness which forced her to read, read, read. Now I'm beginning to see she was not as lonely as I thought. I hope she does some real writing—both poetry & prose.

— JUNE 16 WEDNESDAY

Laid up all day resting the inner man, which manifested [....]

Book 9

[No entries for June 16–July 13, 1943]

⁓ JULY 14, 1943 WEDNESDAY

All dogs in camp rounded up this morning after much delay. Reluctant owners declined to cooperate until a guard finally took a club & started around camp searching for dogs. Guard apparently enjoyed entire procedure.

Yesterday reported at hospital that rabies story false. Dog collection thereby stirred wrath of dog owners, which capped much dissatisfaction with Vliet & Cong. [?] who decided [to] go to camp for vote of confidence.

⁓ JULY 15, 1943 THURSDAY

Vliet resigned. Camp Committee gave block leaders a motion calling for vote of confidence in Camp Leader & Committee. Secret ballot set for tomorrow. I think it will be close but with Committee winning because many people want to get rid of Committee but keep Vliet, since there seems no other man to replace him. I asked Oranje if he would participate officially in camp administration, & he said no. He knows his countrymen, he said, & they would vilify any man who held office as Camp Leader & work against him, merely because it is their nature to rebel against authority unless that authority is their boss & controls their paycheck. He does not wish to make enemies here in camp who will remain so after the war.

All dogs returned to camp today on payment of license fees 3 & 5 guilders, plus tip to guard (native) so rabies story probably fake, although it probably was the original reason given to Vliet by the municipality official.

⁓ JULY 16 FRIDAY

Camp election voted *non-confidence* in Camp Leader & Committee by 191 to 186. There were 43 non-voters, 17 spoiled ballots & 6 blanks. Vote considerably shook committee, especially Penrice & Philipps, who reportedly assured Vliet & Oranje they had 100% British support. Although [previously] refusing to participate officially in camp administration, Oranje now may change his mind. Otherwise Von Asbeck & oil boys will take over.

West told [a] striking story tonight of how Eurasians revert to Asiatic ways or fly completely to pieces in time of crises. One of [the] best gyne-cologists in Malaya personally known to West & who studied in England & who West himself would have called to attend to his own wife, called in a native Hindu woman midwife to attend his wife, a high caste Hindu woman herself, in childbirth. His wife died of sepsis. Malays & Indians revert to age old superstition, whereas Chinese call in best European doctor in such times, he said.

In Debate tonight Van Gluns defeated Schief 14 to 12 on Schief's motion, "Convention is based on hypocrisy."

― July 17 Saturday

Lobbied intensely for camp election of representatives on new Camp Committee headed by Resident Oranje, with provision for regular elec-tions every 3 months. Drysdale as representative of British. During my talking this evening I aroused wrath of several British Committee mem-bers—Blum, Gill, Secretary Starkey—by declaring Committee accom-plished only 1 thing in its history—interview last October largely resulting from Drysdale's efforts. Surprising how many Britons afraid of Drysdale because he [ ] successfully—in Pladjoe.

Oranje finally was forced to assume authority he shirked from begin-ning because, he told me, of his unwillingness to govern a community in which there are no laws or enforcing agency, also because he had no desire to make enemies—to vilify him after war—as has V. D. Vliet. I hope Oranje displays more courage as Camp Leader than that. However, I fear that unless there are strong aggressive men on the committee to force him into contact with outside authorities on communications & other matters, he will not push a progressive program.

― July 18 Sunday

Spent another day lobbying for Drysdale, but he has so many enemies a candidate with no more qualifications than his former job as a British Civil Servant in Malaya & a record of having done absolutely nothing in camp—Hammett—may win.

― July 19 Monday

Banker Traubel entered Dutch political arena against Von Asbeck. Drysdale, Hammett & D. C. Thompson are candidates for British. Jimmy Martin, rotund jockey, circulated Drysdale's nominating petition which I prepared & pushed. We had difficulty getting 21 signatures. It obviously is a losing fight, Drysdale is too unpopular. Australian Gill, member of Brit. Committee, & a big, dumb miner, castigated Ritchie, former chairman of [ ] finance committee in a meeting in Block 5 to which all British invited. But Gill & Blockleader Thompson refused to allow anyone to reply or ask questions outside Block 5. Martin called Gill's hand & forced vote on asking Ritchie to defend himself, but R. declined, telling Gill to put his charges in writing & before a meeting of entire British community.

Taubel's nomination certainly a commentary on human nature. He is one of most generally disliked men in camp because of his food deals, but he is a prominent Dutch banker & faction led by Eurasian Lublik Weddig, Oranje's secretary, hate Von Asbek so much they are backing Taubel against him, although Taubel hasn't a chance.

⤙ July 20 Tuesday

Election Day tomorrow. Poggemier returned to camp after 11 months hospital. Sr. Z. still missing. Town terrorized.

⤙ July 21 Wednesday

Asbek & Hammett elected to Committee. Asbek 256 to 56 for Taubel & Hammett, 77, Thompson 48, Drysdale 26. Despite all Drysdale's good efforts for camp, his inability to conciliate belief [?] of conflicting factions or the unreasoning fear in minds of many he will get us in trouble with Js because at Pladjoe he stood his ground on demanding—*& getting for all workers—rest periods* despite bayonet threats, he is spurned by camp for leadership.

⤙ July 22 Thursday

Koot made ten containers for me, tube shaped. Niposh said Rome bombed. Italy's collapse must [be] near.

⤙ July 23 Friday

Christie & I translating Malay book "Perang Armageddon Apokok Itoe" published [in] Java by Seventh Day Adventists.

Aussie Dredger Marning completed mortar & pestle for grinding maize. He hollowed out a tree stump by drilling a hole through it then burning it larger by building small fire into a clay packed base. Flour ground from corn, soya beans, Ubi Kajoe (tapioca root) is in great demand for cooking.

We make pudding cakes of maize & soya bean flour almost every other day. Bullet hard soya beans are first roasted, then ground in small stone mortar, mixed with maize flour similarly ground & sometimes gaplek flour (from tapioca) is added for consistency. Makes a welcome & assimilable addition to diet, especially for those unable to digest soya beans.

— July 24 Saturday

Camp inspected carefully; Taow stricken apparently with chicken pox & taken to Charitas. Inquiries made for Quinn & Wootton & 3rd man, reason or source not disclosed but I have a hunch another exchange is in progress. I have felt so for past two months.

Niposh said Allies landed [in] Sicily but since it [is] only [an] island [it is] not important unless Allies advance to mainland.

Camp morale highest months long.

Vliet's birthday passed eventless [in] contrast [to] big celebration last yr. Block 2. We haven't wherewithal to celebrate anymore.

— July 25 Sunday

Dutch Civil Officer Tiking baptized 4 a.m. rites, second convert in camp. Interestingly, he was congratulated afterward by staunch Protestants A. Colijn & J. A. H. (Palmbil) Colijn; also by De May & unbeliever Vliet. Fr. Elling's work bearing fruit. Additionally several fallen away Catholics returned & one who [was] baptized but never educated or lived Catholic, Routjey received first Communion.

— July 26 Monday

Movement to oust Beisel from kitchen chief & put Weddington seems to have failed.

Rumor—Duce fled [to] Switzerland.

— July 27 Tuesday

Niposh dead silence re Duce, Sicily, etc.

— July 28 Wednesday

Japanese today asked if [there are] any journalists, actors or singers [in] camp. I was presented & on being questioned said 5 yrs. with Uni[ted] Press, whereof 2 [years were] stateside. They presented papers whereon written names of obscure organizations unknown to me, such as "White

Shirts & Black Crusader." Also "C.I.O.A.F.L.," whereof I said two *labor* organizations, "C.I.O & A. F. of L." British Camp Committeeman Hammett said before I called J. asked if I could sing. Hammett said "No." I informed Hammett I was grossly insulted & threatened retaliation. Ha!

— JULY 29 THURSDAY

Joy swept camp when paper said Duce resigned, succeeded by Badoglio. New high camp morale, singing, laughter, animated voices. Also Guam bombed; Stalin to one sector.

Made bet with Harley Clark that Sicily [was] *not* captured by 3rd week in May. He believes it was. My guess is last week in June or first week in July. Duce probably resigned 10 days ago—July 18 or 19.

Tokyo said J[apanese] would pursue war unaffected [by] Italian cabinet changes, until victory.

Latest name for an old nuisance in Block 5 "Sinex Infandus."

— JULY 30 FRIDAY

Arthritis crippling Allen suddenly. I massage him twice daily. Germann & I playing American Man & Wife in forthcoming camp show. Rehearsing daily.

— JULY 31 SATURDAY

New J. guard asked Koot, who [was] busy building stage, "Where is Einstein"? Then asked "How far is [it] to the moon"? Educated Methodist mission school, Tokyo.

Medan Sumatra Shimbun of 7/9 said U.S. Congress threatened bomb [ ], quoted volcanologist Imanura saying 3 or 4 ton bomb dropped [in] live volcanoes might produce big explosions causing local earthquakes & local damage—but said few cities near live volcanoes, therefore damage not as widespread as would [be if] same bomb dropped [on a] populous area. Anyway—government taking secret but appropriate steps [to] combat [the] menace. Also revealed Vladislaw Sikorsky killed [in] plane crash near Gibraltar.

— AUGUST 1, 1943—SUNDAY

Reading Patrick M. Synge's "Mountains of the Moon," an account of botanical mountain climbing expedition to Ruwenzori Mountains, Africa, near source of Nile. Synge was a contemporary of Allen's at Cambridge and "last man on earth one would imagine doing that sort of thing," Allen said.

⌐ Aug. 2 Monday

Began rehearsals for show, 2 to 3 hours each morning.

⌐ August 3 Tuesday

Allen went to Charitas for a stay. J. guard forbade lecture which was scheduled—Fr. Elling on Calvinism.

Dutchmen Van Hilton & Van Arkle, showed their true colors when they tried to stop Elling from being allowed to lecture on Tuesday nite. Although my Tuesday night lectures are for English & solely under my control, they told Lawson, entertainment committee chairman, Elling must be prevented from beginning lectures under me & he must be confined to Sundays. They said it was a shame he had succeeded in getting me to put him on after he had so cleverly & quietly been deprived of his Thursday night time for English lectures. As a matter of fact, I requested Elling to lecture on Church of England as did Strugnell, for his Monday night session. So Strugnell & I arranged to split 3 lectures to which Elling consented.

⌐ Aug 4 Wednesday

Bismark rumored partially evacuated.

I'm planning elaborate female costume changes for show & scouring camp for same.

⌐ Aug. 5 Thursday

Tied hand & foot 2X2. Fed twice, water once.

⌐ Aug 6 Friday

Hospital kitchen now making good pudding or cake from maize & soya bean flour, with gaplek flour for stiffening—steamed in boiler several hours.

⌐ Aug 7 Saturday

Concert rained out but since we were in costume we staged full dress rehearsal. This morning guard allowed Koot & me to go outside for foliage for stage decorations.

⇀ Aug. 8 Sunday

Clear weather, good guard allowed show [to] go on, hugely successful—called best yet. Series [of] comic episodes beginning [with] two ultra-ultra old school tie boys on raft—Pratt & Hammett—being picked up by Dutch ship whereon American couple—Germann & I; Dutch couple—deJong & Paow; Frenchman—van Arkle; Spaniard—Gordon Burt. Next scene Paris café, street scenes, then Folies Bergeres. Dutch peasant dance, Hawaiian scene & Singapore [ ] Way, with more dialogue interludes by Pratt & Hammett, comprised second half. Harold Lawson directed. For first time in camp concert history a character changed costume three times—myself. My Folies Bergere costume—black, shoulderless evening gown (fashioned from Lely's dressing gown worn backwards & topped by white turban, silver paper earrings & necklace) brought down the house. Germann played his part well.

⇀ Aug 9 Monday

Resident Oranje, Lublik-Weddig, his secretary & assistant de Boer taken away by J. [Later note:] (Note—Lublik-Weddig executed by beheading; Ziesel beheaded also, believed but not sure, possibly [committed] suicide Eight Dutch Civil Servants executed—beheading) Oct. '43.

⇀ Aug 10 Tuesday

Chief of Police Lake & P. J. A. Ronkers-Agerbeek today taken away—both Indo-Europeans & latter talented cartoonist.

Native youths 16 to 20 recruited [for] various purposes, wear uniform—white for military [?], etc.

⇀ Aug 11 Wednesday

More Dutch Civil Servants taken. Assistant Resident Steuerman of Lahat; Fanoy of Palembang & Overbeek also of Palembang. Purpose unknown.

⇀ Aug. 12 Thursday

Reported Oranje, etc. jailed. That perhaps suspected relation AS [?], which absolutely untrue if so.

⟶ AUG. 13 FRIDAY

Wilson's asthma has him down again. Poor fellow, for weeks on end he never lies down, but sleeps sitting up, crouched on bench in surgery, his head resting on table, wheezing like a leaky old organ. A throat spray helps him somewhat, as does a tea-like mixture of boiled Joha leaves.

⟶ AUG 14 SATURDAY

Wilder grow rumors—Latest Germans withdrawn all troops from occupied countries for defense of fatherland & Russian breakthrough hurled Nazis from Russia.

Latest camp enterprise—making milk from soya leaves & which resembles in flavor & appearance real milk & supposedly contains same vitamins, proteins, etc. Oil experts doing it with great labor & pains.

Hosp[ital] acquired a large grinder for grinding flour, & Carl [?] now makes big cake thrice weekly.

Poggemier again teaching me Malay.

⟶ AUG 15 SUNDAY

All Catholics to Mass & Communion for soon & righteous peace. (I hope Hollweg, etc. ok too.)

Dutch banker Geroms taken away. [Later note:] (Geroms beaten to death in [his] own house which now Kempai headquarters) Poekoel Saya!

⟶ AUG 17 TUESDAY

Elling lectured on Calvin. Public lectures henceforth will return to Thursday nights as formerly.

Allen's birthday today, but he is still in hospital, his rheumatism still plaguing him.

⟶ AUG 18 WEDNESDAY

The bob-tailed ginger haired Kampon cat which has "adopted" the clinic, had a kitten several days ago in the library bookbinders box of old rags. Today she began exploring our room, as if searching for a new home. I thrust some old newspapers in a broken suitcase, put her in it, she investigated extensively, then left, returning with her kitten, its eyes still closed, & hanging from mother's mouth. So it looks as though she will stay. [Later note:] Mother & daughter killed & eaten Oct. '44.

⌐ Aug 19 Thursday

Spending all spare time & until late night writing letters to Jean describing camp life.

Announced will be blackout rehearsals Friday through Sunday a.m.

Dutch coal miners W. Van Dam & Walter, from Pubat district taken away. [Later note:] Never returned; believe executed.

⌐ Aug. 20 Friday

Dutch banker J. F. Traubel taken away. [Later note:] D. R. Matheson, 44, Malayan Police, added to hospital staff.

⌐ Aug. 21 Saturday

Been working day shift on letters to Jean.

⌐ Aug 22 Sunday

Japanese inquired [as to] whereabouts [of] Msgr. Mekkelholt—ominous in these circumstances.

⌐ Aug 23, 1943 Monday

From now on I'm using Pitman shorthand to practice what I've been studying for the past year.

[Entries from here through September 15, 1943, transcribed from shorthand.]

Banker Shenk [?] ... taken away. He was in a hospital with [a] septic foot but was compelled to go [when?] told a ... doctor was available.

Finished my letters and diary to date.

⌐ August Twenty Fourth Tuesday [1943]

Two more Dutchmen taken away—Tromp and Roteer—but in the afternoon they returned with Shenk after being questioned about the Dutch Home Guard previous to the war.

⌐ August Twenty Fifth Wednesday

Hereafter I will write all diary in Cable-ese [he means telegram abbreviations]. Radical change between Japan's tone now [and a] year ago. Even in *Nippon Palembang Shimbun* recent questioning internees. South Sumatra's Governor General.

Loutening General [Kasao or Kasai] writing Nip-ah-sh warned Indonesia's war will [be] longest warfare must [be] prepared coming hardships including various shortages. Secondly certain men Palembang who spread rumors Allied attacks punished severely, others will [be] similarly dealt [with].

Naturally since war still ongoing both sides attacking but nearest allies now Australia [and] India. Japanese navy will halt any enemy sea attacks and army any land attacks—admitted possibility enemy attack Palembang. But no need fear account strong advances.

Also said Sumatra's condition best compared Japan Germany England America regards food stuffs.

Previously Nip-ah-sh ask why United States attacking since no one attacking her—said only conclusion drawable [is] U.S. intends [to] rule [the] world.

— AUGUST 26 THURSDAY

New Indonesian guards some speaking excellent English trying [to] draw Internees into conversation [about] warfare. Suspect agents-provocateur.

— AUGUST 27 FRIDAY

Earl David Van Arkel 23 to 3 opposing Van Arkel's motion "Civilization destroys initiative." Van's discourse among [the] worst we have heard.

— AUGUST 28 SATURDAY

Jones North East corner 273033; he said has [my] horoscope indicating years 1927, '30 & '33 were my lucky years but I remember nothing special[ly] lucky about them.

Koeboes: primitive jungle nomads whom Malays regard as animals and for whom Dutch government makes no provisions. Malay opinion of Koeboes typified by Loeboek Linggay taxidermist who asked permission to stuff and mount a Koeboe. American missionaries (probably Adventists) successfully worked among Koeboes however could not use native Indonesian assistants because Indos despise Koeboes, distrust each other.

— AUGUST 29 SUNDAY

Chinese food contractor paid F.100 for one large tin [container?] Klim which he sold us last year for F.8. The new improvements buy tins for which we pay F.7.50 for coffee worth F.5 for tin and F.2.50 for coffee.

Old Mellor, 78, died last night in insane asylum where he had been past nine months. His daughter in women's camp now has lost parents who died here and husband who drowned Bangka Straits.

⚊ AUGUST 30 MONDAY

Rumors persist heavy fighting Burma and Rangoon captured. I am unable to believe, impossible during rainy season.

⚊ AUGUST 31 TUESDAY

Queen Wilhemina birthday marked by private reception by camp senior Dutch civil servants in absence Oranje, Santwick, for block leaders and camp officials plus Worth and myself as Australian and American representatives.

After dinner hospital staff, patients and campleaders enjoyed cake [and] coffee with white sugar which West hoarded more than a year.

⚊ SEPTEMBER 1, '43 AND SEPTEMBER 2 '43

Reading "Duke" of Wellington by Philip Guedalla.

⚊ SEPTEMBER 3 FRIDAY

Wrote my views [on] disarmament and read at Debating Society discussion.

I believe world disarmament impossible unless all peoples and nations united by common idea [which] points to one universal religion—Christianity.

SEPTEMBER 4 SATURDAY

Japanese interrogated many [Jub, Jupa?] civil officers concerning former air raid precaution system.

⚊ SEPTEMBER 5 SUNDAY

Coolies begin digging what resembles pill box foundation at camp entrance.

⚊ SEPTEMBER 6 MONDAY

Began documenting proofs Christ founded one church.

⌐ SEPTEMBER 7 TUESDAY

Letters from England received by several Britons. All dates [were] June and July [slipped in: August] 1942. Letters showed ships *Empress [of] Japan* and *Gorgon* arrived safely.

All indicated relatives had not heard anything concerning us.

Mrs. Begg in August wrote she had vainly explored every possible channel of information.

Two letters to Hoy from India [with] 1 October date from his mother said she heard from his wife, although earlier letter said had not. Leading to speculation, wife possibly interned somewhere after shipwreck. She sailed *Felix Roussel* from Singapore.

⌐ SEPTEMBER 8 WEDNESDAY

Sunday after Pentecost [Nipash] admitted British landings Reggio but said only 400 [were] all wiped out except 50 who fled hillwards.

Cat and kitten keeping us busy nights since she insisted [on] kitten sleeping inside mosquito net while she roams and hunts but frequently returns to check up.

⌐ SEPTEMBER 9 THURSDAY

Nipash now decrying British advance from Reggio to Palmi, saying such an offensive will only prolong war.

⌐ SEPTEMBER 10 FRIDAY

Began reading Margaret Mitchell's "Gone With the Wind."

⌐ SEPTEMBER 11 SATURDAY

Room communique Nipash saying 081745 Italian government surrender unconditionally. British dispatch said Mussolini set up Fascist government [in] northern Italy where German troops move into position smoothly.

Nipash officially warned populace against Allied propaganda. Also said "If enemy suddenly changes its tactics Japanese prepared [to] change theirs also. [Wherefore] do not criticize officials who [are] carrying out operations."

⌐ SEPTEMBER 12 SUNDAY

Reading all day.

~ SEPTEMBER 13 MONDAY

Charitas hospital closed. 32 [Malay?] civilian patients also Dr. Peter Tekelenburg and Bishop Mekkleholt came here. Nuns sent to women's camp, soldiers to service camp. Our camp population now 501 men including children.

~ SEPTEMBER 14 TUESDAY

5 Dutch civil officers including [Resident] Oranje returned [to] camp after several weeks intensive questioning.

~ SEPTEMBER 15 WEDNESDAY

Japanese announced entire camp moving. This section goes tomorrow with half hospital and West… [rest in plain text]

[First set of shorthand entries ends here and Muntok Prison diary begins.]

~ SEPT. 16, 1943

Coffee served 2 a.m., then breakfast & trucks arrived. Our section of 230 men, laden with luggage, hiked in dawn grayness through silent Palembang to Moesi Riverside where we were joined by 57 Pladjoe oil workers who have been quartered in town since Pladjoe move last January.

Trucks moved all baggage set out—including chickens & ducks—[onto] a ferry packet, 300 ton former "Bagan" of Penang, which had evacuated 100-odd Harbor Board men from Singapore, then took us to Muntok, Bangka Island, in the straits between Sumatra & Malaya, 6 hours sailing time downstream. Leaving 6:20 a.m., passed 5 big tankers anchored. Elaborate precautions guard our route. Japanese & Indonesian soldiers posted at all intersections, fields, etc. Launch followed us & Muntok route same.

Most vivid impression [was] the somber atmosphere of Muntok. Town completely deserted, dead silence reigned. And our destination chilled every heart—the grim, triple ringed jail which formerly housed only life termers for one section of Dutch East Indies, and which was the scene of much horror in February, 1942. The grim silence was utter & absolute, so much so that its influence reduced to whispers the few words men spoke to each other as we were lined up, counted, luggage inspected & assigned to cells. One huge room had a wooden shelf along the wall for a bed. Other cells held about 50 men each, lying side by side in 3 rows on concrete floor with only a grass mat beneath. But most of us were so tired we slept, loglike, all night.

Japanese supplied us with hot meal of rice & boiled fish—pleasant surprise in contrast with previous moves. In fact they conducted the entire move with almost apologetic consideration. [The] move [was] not explained.

⏤ Sept. 17 Friday

Opened clinic in square, wooden tile roofed building [in the] center [of the] jail compound. Men [were] busy rustling nails, bits of wood, anything which might possibly [be] used. Drysdale noticed a hen scratching vigorously beneath papaya trees which were growing from a former bomb crater. [He] investigated, and dug up an aluminum mess tin. He reached his hand into a hole under the logs and got a good pair of shorts.

⏤ Sept. 18, Saturday

New Pladjoers have 3 violins, two cellos—staged good concert last night in the big Block.

⏤ Sept. 19, Sunday

Mass said in large empty cell block.
Second half of camp arrived, bringing total population to 538. As he walked through the gate & saw our new home, Hollweg's face was a study in rage.

⏤ Sept. 20, Monday

Clinic swamped.

⏤ Sept. 21, Tuesday

Japanese guard by gestures said San Francisco and Vancouver bombed. Finished "Gone With the Wind."

⏤ Sept. 22 Wednesday

Fortunately able to get fish daily. Food much tastier here than formerly, but quantity smaller.

⏤ Sept. 23 Thursday

New orchestra of violins, cello & 2 guitars gave concert tonight, standing in covered veranda of block 1 because rain threatened. Clad only in shorts, they had an unconcertlike appearance, but good musicians. Cellist, tall, lean, bushy bearded, cavern eyed, looked like a cartoon of wild IWW, named Schepero McGillivere. Despite chilly breeze, campers clustered around stone bathing tanks fronting the veranda and loudly applauded.

⁓ Sept. 24 Friday

Clinic business growing—183 outpatients yesterday.

Camp rooms 45x22; Block II 50x30; & Big Block 139x40. Verandas 185 feet. Yard 150 wide, verandas 11 feet wide.

[Entries from September 25 through October 16, 1943, transcribed from shorthand.]

⁓ Sept. 25 Saturday

Food looms largest of matters [in] camp life. Because quantity insufficient men continuously hungry all but two woodcutter crews struck when privilege getting food is withdrawn. Now all camp members regardless [of] job eat with blocks.

⁓ Sept. 26 Sunday

Bishop sermoned inspiringly with "if we live true spiritual life [in] these circumstances discomfort will not matter."

Mass said large empty cell wherein we knelt [on] bare concrete floor unless we had cushions.

⁓ Sept. 27 Monday

Experimented [with] calling clinic patients by blocks today and treated 119.

⁓ Sept. 28 Tuesday [partly in handwriting]

140 internees from … [places given in handwriting] and 2 doctors A. P. A. Boerma of [Siman/Simay?] Gold Mine, Tandai, Sumatra & Willem van Woerkom, an estate doctor

entered camp bringing population of 673 with 38 priests and brothers.

⁓ Sept. 29 Wednesday

Clinic cases rose to 162 keeping 3 dressers going 5-1/2 hours.

⌁ Sept. 30 Thursday

Norwegian ship capt. Halvorsen who abandoned sunk [ship] 140 miles off Tjilatjap Mar. 7. He sailed alone 18 days landing same island we did.

⌁ Oct. 1 Friday

Fish issued twice daily although no fruit such as bananas or pineapples.

⌁ Oct. 2 Saturday

Sir John Campbell 69 Malayan tin baron now ill [despondent?]—example of man who lived entirely for world and in old age has [nothing] to cling [to].

⌁ Oct. 3 Sunday

Mass said on Block 10 veranda alongside water tanks our/hour [?] morning. Blankets hung from lines give vestige [of] privacy but not much as bathers splash and men wash dishes.

⌁ Oct. 4 Monday

Block 11 remodelled and rooms built for clinic and committee.

⌁ Oct. 5 Tuesday

Japs gave 25 eggs [to the] hospital—first time Japs ever gave eggs [to] camp. Also promised supply sugar regularly, 100 kilos weekly—30 grams per man per day.

⌁ Oct. 6 Wednesday

Report German leaders fired similar [to] Mussolini. Burma rumor factual.

When permission sought [to] buy cakes for children guard refused, saying Japanese children unable to buy cakes because of bombing.

⌁ Oct. 7 Thursday

Acute water shortage, taps dry, two wells low. Men ration[ed] one bucket each for washing, one bottle for drinking.

[Our] morning meal long has been gaplek—tasteless sticky porridge of ground tapioca root. Gaplek basis for many wry jokes.

⟿ Oct. 8 Friday

[Text of postcard to another POW from POW in another camp, copied here by McDougall and irrelevant to him.]

⟿ Oct. 9 Saturday

Sir John Campbell made second attempt at [suicide?] when at 11 p.m. he dived head first from his bed onto concrete floor.

⟿ Oct. 10 Sunday

R. W. Morris, British planter, among Djambe internees lived 3 months Singkao Lunga islands before captured after sinking Malacca Straits Feb. 4. Swam ashore 7 hours off Kuala, sank with about 350 aboard. Hired Javanese fishermen, travelled sampan by night because natives unwilling [to] travel by day. Morris did not attempt [to] sail [to] India [or] Australia because insufficient money [to] buy boat and also thought trip impossible.

⟿ Oct. 11 Monday

Jennings & Hall landed Benkoelen after some 3 months at sea in open boat trying for Australia, apparently never sailed south of Sumatra. Lived for weeks [on] seagulls caught with bare hands which alighted [on] boat. Hall lowered himself over side [and] chewed barnacles off bottom.

⟿ Oct. 12 Tuesday

Nightly "[brownout?]" began with Muntok on perpetual alert.

⟿ Oct. 13 Wednesday

Wildest reports Wilhelmina in the Hague, Yanks northern Sumatra; also that Japanese mistrust native police.

⟿ Oct. 14 Thursday

Sir John Campbell died 7:15 p.m. [of] heart disease "auricular [fibrillation?]." Buried this afternoon Christian cemetery where lie [9?] British who died Feb. '42. Japanese supplied two large beautiful wreaths of huge yellow frangipani; purple and dark pink bougainvillea, sweetpea-like Honolulus and other blossoms—beautiful but odorless like all tropical flowers. Coffin carried to cemetery on shoulders [of] six men.

⌐ October 15 Friday

M. V. de Visser, 35, died 1:45 a.m.—15th since internment—unknown cause after entering hospital last night. Died in high fever [of] suspected septicemia resulting from septic sores. Buried similarly to Sir John Campbell yesterday.

⌐ October 16 Saturday

Peanut said Allies occupy all Italy and that news from [Japan] is always beautiful.

Japanese civil officer in charge our camp named Takimura, is by far [the] best official we have ever had. Today he gave long interview, Asbek & West—first such ever granted us—concerning food situation. Taki seems trying hard [to] improve our lot.

[Second set of shorthand entries ends here.]

⌐ Oct. 17 to 23

Sunday Prior's 60th birthday. I found a cigar for him—his first in 8 months & he is the happiest. Prior unqualifiedly predicts the collapse of Germany between Oct. 23 & Nov. 7, when she'll ask for an armistice. He says Japan will collapse sooner.

Morris Philipps, Malayan gambler, horse race man & promoter offered to bet 25,000 guilders *we* are free of Japanese supervision by Jan. 1, 1944. My opinion: of 100 chances when war ends some free southern regions—10% by 1/1/44, 70% by 4/30/44; 90% by 9/1/44.

Read P. Buck's "House Divided" & Charles Brooks' "The General Died at Dawn." Reading R. A. Saville-Sneath's "Aircraft Recognition."

After Poggemier asked protection over himself, Civil Service last night established 2 hr. shifts beside his bed.

[Entries from October 24 through November 1, 1943, transcribed from shorthand.]

⌐ Oct. 24 Sunday

Wildest rumors—40 th[ousand] Allied troops landed near Soerabaja fighting 7 [hundred] kilometers from here, Russians in Danzig. Eric and I have been lying off with diarrhea all week but now up again.

⁓ Oct. 25 Monday

Despite acute shortage [of] wood, flourishing chair stool manufacturing going on. Beds and tables also appear seemingly from thin air. Men ingeniously using firewood, bamboo and planks lifted from bed frames [or] brought from former camp.

⁓ Oct. 26 Tuesday

Palem. Japanese ordered rice ration reduced from 150 to 100 kilos daily. Thus cutting individual rations from 220 to 140 grams per man.

⁓ Oct. 27 Wednesday

36 [more] men arrived from Palembang including Dr. Holweg who [did?] 7 months jail; Fanoy and other civil servant from jail; and various civilians who [were] arrested 37 days ago. 2 doctors, Charitas Mother Superior and 4 other civil officers still held.

⁓ Oct. 28 Thursday

One serious dysentery case among new arrivals.

[paragraph sign] Reports Allies reached Macasser [spelling?] Straits; captured all Burma, half Siam. Nipash said Russians offensiving entire front from Sea Azov ... to Lake Ilmes.

⁓ Oct. 29 Friday

First adverse rumor—Japanese recaptured Boona N.G. [New Guinea?]. Vandervliet and Dorrestier taken away by Japanese.

⁓ Oct. 30 Saturday

Work party brought in weatherbeaten piano on veranda of closed house near outside gate. One day work party members [were] bathing at wall and chopping wood while one member played piano—all stark naked. We have been trying [two marks ( ) which could mean "for year"?] to obtain piano. Camp now has 3 orchestras—swing, Hawaiian and stringed.

⁓ October 31 Sunday

Bishop M. confirmed 8 persons colorful ceremony wherein he used my crozier. Episcopal ceremonies strange in place like this. Roses and palms on aisle are setup on veranda block 10. Sarongs and blankets hanging from iron fence and lines afford partial privacy. Worship[pers] use wooden stools and benches and kneel on cement of well of bathing atrium and veranda. Men in block 11 sometimes lean(ed) over their wall to watch.

⇀ Nov. 1 Monday

"All Saints Day" began with two masses—one by Bishop M.—and continued with heavy clinic runs of 158 cases. So much clinic work this camp I have little time for study and I am seriously thinking of quitting hospital and going into camp.

[Third set of shorthand entries ends here.]

⇀ Nov. 2 Tuesday

Kendall decommissioned by bad heart, so I [was] transferred from clinic to hospital ward assisting Harrison, washing patients, taking temperatures, etc. Simultaneously Rust, M. van Zijl's condition turned grave & I had job of nursing him. Van Zijl, 44, tremendously fat school principal of Lahat, entered hospital Nov. 21 with undiagnosable stomach ailment, continuous vomiting, etc. 2 of his 5 children are here, the most well behaved boys I recall ever meeting, 11 & 13 yrs. old. Eldest in hospital with sores Nov. 9 to 26. Zijl critical after we moved him from ward to vacant cell we are using as workshop, about 8 feet square, small barred window high up—one of the condemned cells. Priest gave him last Sacraments Thursday the 4th & priests stayed beside him next 24 hours till death at 10:22 a.m. 11/5/43. First time I ever pronounced death. When I was certain he would last only a short time longer I summoned Bishop & priest, thermometer in his armpit. He gasped what I thought was his last breath at 10:20 a.m., then unexpectedly two minutes later took another deep, slow breath & gasped it out—his last. Displayed remarkable self control. Bishop celebrated solemn requiem High Mass 7 a.m. 11/6 & 12 pallbearers, alternating 6 at a time, carried the heavy burden ¾ mile to cemetery. I was a pallbearer. Z.'s death was the third in Muntok jail camp; Campbell & Visser died Oct. 14 & 15 respectively.

So pressed by work this week, no time even to write in diary, which I am doing now, Sunday, Nov. 7.

[Entries from November 8 through December 6, 1943, transcribed from shorthand.]

⟶ Nov. 8 Monday

First time since entering Muntok jail week began without [at] least one patient seriously ill [in] hospital.

Gave Eric pair trousers for resewing my knapsack.

⟶ Nov. 9 Tuesday

Narrow way between wall and cell block crowded with various [projects?]—woodcutters, workshop wherein camp technical jobs done—piano being repaired, organ built, etc.; chairmakers busy, chicken houses located and children's school held. However, ¼ section extending from hospital shut off by fence makes good sunbathing spot for us. Since dysentery cases guards do not come here for post duties.

⟶ Nov. 10 Wednesday

Camp Committee trying to halt black market buying by saying Japs prohibit, also Dutch strongarm squad rumor inferring Committee [appealed?] for cooperation.

⟶ Nov. 11 Thursday—"Armistice Day"

British held memorial service attended by about 100. Parson Wardle spoke, two hymns sung, several prayers recited.

⟶ Nov. 12 Friday

N.R.P.M. man Bouchard attempted suicide by inflicting [four?] shallow wounds over heart with heavy knife while cleaning fingernails as he stood in yard with dinner being served. Although wound slight, subsequent shock nearly killed him. I have never seen such a case of shock from such a seemingly small wound. Of course the mental [psychosis] promoting act and following it was responsible for the shock. A cool Dutchman who saw him quietly asked him "What [would] your wife and children think? Come to the hospital." Brought him over here, telling curious he fell on his knife.

⟶ Nov. 13 Saturday

[Began] reading Rachel Field's "All This and Heaven Too," which has one of the most intriguing introductions I have read in a long time.

⟿ Nov. 14 Sunday

Seven more men from Benk. with news three men sentenced ten years each and one eight years on charges presumed [to] be espionage but unrevealed by Japanese. They also said Charitas Hospital mother superior sentenced ten years in Palembang Jail.

⟿ Nov. 15 Monday

Reports 10 m[illion] men fighting K., Allies occupy only Southern Italy. Solomons, half New G [New Guinea?], Yan. [died?] Rend, Allies piling-up men [and] material Northern Burma, new six-ton bombs devastating BrLn [Berlin?].

⟿ Nov. 16 Tuesday

Finished "All This and Heaven Too."
Paid five guilders for chair built for my desk.

⟿ Nov. 17 Wednesday

First *Nippon Palembang Shimbun* given to camp by Japanese described heavy fighting around R. & B.
Learned Padang [internees?] [number] 900 men 2500 [women] and children—about 200 men from Singapore, rest Dutch.

⟿ Nov. 18 Thursday

My weight down to 50 kilos or 110 pounds—lightest since high school days. Although I tire easily my general health is good.

⟿ Nov. 19 Friday

Mother's birthday. I wrote letter to her and offered a mass and communion for her.

⟿ Nov. 20 Saturday

Read F. S. Packard's "Night Operator" and other railroad stories.

⟿ Nov. 21 Sunday

H. V. M. Woods, 42, GV [government?] board officer Penang died 9:15 a.m. pulmonary embolism his block, buried 3 p.m. His wife in Australia.

Today I acquired only private room in camp when I moved into 6' x 6' cubicle next [to] hospital toilet, formerly used as dysentery room and mortuary.

⌐ Nov. 22–28

Last night 8 new men from Tandjong Karong [?] arrived, 7 civil officers and one priest.

During week I read Steinbeck's "Grapes of Wrath."

Camp looney bin opened with Pogg & Buchard transferred from block 6 to special small cell with [keepers] Van Dam & Van Diemen.

Japanese finally allowed recreation outside walls with hour a day 40 men permitted out to play football.

Thursday Woods' possessions auctioned bringing F 252. I bought pair socks for Fl. 3.75. Incredible [record/regret?] I has/as Fl. 40 bid for worn tower.

First full-fledged concert staged this camp Saturday halted in middle by [guard?] who said must end by 8:30 p.m.

Biggest event of week for [me] personally was "Thanksgiving Day" feast participated in by German, Christie, Collin Campbell, Attenborough, Van Geyyel and me. By devious means I got small amount [of] saffron, coriander seeds, leeks which were pounded into powder and mixed into mashed ubi Kaya and fried over block kitchen fire into patties similar [to] potato cakes. 5 coconuts used to make "Santan," milk for coffee and pudding are baked in hot water boiler fire boxes.

⌐ Nov. 30 Tuesday

Peanut said British exchange slated early next year. Boat coming here.

. St. Andrew's Day celebration by Scots who ate ubi kaya "Hagis," drank coffee, made speeches with Chieftain Jock Brody presiding. Concert [of] Scotch songs held evening but lacked old enthusiasm. In fact entire camp seems falling under lassitude wherein studies [are] neglected, men "fed-up," lack ambition for anything.

⌐ December 1 Wednesday

Chief civil officer Muntok Takaimura in charge [of] camp, is good man for us, kind [and] courteous. He corrected my letter to Hori and said he would take it to Pangkal Penang, Bangka capital, himself. J. Schuurman,

Palembang Postmaster, who began Japanese studies only year ago translated letter, and written Japanese characters in English.

➤ DECEMBER 2 THURSDAY

Official camp canteen opened selling coffee on contract basis 4 months one cup daily.

Private "block kitchen" frying ubi cakes 50 [cent sign?] weekly, customers supplying ubi from their meal rations.

Japanese guard changed, new ones from P.P. seem good lot.

➤ DECEMBER 3 FRIDAY

Japanese told group [of] men Japan, Britain, America, planning [to] exchange nationals soon—confirming Peanut's story to West of exchange ship due here early next year.

➤ DECEMBER 4 SATURDAY

Hospital kitchen busy making sweets for children for St. Nicholas day December 5.

➤ DECEMBER 5 SUNDAY

Using tapioca flour, sugar, coconut, and [a] few eggs, hospital cooking experts made cookies and sweets for children and our staff. Remarkable how much good can be done with so little.

➤ DECEMBER 6 MONDAY

Peanut said he took my letter to P.P. but could not reply to my question whether it [would] be sent to Tokio. He said America[n]s would be exchanged next year but did not know whether would include Muntok internees.

[Fourth set of shorthand entries ends here.]

➤ JANUARY 11, 1944, TUESDAY

I have practically recovered from a severe attack of subtertian (cerebral) malaria. There have been no proven new cases of malaria either in Muntok or Palembang (contracted in those places) since internment. This time fever lasted 14 days—Dec. 12 to 26 inclusive, during about 10 days of which I remember nothing, having been semi or unconscious. Fever ranged from 39 on Dec. 12 to 40.2 Dec. 17, subsided to around 38 & 37 the 19, 22 during the crisis. During the crisis, of which I remember nothing, priests stood by to give me last sacraments, because for a while doctors feared I might die. West fed me 30 grams quinine daily & said I kept it down, vomiting only once. For a number of days they were unable to get food into me. During 2 nights towards the early part of the attack, volunteers in hourly shifts watched by my bedside because too weak to get up & because I wanted someone to talk to. My mind was beginning to [ ] to my own knowledge & I feared the brain fever which killed de Visser. I distinctly remember several times trying vainly to tell Dr. West something but all I could speak was nonsense—my brain & my tongue wouldn't coordinate. Nor could I concentrate long enough to remember one sentence until I had spoken it. A thought would flash into my mind but before I could express it, it was gone, leaving me with the impression it had been a good thought but with no recollection of its substance. So my conversations with West were disjointed nonsense, of which I was helplessly & miserably aware at the time.

I remember a few of the watchers the first two nights. My next conscious period was Dec. 24. Prior to my illness I had requested Fr. Elling that a Mass be said for my father on his birthday, day before Christmas. On the 24th I awakened in the hospital ward—into which I had been carried from my room a few days previously so it could be occupied by C. J. (Corky) Arnold, 69, gnome-like little Perak planter, dying of dysentery. [Later note:] My room tiny cubbyhole used for death cell—a private place for men to die.

Elling that day told me the first Mass had been said for Dad & the second for me. Christmas Day I was aware of everything going on around me but was extremely deaf—quinine—& unable to hear the sound of a single note of the Christmas music sung by the Church or the Camp Choir. Bakker conducted Camp Choir in program identical to Christmas, '43. Allen read Dickens Christmas Carol same as last year, also.

By New Years Day I was well on road of convalescence but still very weak. New Years Eve Lawson directed a Camp Concert which was excellent, by all reports. I didn't see it. Camp bought two pigs which were consumed New Years Day, hospital patients getting the liver.

Germann & I had long planned a special feed Xmas, but my illness stopped it. Both he & Christie also have been experiencing fever attacks. Mike Treurniet had scheduled a duck dinner for New Years, but he postponed it until Sund. Jan. 9 for my sake & so I had a generous helping of duck to put on my Sunday rice. [Later note:] Ducks brought into jail from Pladjoe by new prisoners.

My mind was fuzzy for a considerable time after Dec. 26. Several people told me they spoke to me & I answered nonsensically. On Jan. 1 or 2 we had to fill in some forms for the Js. Harrison wisely had me write mine out on a slate, for him to copy. Later he & Doc West said the answers were terribly misspelled, as, New York "ben Yourrk," & many others. Even now I'm suspicious of myself.

And so for the second time in less than 2 yrs. I have gone down into the Valley of the Shadow of Death—and come out through the mercy of God. The first time was when the *Poelau Bras* sank. I was keenly aware of everything down to the smallest detail then. This time I knew nothing of my danger until well afterwards—was not even aware I was very sick. How blindly and in ignorance of one's peril can one slip out of life.

On Jan. 3, C. J. Corky Arnold, Selamgor planter, died of heart failure following chronic dysentery. He died a lonely death at 6:15 p.m. in my bed. I was unable to sleep at all the previous night, & heard Corky's cries. Whether they were cries of pain or only of loneliness, or despair, or because he cried—a long exclamation of woe—merely for the sake of crying, I don't know. Somewhere outside the walls, but close by, a dog howled mournfully much of the night. Corky was carried to the cemetery at 3 p.m. Volunteers were asked for because Corky was a lonely old man with few friends.

I began reading about New Year's & have read John Buchan's "The Isle of Sheep," "Sick Heart River," & "Path of the King"; E. Phillips Oppenheim's "Ask Miss Mott" & am today beginning his "Mr. Billingham the Marquis & Madelon"; reread a number of Edgar Allan Poe's short stories & best of all, Taylor Caldwell's "Dynasty of Death," a gripping novel based on early years of munitions industry in America, seemingly based on fact. Elling brought me Holy Communion Christmas & New Year's Day & Epiphany (which was Gertrude's birthday).

⟶ JAN. 14 FRIDAY

I lie here doing nothing all day except read, and hear little of camp gossip, so there is not much use in a daily diary.

E. H. Tunn, retired Malaya policeman, died Jan 13, 1 a.m., dysentery. His wife in Women's Camp.

A few days ago Block 1 acquired a British Block Leader, W. D. Peterkin, after their former leader, one of [the] best men in camp, Scheffer, a Dutchman, resigned because of so much grousing. The block voted to exclude the kitchen staff from its membership. The election became partisan & bitter over British-Dutch question, whereupon Dutch candidate withdrew, leaving British to squabble among themselves.

Read Max Brand's "King Bird Rides" & starting H. G. Wells "Apropos of Dolores."

⟶ Jan 15 Saturday

Weighed today—46½ kilos, 102.3 pounds! Height 1 meter 77 cent., 5'9.3 Finished "Apropos of Dolores."

⟶ Jan 20 Thursday

Still convalescing, but about ready to return to work. Read Edmond's "Chad Hanna" & Upton Sinclair's "Wet Parade." Japanese announced 200 more internees, from Pangkal Penang will be put in here, where we already are jammed like sardines.

⟶ Jan 24 Monday

Went back to work on hospital staff.

⟶ February 6 Sunday

Resident Oranje yesterday returned from Pangkal Penang, where [he was] taken 3 weeks ago with 3 other civil servants who returned last Sunday. This week read Inglis Fletcher's "Raleigh's Eden" & Louis Bromfield's "Green Bay Tree."

I seem to be falling into the apathy of many other camp members, as regards study. Haven't studied a bit since illness. Mental concentration becomes more & more difficult. Doctor says it's lack of proteins in diet.

"Peanut" [Later note:] (Jap Commandant) says war endable spring 1945. Eastern front stalemated, Burma quiet.

Read Herman Melville's "Typee."

⟶ Feb 10 Thursday

Finished vol. 1 Hervey Allen's "Anthony Adverse." Yesterday began dismantling fence to make way for building hospital wing.

⟶ Feb. 12 Sat.

Read H. G. Durnford's "The Tunnelers of Holyminden"; also R.O.T.C. Manual.

Died malaria G. B. W. Gray, 60, Malaya planter. First death directly attributable [to] malaria. However, Gray made no apparent effort [to] fight illness. Made up [his] mind he [was] going [to] die before [entering the] hospital ward, perhaps [on] account [of] once being told "avoid all serious illnesses" [on] account [of] bad heart.

— **Feb. 15 Tuesday**

Finished vol. 2 "Anthony Adverse."

— **Feb. 24 Thursday**

Jean's birthday.
Finished Anthony Adverse vol. 3 & began Kenneth Roberts' "Oliver Wiswell" & Pearson & Allen's "More Merry-go-Round."

— **Feb. 25 Friday**

Tussenbroek cooked onions in coconut oil for me.

— **March 1 Wed.**

Began Dr. Victor Heiser's "An American Doctor's Odyssey."

— **March 2 Thurs.**

Prisonier de guerre cards issued for writing U.S.A., England, Holland. Takimura read Christmas & New Year Greetings from Red Cross Societies. English speaking Allied countries including one from "Washington Sanba-cho Marshal."

Japanese Red + requested checking lists [of] *Poelau Bras* survivors. 90 names of persons rescued were missing from lists & Hancock's not among them.

— **March 7 Tues.**

Wrote card home: "Sumatra, March 1944. Dear Mother & Dad—I'm enjoying good health & spirits & sufficient food & drink, adequate quarters & reasonable happiness. I need nothing from home except word the family is well.

I attend Catholic Holy Mass each morning & Lenten services at night.

Am busy daily reading, studying Malay, shorthand & assisting the doctors in our little hospital.

Cool sea breezes make this tropic climate pleasant. Am well suntanned

& weight normal. Best wishes to you both & to Jean & Pete, Gertrude & Paul & a kiss for baby Jean Francis on her fourth birthday.

Love from your son."

Today second anniversary [of] *Poelau Bras* sinking.

⇀ MARCH 13 MONDAY

Japanese took prisoner of war cards, including a second one of mine—to Mary Bell: "Have not heard from either you, Gertrude, Mother, or Hori. Please tell them I am well & wondering if repatriation or exchange is possible.

I'm in good health, reasonably comfortable & happy. Need nothing urgently except word you all are well.

Life here has changed little since I wrote you a year ago.

Give my regards to Mrs. Bell, Dick, Father Bill & the rest. We have Catholic Mass here each morning. God bless you & keep you. With all my love, Mac."

Also succeeded in getting camp officials to approve acknowledging Red + greetings from Washington as follows: "Prisoners of War Dept. American Red Cross, Washington, D.C. Many thanks your Christmas & New Years greetings which were especially appreciated by the two Americans here, W. H. McDougall, Jr. of Salt Lake City, United Press Correspondent, & E. H. Germann, No. 1 Massachusetts Ave., Buffalo, N.Y."

Japanese so pleased with [the] idea they gave camp 12 more cards for acknowledging similar greetings from Red + Societies in Canada, England, Australia, South Africa.

Two years ago today my lifeboat landed on Poeloe Laboean Island.

⇀ MARCH 15 WEDNESDAY

Reading Abbe Constant Frouard's "The Christ, the Son of God." Also "Regency"

Concerted effort by oil group to oust Biesel from kitchen, alleging maladministration, notably example "coffee war"—difference of 100 Gs. Jan to Feb after halting serving coffee in kitchen.

Weighed 51½ kilos, up 2.

⇀ MARCH 17 FRIDAY

Biesel & Bakker resigned as kitchen chiefs, under fire, effective April 1.

Hospital staff celebrated St. Pat's with tasty bit of canned sardines fish

& tomato sauce with onions on fried ubi bread. The cans from Helling's treasure.

➝ MARCH 19 SUNDAY

Camp lottery being conducted for indigent loan fund, which provides F.150 monthly for paupers, who [are] increasing monthly.

T. L. Dee, 48, Dutch Postmaster Pandjong Karang, died 5:10 p.m., diabetic coma.

➝ MARCH 20 MONDAY

Dee buried after requiem High Mass at 1 p.m.. F. M. Joseph, 40, Dutch Civil Servant Palembang municipality, died pneumonia following suspected paratyphoid fever. [Later note:] Died in terror in my room.

➝ MARCH 23 THURSDAY

Finished John Buchan's "A Prince of the Captivity."

Received receipt for F.1200 from Camp Committee as kitchen fund balance applied to loan fund. Redeemable after war.

➝ MARCH 29 WEDNESDAY

Herbert G. (Bert) Smallwood, 51, burly cockney roustabout & one of my favorite camp characters, died 1:30 p.m. pneumonia following myocarditis, in my room. H. G. Hammett, Brit. Representative, led graveside prayers. Fr. Bakker's choir sang at jail gates before coffin left, followed by 30 friends, including Germann, Christie & me.

Takimura accepted my letter to Syonan Governor concerning repatriation. Taki told Asbeck he would give it to Resident of Pangkal Penang. I think it will never reach governor.

➝ MARCH 30 THURSDAY

Have gained 1 kilo since 16th. Afraid may be water. Many men suffering oedemia [on] account [of] heavy starch diet unbalanced by other foods.

➝ MARCH 31 FRIDAY

Japanese military took over command of us from J. civilian administrators at 3 p.m. Camp Hall wherein all nationalities segregated.

⇀ APRIL 9 SUNDAY EASTER

My third Easter in prison camp. Rumors McA[rthur] reached Philippines, Germans collapsed February.

J. guard said Japanese captured Hawaii from where [they are] bombing New York.

Australia being bombed from Sumatra, Java, & New Guinea. Germans in North Africa & all will end within year when Nippons will dominate Asia & Western Hemisphere, & Germans Europe & Africa.

Move afoot [to] oust Oranje from camp administration.

Two days ago began receiving maize from Japanese. Ubi (tapioca) ration nearly ceased. Food quantity steadily decreasing. Beri beri incidence increasing, especially among middle aged & elderly. Penrice one worst example, losing control limbs. Burnside, Prior, Jeffrey also examples.

⇀ APRIL 13 THURSDAY

J's officially promised [to] give each internee F.1.50 monthly "for soap & kind." Inflation, near famine, etc. outside resulting [in] prices F.500 one bag sugar of 100 kilos, coconut oil F.80 for 4 gallon tin; rice, coconuts unpurchasable; black market chickens for 1 pair shoes, 3 or 4 chickens 1 shirt; rationed tobacco in camp 80 cents lempeng (40 grams); package cigarettes outside F.2.

However J's showing more interest [in] our welfare than ever before, inquiring & promising. But today confiscated large scales whereon we weigh all food issues to check accuracy of contractor's sales & J. rations, with words, "Japanese army honest. Always gives full weight as promised." And if not full weight it's because "there isn't enough to be given."

Yesterday began Malay lessons with Biessel.

Camp toko discontinued.

⇀ APRIL 17 MONDAY

Weighed 52 kilos today.

C. M. J. Kirk British policeman received copy [of] telegram from South Africa via Geneva & Tokyo addressed British internment camp Sumatra saying son Colijn born 28/8/42, indicating his whereabouts known. No date except day transmitted "24" no month, year.

⇀ APRIL 21 FRIDAY

Bet 50 guilders with de Raadt, E.A.P. Controleur B.B. Dept. van Binnenlandsch Bestuur, Batavia—C. that Nippon will not capitulate by October 30, 1944. If still fighting Nov. 1, 1944 I win. If capitulates by Oct. 31, I lose.

Ration squabbles continue, but committee decided [to] give certain class B workers, including hospital staff, 100 grams extra maize porridge daily 10 a.m.

→ April 22 Saturday

100 men daily now permitted outside jail for 1 hour's walking or lounging football field. 50 go 8–9 a.m. & 50 go 3–4 p.m.

→ April 30 Sunday

Nippon increased monthly cash allotment to 4.50 per man same day (27th) a Major General inspected us. Yesterday Nip. Anniversary Jimmu Tenro [?] & 11 camp officials [were] guests Commandant his house for dinner duck, chicken, brandy, sake. Nips. becoming increasingly cordial. Have promised outside hospital & removal 250 men to decrease camp crowding. Nips. gave us 2 cookies, 7 bananas & 2 ounces Arak each man yesterday & commandant attended Sat. nite concert wherein before his arrival, band played "Yanks Are Coming."

Princess Juliana's birthday but wood situation so bad, didn't eat till 3 p.m.

Nip. Commander after roll call told camp tin mining company angry because we [are] taking up some [of] their land for gardening, other purposes, demanded 25 light globes lent us last fall, by tonight. Committee apologized for taking globes, promised see his superiors Palembang next week [ ] in reprisal.

Mike Frurniet last night opened can sweet condensed milk & tonight a tin of Camel cigarettes. [Later note:] saved since 1941.

→ May 1 Monday

Nippon doctor examined many [ ] & beri beri cases, but refused [to] enter hospital so we carried sick men out to him.

→ May 2 Tuesday

Died 5:40 a.m. L. B. G. Jeffery, 53, British engineer, long time Hangkow Tientsin, beri beri.

⚊ May 4 Thursday

Yesterday Asbeck told Nippon he [was] unable [any] longer [to] control black market account men so hungry. Last night 100 bottles coco oil smuggled in. This morning a Dutch civil servant caught on garden party with 25 kilos fish, which Nippon gave kitchen. This afternoon Djambe Assistant Resident coming in from garden party caught with big fish concealed [in] clothing. Our diet now tapioca with sprinkling [of] maize breakfast & dinner. Tiffin about 13 grams rice, few vegetable leaves, fish sauce. Average weight dropped 1 kilo last month. Yesterday block leaders demanded Asbeck take vigorous policy toward Nippon over food.

⚊ May 5 Friday

Out for hour with walking party in field approximately 50 yds. Square [in] front [of] jail bounded by our gardens on two sides. Greenery, trees, & breeze pleasant. Through break in foliage a narrow strip [of] sea visible [in] distance. Although we [are] on [a] hill few hundred feet above sea level, the sea appears to slope sharply upward toward horizon, as though it were a flat, gray rising plain.

Medical report listed 69 beri beri cases last month.

⚊ May 6 Sat

Round robin letter sent Womens Camp but not allowed [to] state health conditions or mention even skin spots. Black market peanuts 15 G kilo; fish 50 G kilo.

⚊ May 13 Sat

Last evening died F. L. Llewelyn, 47, Brit electrical engineer with FMS, Palembang. T.B. after many years illness, last two acute. Suffered much but always courageous & optimistic. His last days were agony. Buried today.

Food situation graver daily, reflected in declining health [of] camp members, increasingly difficult [to] cure sores, fever, beri beri. Medicines rapidly being used up. Decided [to] ration hospital & clinic at 700 cc's fortnitely each, means 50 cc's daily for entire hospital, or about 1 cc daily carbolic ointment. Dressing job getting more difficult & takes until 12 & 1 p.m. daily despite assistance [of] D. Banks, cable & wireless man.

Wrote letter to Capt. Seki, Chief South Sumatra Internment Camps, duplicate letter of one addressed to Gov. Syonan. Seki arrived here this week, [gave] speech [to] camp members [in an] apologetical vein, assuring us Nippon [are] concerned [for] our welfare & vaguely promising better conditions, more food next month, when military administration organized & functioning.

⇀ May 14 Sun.

Medical report 4/1/43 to 3/31/44. Population 4/1/43–455; 3/31/44–730. Pop increased over 60% when moved from Palembang to Muntok. Outpatient treatments 35, 784. Patients admitted camp hosp. 339. Patients transferred Charitas first 6 months only 72, Cases dysentery & diarrhoea 305. First 6 months 151; 2nd 6 months 154. Malaria, 353; first 6–22; 2nd 6–331. Beri-beri, 88; 1st 6 nil; 2nd 6 88. Deaths, 15; 1st 6–4; 2nd 6–11. Death causes, 1st 6–heart disease, 2; cancer, 1; senility, 1; 2nd 6–heart, 2; pneumonia, 2; dysentery, 2; malaria, 2; diabetic coma, 1; intestinal obstruction, 1; cirrhosis liver, 1. Death rate per 1,000–24.6. Average weight variation per man over 12 months period, a decrease [of] 5.6 kg (11.2 pounds).

⇀ May 17 Wednesday

Resting after fever attack Monday. Mike Treurniet, clinic dresser, substituting, assisted by Banks.

Natives now permitted [to] bring food products to gate for sale, therefore small quantities ubi cookies, dried fish, peanuts, etc. coming in, but *no fruit.*

Committee also has permitted organization of black market for camp benefit.

Cat last night moved her kittens from our room to committee room, their eyes now open.

⇀ May 19, Frid

Read W. H. Hudson's "The Purple Land," story of wanderings in Uruguay or Banda Orient in 1860s & 70s.

⇀ May 21 Sunday

Two men died today: A. J. Schonzetter, 68, Dutch planter; & J. Schmidt, 60, German-Dutch small planter & Mohammedan, who 2 yrs. ago was suspected [of] making hole in wall. Schmidt was Catholic in youth but turned Mohammedan. Fr. Elling conditionally absolved & annointed while S. unconscious.

Schonzetter died 1:40 p.m. pneumonia; Schmidt, 5:40 p.m.

N. today announced rice ration doubled next week, & 210 people coming Pangkal Penang end May.

Returned to work today after a week off because of fever. But attack a mild one & no high temperatures.

⟶ May 28 Sunday

Entire hospital moved next door to tin mining coolie quarters. Holderness died dysentery 11:10 a.m.

⟶ May 30 Tuesday

Pangkal Penang internees [later note: 200 skeletons] arrived. Spandan died during tiffin, about 1 p.m.

⟶ June 11 Sunday

Five deaths since June 1—H. C. Schroder, 48, cerebral malaria 6/1, W. J. Ockhuysen, 52, D. Police, dysentery & beri beri, 6/6, R. W. Morris, 40, British planter, beri-beri 6/8, F. Fletcher, British planter, myocarditis & beri-beri, H. Zimmerman, 42, British clerk, beri-beri 6:45 a.m. today, my shorthand teacher.

My birthday uneventful. Monday 6/5 W. resigned after scurrilous gossip from certain quarters & anti-hosp[ital] attack by Bl 10 leader Schol in Blk. Leaders' meeting Sat. which I believe resulted from movement begun by Oosten or B.P.M. leaders against hospital some time ago. Tues. nite I talked with Oosten, accusing him of being motivating force [behind] this, [as] well [a]s other camp changes. He denied hospital episode, admitted some others & made some good suggestions concerning hospital reorganization & we parted amicably. I also interviewed Bishop & generally acted as compromiser, bringing opposing factions together.

Eric German joined staff as dresser last Saturday. 6/9 got another dresser, Indo-European Rollofsma.

Dressing job grows daily, occupying us to 1 & 1:30 p.m. daily & again from 4 p.m. to 5 or 6 p.m. Trelemiet laid up since 1st day here & I wonder if he's lost his spirit.

I began atebrine course 6/9 Frid night with 2 pills. Will take 2 each Friday night & 1 each Saturday nite henceforth. West gave me 80, sufficient until 1/1/45.

Zimmerman 7th beri-beri death & I expect many more.

My money going fast. Am on last 100 G & lent 60 of it to West.

5 men jailed this week when caught outside fence or coming through fence early morning, presumably after nite out black marketing or frolicking. Much easier [to] get out now since tin mining surrounded only by wire fence & gate through wall into jail open until 10 p.m. & opened again 4 a.m. 2 men caught & tied up, one [at the] beginning [of the] week & other tonight, who escaped his bonds when left unguarded, whereupon camp roll called. 1st man got 3 days native jail in town but fate [of] others yet unknown.

Nippon gave camp 300 liters drum oil, 100 kilos peas & some peanuts today, on Zimmerman's death.

— 6/18 SUNDAY

8th beri-beri death & youngest man yet to die when G. D. W. Roberts, 29, 4:45 p.m. 6/16 after spasms of over an hour from 7 a.m. He quieted after Prontopon injection & saltwater by mouth. Spasms similar to Morris, but Roberts continually cried loudly & hoarsely, body rigid, eyeballs turned sharply down & lids drawn back, mouth twisted, giving ghastly cast to face. Throat muscles taut, breathing cramped. He [was] conscious throughout spasms, but slid into coma several hours later & never came out—which reminds me that of all men who've died in our hospital, only one, Llewellyn, was conscious shortly before the end & fully aware he was about to go. Others, except heart attack victims, in apparent good health when seized, were unconscious from 8 to 24 & 48 hours before death & usually slid into death without realizing seriousness [of] their case. On other hand, a few came into hospital no serious cases but convinced they [were] going [to] die—and eventually they invariably did. A man's spirit certainly plays a large part in whether he lives or dies—the quitter always losing, the fighter frequently fighting his way back to life & health.

Kempetai invaded camp [with the] result [that] men [were] caught outside & gates between camp closed 11 a.m. 6/19, isolating both. Only workers under guard & in groups permitted [to] move between camps. Camp store closed, thus shutting off even tobacco supplies. Only camp rations & small amount extra food for hospital sick admitted. Men jailed still unheard of. Jockey Bagby who [was] tied up & escaped later, upsetting guard taken from camp Monday morning but allowed [to] return in afternoon. Kempetai left camp Friday to everyone's relief including Nippon Commmander, but gates still shut, handicapping greatly camp activities &

complicating hospital hot water situation which [is] already bad because of distance from boiler & shortage of firewood.

Apparently no motorized transport [of] any sort hereabouts now.

During Roberts' funeral walkers noted fresh air raid shelters dug, barbed wire & sandbagged barriers surrounding house which previously [housed] radio transmitter, etc. All available land planted in ubi kajoe or other vegetables, indicating more stringent food conditions. Our rations daily decreasing.

Got another dresser, Brother Everdining, whom I'm training—making six men in all—Mike Treurniet, R. Banks, Eric German, Rollofsma, Everdining & I.

I suffered fever attack Friday p.m. & Mike returned [to] work Saturday. This attack mild—39.4 peak & no fever today, also no shivers, so I'm sure it has been thrown off & I'm okay. Also convinced that fever relapse follows [a] period [of] exhausting work & strikes when body utterly tired, resistance low.

Hospital staff increased by addition [of] more priests, brothers, also Betenhausen, English speaking Dutch Block leader joined staff in executive capacity, [as a] result [of] demands [of] Oosten & Dutch sector camp. Oosten wanted Schaeffer, but Dr. West preferred Betenhausen since Schaeffer already thrice declined invitations [to] work [in] hospital His job supposedly Hospital Superintendent.

Capt. Seki arrived this afternoon, inspected hospital this evening.

— 6/19 Mon.

Gates between camp opened & Seki [gave a] speech [to] camp, saying our prospects were more work, less food. He [is] sorry for old men & sick, but Nippons didn't start war. Ended by advising us not to get sick, to which camp members responded with derisive laughter, whereupon interpreter exploded, shouting tirade [of] abuse which Asbek & Hammett did not translate. Later, Gunsol Sergeant Tokin, Camp Commmandant demand[ed] 200 men daily for new gardening work, saying we must work or starve since no food from Palembang. Local food situation serious. Also that women arriving shortly. Seki said this [is] a theater of war with possibility of action & that soldiers must come first in food consideration. We [are] not fighting, therefore must [be] thankful.

⌐ 6/23

12 men jailed [for] blackmarketing released, returned [to] camp Tuesday night, gaunt, thin, slept [on] stone floor sans clothing, mats, but never questioned.

Tues, 6/21 borrowed 100 guilders from Bishop & 186 guilders from Koot. Bishop's loan even money & Koot's at exchange F.186 for $1. I gave letter of acceptance on United Press for American dollars gold $100 to each. So I must repay $20 D gold after war. Bishop's loan I used to finance Kongsee as Dr. West, Harrison, Earl Thompson & I for buying food stock to save against emergency. Each man took $20 share payable to me after war. Dr. West gave me his "I.O.U." for $80 [on] behalf of himself & others. I will finance Germann for about $22.50 for 10 kilos beans, peas, soya beans, same as us. We [are] stocking 5.2 kilos each divided into brown beans, green peas (katjang hsidjau) & soya beans (katjang kedeleh). Each man also gets 1 bottle palm oil to stock.

The 186 G loan will be my emergency fund not touchable unless acutely needed—kept preferably for use after release.

Wrote letter in Malay & English to Capt. Seki, which Van Asbek & Hammett agreed to give him at their scheduled official interview which will be interpreted by Nippon speaking Dutch Pangkal Penang postmaster, den Voorden.

Pangkal Penang men this week killed & ate our three camp cats! This morning hide & head of mother cat found in septic tank. Mother & son we lavished our food, even pork fat, on in Boekit Besar camp. Wilson & I spent many restless nights keeping kitten in room, satisfying prowling, apprehensive mother—all for [the] sake of keeping rats & mice down. Now some selfish, ravenous wolves who are hungrier than anyone else in camp, kill them. Since Penang personnel came here thefts of clothing, etc. sharply increased.

Loans, letters, etc. kept me busy all week, during which I have not worked hospital, taking week off account [of] fever last Thursday & Friday. Hit 39.4 Friday p.m., so laid off. However my fever now seems under control of aldrine, but latent, ready [to] flare up when [I] become physically dog tired several days [in] succession.

⌐ 6/25 SUNDAY

Died 1:25 p.m. T. H. (Flash) Roberts, 38, British seaman, beri-beri— 9th beri-beri victim. I sat beside him last few hours, until end. Remarkable how all beri-beri suddenly lose [their] mind & go into spasms several hours before end. Last few cases seized early morning, 6 to 8 a.m. & died [in the] afternoon.

Also dying tonight are 2 others [of] beri-beri, one the oldest camp member, veteran Dutch soldier, de Groot, who tonight, in his slow, dry, perfectly enunciated Malay, told West, "Doctor, I'm already finished. Soon I will be a dead man. Thank you very much (for care)." West gave him a shot of morphine to ease his breathing pains.

Nippon Major inspected camp today.

I resumed work today after a week's rest.

Many men in camp selling food, to get money to buy odd bits of fish, oebi cakes, etc., but to great danger [to their] own health. Latest beri-beri deaths were of men who long had sold their rice or entire meal in order buy tobacco, cakes, etc.

⇀ 7/2 JULY

Dutchman dying [of] beri-beri in hospital worships money more than his life, although already financially secure, he has been *selling—or trying to sell—Vitamin B* tablets, [the] very things which might have saved his life. Now it may be too late. Another man, an Englishman, has been selling his food so long & so successfully he was able to pay his kitchen fund which he did in order to increase his toko (camp store) spending power & buy bits of fish, prawns, etc. He also has phobia against coming into hospital.

This week N. K. P. M. (Standard Oil) James named camp labor controller & B. P. M. (Shell) de Bruyn named camp police officer.

Capt. Seki replied to camp requests largely in negative, but promised, on [his] own authority, to supply more ubi to supplement camp ration. This ubi he promised would not mean reduction in rice ration. 2,000 kilos ubi arrived few days later & rice ration [was] promptly reduced.

V. Asbek failed [to] give Seki my letter, but took me to [the] interpreter who swore my previous letter [had been] sent to Tokyo & promised [to] give this one [to] Seki.

Six deaths this week, 4 beri-beri, 1 dysentery, & 1 heart disease, making 30 deaths since moving to Muntok, 45 total. Deaths: A. J. Taylor, 50, British planter 6/26, beri-beri, A. N. Saybourne, 54, British Cable & Wireless, heart failure following beri-beri, & B. de Groot, 72, Dutch soldier veteran, both 6/28, & thus causing our first double funeral; Ch. F. Ridder, 48, Dutch, TB & dysentery 6/29; F. A. Schylenburch, 60, Dutch, heart disease 6/29; M. F. Enright, 64, New Zealand miner, 6/30.

Enright calmest man yet to die. A Catholic, he wanted to have ample forewarning, so, several days previously I advised it & he was warned. The morning of the 30th he looked nearly finished, but his mind was clear. He received last sacraments, gave instructions regarding his effects & said he was ready to go. Spoke as matter of factly as if he were merely moving into the next ward. He died about 6:30 p.m.

⟶ July 16 Sunday

10 deaths so far this month, whereof 7 beri-beri: W. Blom, 60, cerebral malaria; H. van Geel, 44, dysentery & beri-beri; W. J. J. Karstel, 55, dysentery & beri-beri; F. A. D. Lang, 57, pulmonary TB; B. A. Bruins, 43, beri-beri; Boswell, F. V., 51, beri-beri; Fisscher, C. J., 47, beri-beri; Wiegand, B. B., 53, beri-beri; Stork, B. H., 48, dysentery & beri-beri. All but Blom, Bruins & Boswell were of Pangkal Penang group. Stork was chief engineer Bangka Tin, big job. He partially lost his mind in Pangkal Penang jail & while here was subject to many hallucinations. Bruins was civil servant of Djambe district. He was food seller & the man who would sell Vitamin B tablets when dying of beri-beri. Total deaths now 55, whereof 40 in Muntok.

Germann & I celebrated July 4 with pleasant dinner of brown beans & Bully Beef, coconut milk for coffee & beans & ubi-coconut cakes. Later in the week, West, Harrison, Earl Thompson & I gave Kendall a dinner, at which McKern was also a guest, on [the] occasion [of] Kendall's official retirement from hospital staff & move into Ward B, old men's ward. Kendall, a big, bluff, white haired, red-faced British planter of some 60-odd years who once was Hospital Ward Master [at] Clumay, & poor sighted, he was good worker, but bored us to tears with continual, interminable reminiscences of planting & World War I. However, we all liked him & his good spirit & good will. Dinner included nayi goreng, fried salt fish, coconut-ubi cookies, pineapple stew, Japanese army cigarettes & glass of arak (coconut wine) each. The two dinners were first time since our feed last Thanksgiving that I have really eaten my fill. We are continually hungry now, a perpetual inner gnawing only possible to forget if so mentally occupied the hunger pangs are temporarily forgotten.

I've been busy writing letters & telegrams which I hope to get permission to send. Also read T. E. Lawrence's "Seven Pillars of Wisdom," a somewhat monumental work, albeit fascinating. His frequent introspection & analysis of self & surrounding persons, religions & customs, were far more interesting to me than the real action of the successful revolt, which climaxed in capture of Damascus from Turks while Lawrence was still in his 30th year of age.

My hardest personal battle [in] recent years has been with tobacco, which I vowed never [to] touch again, but which resolves [have been] broken numerous times, including July 4 to 15, wherein I smoked considerably. Today I'm beginning a new tobaccoless period & hope to make it permanent. Non-smoking is doubly difficult now that we are perpetually hungry—a cigarette lessens the ache. However, I am determined to persevere. If I lose this fight I lose not only my own powers of self-discipline & respect, but break a sacred vow permanently. One of the psychological factors involved is the lack of a definite time period of abstinence. A lifetime is too vague. When I quit in normal life, I did so for specified periods, usually 3 or 6 months & stuck to it, never breaking down once, but resuming at the end of the period. So this time I have set a time limit of 6 months from today—to Jan. 16, 1945, when I will renew for another 6, etc. [Later note: Priest dispensed me from this vow, substituting daily litany Blessed Virgin Mary, August 6, 1944.]

─ JULY 19, WEDNESDAY

Politics interesting camp with Aug. 1 election [of] Camp Committee nearing. Opposition circulated petition calling for new committee of 5 men to be named by petition sponsors of camp approved by voting confidence in sponsors who are Van Roy, domestic troop, Limberg; A. N. Colijn, Camp Committee tardily countered with letter recommending 7 man committee.

Of late, camp administration problem growing more serious because of rift between Resident Oranje & oil magnate Oosten. Various attempts [to] bring them together failed. On my own initiative & M.M.'s recommendation, I talked [to] both men privately—urged Oosten [to] come into open, take place [on] Camp Committee & meet Oranje. Oosten agreed. I then got Oranje to agree to meet Oosten. Yesterday they did & after[wards] thanked me profusely for effecting rapprochement. However, I trust neither of them—Oranje being too weak to resist Oosten & fearing Nips; Oosten being totally unscrupulous & in my opinion planning [to] get complete control [of] camp, especially hospital & toko, so he will [be] able [to] control [the] stock [of] food, medicine for sole benefit B.P.M., so that, when liberation comes, he can wire London, "I'm here, with my men in good

health & ready immediately [to] begin rebuilding B.P.M. in East Indies."
I hope I am wrong in my suspicions, but we at hospital are planning ac-
cordingly. Oosten told Oranje & me he intends ousting Everstien as toko
chief & that toko will be test case of his strength on committee [of] which
he thinks, & probably correctly, he will [be] chairman if elected. Van Roy
sponsors immediately after Oranje & Oosten conference, named their candidates as Oosten chairman, Van Hoek, Pangkal Penang camp leader & no.
2 in Bangka in British Rep. Hammett, planter Domestic & Government
Civil Servant who coinspector teacher Vander Wetering.

Report today Nip. Suzuki said Allied landing Cheribon.

Death is continuing with former British camp leader W. Penrice dying
[of] beri-beri; oil man Marenius died 3 a.m. today & Brother Superior Ricardus received last rites [this] morning. Ricardus's mind clear & he [was]
cheerful, even joking with me about getting him a Doerian [?]!

— July 24 Monday

At home today is Utah's biggest state holiday: Mormondom's coming
to Great Salt Lake. But here in Muntok Internment Camp it was only another day of death—taken casually in stride—and politics. Deaths are now
64, of which 49 in Muntok. Politics taking on more sinister complexion
as I piece together bits of evidence showing Oosten's hand more plainly
in hospital grab attempt. I've spotted his finger man on our staff, whom I
thought well of & trustworthy & anti-Oosten.

Today's death a remarkable case of deathbed conversion & repentance.
T. J. Kuh [?], 54, fallen away Dutch Catholic, [was] dying [of] beri-beri.
Learning he was an R.C. & had recently declined ministrations of a priest,
I spoke to him about 10 a.m., warning him he was seriously ill & should
settle his affairs spiritual & temporal. He declined to call a priest. Later,
while talking with Dr. West, he requested West to "keep the brothers &
pastors away from me. They bother me—don't feel like talking." He still
later flatly refused to talk with Father Alberts. While we were eating tiffin
about 2 p.m., he suddenly called for Dr. West, asked if he were beyond
hope, & on being told yes, told West to be his local executor—taking all
his possessions to dispose of as West saw fit because he, Kuh, didn't trust
the Camp Committee. West called in Bettenhausen as witness. Kuh's last
request of West then was [for] West [to] put Kuh's rosary in the coffin with
him. About 2:40 p.m. Kuh suddenly sent for Fr. Alberts, made his confession, received Extreme Unction, and, while Fr. Alberts was pronouncing

the last words of the service, Kuh died. While all this was transpiring a Chinese workman was busy outside the fence building a coffin. He completed it just in time. Kuh, dripping water & serum from his corpse & leaking from the coffin, was buried within an hour.

Tonight—returning to politics-West & Hammett will decide whether I am to be candidate for hospital wing commander under new plan of 5 wing commanders to govern camp [in] conjunction with Committee. Other possibility is our present Block Leader, D. C. Thompson.

This week read Alice Tisdale Hobart's "Oil for the Lamps of China," which gives a well put & accurate insight—from the foreigner's viewpoint—into the Chinese mind & custom & describes squeeze more understandably than I have read anywhere before.

[Later note: Decision favored Thompson as wing Com.]

— JULY 28 FRIDAY

Three deaths today, setting new camp record for 24 hours. Two dysentery & beri-beri cases, Dutchmen W. Schoe, 44, B.P.M. driller, who [was] sick only [a] week, lacked spirit to fight. When left Java 2 1/2 years ago, told friend, "I'll die just before victory (Allied)" & when entered hospital, altho not seriously ill, told friends, "I'll never come back to that block (of which he [was] Block Leader 10)." Kasteren died shortly after confession 1st time [in] 30 years. "Now I'm happy," he said. "I'm at one with my Creator."

Then death [of] R. F. L. Lanauze, 53, British Manager, Cable & Wireless, Penang, Malaya Branch, of beri-beri. He [was] so swollen [he] had to be jammed into narrow coffin & body leaked copiously.

Camp election committee chairman A. N. Wootton, Australian, resigned because political factions [were] bickering under his preferential election system, which it appears he may have designed incorrectly.

Finished Eric Linklater's "Juan in America," amusing, sometimes hilarious satire, full as usual of Linklater's refreshing description, albeit packed with rare[ly] used 4 & 5 syllable words.

Random thought:—Of all things I missed most acutely after internment was a watch. I've lived by the clock so long, its command insisted on guiding my daily life even in jail. And although I still want to know the time continuously, the sharpness of the desire is dulling, fading almost imperceptibly into mere interest instead of restless annoyance at having to visit the hospital clock frequently.

⇀ July 31 Monday

Camp Committee election results British Hammett 95, Drysdale 48, Dutch—Oosten 323, Vorstman 193, Dorrestien 189, Wetering 150, James 135, Broerse 100, Fanoy 58: electing Hammett & Oosten, eliminating Broerse & Fanoy, forcing runoff election of Vorstman, Dorrestien, Wetering & James.

⇀ Aug 1 Tues

2nd election results—Vorstman 232, V. D. Wetering & Dorrestien 187 each, James 100. Wetering & Dorrestien tossed coin to decide tie, Wetering winning. Committee now: W. H. Oosten, B.P.M. oil magnate; A. van Hook, 58, No. 2 Bangka Tin; Vorstman, 40 Controleur Palembang Residency; J. R. vander Wetering, 37, government inspector schools & J. H. G. Hammett, 38, Secretary to Resident Negeri Sembilan, F.M.S. making Oosten only non- government man on Committee—if he accepts to serve on it in view [of] its present set-up. If not, he completely will lose face.

Today two men in hospital [were] caught selling food to outsiders. Another man violently ill after eating smuggled black market cookies—and he on a soft rice diet!

Yesterday morning I gave to Camp Commandant Serg.-Maj. Tokin a letter to Captain Seki requesting permission to send to proper authorities an application for transfer to Manila, Shanghai, or Bandoeng; & three telegrams, one to Hori in Tokyo, & 2 to International Red Cross for forwarding to A.P. & my home, respectively. All these letters & telegrams written in Nippon go by Scheuerman.

⇀ Aug. 4 Friday

Oosten & other elected committee members took office, elected Oosten chairman & Hammett vice-chairman, selected van Asbek [to] continue as Camp Liason Officer with Nipponese.

Sergeant Tokin yesterday returned my letters to Van Asbek saying Capt. Seki refused [to] accept them, after reading them was "a little angry" & declared he could not be bothered with such things.

Committee wrote Seki very strong letter directly blaming Nips for camp deaths due [to] malnutrition. Strongest letter yet.

Two more died—Aug. 2—C. D. Campbell, 54, planter, & W. A. Nesfield, 53, British Ship officer. Campbell of dysentery & beri-beri, & Nesfield latent beri-beri.

⚊ Aug 6 Sunday

Another death today [ ] Dutch tin miner M. J. Tesser, 44, dysentery & beri-beri.

Dysentery epidemic sweeping camp, 45 cases total now & West strenuously [making] effort [to] get isolation hospital outside camp to remove cases & check spread. Greatest number [of] cases yet in hospital—126 today, with more needing admission.

Mike Truerniet's spirit seems waning, so gave him 2 weeks vacation from dressing job which adds yet more to our load.

⚊ Aug 13 Sunday

Camp Wing Commanders elected yesterday, F. Drysdale, 46, Scotch Engineer & Businessman Malaya for Blocks 1, 2, & 3; D. Barnaud-Gerrens, 34, Dutch B.P.M., Blocks 4, 5, 6, & 7; R. A. H. Beissel von Gymnich, 38, Dutch Civil Servant, Blocks 8, 9, 10, & 11; J. J. Prins, 35, Banka tin miner, Perak, Malaya, Hospital. New Committee appointed as secretary H. Pomes, 39, Banka Tin.

Nips gave us new isolation hospital, capacity 65 for dysentery & TB cases, 1/2 mile from here, to be completely staffed and managed by priests of Block 6, with Father A. Hermelink as superintendent & Dr. A. P. A. Boerma, 32.

⚊ Aug 17 Thursday

Reliably—Allies France crossed Siegfried Line, Russians [ ] Poland close German frontier: persistent unconfirmed: Java & Borneo recaptured.

Locally we are in air raid alarm period [with] blackouts nightly. Today real alarm caused much apprehension among Nips & Hihos & hurrying up of double funeral party. Natives took to shelters.

R. H. Prior, 60, picturesque character of Palembang Jail dysentery days, died 8/15, 11 p.m. [of] beri-beri. He appeared aware of his danger, before losing senses completely, & took it quite matter of factly. Today 2 more deaths, bringing total to 80, of which 40 British & 40 Dutch. Of 46 beri-beri deaths, 11 were [ ] or atrophic beri-beri & remainder hydropic or wet cases, of which 7 developed hydropic necrosis of subcutaneous tissues resulting [in] general toxemia.

⚊ Aug. 20 Sunday

Have read several good books recently: Duff Cooper's biography of Talleyrand; "Autobiography of Benvenuto Cellini"; Sinclair Lewis's "Work of Art." But reading standard dropped today, when for lack of anything else, read Charles Setzer's "Gone North," a thriller of the North—hack writing. I'm fed up with such fare and can find enjoyment only in well written, meaty works.

Two deaths today, both Dutchmen 61 & 43 years respectively. Latter, B.P.M. group leader Pladjoe camp, put up good fight until yesterday when [he] gave up, begged injections to end his life & suffering. The older man, contrarily, fought to [the] last despite real agony—days of violent hiccoughing. He confessed & received sacraments for first time since youth, died happily & gamely, insisting on going to W.C. & refusing bedpan to the last. Because of B.P.M. pressure, attention lavished on P. H. deJong, 43, in vain. T. J. von Balgooy, 61, died without special help of extra eggs of injections or attention, but he died like a man. The other probably too tired of fighting with no spiritual background, lacked the most essential thing of all.

⤙ Aug. 25 Friday

Finished Robert Penn Warren's "Night Rider."

Two deaths today, Dutch Pangkal Penangers—beri-beri & dysentery. Beri-beri Dutch deaths now 44 to British 40 & will always probably remain ahead because of more material "to draw from"—especially from among Pangkal Penang group of long undernourished & borderline men. British population in camp now 158.

⤙ Aug 27 Sunday

New note in the ludicrous: grown men, government, business & planting tycoons line up to receive three roasted peanuts each, "seconds" on distribution of 20 grams per man for 13 cents.

Chief camp duty officer, Doef, resigned because of ill health after Oosten severely censured him before Committee. "Poor Doef," Oosten said to me today, "he got sick."

⤙ Sept. 1, 1944

Camp feasted yesterday—Queen Wilhelmina's birthday, 64th. Even Japanese Commandant extended his good wishes to camp on the occasion & donated a pig. By careful husbanding [of] rice & other meager supplies & by camp individual donations totalling some 400 odd guilders, a real feast eaten. Morning pop [?] extra large portion with katjang hsidjau "green peas." A large maize cake & coffee at 11. Double portion rice, plus peanuts, pork bits, sauce coconut, salt fish bits & plenty vegetable for tiffin; Nayi goreng, more nuts & coconut for dinner. Our hospital staff had "internal rewards" which I & many others [were] unable to eat. Our stomachs have shrunk so much that an amount of food which merely would be a comfortably large dinner in ordinary life is now an unprecedented & too large amount to consume. Outstanding is the psychological effect of such abundance. Camp morale soared, deaths & privations were forgotten. The orchestra played from 10 a.m. to 12:30 noon. Most of us sat in the moonlite until 1 or 2 a.m. this morning, too full to sleep.

A few hospital staffers drank small shot of "brandy" with Resident Oranje & smoked cigars after dinner. Oranje earlier today had spoken at the "reception" for camp officials, eulogizing hospital, drawing attention to recent political tempest, "election quarrels" & platitudinously stated Wilhelmina's birthday once more unified camp, providing atmosphere [of] brotherly love, etc.—truly remarkable what a little food can do.

Am reading "Sappers," Bulldog Drummond stories, also exchanging English for Malay practice with Father Bakker, our choir leader, my lessons being translating story of New Testament into English from simple Malay version.

August deaths totalled 21.

Entire camp given Typhus A & B inoculations today. Japanese gave serum. 2nd injection Sept. 7. I got certificate from Doctor G. F. West for inoculation for typhoid, paratyphoid A & B, cholera, plague, dysentery, & cerebro-spinal fever vaccine.

Recent reading includes third reading of Allen's "Only Yesterday"; also Patrick MacGill's "The Great Priest."

⇀ SEPT 7

Bought 3 ½ kilos peanuts for 35 guilders from West for resale, effort make little profit.

⇀ SEPT 11 MONDAY

Finished 3rd reading "Only Yesterday." Read Robert Service's "The Roughneck," first I've read of his prose, & am now beginning Eric Linklater's "Poet's Pub."

Today wrote two postcards, one home & one to Mary Bell. Cards limited to 50 words in English, Malay, or Japanese; only blue or black ink—no other colors allowed for some unknown reason, possibly prevent code; &

confined to three subjects—for which title in Malay & space allotted, viz.: 1. Kesehatan, or condition of health, 2, Kehidoepan, or living conditions, & 3. Lain-lain, or other particulars. My card home said, "Sept. 10, 1944, Dear Mother & Dad: I am safe, health good, weight normal. (2) living comfortably in pleasant, warm climate. Need nothing from home. (3) Hope you received previous postcards. Have not heard from you. Love to you, Jean, Gertrude, Paul, Jean Francis. God bless you. Son W.H.M., Jr."

Card to Mary said: "Sept. 11, 1944. Dear Mary, Despite occasional malaria, my health continues good. Still weigh 115 pound. (2) Am working Camp Hospital, living comfortably under circumstances. (3) Sent you telegram & three previous cards. Tell Mother, Jean, Gertrude I'm okay, and still have Bill's prayer book. Love, Mac W.H.M., Jr."

Ward B, or old men's ward, this day moved across Pendopo to other side of the square, in order [to] provide more room for hospital patients.

Due to wet & insufficient firewood we had only two meals today—Breakfast pop & 3:30 p.m. dinner. However, gap broken by midday coffee & handful roasted peanuts.

I spent 22 guilders in August. Must reduce or I'll soon be broke.

Letter from Palambang Resident A. Oranje to Dr. G. F. West…Head Camp Medical Dept. Muntok Internment Camp, Sept. 4, 1944

Dear Dr. West:

I feel it my duty to express my gratitude to you and all members of the hospital staff, who assist in whatever respect in nursing treatment & general care for the patients for the food & kind treatment which I received during my stay in hospital for the period 6th August–2nd September.

Not everyone expresses his thankfulness on the occasion of his departure, but I assure you that most patients in hospital are full of praise for the care experienced. Everyone who realizes under which circumstances the work has been achieved & how much good work is being done "con amore."

My desire is that everybody be & shall remain fully convinced hereof, I for one shall not easily forget this.

I am handing a copy of this letter (together with a translation in Dutch) to the Camp Management for their information.

Yours faithfully, A. Oranje, Resident van Palembang.

— SEPT. 15

One year ago tonight we were feverishly preparing to move camp—we knew not where.

And today another move is scheduled, not the camp, only one individual, but that individual—Dr. G. F. West—has become during our internment a stalwart institution, a bulwark of the British community against Dutch oppression & a man who has exercised a great influence for good of the camp in general. He has kept the hospital from becoming a political football or a B.P.M. monopoly. He has done his best for the down & out. His barbed tongue & brusque manner have made enemies, but now that he is leaving I think most of the enemies—especially the British—realize how much good he has done. Yesterday the new Japanese camp commandant arrived & took over from Sergeant Tokin, who informed West the doctor must go to Palembang, at Capt. Seki's orders, to work. We know not where or under what circumstances but believe it will be in some military hospital. West is a Colonel in British Medical Corps & was wounded in Malaya—losing two fingers & suffering severe leg wound. Nips said 3 European doctors will come here from Pangkal Penang to work in hospital. The new Commandant is a bull necked, square-jawed, 1st class sergeant serving in medical side of J. army. May signify further camp & hospital changes—having a medical officer in charge of camp.

Although I hope I'm wrong, I fear Oosten & the B.P.M. will attempt to seize hospital control for benefit of B.P.M. Oosten has never shown the slightest interest in any sick men outside the B.P.M. & is doing his best to preserve "his boys" so they'll be able to start work immediately upon release. He now, through Jussenbrook & B.P.M. Eurasians, completely controls the kitchen, as well as the work parties, has emasculated the camp toko (store) & is proceeding with dictatorial high hand to run the camp as though it was a B.P.M. outfit & the men were serfs to do his bidding. He has disappointed me greatly—both as a man & as an executive. Undoubtedly he is a man of great ability or he would never have risen to his high position. But he is a bull with cunning. Not a leader with understanding, tolerance, or tact. I & others have caught him in so many subterfuges, rank lies & double dealings, I can plan absolutely no reliance on his word. Until now—and presumably for a great deal of his life—he has preferred to work behind the scenes—getting information from his spies, pulling the proper strings & ruthlessly carving out of his company & life—for his company is his life—all who in any way obstruct or displease him or who may not act according to his purpose. His devious methods have become so much a part of him that I believe he is utterly unable to think or act in any other way. He cannot be sincere. Maybe I have grossly misjudged him. I hope so.

But this estimate herein is my opinion now—a far different one from 2½ years ago in South Sumatran jungles.

This day of beri-beri died Bill Tickle, a jovial Britisher of 37, likeable, big-hearted & game. Hard luck dogged him ever since his internment—spots, boils, hernia, lame knee from old football injury, fever, dysentery, & finally beri-beri. As he hovered on the border of semi-consciousness this morning, his lips writhed the now too familiar, open-mouthed ghastly beri-beri smile, he held my hand and said, "Oh Mac, what a fool I've been"! I wonder what he meant & if he knew he was dying. They were his last intelligible words to me.

⟶ SEPT 17, 1944 SUNDAY

Last night we held our last "Kongsie" party together for Dr. West. He, Harrison, Earl, Thompson, Matheson, Betenhausen & myself ate one of tastiest dinners yet. Earl, assisted by Quinn, cooked it in new hospital kitchen, Harrison printed an amusing Irish menu complete with harp, & we ate poached egg on spinach-like vegetable, nayi goreng & ikan pede (a small fish), a pudding of peanuts & peas ground—very good; Campbell's Cream of Chicken soup—from a precious hoarded tin—fried tempe, banana, coffee & arak kept from last March & mellow. Spent most [enjoyable?] evening.

Today Camp Committee tendered West rather elaborate dinner—nayi goreng & delicious sambals, light beans, prawns, Nip cigarettes, cigars, bananas & speeches by Chairman Oosten, Resident Oranje, British Committeeman Hammett, Hospital Harrison & lastly West, whose emotion plainly evident in his voice. Oosten's words were polished, clever, amusing, but too much Shakespeare & the hand of his tutor Curran-Sharpe. Not up to his own original & effective style. Oranje was emotionally sincere & lavish with his praise of West & said that whereas once before (West's jail birthday dinner, 1943) Oosten cleverly paraphrased Kipling's East is East, etc., but that tonight East (Oosten) & West had met & were together—today West & *Orange*, the House of Orange as represented by the Resident of Palembang had met & Orange would be ever grateful. Harrison skillfully delineated West's character—bad as well as good points—pointedly stressed West's program of impartiality & urged its continuance & pledged loyalty of hospital staff to West's successor, Boerma. Boerma briefly replied, Hammett expressed gratitude & West paid loyal & sincere tribute to his staff, not because a few staff members were present, but because he meant it &

for the benefit of the Committee in general & Oosten in particular. He urged continuance of present staff & policy.

Finished first column of Eric Locke's "Salute to Freedom," an absorbing & knowledgeable story of Australian ranch—or station—life.

— Sept 18 Monday

Entire hospital staff noon today special tiffin for Dr. West, followed by a few short speeches & marked by lumpy throats—especially in West's when he bid us formal farewell, traced the history of our hospital, enumerating veteran staff members, beginning with Harrison, in this same building in Feb. '42 when wounded & dying survivors of Bangka Straits were jammed in here with men & women refugees. I was the second member—in Palembang jail when, West said, "Mac began his study of the human form by painting Palembang bottoms."

No mention of Allen, who long since has dropped from our midst, alienated himself from us & in fact been anti-hospital, firing futile sour grapes pot shots from his clinic sancture [sanctuary]. I wonder what his thoughts [are] these days?

Last night died the camp's "Trader Horn," tall, cadaverous [blank spaces] Meister, 47, Dutch Borneo Trading Co. man. Meister was the camp's biggest barter man, even doing a large business in food, even brokering meals of men willing to sell their food—(and died as a result)—for money. He also loaned money, guilders repayable in American dollars at $4^1/2$ times the amount borrowed. A loan of 100 guilders must be repaid by 250 *American dollars* after war. Col—borrowed such an amount, signed a note but received only 506 down & was to collect the rest this week. But Meister died. Because M. had a great amount of other men's belongings in his possession for sale, Camp Committee appointed 2 trusty men to guard his bunk quarters immediately [after] he died, and luckily, for there was a great rush scramble to get at his stuff. Early this morning C. went to Oosten & said he had to get at Meister's papers before Committee opened them. Then the story came out. "Are you mad?" Oosten, his former best friend & life companion asked. "You, a lawyer, expect to break into a dead man's private papers after the Committee has formally taken over his estate for administration?" More & more every day does C's nickname of "Mad Jack" fit him. To what depths indeed have the mighty fallen.

An indication of Oosten's change of front vis-à-vis hospital shown today when he refused Boerma's request to bring Senenhausen into hospital staff with him. Oosten even said Senenhausen must leave his present quarters in the Clinic, where he lived with B. & Hollweg, & return to the block. What a come down for S. He was given enough rope & hanged himself despite plenty of warning. And when he was O's fair-haired boy & even hospital representative at block leaders meetings.

Today I wrote a letter to West of appreciation & advice, for him to open when he arrives at his destination. I hope it is read in the spirit of goodwill [in which] it was written & that the advice accomplishes some purpose.

⌐ SEPT 19 TUESDAY

Many letters & cards received by camp members from Holland, Britain, Australia, South Africa, Scotland & even one from Jerusalem & Vancouver, B.C. all mailed over period from Oct. '42 to March '43. Christie's letter said his card, mailed Palembang 3/14/42 received Vancouver 3/15/43. Nothing from America for Germann & me. Some men received 12 letters.

Last night read Somerset Maugham's "Moon & Sixpence."

⌐ SEPT 22 FRIDAY

Finished Book II "Salute to Freedom."

Second youngest man to die beri-beri, W. Keizer, 34, Dutch lighter (ship) man went this morning, a game, cheerful, likeable fellow, always appreciative of our nursing, he suffered much for months, fever, serious bed sore which I months ago thought would kill him, dysentery & finally beri-beri. He knew he was almost sure to die, but fought on, smiling to the end. I spent two hours dressing & easing his position right before he died. His agony [was] intense, so Dr. West gave him shot [of] morphine to ease pain while we worked on him. I got him a Nip cigarette, his first real one for [a] long, long time, & told him to smoke it before he went to sleep—from which I knew he would never awaken. He smoked it gratefully, deeply, thanked us all, sank into unconsciousness & died 12 hours later, without recovering consciousness.

Sold peanuts for $32.50, plus 200 grams @2, suffering loss account ½ kilo short weight, but Doc big-heartedly paid ½ loss because of short weight. I bought them from him, but he was shorted too in deal.

⌐ SEPT. 26, '44 TUESDAY

Dr. West left today before dawn, ostensibly for Palembang & work in military hospital. He gave me 40 stebrine [?] tablets before he left, to fill out this year, & to Harrison gave 2 months supply for Harrison, Earl & me, which should keep us free of fever until April. I gave West my 35 American bill as a parting gift. He previously bought my last small Travelers Check for $20, for 37.50 guilders. Now have left only the $250 Travelers Check draft. Am spending between 15 and 20 guilders monthly—mostly for tempe katchora hidjan (green peas) & occasional fish. Hope we get out before my money ends for the end might mean beri-beri.

➤ Oct. 1 Sunday

Sick in camp today 371 (of which 131 in hospital) or 41% [of] camp's 851 population.

Japanese refused [to] provide extra food for workers despite increasing inability [of] workers [to] carry on [on] such short rations. Available workers decreasing so rapidly camp asked J's [to] provide coolie labor, which [was] also refused. Water shortage so acute, water being carried from distant wells & camp unable [to] obtain sufficient water for tea, coffee & barely enough for cooking.

➤ Oct. 2 Monday

Rain alleviated water shortage.

➤ Oct. 5 Tuesday

R. St. G Johnston died this evening. Number [of] men in camp losing their minds—not violent, but talking irrationally, acting strangely.

224 women arrived for women's camp.

➤ Oct 6 Friday

7th death in 6 days (4 in last 24 hours)

➤ Oct. 7 Sat.

A. M. Red Cross Invalid food supplies & U.S. Army supplies received consisting [of] tinned foods & small am't soap, Vitamin Concentrates & 15,391 cigarettes—Camels, Chesterfields, Old Golds, Raleigh (no Luckies). No medicines (see inventory attached). Japs opened all paper wrapped articles, such as cigarettes, packing material, etc., & burned them, helping themselves to cigarettes at least & even opened all tins of Rose Mill

Patte [?] for some strange reason. Opened cans given to kitchen & served tonight's supper as "Sauce American." Every man in camp got 18 cigarettes. One empty package Camels bore U.S. tax free stamp May, 1943, cigs in poor condition. A Red Cross receipt which also escaped bore printing date April, '43. Camp Committee did excellent job apportioning goods, called meeting, to which I [was] invited as American, announced plan distribution, thanked Red + via me. Camp elated, especially at cigarettes. Probably will be a tremendous trade [of] goods in camp with fancy prices. Goods split [into] 6 groups for distribution, [on] account [of the] variety [of] kinds & sizes packages. Group I divided into units totaling 996—one unit per man (847 including 4 p.p. women) & remaining 149 units for hosp. stock & patients. Group II for hosp. stock & block patients. Group III general camp distribution; IV, kitchen; V children (in lieu [of] cigarettes), VI camp lottery.

Inventory:—(no. tins or packages parenthesis) Group I Pork with carrots & [ ] (223), ham & eggs (148), pork loaf (21) prem pork etc. (46) corned beef (85), Spam (pork ham) (8) salmon (74) Group II Butter (252) powdered milk (82) cocoa (8) orange juice (8) Vit ration cakes (140 cakes) bouillon powder (8 kg) ascorbic acid v.t.c, (66 packs) Rose Mill Patte (1 tin intact) dried soup powder (32 pcs.) III—Kraft cheese (82 ps) Kup Kafay (156); cigarettes, (15,391). IV—Dried prunes (78 ps) sugar lump (8½ pgs) raisins (8 pg) V Biscuits 8 ps VI grape jam (66) other jams (7) soap (150 cakes). Tins varied from 8½ to 12 ounces, pkgs from 2½ to 8 oz.

Camp received 1 drum, 200 liters palm oil, which distributed 10 ccs daily will decrease skin spots as [it] did before—we hope.

Camp telegraphed Palembang & wrote Red Cross Tokyo begging for food & medicines [on] account [of] so many deaths (4 yesterday).

With 3 men off sick, dressers working top speed 6:20 a.m. to 5 p.m. with 1 hour off for lunch—exhausting work on empty stomach. Wonder how long we can keep it up.

Today Eric Germann's birthday (31), made pleasant by cigarettes & other things, including few dried salt fish issued.

— OCT 8 SUNDAY

On general camp distribution I shared a 12 oz. tin of "Prem" sausage-like pork concentrate, which E[ric], Mike Treurniet & I will open Thanksgiving Day. Traded Fr. Nielen ½ stick camp tobacco for 10 Camels Chesterfields.

Today [at] lunch Germann & I received first & only concrete expression gratitude towards America, through us, for Red Cross goods, when food server de Raat gave us extra spoon boiled cucumbers. Altho we might have refused, seems Camp Committee might, as a gesture, might have given us leastly our choice of units. As [it] was, we had to trade in order to share together & German lost on deal.

‒ Oct. 9 Monday

Today camp general distribution of Group III—Kraft cheese & "Cup Kawfay." Each man got 1 slice spoiled & damaged cheese, chickory-like stuff. So of Am Red Cross goods I've received 4 oz. sausage, 1 thin slice cheese 1½" square & 1 cup weak coffee. Small potatoes after 2½ years waiting—not even a letter.

Exhausted after today's 10 hours dressings—119, a new record. Began 6:30 a.m., finished 5:30 p.m. with 1 hr. off for lunch occupied in 15 minutes eating & cleaning up trays & persons 45 minutes. We cannot maintain this pace on semi-starvation diet. Men near collapse & fever gripping them. Such continuous work—day after day—is bound to have serious effects as our last physical strength is exhausted. Nerve alone does not prevent beri-beri.

Last night 3 doctors arrived from Pangkal Penang—2 white Dutch & one Indonesian, the latter a surgeon named [P. E.] Lentze, this morning named chief camp medical dept., succeeding Dr. West. He is government doctor & formerly chief doctor of Bangka Tin in this island, speaks extremely little English & such rapid Dutch that Dutch speaking British find difficulty understanding him. Other two men Kramer & Hampskhuor. Boerma transferred work to caring for Pangkal Penang block.

‒ Oct 14

1 year ago today occurred first death in Muntok camp—Sir John Campbell. Today the 100th death—Br. Mathair and also 101st—Hookstra.

‒ Oct 22 Sunday

Camp today received 12,474.70 guilders (in Jap. Guilder notes) from American Red +. Japs handed it over accompanied by a piece of Cross paper, allegedly a receipt, entitled, "Grants in Aid." No written indication of Am Red Cross, but Japanese told Committee it came from American Red Cross.

Last Sunday dressers decided to ask for more men & reduce working hours to 4 daily, effective Wednesday. After considerable trouble involving Camp Labour Office, Drs. Lentze, Boerma & myself, today we got 4 men who [are] scheduled to begin tomorrow. One of them, Buy, started yesterday. We are becoming so weak physically [on] account [of] malnutrition it's impossible to carry on at the pace recently—average 105 treatments daily. Many bad cases, working 8–16 hours daily. Sickness & death increasing—20 deaths already this month, of whom this week were Palambang Burgomaster P. H. M. Hildebrand, 44, who bid against me in the Queen's birthday "horserace" auction Aug. 31, 1942; L. A. Siedel, 47, 1st officer of *Poelau Bras*, who piloted a lifeboat to Kroe in 4 days with 58 aboard, & Rev. F. G. M. van Iersel, 36, R.C. priest & one of our ward attendants, who died today 4 a.m. [of] malaria. I attended his funeral 9 a.m. acting as pall bearer ("carrier," we call it), for another man, a Dutch planter Veldhuis, who died last night. Priests carried V. Iersel's coffin to waiting truck outside jail gate, & six of us carried both coffins from truck to grave. Double funerals nowadays are commonplace. I walked into the main camp one day last week during a triple funeral & the camp seemed as silent, desolate, and sad as a lonely grave. Of 837 men here, 462 were on sick rolls yesterday (138 of them in hospital). To worsen matters, a further 15% reduction in food rations went into effect this week. If we are prisoners another year, at least 50% of us will be dead & another 25% unable to walk out. Haven't been able to study at all lately, only after 2 weeks finished a book, Maurice Hindus' "Green Worlds."

‒ Oct. 24

Today Germann & I petitioned Camp Committee for grant of 300 guilders from Red Cross gift, on grounds we are Americans & entitled to share in gift from American public to needy war prisoners. Petition coldly received.

‒ Oct 26 Thursday

Last night died four men, including K. G. A. Dohoo, 38, British civil servant in Malaya, a real gentleman & to me personally the most tragic death yet in camp. Dohoo died of malnutrition & malaria—lack of food & lack of quinine, as so many others now are dying daily. His story is the story of the British community here. Bombed, shelled, wounded, sunk in Malacca Straits, swam for life & won, landed & interned penniless, clothesless. Never had a cent except occasional infinitesimal loans in camp, uncomplaining & cheerful, tolerant, cultured—but one of those persons constitutionally inept at almost every practical aspect of living. Completely unable to successfully care for himself. Septic sores & chronic malaria, coupled with malnutrition, sapped his physical reserve until he collapsed a few days ago, was brought into hospital & died. Always active in camp life, always willing to work on many jobs, but never succeeded at any of them. He just couldn't work with his hands without spilling something, or dropping something or burning the rice. But he was [a] man other men loved because he was a genuine gentleman—heart & soul. I was with him when he died at 8:45 p.m. after 24 hours of coma. Hasseluhn & I carried him to our makeshift mortuary where were four coffins. We opened one—the wrong one, for it contained the corpse of a man who died a few hours earlier—Trompeder, head of the Camp Central Accounts Administration—who literally worked himself to death—long hours [of] unremitting toil. Later during the night 2 more men died. This afternoon the camp held its first quadruple funeral. The four coffins placed on the Pendopo before the hospital while Hasseluhn & V. Asbeck read English & Dutch services.

Today Camp Committee conferred with Capt. Seki, Commander South Sumatra Internment Camps, who [is] now permanently located here. He agreed [to] allow us to send out hunting & fishing parties, but would promise no more food.

Dressing staff reduced to 4 men today—Starkey, West, Marcus & I—& we are nearly on our last legs.

Compilation of last mail: camp received 1371 letters of which 666 [were] for living camp members, 134 for dead, 551 for persons not here, & 19 miscellaneous—for women's camp, Dr. West, & 2 for Americans from New York City. One of them addressed to W. Clark & E. E. Probstfield, F. L. Tobby & V. Madalin "New York" North Sumatra; the other to Probstfield, Kisaran, East Coast, Sumatra.

⟶ Oct. 29 Sunday

Dressers & ward attendants today put on workers' calory basis, climaxing our dressers' long fight for more food or more men. Friday nite Dr. Lentze examined me & said I had combination of spinal trouble & bronchitis & that he suspected T.B. Ordered me off dressing or other heavy work indefinitely, but permitted me [to] supervise & train dressers. Perhaps I'll get a long rest, perhaps not. [Later note: Lentze's diagnosis all wrong—just starved.] At any rate, his order cut dressers to 2 experienced & 1 new man—impossible situation & exactly what I predicted to Doctor's Committee in petition of 2 weeks ago & to Oosten nearly 2 months ago. Sat. a.m. Lentze & I visited Committee, said [it was] imperative [that] hospital get more men & extra food. By noon Committee granted extra calories on same basis [as] working party to dressers & ward attendants, latter of whom [have] long been receiving 100 grams rice extra.

Friday Committee refused G.'s & my petition for 300 guilders grant, but neither referred it to Wing Commanders or gave us written answer as we had requested. We again asked for both & I personally demanded both from Oosten Sat. a.m.

News of Allied landing Holland Sept. 18 & U.S. attack east Philippines Oct. 24 cheering camp. No details of either, however.

— Nov. 5 SUNDAY

Week's events included arrival today [of] small quantity Red Cross tinned goods, & 9 deaths, including Pastor P. J. V. Eyk, 37, another hospital staffer, who died of exhaustion & malaria, collapsing suddenly 10 a.m. & dying 11:20 a.m. in Block X, surrounded by priests & brothers reciting the Holy Rosary. The doctor was not called until after death, since it was obvious he was dying & nothing could be done. Brown, known as "Vulgar," because of his foul language, was a salesman in Malaya for General Electric. The only Britisher attending his funeral was Hasselhuhn who conducted services. A sad epitaph.

Men are collapsing suddenly & dying every day now, within a few hours. Yesterday so collapsed & died H. J. De Boer, Controler, who once wrote Malay letters for me & long was a fever & spot patient.

Wednesday Oosten gave to Doctor Lentze, for me, 1 tin "Milko" & 2 tins army ration butter, which he said was for 1 week's consumption & next week he would give me more, in order [to] build up my strength & ward off T.B. I'm definitely off work now, having spent last week training new men & preparing dept. to carry on.

Saturday H. van Asbeck, 35, N.K.P.M. Pendoppo Sumatra (Standard Oil, N.J. here) lent me 30 guilders for which I gave him note on U.P. He volunteered the loan, much to my surprise, explaining he & his fellow N.K.P.M. men owed much to America & since, in our petition, we pointed out that we could get help from no other group in camp because of our nationality, he wished to advance Germann & me this amount & possibly more later.

Fr. Elling has severe dysentery & malaria now, contracted while working hospital dysentery ward.

Yesterday I made a brief will, leaving my camp possessions & money to Germann with instructions to forward my papers & Travelers Draft for $250 to my family afterward. If he also should die, Bishop Mekkelholt or Father Elling were named beneficiaries & executors.

⤚ Nov. 8 Wednesday

Death is scourging the camp. 6 men died between 7:30 a.m. yesterday & 11:30 today. More will go tonight.

Oosten again is out to change hospital administration, this time appearing genuinely & sincerely alarmed, in effort to get stronger medical leadership. He sought me out this morning to reveal his plans & ask my opinion. I gave it flatly. He proposes to remove Lentze to other camp & put Kramer in. I fear such a move will cause more trouble & bitterness than it's worth—and we know not if Kramer is the man for leader. I also brought about a meeting—for [the] first time—between Oosten & Harrison. Hope it bears fruit. Since this morning's conversation I've been told Oosten is playing a double game again—intends to clear British from hospital. Also what he said regarding K's desire *not* working with L. appears to be untrue & [the] converse the case.

⤚ Nov. 16 Thursday

Kramer named hospital head Monday with Dr. Hollweg as "advisor" to hospital. Hollweg's appointment stunned us because he is notoriously anti-British & long has been nothing but a troublemaker in camp. Before his appointment [was] officially announced, Friday, he stormed into hospital office, demanded to see Red Cross stocks, because his figures did not jibe with ours, accused Quartermaster D. C. Thomsen of irregularities. His tirade practically amounted to accusation of theft. Thomsen produced his books, proved their accuracy & it showed that the discrepancies were the fault of whoever booked out supplies in camp & *not* hospital's, whereupon Hollweg, & Oosten, who accompanied him, stormed out. Saturday Thomsen read a letter to Committee requesting definition of Hollweg's official camp status & accusing Hollweg of being anti-British. Committee tried for two days to have Thomsen delete anti-British references from letter, but he refused—and wisely, for Hollweg & Kramer have been trying to get Thomsen fired, but—all this is still very sub rosa—Oosten & Hammett resisting because afraid of anti-British aspect. Hollweg & Kramer also nominated another camp troublemaker & busybody to the job replacing Bettenhausen, Thomsen & me as a sort of super—hospital superintendent—Fanoy—who is a standing joke in camp. Oosten flatly refused [to] allow Fanoy on hospital staff & said he would resign his chairmanship first. Hollweg & Fanoy are the Dutch Red Cross Chairman & Secretary, respectively, of Palembang.

First death of Black Water Fever killed British R. A. J. Lyng, 21, (real name Lowe), 12th youngest man yet to die. He was an army deserter & took assumed name when captured, posing as son of man in camp named Lyng.

— Nov. 27

Hospital affairs rapidly worsened until today Doctors Kramer, Kampochnur, Hollweg & Boerma "struck" without warning. Dr. Lentze, however, continued working in the blocks & agreed to look after the seriously ill in hospital. F. Thompson, 36, British engineer, died this morning. Harrison went to inform Dr. Kramer & found him playing cards in Hollweg's office. Kramer did not come, so Thompson was [placed in a] coffin without officially being declared dead. No medicines have been dispensed or patients waited—except Pastor V. Oort who died this afternoon—[ ] doctor so far—3 p.m. today.

Kramer took extremely highhanded attitude immediately upon assuming charge of hospital. Obviously poisoned by Hollweg's stories, he openly mistrusted the staff in general & Harrison, Thompson & me in particular. He, however, showed especial favoritism to Roellsma, whom he allowed free access to medicine cabinet & whom he treated as head dresser. When doctors moved into an adjoining room—former Hiho sleeping quarters & Jap Sergeant ordered Harrison to sleep in office, so, when room was made available, we moved dressing cabinet back into office where it had been formerly. That night I discovered cabinet locked—first time it had ever been locked because hitherto we had been unable to obtain lock. Roellsma obviously had instigated the business by telling Hollweg & Kramer it should be locked. But he said nothing to me & took the key to other camp at night. I inquired of Kramer, who said he had ordered it locked at night. But Roellsma locked it also in afternoon, whereupon I took the lock. Next day another lock appeared, whereupon I asked Kramer as aforementioned.

I ordered the cabinet be not locked until I went to bed or removed bar so it wouldn't be. Roellsma, without more ado, went to Kramer, who went to Committee. Hammett came over here & together we asked Kramer to explain the business. I explained cabinet was now in office where Harrison slept & no necessity for locking, but if it must be locked, could I keep the key in case of emergency night calls. Kramer said *no*. Pressed if he did not trust me, he replied, "Let me say that I trust no one." Later that evening, I talked with him again & he said he couldn't understand why the *staff mistrusted* him (Kramer). "If you publicly say you do not trust us, how can you expect us to trust you?" I replied.

K's general attitude toward us was that of a bullying white overseer toward menial coolies. Harrison & I never went near the medicine cabinet without Kramer being there & lately not unless third party was there as a witness, because of a bottle of Clark's Blood Mixture, which Harrison had placed back in the cabinet, disappearing. Harrison was held responsible. We, & Asbeck also, believe Hollweg took it. The bottle later reappeared, nearly empty. A few days ago Harrison & I were accused by Kramer of making away with 10 quinine pills—had been given Roellsma for [ ]. Kramer did not apologize, but went to Committee & demanded investigation, saying that after he had made a public fuss about it, the pills had reappeared. What actually happened was that he gave Harrison 185 pills & told him there were 175. Harrison counted them, discovered 185, immediately informed Kramer & K's little trap collapsed. Several times thereafter he gave us wrong counts of [ ], but on being checked in his presence, he was forced to correct the count.

What brought on the strike, however, was the action of Camp Committee in taking direct charge of hospital personnel. Hospital divided into 3 departments: Medical, under doctors; 2—Household, under a new superintendent; Sengers, & 3, Accounts, under Hilling.

Oosten & Hammett were named as Committee members to have direct charge of hospital. No staff changes could be made without Committee approval. Kramer argued he should have sole control of hospital & personnel. Committee refused. At a meeting last Saturday of Oosten, Hammett, Kramer & hospital department heads—Harrison, Thompson, Bettenhauser, Fr. Hermelink & I, Kramer acquiesced in the new plan. But this morning, when doctors went on unannounced "sit down" strike, Asbeck asked Kramer to explain. K. refused to explain anything except in a meeting of all doctors & Committee. He said only that Kramer, Kampchnur &

Hollweg were not going to work. Boerma—the coward—pleaded *sick* as his excuse. Lentze declined to be a party to the whole affair, but continued working in block & agreed to look after most seriously ill.

It is nearly incredible that doctors could or would refuse to treat sick & dying men for any reason whatever. And the only reason in this case is politics—dirty Dutch politics. They want to wield certain power. The Committee refuses to allow them to wield such power because the Committee feels—& rightly—it would be detrimental to the camp & to the hospital to allow such irresponsible & twisted personalities as Hollweg, Fanoy & few others to be placed in position of such grave responsibility.

I say—that if a soldier deserts in time of war he is shot. If an officer deserts he is court martialled & shot. If doctors in such a time as this desert helpless sick & dying men they should suffer at least to have their license to practice revoked by the Dutch government after the war.

Doctors 4:30 p.m. suddenly called Wing Commanders & block leaders into clinic (Thompson not informed or invited) & read a statement blaming Camp Committee for noncooperation & failing to meet the doctors & discuss hospital reorganization. After repeated but futile efforts to get cooperation from committee, said the statement, the doctors as sign of protest did not make their customary morning rounds in hospital or blocks (except Lentze's block) but would make the rounds this afternoon. Doctors then began rounds in hospital, Kampochnur about 5 p.m. & Kramer 6:30 or 7 p.m., after which Harrison & I dispensed medicines—mostly opium. I put out Vit. B powder between 5 & 6 p.m. with a few Elasto & Creosote pills.

At 6:30 p.m. Committee met with Wing Commanders to explain their side of story. Among other things, Committee said doctors had been so busy during the morning in conferences they had been unable to make their morning rounds. Doctors were not in conference all morning, as a matter of fact, & as I previously mentioned, spent a large part of morning playing cards.

⌐ Nov. 28

Kramer hurried around wards *before* roll call this morning, finished shortly after roll call & before breakfast, then came no more into hospital until 10 p.m.—tonight when he looked into Ward F. Kampochnur made his rounds as usual.

Resident Oranje sought a private interview with Dr. Lentze, which Lentze agreed to at 11:30 a.m. But at 11:15 he told Oranje he could not talk with him because other doctors forbade any doctor talking individually with anyone of camp officials without presence of all other doctors in the meeting. Lentze added that his fellow *doctors censured him* severely for *working yesterday morning*—making his rounds of the sick in the blocks! One of the blackest & dirtiest criticisms I've ever heard—*doctors* censuring a fellow doctor because instead of *striking* he cared for the sick while they played cards & talked.

It is our impression that the real reason for all this trouble is that Oosten privately & secretly promised the doctors certain concessions in reorganization of [the] hospital, particularly regarding staff changes, but was unable to fulfill the promises because of Committee's opposition. This is borne out by Hollweg's appointment as advisor to hospital & the combined descent of Hollweg & Oosten on Thompson Nov. 10, also by certain remarks from other sources, Oosten's former close contact with Hollweg—whom Oosten now denounces & Hollweg's violent anti-British hospital staffers remarks.

Oranje has privately let Oosten know that Oosten's only salvation now is to go sick. It appears that Oosten will either have to resign or go sick so discussion can be carried on without him. His tactics of intrigue have finally proved his undoing.

Today Asbeck had strong words with Honjo, the Jap interpreter, whose highhanded & obstructive tactics are making contact with Capt. Seki very difficult.

⇀ Nov. 29 Wed

Committee verbally invited doctors to meet them. Kramer before replying consulted Hollweg & returned saying doctors would not talk with Committee except in presence of Wing Commanders. In other words, doctors intended to put Committee on trial before Wing C[ommnders]. Oosten asked my advice, which was to put [the] boot on [the] other foot by informing doctors they (doctors) would be summoned before Wing Commanders to answer charges of neglect of duty by their strike Monday. If doctors refused them then they would have to meet Committee privately or settle matters internally as Committee wishes, or they would have to refuse any meeting. But in meantime they would have to carry on their work as they are doing today, or strike again, which would bring a storm of camp protest on their heads.

Committee then met & drafted a letter to doctors inviting them to meet Committee. If doctors still insist on Wing Commanders presence,

Committee will show letters to W.C.s, ask for a vote of confidence by W.C.s to carry on negotiations privately. If W.C.s insist on being present Committee will resign & leave W.C.s holding the baby.

Bishop advised Oosten to "kick out Hollweg at all costs."

Kramer had long talk today with Fanoy & later with Van Santwijk.

Now reading Fedor Dostoieffsky's [*sic*] "The Idiot." Last week finished George Meredith's "The Ordeal of Richard Feverel," also Neville Henderson's "Failure of a Mission."

⁓ Nov. 30 Thursday

Doctors refused to meet Committee alone, therefore Committee tomorrow will ask W.C.s for vote of confidence.

This evening Germann & I had a Thanksgiving Day feast of brown beans, Bully beef & Pap[aya] sauce, topped off by Camel cigarettes I saved since Red + issue. Cooked beans 2 days, opened can corned beef purchased May '42 & made sauce of milk, soft rice, butter & palm oil (Klappah sauce).

⁓ Dec. 1 Friday

This morning Dr. Kramer staged the most ridiculous & undignified performance in experience of doctors. He informed Biesel [?], Wing Commander of Blocks 9, 10, & 11, that since Biesel & his block leaders refused to attend the meeting called by the doctors Monday afternoon, that the doctors considered Biesel & his block leaders as no longer true representatives of the camp. Therefore in future the doctors would deal only with persons *they* considered true representatives of camp! Biesel declined to attend the meeting because he said, & correctly, that doctors had no authority to call such a meeting without asking permission of Camp Committee. Actually only W.C.s *or* the Comm. can summon a W.C. meeting.

Dr. Lentze told me today that Committee promised Dr. Boerma hospital would be reorganized (when Boerma took over after West's departure). However Committee did not agree with Boerma's recommendations. Some of the recommendations concerned staff changes. When Kramer succeeded Dr. Lentze as hosp. head, Com. promised Kramer there would be reorganization. But Committee refused to agree with Kramer's recommendations for personnel changes. "Committee wanted to have their own men in hospital," said Lentze. I told Lentze the staff wished him to return to hospital, but Lentze said it was impossible. "The Committee dismissed me & I will not return," he said.

At 11:15 a.m. Kramer entered staff room & made a long statement, an approved translation of which, much condensed ([ ] okayed by Kramer) follows: "A conflict has arisen between the doctors & the Committee. Both doctors & Committee had been of the opinion that an immediate reorganization of the hospital & certain changes in personnel were necessary. The doctors considered that the reorganization & changes in personnel were not being carried out by the Committee with reasonable promptitude, bearing in mind that the matter had been pending since the departure of Dr. West. For this reason, & in order to point to the Committee's laxity in the matter, the doctors on last Monday, *went on strike*. Of course it was not a strike, but this unpleasant name was purposely chosen by us in order to make it clear to the camp that the question was a serious one. Of course the doctors realize that the camp should not be made to suffer & that the doctors' visits must continue to be made, and therefore after our 'strike' on Monday, we made our usual morning rounds in the afternoon of the same day.

"In order to acquaint the whole camp with all the facts surrounding this case, we called the Wing Commanders & block leaders to meet us on Monday afternoon, when a statement was made (see below). Wing Commander Biesel & the block leaders of his wing did not attend the meeting & for this reason the doctors no longer regard them as suitable representatives of their section of the camp, & therefore, for any future meetings the doctors will select & invite responsible camp members to represent their section in their place.

"In the meantime the Committee has approached the doctors in writing, inviting them to confer with the Committee. The doctors have replied that they were willing to attend a conference provided that all the Wing Commanders & block leaders were also invited to attend, because it has become clear to the doctors that the camp as a whole was badly informed with regard to the doctors' attitudes The Committee, however, refused to meet the doctors on these terms with the result that a deadlock has arisen. This statement is therefore now issued by the doctors in order to enable the camp to form a sound opinion as to whether the doctors of the Committee should undertake the reorganization of the hospital."

Doctors' statement to Wing Commanders & block leaders Monday afternoon: "The Committee & the doctors were of the opinion that a thorough reorganization of the hospital, & certain changes of personnel, were necessary. The doctors are of the opinion that these questions were not handled sufficiently quickly by the Committee. These questions have been

awaiting settlement since the departure of Dr. West. By way of protest &
as the ultimate method of making clear to the camp this need, the doctors
have this morning made no visits! As the camp welfare demands a round
by the doctors they will make their visits this afternoon. They request camp
members to signify as quickly as possible who should take in hand the reorganization of the hospital, namely, either the Committee or the doctors."

After meeting of Committee & Wing Commanders this morning,
W.C.s gave Committee vote of confidence & censured actions of doctor[s].
Com. was empowered to settle the matter. At the meeting it was disclosed
by Com that 1—Kramer & doctors nominated *Fanoy* as Hospital Supt.
& other men, not named, to other positions. Fanoy & others rejected by
Committee on grounds [of] unsuitability. On Nov. 16 doctors said, "All
right, if you do not accept our suggestions, run the hospital yourself as a
private hospital & we will be visiting doctors." Committee agreed & drafted
beforementioned plan of 3 depts. & [ ]. Doctors agreed & at meeting Sat.
Nov. 25, hosp. heads [were] notified in Kramer's presence & he acquiesced.

Mond. Morning, Nov. 27, camp Dutch officer de Prijn, summoned
by Doctors Kramer, Kampochnur, Hollweg & Boerma & found them examining each other & certifying each other as fit for convey & other light
work duties. "Why," asked de Prijn. "Because we are not working as doctors
anymore," they answered.

During meeting a slate was handed to Committee with message from
Kramer saying doctors were informing camp of their side of story—reading
statement in all blocks—& henceforth would meet the Committee only
in presence of W.C., block leaders, & certain other camp representatives
selected by doctors.

When Sengers approached Dr. Kramer this morning to inform him
of Senger's findings & recommendations concerning Hosp. & to ask K's
opinion, K. told him K would have nothing to do with Sengers now or in
future.

November deaths totalled 58, highest yet & nearly 2 a day average.

⌐ DEC. 4 MONDAY

Kramer began his invasion of staff today with flank attack on me. Harrison had a bit of fever, 1st in long time. K., on seeing Harrison sick, did
the unexpected thing of whipping 12 Kinin pills from his pocket & ordering Harrison [to] lay off 4 days. K. then marched into staff room & in loud
voice informed Bettenhausen & Sengers he wished Vink, a little Eurasian

ward attendant who joined staff at K's appointment, last week, to deal out the medicines, a job which I have been doing nearly 3 weeks as assistant to Harrison. Kramer further said his reason was that he "was tired of all the mistakes made by McDougall." Never once before has Kramer accused either Harrison or me of making a mistake in giving out medicines. The Kinin episode was, in his eyes, a theft, not a mistake, such as giving wrong medicine to a patient or missing a patient. Sengers consulted Committee because he did not want Vink taken away from ward attendant duties as we are very short of ward men, but Committee said doctor must be allowed to choose his own medical assistant.

Kramer next ordered Germann & Verdunk shifted from staff room to a ward as sick patients, despite fact Germann went sick only yesterday—the first time he's been sick since Kramer came to hospital. Germann has lost on[ly] 24 days due to sickness since July 11, whereas several other staff members such as [ ] & Nagelkirk have not averaged more than one week's work a month since being on staff—laying off sick [the] rest of [the] time.

I think Kramer's game is to shift Germ. & Verdunk—who has been a good ward man, but is anti-doctors—out of staff room, give their places to two Kramer appointees so they can not return. He must be after Germann simply because G. is my friend & does not kowtow to K.

I am in a somewhat precarious position because I am listed as a "permanent patient."

However, the problem must be solved tomorrow as Oranje is determined that Committee must dismiss Kramer from hospital tomorrow.

Following is Committee's statement of 12/2/44 answering doctors' statement:

"1. Up till now the Committee has refrained from informing the camp about the difficulties which have arisen between the committee & the doctors as the Com. preferred to settle these difficulties in a frank talk with the doctors. However, the doctors have thought it necessary to approach the Camp direct & that action forces the Com. to do the same so that the camp shall learn both sides of this question.

"2. A few weeks ago, after discussion with the doctors a new arrangement of the respective duties of the doctors was agreed upon. Dr. Kramer was given charge of the hospital & was requested to review the organization as soon as possible. A few days later Dr. Kramer drew up a new scheme to which the Comm. agreed. However, a difference of opinion arose about the appointment of the managers of the Household Dept. because the Com. strongly objected to the appointment of a man who in their opinion was entirely unsuitable. This raised a question of principle—whether the doctors or the Com. should have the final decision in the appointment of important staff members.

"3. As a result Dr. Kramer informed the Com. that under these circumstances he could not take over the management of the hospital & that the suggestion of the doctors was that the camp hospital should be managed by the Com. itself as a private hospital so that the doctors would only visit the patients & give their prescriptions.

"4. As there was no other out, the Com. informed the doctors that they would follow their suggestions but pointed out:

a. that this could only be done in close contact & cooperation with the doctors,

b. that the Com. would agree for the time being as in their opinion a doctor should be in charge of the hospital.

The doctors replied to this in writing that they did not wish to give any comment & that they were no longer interested in the matter.

The management of the hospital was divided into three departments:

a. the medical dept. under Dr. Kramer; the appointment of staff to be agreed by the Com. to safeguard a smooth running of *all* the camp services.

b. accounting & household depts. Respectively under Mr. Hilling & Mr. Sengers.

"5. For a few days up till Sat. 20 November, there was a daily conference between Drs. Kramer & Kampochnur & Mr. Oosten & Mr. Hammett in a pleasant way.

Last Monday morning (Nov. 27) it appeared that the doctors suddenly had strong objections; however, they did not inform the Com. & some of the doctors took an attitude which the Com. considers most regrettable.

The Com has since Monday tried to get into contact with the doctors to find out the reason of this change of attitude but without success.

The doctors declared themselves only willing to express their complaints in presence of the representatives of the camp, namely the wing Commanders & the block leaders & later on the doctors wanted to include such camp members as they wished to invite.

"6. According to the information given to the Wing Commanders the doctors want the camp to decide whether the doctors or the Committee are to run the hospital. This controversy is wrong as the hospital is one of the Camp Services & therefore must always be under supervision of the Committee who are the only body which is responsible to the camp. As long as this Committee exists the doctors have to recognize it as the elected representative of the camp & cannot ignore it as they have done during the last few days. If the doctors are not content with the present Comm. they have the fullest right to suggest to the camp a declaration of non-confidence.

"7. The points mentioned above were fully discussed with the Wing Commanders on Friday morning & their joint opinion was

a. that the Committee alone should deal with the question as they constitute the management of the camp as a whole.

b. that the Wing Comm. were quite willing to give their advice on this question after the Comm. have had a talk with the doctors, but only on the request of the Comm.

c. that the W.C.s were not prepared to attend any further meeting that may be arranged by the doctors for the discussion of this subject.

"8. The Comm. is grateful to the W.C.s for their vote of confidence. They wish to point out clearly that they are fully prepared for a frank talk with the doctors & that in their opinion a settlement can be reached, provided that there is a genuine wish from both sides to come to an agreement. Such an agreement must be reached as soon as possible because everybody under the present circumstances ought to cooperate not only for the special benefit of the many sick, but for the welfare of the camp as a whole.

Signed—the Camp Comm. Muntok, 2 Dec. 1944."

Last night we learned some more of Kramer's original proposals:—Fanoy as Hosp. Supt., Treverron as Quartermaster, Barnevelt & Roopal as kitchen cooks, replacing Bellenhause as Supt., Thomson as Quartermaster, & Earle & Quinn in kitchen.

Fanoy, Hollweg, Colijn & others are now engaged in a concerted campaign to discredit Oosten, accusing him of 1—moving from his block to Camp Duty Office despite his campaign promise to stay in block; 2—buying from black market, although he officially condemned it; 3—buying another man's breakfast pap [ ]. (Oosten says he traded a can of Quaker Oats for so many portions pap). 4—eating the kidneys of the deer & pigs hunting party shot (Oosten disgustedly replied kidneys are one meat dish he [is] never able to stomach).

Reliably—women's camp population 704. 7 women died since Nov. 1. Our camp 714.

⁓ Dec. 6 Wednesday

Last night Harrison, Thompson & I drafted a petition to Camp Committee urging removal of Kramer & reinstatement of Lentze. Today 31 staff members signed it & I read it to Committee & lodged it with them. Committee decided that one of its members—Van Hoek, Bangka Tin official & therefore Lentze's superior, to officially inform Lentze that hospital staff, Wing Commanders & Camp asked Com. to induce Lentze to return. Com. joins in request & apologizes for its previous action. Our petition follows:

"Hospital Dec. 6, 1944.

To Camp Committee.

"We, the undersigned members of the hosp. staff, most strongly urge that the Comm. remove, immediately, Dr. Kramer from the post of head of the hospital, for the following reasons:

1. Since his appointment as head of the hospital, Dr. Kramer has failed to cooperate with or to consult the heads of the hospital depts.

2. The basis on which an organization of this nature must be conducted, under the present circumstances, is one of cooperation between persons drawn from many walks of life. Dr. Kramer has not acted upon this basis, but upon the basis of regarding the members of the staff as mere employees with no voice whatever in the direction of affairs. Indeed Dr. Kramer has stated openly that he does not trust the staff & has gone so far as to suggest that responsible members of the staff have been guilty of embezzlement of hospital stocks.

3. In a voluntary cooperative organization such as this, the success of the head of the hospital must rest upon the quality of good leadership & the respect won from the staff. Dr. Kramer clearly lacks good leadership & has failed to win the respect of the staff. The espirit de corps of the staff has deteriorated & as a consequence the efficiency of the whole organization has suffered severely. This state of affairs has been observed & commented upon by the patients themselves.

4. Dr. Kramer has done nothing to implement the scheme of reorganization recently approved by the Committee & announced by the chairman of the Committee to the heads of the hospital staff at a meeting at which Dr. Kramer was present.

5. Dr. Kramer has, in our opinion, been guilty of unprofessional conduct by his leadership of the 'strike' of Monday 27th Nov.

Further, we strongly urge that, in the room of Dr. Kramer, the Committee should induce Dr. Lentze to allow himself to be reinstated as head of the hospital. We deeply deplore the Committee's action in giving approval to the removal of Dr. Lentze from the post of head of the hospital in the first instance, & we urge that every step necessary for his reinstatement be taken at once.

Further, we demand that the appointment of Dr. Hollweg as advisor to the hospital be cancelled & the post be abolished.

Signed Harrison, Thomson, Bettenhaussen, McDougall, Matheson, Helling, de Beyer, Jones, Earle, Nagelkerke, Biesiot, Quinn, Bryant, Wrigley, Hageman, Banks, Anderson, Brodie, Treurniet, Miller, Drost, Starkie, West, Verdona, Germann, Christie, Jackson, Husselhuhn, V. Diemen de Jel, Wilson, Herridge."

Another evidence of the times—Japs report natives refuse to sell firewood for money, demanding food instead. Camp has only two meals daily now because of food shortage.

— DEC. 8 FRIDAY

4 men in their 30s & one only 30 died last night & today of beri-beri & dysentery. Pastor Hoffman Javanese expert one of them.

Camp Committee today replied to our request for aid from Red Cross grant. Reply follows:

"Muntok, Dec. 7, 1944

Messrs. W. H. McDougall, Jr. & E. H. Germann

Gentlemen:

With reference to your letter requesting the grant to you of a suggested sum of 300 guilders from the Red + 'Grant in Aid' allotted to this camp, I am directed by the Camp Committee to inform you that the matter has been discussed with the Wing Commanders at your request, & that the latter agree with the Committee that it is impossible to consider the grant to individual camp members of sums of money from these funds.

I am to point out in the first place, that there is no direct evidence that this grant was made *exclusively* by the American Red + while in the second place it was expressly stated by the occupying authorities, when the money was handed over, that the grant was to be distributed *equally* to all camp members, irrespective of nationality.

The Committee therefore regrets that it is unable to see its way to accede to your request for special monetary grants to the two U.S. citizens interned in this camp.

Secretary Camp Committee, H. Pomes."

Yesterday afternoon I urged Oosten to apologize personally to Lentze for any possible offense O. might have caused him. To my surprise he agreed immediately & informed him he was willing to make a public apology if Lentze wished.

Meanwhile Oranje wrote letter to Lentze stressing [the] fact Oranje [was] speaking as [an] official [of the] N[etherlands] E[ast] I[ndies] government to a government doctor, urging L. for sake of camp to return to his post.

Lentze's strongest fear, I feel, is his fear of being ostracized by his fellow doctors here if he accepts. I pointed out to him, however, that Kramer grabbed the job on it being offered him which showed he was not "one" with Lentze then, so why should K's feelings be considered now?

⁓ DEC. 9 SATURDAY

Kramer attended Committee meeting & resigned when informed of staff petition. Since Lentze will not return, Harrison named head [of] medical dept. & in charge of medicines. Doctors continued regular rounds & K. remains in present quarters, which will lead to much trouble, I'm afraid, as Doctors are determined *not* to cooperate with Committee & K will be against us.

⁓ DEC. 10, SUNDAY

Today I began active work to get Dr. A. S. McKern, 60, Penang physician who has been hospital patient since internment, but who [is] now ready [to] assume active duty if possible, to take over job of head doctor, or, failing that, to come on staff as consultant available to those wishing his services. He is willing. Bishop Mekkelholt, when approached, advised me to push the campaign. Oosten is against 1st plan but may favor second. Asbeck against both plans; Oranje undetermined [?]. Hilling favors first or second.

Lentze has diagnosed my trouble as "spandylitis," or an inflammation of the spine. McKern, merely hazarding an opinion, does not think it serious.

I am now typing death record forms for Japs, including a few from women's camp—one of them a Mrs. Gladys Irene Jones, possibly wife of P. L. Jones, publisher *Malay Mail*; another Sister Wybrechta, Lahat R[oman] C[atholic] nun.

⟶ Dec. 11, '44

Yesterday mail received by some camp members on forms via Jap. Red Cross & other via Apostolic Legation Australia, all mailed Dec. 1943, informing that first word received from us received in Dec. '43 Delegation.

⟶ Dec. 12, 1944, Tues.

Today Oosten came to blows with a B.P.M. employee, J. Nuytern, 40, who earlier in day had fought with block leader Sevenhausen, also B.P.M. man & Oosten's former "fair haired boy," over a bottle of coconut oil. Sevenhausen went to Oosten, who decreed Nuytern must pay for bottle. He refused on grounds he would admit he was wrong if he paid. During second meeting with Oosten, Nuytern attacked Oosten after first overturning a table in the doorway so none could enter for nearly a minute. Both men reportedly were fighting fiercely. De Bruyn, James, & 2 others pulled Nuytern off & subdued him, after which he was taken to clinic where he accused Oosten of being a dictator & cruel to his employees.

⟶ Dec. 14 Thurs

Kramer's efficiency as a *doctor* as well as administrator indicated today when I asked K. for Visform which Dr. Kamposhuur prescribed for patients in Wards C & E. Kramer replied "Visform? Visform? What is Visform? I don't know what it is or that we have any." Kamposhuur himself didn't know Visform was in medicine cabinet until Harrison suggested that he use it.

Another attempt by Kramer & Hollweg to get Harrison was made today. Harrison summoned to meeting of Oosten, Hammett, Kramer, Hollweg & Lawson, wherein doctors attempted [to] accuse Harrison of telling Lawson that on Nov. 27 strike Kramer was called 3 times to see Thompson who was dying & refused to come. Harrison never said such a thing or even discussed case with Lawson. Lawson confirmed this, said his information came from a member of hospital staff whose identity he refused to disclose. Traubel was called in to substantiate this & did so—he being a member of Kramer's bridge four last Sunday when K called for Lawson & threatened to "punch Lawson's head" if Lawson made any more such accusations in camp.

The facts are that Kramer couldn't be found when Thompson was dying & that when he was notified of Thompson's death he continued playing cards in Hollweg's office & Thompson was put in coffin without being seen by doctor.

Yesterday Kramer called Jock Brodie before Committee because Brodie removed Hensen's body from Ward F before Kramer had been to see it. Hensen's corpse was fouled & the stench was so bad Jock moved it as soon as possible after death.

Finished Stephen Gwynn's "Captain Scott," a gripping character study of the ill fated polar explorer & a lesson to all men who face adversity.

Rapid decline of men's physical condition becoming ever more noticeable. Men wasting away to skeletons. McKern says mainly due to lack of proteins in diet. However, a small portion of the camp are weathering conditions fairly well & a few of them even putting on weight. They are the workers who in addition to getting extra "calories" allotted for certain jobs, also manage to supplement their diet by extra food obtained in various ways or bought on black market. Kitchen workers, of course, are foremost. Then come working party men who carry stores from godown outside into camp—& manage to steal a bit; then a portion of garden party men who get extra vegetables, hospital workers on calories & who until recently got "internal seconds," Camp Committee who grow fat from black marketing, & finally "black market" operators & their more prosperous customers, probably 150 to 200 persons in all who get extra food in small or large amounts. The rest of the camp must exist on regular rations only & so they slowly starve. Even the workers, however, suffer—men who burn up more energy than they can replenish drop out of the working parties—victims of beri-beri, protein deficiencies or fever—and sicken & die. Truly, as Englishman named Robertson wrote to Committee only those fortunate to get extra food in one way or another will walk out of this camp when freedom comes. So it is understandable why some men lick their plates like dogs after eating the last bit of food.

⇀ Dec. 15 Friday

Yesterday New Zealander Gordon Burt carried into Ward F [in a] dying condition. About noon I informed Kramer, Burt nearly finished. Kramer came & looked at him, walked away telling Hollweg "He'll last only a few more hours." K. did nothing for him but earlier Lentze, while Burt [was] still in block, prescribed quinine which I gave Burt. Last night Harrison asked Lentze if [there was] any Vita Camphor or other heart stimulant in hospital. Lentze secretly then got 3 Coramin tablets from cabinet I gave to Harrison for Burt. Lentze worried about Burt all night & this morning gave Harrison 3 more. Today Burt is conscious & sitting up—his life saved by the Coramine. But what will his fate be if K. keeps on neglecting him & we are unable to get more heart stimulants for him? And what of other patients in like condition if K. continues his policy of neglect? Something must be done to get K out of here.

Book 10

↞ Dec. 16, 1944 Saturday

Pendopo scene: Calorie beans being served [to] queue of men. 5 feet from bean pot a freshly filled coffin. Flowers on table beside pot, being arranged for coffin. Funeral service awaiting end of bean serving. A second coffin arrives.

Second Scene: 2 a.m. Dysentery ward, Anderson on duty. 5 patients call simultaneously for pots. Rapid dealing gets 4 in time. Fifth can't wait. Anderson shoots pot under him, but fraction of a second too late. Fouled bed. Pots whisked away, dumped, rushed [to] other patients. Urinal tins fly around as Andy works furiously. Hand disinfected pans passed patient to patient. Then a lull. Breathless, Andy washes his hands, sinks onto a bench, "Reminds me of the quick lunch counter."

↞ Dec. 18 Monday

Roelfsma today named Head Dresser by Harrison & approved [by] Committee after, we agreed he [is the] only man available. We regretted having to do so, but no other way possible. I am now listed as a *permanent* hospital patient but allowed [to do] light work. Lentze today gave me calcium injection.

To date dead 58 of 201 Pangkal Penang; 85 of 570 Dutch from Sumatra, 55 of 172 British. Present camp population should be 943 if [there] had been no deaths. It is now 744—198 died & 1 (Dr. West) left. 21% of population died—rate of 210 per 1,000. [Later note:] This figure not exact percent because many camps now combined in Muntok Jail.

↞ Dec. 20 Wed.

Kramer's position rapidly weakening. Sunday he wrote a letter to Committee which is being kept secret but which I was informed was "the letter of a mad man." 2 a.m. today a dysentery patient, de Jong, died. Harrison awakened Kramer but K suddenly fell asleep again & body lay until after 6 p.m. roll call when H. reminded K. of death—and this performance on heels of Kr's attempt to fire Jock Brodie for removing a body last week before K. saw it. Yesterday Foulds [?] asked Kr. to let him have another doctor. Other doctors also are getting fed up with his neglect of patients. When Harrison appointed & today signed notice that Roelfsma was head of dressers & Fr. Hermelink named Harrison's assistant—without K being consulted—it was another blow. Today I learned Kr. this a.m. told Oosten he wished to leave hospital entirely.

Read Sinclair Lewis' "The Job."

Monday night dreamed war ended & I arrived home to Mother, Dad, Jean & Gertrude. First dream I remembered them all in together.

Chinese contractor yesterday told Pete V. S. Berg war [was] endable soon "tida djooeh"—"not far." First time he ever opened his mouth about anything but [the] business of supplying our food.

Large poster outside exhorts populace to support Japs against enemy.

— Dec. 23 Sat.

Yesterday Dr. Lentze stricken with appendicitis & taken to Pangkal Penang.

Japanese gave permission for priest to say Mass Christmas in Women's Camp, where women dying nearly 1 a day according [to] death certificates I'm typing. A nun, Sister Hermina, died Dec. 19 of *appendicitis*—with 2 surgeons in this camp.

Kramer today told Asbeck the 10 tins of milk powder kept for *emergency* by Hollweg are *gone*. 5 of the tins were for *hospital* use. Incidentally, Hollweg is seriously ill—malaria.

One year ago today was the crisis in my illness, doctors thought I would die.

— Dec. 24 Sund. Christmas Eve

I have just assisted a priest who administered the last rites to M. P. V. Bekaert, 54, Dutch Rubber Restriction Officer, who returned to the Church this week after 30 years away. Another man, J. Freriks, 49, Dutch Policeman who cheered us all with a few bottles of cognac & liqueurs in [ ] April 3, 1942, also is dying tonight.

This evening after roll call Fr. B. Hermelink led an emaciated choir of 11 singers in a Christmas carol on the hospital veranda. They sang the story of the Nativity as did the full choir led by Fr. Bakker last Christmas & the first Christmas in Palembang Jail. Biesel & Allen, standing on a bed at the back of Ward D (occupied by a patient, too), read the Dutch & English story between songs. Their voices carried well throughout the hospital, where men lay side by side—14 & 16 to the row—on the stone shelves of the wards. But it was a grim night—this—compared to last year & 1943 [sic] when there were no serious cases—except myself & I had turned the corner. But tonight many men heard & knew they were hearing the strains of "Silent Night, Holy Night," "Adeste Fideles" for the last time on this earth. Although all was silent in the wards—dysentery victims in Ward F could not wait & whispered urgently for bedpans to tiptoeing attendants. Their lives slowly draining away, they lie & hope something will save them—something. But there is nothing. Little or no medicine, no doctor in whom they trust—because Kramer still has charge of [Wards] D & F & declines to call in any other doctor despite at least one request for another doctor—from Britisher Foulds [?].

And so Biesel & Allen read the story of the Nativity & the choir, tottering remnant of a once splendid chorus—sang. When finished, they were marched back to the jail camp under guard—for we are shut off from each other after dark.

Then Bekaert suddenly became worse. I called a priest & assisted him by the light of a kerosene lamp, in the stench of Ward F. Fr. Van Thiel, 36, stood on the bench, asked Bekaert if he wished the last Sacraments (because, although B. had been receiving the Sacraments this week he refused Extreme Unction—because it would be too much like giving up the fight for life. "They'd all say 'Old Bekaert is dying' and I don't like that," he explained.

Germann gave me 3 American cigarettes he saved since the Red + issue for this occasion—a real Christmas present under these circumstances.

— DEC. 25 CHRISTMAS MONDAY

Bishop Mekkelholt celebrated High Mass at Women's Camp, which he said [in] a large, well built, airy place of 7 barracks, Guardroom & hall. Hospital & wash rooms in good location, healthier air than here. Some 350 women, many crying with joy, attended Mass. 182 received Communion. Sisters had prepared everything well—had all vestments, etc., from Charitas Hospital. 23 [?] nuns in camp, 160 children. He was not permitted to speak to anyone, but was allowed [to] give sermon in Dutch. Two Japanese guards sat close to the altar—one on either side. 2 altar boys, trained by the nuns, served. The Women's Choir, well trained & in good voice, sang. Women seemed [in] better health generally than men of this camp. Bishop happiest—elated over success of occasion—the first Mass said in Women's camp since women interned. Capt. Seki & other Japanese treated Bishop very respectfully & with grave courtesy—in contrast with the free & easy attitude adopted in past with Liaison Officer Von Asbek. 340 host particles left there.

Christmas atmosphere lacking in camp today, except for religious services this morning & usual congratulatory exchanges. But 100 grams of pork per man at dinner was tasty exception. We had a double funeral, Van Stiely & Bekaert died during the night, but we have become so calloused to death that it made little difference to camp members. Coffee served 3 times, & in Block 10, Catholics this evening had coffee & cakes. We on this side unable to participate [on] account gates locked [after] roll call.

Rumor persists [that] German army surrendered but SS & Gestapo still fighting in Bavaria. Also that Manila radio (American) now broadcasting.

— DEC. 28

Last nite Dr. Kampochuur, assisted by his pal Hartog, Pangka Penang black market king, killed a dog to eat. Thus P.P. men have now eaten 2 cats, 1 monkey & 1 dog—at least. Also being caught & eaten—by butterfly net method, are bats. They'll be eating rats & mice next. Several people are cooking various plants & grasses. Part of the camp diet consists of various leaves, ubi, palm, papaya, bayam, Seri awan, terassi—compressed rotted fish is another delicacy—now being sold at 1.50 per ounce & when boiled or fried makes tasty sambal—or garnish for rice. In ordinary life, they say, a European wouldn't be caught dead with terassi in his possession.

The doerian season is in full swing & today for [the] first time in camp history, camp members all got at least part of one. Doerians are great delicacy—a large fruit, weighing several pounds, tough spined skin, inside a creamy meat surrounding hard chestnut sized seeds or pits. The pits are good when roasted. Doerians have a strong, sourish smell, but like limburger cheese, its devotees are fanatical eaters. They must not be picked from the tree, but ripen & fall naturally. Trees are large, 50 ft. high sometimes, & fruit falls with loud thud.

Yesterday night *dreamed* Kampschuur told me [to] give special medicine to a person who died as [a] result, whereupon K told me I must shoot myself to save [the] honor of [the] doctors. I didn't want to but was compelled. Three times I tried, but couldn't pull the trigger first two times.

3rd time I pulled trigger, felt a pop in my head, but it [was] only [a] reaction—hammer clicked on a dud bullet. So I went to Dr. West & asked him [the] best way of shooting myself, explaining that I didn't see why I should kill myself in order to save honor of doctors whose mistake it was. West said I could shoot him thru the eye to demonstrate how [there was] another way, but I demurred, whereupon he took a rifle, explaining the revolver was too small, pointed it at his left temple & fired trigger with his thumb, killing himself. As he collapsed in my arms, he told me to call Thompson & Harrison.

⟶ Jan. 5, 1945 Friday

204 deaths in camp during 1944 of total 229 to date.

New Year's passed as uneventfully as Christmas. Two cakes, made of Kedeleld soya beans, sugar & few Katchang (peas) & few other ingredients was our only private celebration. Most of the hospital was awake at midnite for a round of handshaking & one man died in Ward F just after the clock struck 12. However Japs gave each man in camp 1 package of cigarettes & supplied a large wild pig—some 170 kilos & 1 small pig, both of which we divided, sending ½ to Women's Camp.

Old newspapers show southern Philippines occupied in September & Germans almost finished in Oct.-Nov. Jap attitude here definitely changing to one of frigidity. Building being camouflaged & barricaded & soldiers for first time carrying live bullets in their belts & guns. Formerly cartridge holders used as spare pockets for cigarettes.

⟶ Jan. 6 Saturday

Gertrude's birthday. To Mass & Communion for her today. I strongly advised Oosten to resign & set election Jan. 31 & not run for reelection. Camp is very anti-O now. Commmittee is only his rubber stamp & thus arouses widespread antagonism. No guts & seemingly completely out of touch with camp life. For sake of peace, etc., better that O. get out.

From typing death certificates today I learned 7 women died in November.

⟶ Jan. 8

Dr. Lentze returned from Pangkal Penang, operation success.

⇀ Jan. 11, Thurs

Three letters received this afternoon—two from Jean & one from Lyle Harrington & wife Annah. Jean's dated March 24, '44 said: "Had three of your pictures made up for Mary for Easter. We have wonderful plans for the day we are all together again. Love, Jean"

May 29's said: "Gertrude, Jeannie & Peter are visiting us for a month. At thirteen months Peter looks just like you as you shall see. All my love, Jean."

Lyle's of June 13, '44 said: "If I didn't know you I would worry more. You will be home, it can't be soon enough for your friends. Good luck, Annah & Lyle. P.O. Box 47, Riverside, Cal." Postmarked Camp Haan.

⇀ Jan. 12 Frid

On rereading for dozenth time—trying [to] extract from between lines—believe [there] must be good communication between States & Shanghai if on March 24 Jean recently had made up pictures for Mary in Shanghai. Also Jean's letters certainly [are] only two of [a] series, else [they] would refer to receiving my card or cards, although I'm a bit worried over no reference to Mother & Dad—since Jean said "visiting us" & if she's still at home, one or both must still be alive. I pray both. And Gertrude has another baby—a boy now nearly 2 years old. My card must have been received not early [*sic*] than March '42, else Lyle's message, presumably his first, would have been earlier. Presumably Lyle is in Army, as card from Camp Haan, but Anne must be nearby. Also, Mary's affections remain steadfast. I hope she doesn't pass up any opportunity for her own happiness because of me.

Food situation here becoming grimmer. Noon meal now only small amount rice & small scoop of vegetable with fish occasionally. Camp is slowly starving to death. Only we fortunate few who have money & can tap the black market outside will survive another six months. And if the quinine ends completely—& my atebrine gives out—who knows? However, I feel sure I'll make it. And if my present plans materialize I may succeed once more in getting away. It all hangs on my "contact."

We now know positively Palembang drone bombed by night last Sept.; therefore probable it has been raided frequently since, as rumors said. Baskets of sand yesterday placed in front of guard rooms.

Wednesday children here taken to Women's Camp in a truck & allowed to talk with their mothers 5 minutes—first time they'd seen them since Palembang—Aug. '43.

⇀ JAN. 13 SAT.

Each morning Capt. Seki brings 3 eggs & 3 bananas & a cup of Idjoe soup to Guersen, mgr. of Bangka Tin, who is critically ill of dysentery in Ward F. Fine for Guersen, but hard on other patients who are dying alongside him—with no medicine, no food. De. Bruyn, 35, who died Thurs. night, cursed Japs who brought eggs but let him starve. When P[angkal] P[enang] Jap doctor Hasegawa, who saved many P.P. lives there, brought Lentze back last week, he visited Guersen, whom he'd previously known.

⇀ JAN. 14

Last nite "X" left camp. Shortly after a spy, thought to be one of his fellow A's, threw a scrap of paper into Hiho's room informing that [Malay phrase translated as:] "after roll call a man escaped." A checkup by Jap guard failed to disclose anyone missing, due to clever work in his block. He returned safely, but narrow escape as Japs waited for him at a hole in the fence while he lay for 2 hours within 10 feet of them until they went away for a short time & he slipped through.

⇀ JAN 17 WEDNESDAY

Oosten today resigned from Camp Committee on grounds [of] ill health. Told me Dr. Boerma advised it. Tonight Resident Oranje, Liaison Von Asbeck, Harrison, Thompson & I celebrated the "downfall" with coffee & sugar. First sugar in my coffee since West left. For me, however, it was not a celebration. I genuinely regret Oosten's failure. I believe the others—Oranje & Asbeck—are glad chiefly because they want to be "top dogs" when freedom comes & get any medals or other kudos by Dutch government. My advice to Oosten to resign—of Jan. 6—was & still is based on opinion it is best for camp. Whatever the new management, it can't be much worse than this one, but also I think it will be little better. Dutch are Dutch, whatever their individual names, politics, or rackets. They are ruled by their bellies & pocketbooks, vindictive, selfish, unscrupulous & untrustworthy. They do not trust even each other. But pay us the inferred compliment of reposing confidence in us, at least some of the more prominent ones do. The Japs have them sized up accurately, & despise their kowtowing & mimic them to us. The only Dutchmen in the camp I trust are the Bishop, Fr. Elling & a few other priests.

Van der Wethering, another Committee member, also announced he would not run for re-election.

The way is now clear for Baron von Asbeck to step into the Committee Chairmanship, the goal for which he has been working steadily—carefully planting seeds here & there—since he first joined us in Boekit Besar camp. He is a good liaison man, clever, cunning, fairly astute—but no *depth*.

Last night we had long discussion trying to convince v. Asbeck he must try, through Seki, to interview the Jap General due here 19th. He does not wish to, on grounds it might antagonize Seki & even if not, would not accomplish anything. A majority of camp, we think, want efforts made to obtain an interview. Asbeck last night indicated he would refuse. However, he may be forced to. Among other things, Asbeck said Bishop Mekkelholt *agreed* with him. Today I consulted the Bishop, who flatly denied it. For the Bishop only said effort should be *made* but that he himself would be willing to interview him. In fact, Bishop at my suggestion, then & there wrote a letter in Malay to Seki, asking an interview concerning strictly spiritual affairs, especially regarding Women's Camp. Asbeck will have to present that letter to Seki.

Drysdale has written short, brief plea to General beginning, "Pardon us for approaching you, but we are starving." If the letter is not given to Seki to transmit, which Committee declines to do, he told me, he will present it himself, no matter what the consequences. Asbeck & Committee dread such an eventuality. The whole gang is a spineless lot. They have fairly full bellies, through black market connections, & therefore can philosophize a bit. But the men in camp who are dying of starvation are desperate & willing to take desperate measures.

— JAN 18 THURS

Frequently I have speculated on a situation wherein a dying man, perfectly conscious & aware of events about him but so far gone physically as to appear dead & to be thought dead by onlookers—what his thoughts would be. Tonight I witnessed, participated in, such a situation: Bryant informed me van Doueren asked for doctor, say[ing], "I am dying." I called doctor & went to Ward F, stepped up on bench, lifted mosquito net & felt v. Douren's pulse. No pulse, no sign of breathing, open, staring, glazed eyes. To all appearances dead. Bryant stepped up beside me. "My God, he's gone already," said Bryant. "Yes, he's dead," I agreed, looking closely into v. Douren's eyes. And then—still staring blankly—v. Douren shook his head from side to side—in an exhausted but emphatic denial. He could not speak or see—but he could hear and think!

"Do you want a drink?" I asked. His head moved "No." "The doctor?" Yes, he nodded. "A priest?" Yes. The doctor arrived & I called a priest, who prayed beside him. To our surprise, v. Douren continued living—& still is at this writing—3 hours later. About one hour later he managed to speak, "Water—finger." He could not drink, but wished me to dip my finger in water & moisten his lips & tongue. I did. He nodded gratefully. Then I soaked a cloth, squeezed it into his mouth. He later managed to suck on the cloth. I wonder what he felt when he heard those words, "He is dead." Would that he might recover & sometime tell me. But he will not.

While this was transpiring, a report came Harst was dying in Ward C. I went to examine him before calling the priest & the doctor. He was already dead.

⌐ Jan 19 Friday

V. Douren died 4 p.m. today. And he was thought dead a second time before the end. Several hours after my mistake, v.d. Vliet decided he had finally died, so straightened v. Douren's legs & arms, notified us in the office & called the doctor. But v. Douren revived, doctor found him still alive. In the future, I'm not as quickly going to assume a man is dead.

⌐ Jan 24 Wed.

One of the huskiest men in camp, Jimmy Stanners, 32, Singapore Harbor, died Monday—starvation & malaria; offical cause of death—"general weakness." And our rations daily worsen.

Good news yesterday, though, old paper disclosed Foochow, China fell Oct. '44—& Roosevelt would run for fourth term.

Yesterday mail—small amount—from Java & England, year & more old. Java mail thought to be of last August.

⌐ Jan 25 Thurs

For first time since internment Japs today gave mosquito nets to us—for hospital. Capt. Seki said each net was "large enough for 8 Japanese or 12 internees."

Died tonight G. J. Guersen, 54, Dutch Chief engineer & Head of the

Banka Tin mining, of dysentery & general weakness. Banka Tin Chief Mechanical Engineer died last July 14. Japs tried to save Guersen with eggs, bananas & little medicine, but too late. He was [the] only sick man in whom Japs ever showed any interest, & that purely because [of] Hasegawa's visit.

⤛ Jan 26 Friday

Typed today in Seki's office, in a big house outside our confines. Seki himself not there.

Curran-Sharp in hospital & looks as though he will die in a few weeks at most.

⤛ Jan 28 Sunday

Read Arnold Bennett's "Mr. Probak," entertaining.
Gordon Burt, New Zealander, dying.

⤛ Jan 29 Mon

Gordon Burt died last night. One of [the] toughest men, physically, in camp, boundless energy, indefatigable student, he learned & mastered Spanish & the guitar in this camp. He once accompanied an expedition to North Polar Sea. Only survivor of launch shelled in Moesi River, threatened with execution after capture, prisoned in Jap jail & finally sent to Palembang Jail. His ambition to play in camp orchestra never materialized—only once did he play in it. He wanted so to surprise his wife with the guitar & Spanish. Now he's dead—fever, beri-beri—starvation.

Young Rettmier, 20, overgrown boy whose hunger amounted to mania & who several times left camp in order to get food, two weeks ago escaped from hospital but was caught at the gate. Sentenced to 10 days in Jap jail on rice & water, he has not yet been returned. We fear he is dead.

⤛ Jan 31 Wed.

3 free cups coffee issued [in] honor [of] Princess Beatrice's birthday.

Yesterday Drysdale caught, killed, cooked & ate one rat. [Later note:] Drysdale later bought dead rat from a brother for 1 guilder & ate it. Many men eating rats now.

⤛ Feb 4 Sunday

Curran-Sharpe died today. Failing steadily since knew of his wife's death in Women's Camp some months ago, he entered hospital last week.

Lost consciousness 7 a.m. today & died 8:45 a.m. He [was] my first Malay teacher & when I was ill when first interned he brought me my food.

Have been ill of diarrhea & 1 night of fever past few days. Now recovering.

Rettmier returned to camp. Japs had forgotten him & when Asbeck inquired concerning him he was released.

— Feb 7 Wed

Malay Banka-Billiton bulletin—smuggled—120 Allied planes bombed Palembang Jan. 24, whereof 80 shot down, Japs losing 16. Said aircraft carrier base, not stated where. Camp happiest.

Doc says I've intestinal malaria. Two weeks now only soft rice with a banana twice daily.

Camp election results: Von Asbeck, Vorstman & Drysdale form a new Camp Committee of 3. Hammett must be sad today. He could never shake off his civil service inertia. Hence his downfall.

U.S. landings Lingazen Bay 1/9. Report—Naval fighting north Malacca Straits, 12 Allied & 3 Jap ships sunk. Rangoon captured.

— Feb 10 Sat

Read Marquis James "The Raven," biography Sam Houston; M. R. Rinkert's "Temperamental People," & W. J. Perry, "Growth of Civilization": superficial.

Still on soft rice—very weakening. Fr. V. S. Knapp died suddenly during Mass today. Only 34. Long ill, beri-beri, fever, diarrhea, but returned to Block 13 several months ago. Msgr. Bouma also slowly fading out. Another 6 months & most of us will be dead.

— Feb. 11 Sun.

Died last night of black water fever a 16 year old boy, Sporre. Youngest death yet & also second B.W.F. victim. The first such death also was a youth, young Lyng, 21.

Trouble for hospital again looms on horizon. New Committee is considering making Kramer & Lentze *joint* heads & Hollweg, *advisor* to hospital & again we have not been consulted. Looks like a double-cross by v. Asbeck. But we are digging in & will fight. My old conviction that Asbeck can not be trusted is being proven.

⌐ FEB 13 TUES

Yesterday Seki announced because of health conditions here camp will be moved in about 10 days to a more healthful location 3 days journey. Today reported destination Kepajang, 60 kilos east Benhoelen in mountains where Benhoelen women formerly interned. We are glad of the move but believe a number of sick men will die enroute. However, those who will die will die anyway here, only take a bit longer. I am weak from diarrhea & soft rice diet since Jan. 29. Today no food at all, only a dose of salts.

4 men, all Catholics, buried today, including 1 priest, Fr. Coffen, Schuurman, Pambang ass't postmaster, who wrote Jap letters for me.

⌐ FEB. 15 THURS

Bishop Mekkelholt loaned me 25 guilders & I gave him an IOU on United Press for US $25. Camp busy packing but destination & departure time still unknown.

Today Lentze gave me Vitamin B1 injection—very calming to heart & nerves. Feel much better but because of bad sample yesterday—slime—am eating only "kandjang" thin soup of strained & boiled rice.

When sick men miss regular camp food, they are given tickets entitling them to restitution. Mine dates back to Jan. 29. My fear is that we may be moved before I'm well enough to get restitution here & new camp will not provide it.

Rumor armistice, possibly Europe.

⌐ FEB 18 SUNDAY

Today paid 15 guilders for small bottle Seriawan, a native medicine for dysentery, diarrhea, on recommendation of Dr. Lentze. Yesterday Lentze gave me a small quantity of cod liver malt, his last. He is doing everything possible for me—a real doctor & a real man. Twice he gave me injections of B1 for the heart. Worked like magic, stopping palpitation, calming nerves & acting in general as a tonic. Deficiency of Vitamin B1 affects the entire body & weakens the heart & nerve system. Still laid up, as the diarrhea won't stop. Thank God, it's not dysentery, however.

Still no news of our departure date. A general is scheduled to inspect us Tuesday.

⌐ FEB. 19 MOND.

Sangers just (10:30 a.m.) notified me Doctors Kramer & Kampschuur had decided I am unfit for hospital work in new camp. So after 3 years hard work in this hosp. I am through. History doesn't count. Others out are Bettenhausen, Quinn, Nagelberk, Falkeringa, de Beyer & Verdonk, for some reason. In my case, however, the 2 doctors who so ruled have never examined or treated me & apparently did not consult Dr. Lentze, who, on being asked, said I would be fit to work again when the diarrhea stops.

Read D. H. Clark's "Louis Berettin," & E. M. Forster's "A Passage to India."

⤙ Feb 23 Friday

Japs said camp going to Rubber Estate near Loeboek Linggau, in South Sumatra, railhead from Palembang & on eastern edge west coast mountains, in 3 parties of 250, 210, & 200 men each on Feb. 26, March 3 & 9. Fifty British in first group & remainder British & other non-Dutch nationalities second group. Unknown why specified British first [in] two groups— possibly separation or segregation new camp.

⤙ Feb 26 Mon.

First party of 250 given 300 grams rice, ¼ kilo salt fish & spoon ground coconut (sersenden) each man for journey. May have to last until Wed. or Thurs. a.m. Asbeck leading party which includes Oranje, Dr. Kramer, Bishop Mekkelholt & all Block 10 priests, Van Hilton, Sangers.

⤙ March 3 Sat.

Ordered to move Monday—2nd group. Finished Philipp Gibbs, "Back to Life."

Hollweg, who is in complete charge of hospital move—result [of] dirty Dutch politics—made bad botch of job, whether deliberately or thru ignorance I don't know. Example Hollweg's plan for 2nd hosp. group provided 24 bedridden patients, 56 total patients of hosp., 38 Block patients but only 4 male nurses (Versplogers). Kampshuur revised list eliminating all dysentery, 20 bedridden, 51 total hosp., Block 36—total 87 patients, with 8 Versplogers.

Hollweg's own 3rd party originally—13 total hosp. patients of whom 6 bedridden; Block patients unknown (unlisted)—but 19 *Versplogers*.

Revised 3rd party is: 24 total hosp of whom not more than 12 bedridden now & 15 Versplogers.

Harrison recommended 14 Versp. for 2nd group & 9 3rd group, to

Committee. Thus far Hollweg, who knows nothing of hosp., has never consulted or spoken to Harrison. Dr. Kampshuur, who is under Hollweg, is in charge 2nd group, so angry [with] us [he] will not speak to Hollweg & used Vostman as intermediary. How Camp Comm, Oranje, etc., after so vigorously & roundly long denouncing Hollweg, could allow doctors to place Hollweg in charge [of] hospital transfer & thus over the lives of seriously sick & dying men, I can not understand. But they did—& then ran off with 1st party, leaving us holding the bag.

Harrison & Lentze & 7 others are remaining behind entirely with men too sick to be moved at all—they will be moved into the jail.

⏤ March 5 Mond.

Group 2 of 250 men & 25 stretcher cases left Muntok Camp between 12 noon & 3 p.m., staggered along 600 meter pier & onto 600 ton Jap ship where 157 men & luggage [were] stuffed into midships hold 30 X 50 feet & balance into forward hold 30 X 36 feet. Stretcher cases [in] forward hold. Cramped conditions, stifling heat & pitch darkness nightmarish. I was among lucky ones in forward hold. Ship lay in harbor all night & moved off at daybreak. Mid-hold horrible. Men & luggage stacked atop one another, many unable even to sit. Japs allowed them on deck only for toilet.

⏤ March 6 Tues.

Entered mouth of Moesi River about 8 a.m., sailed up it all day, allowed on deck for short periods but at certain places which they didn't wish us to see, probably defense positions & the refineries—also Palembang proper—everyone [was] sent below decks & not allowed up under any circumstances. One man, injured, could not go below & was blindfolded. Before leaving camp each man received 6 rice balls, coconut shreds & fried fish—about 1 big spoon. We docked at Katoe Pati, rail terminal above Palembang, were put into 4 coaches & 1 box car for stretcher cases, windows & blinds slammed shut & left for night on siding. 1½ loaves bread—first tasted since Sept. '42—& tea issued [to] each man. Many men unable [to] find seats & lay on floor. Many stretcher cases also forced [to] walk to train & sit up entire journey. Passed night [in] extreme discomfort & heat as no ventilation account [of] closed windows, also no light.

March 7 Wed.

Train left Katoe Pati 7:30 a.m. & arrived Loeboek Linggau 7 p.m.

Windows closed [at] every station, which [were] numerous. Hihos bought a few things—such as pissans, rice balls—for those willing [to] pay outrageous prices. At L.L., however, Japs bought pissans for working party, 13 for 1 guilder—6 cents each. Paid 30 cents Muntok. Issued 1 cup tea & 1 box bread [at] night & shut in car again. This time German & I slept under seats on floor, so tired [we] slept soundly all night until awakened before dawn & hustled from train.

MARCH 8 THURS.

Trucks brought us [to] Belalau rubber estate, 12 to 15 kilometers from L[oeboek] L[inggau]. Camp consists [of] wooden buildings, mostly concrete floors & galvanized iron or tile roofs. Hospital has the leaf roof & dirt floor—selected because cooler. Our building—Blocks 7 & 8—houses 86 men (42 Bl. 7 & 44 Bl. 8), all British except [a] few working party members are in this building. 4 dregs from Pankal Penang also put in here. Building formerly coolie lives [living quarters] for rubber workers on this estate, which is estimated about 5,000 acres. We appear to be in [the] center of it. Sanitary & water accommodations very poor. A small dirty creek forms one boundary & from it issues all water except that used in kitchen, which [is] drawn from a well dug next to creek. All water must be boiled & all must depend on 4 issues tea per day for drinking or boil more ourselves. Latrines freshly built, one drained into creek until [a] few days ago when [it was] closed. Soil full of hookworm. Food is improving, though, we got *fresh vegetables*—carrots, cabbage, soy beans, for dinner.

Resident Oranje said he felt move keenly because at L.L. he himself used to officially receive thousands [of] Javanese colonists brought here to open new land & relieve congestion [in] Java. They arrived just like we did, jammed in box cars & 3rd class coaches, hungry, tired, loaded with tacky luggage—sacks, baskets, bundles, herded into trucks & driven to jungle clearings. We also got meat—water buffalo—on our arrival meal.

MARCH 14 WED

Camp life is much like camping out. Our barbed wire enclosed area is full of ubi kagoe & ubi manis (crude sweet potato) & other edible leaves, vines, & few berries. We pick the leaves, clean & boil them together with the heart of banana tree, a soft, sweet, fibrous white stalk gained by felling the tree & cutting thru to center, opening it to get heart. Stalk [?] is then diced & boiled. We bathe & wash clothes in creek, boil all water & dare not walk barefoot because of hookworm. In fact footgear problem is acute. Daily rains keep ground muddy. Caked mud tears soles from old shoes & tromped (wooden sandals) slip off feet. Many of us will probably get "hooked" eventually. Food situation still uncertain but looks like [it] will improve—especially vegetables. Camp has 14 Blocks of which some [are a] group [of] small houses on little hill, where all brass hats & most of working party live.

For [the] first time [in] internment history a Jap doctor is taking real, active, constructive interest in us. He inspected all men during a special roll call, increased rice rations 50 grams per man, supplied quinine bark & when Group 3 arrived L.L. station this evening gave 27 stretcher cases injection each & drink [of] arak. He [is] watching diet closely & ordered one latrine changed.

Entire camp cheerful, optimistic. Our surroundings of rubber trees more pleasant, no more walls. Almost everyone's health improved magically—whether a temporary psychological uplift or not remains to be seen.

Block all British or nearly so—block pleasantly quiet. No Dutch jabbering [at the] top [of their] voices, shouting [at] each other as though conversing between passing ships. Hope [it] remains this way.

This [is] my first real taste of block life, hitherto always having lived [in] hospital. Keeps one busy dark till dark, if one cooks, sews, etc.

March 15 Thurs.

Group 3 stretcher cases & few others arrived last nite & balance came out this morning. Two men died since we left Muntok—McGiffin, British, & Dr. Anton Colijn, my old jungle friend & son of Holland's longtime prime minister. 3 men have died [in] this camp—Eurasian Lassacquere, Dutch Pypers & Smulders. His own stubborn folly killed Colijn. A physical culture fanatic, he exercised strenuously several hours each day from [the] very inception [of] internment, despite doctor's warning it would seriously injure, if not kill him ultimately. Having used up all his reserves of strength thus, fever got him, racked him for months, sepus [?] finally infected his whole body. He swelled up all over. Had plenty of money from beginning, sold watch for some 400 guilders & borrowed much more at exorbitant rates, but he had an insatiable sweet tooth & spent most of it on goela java (brown palm sugar) & cakes, instead of nourishing foods as fish & idjay. And so he died, last Tuesday, March 11, & [was] buried [in] Muntok. Oosten did all he could for Colijn, & even more than he should have, using 90 guilders B.P.M.—almost half the remaining kongsie total—to buy sulfanidamides for him. When I said goodbye to Colijn in Muntok, he told me he was "at the end of my strength," & that even a few months more of internment would be "a long time" for him. But he talked of dinners together after [the] war. If he had listened to doctors instead of telling them "I know my own body," he would have survived in good health, for he had the means & the connections.

~ March 25 Palm Sunday

W. P. Allen, 34, Far Eastern representative of Boots Ltd., Nottingham, England, chemist & drug manufacturer & long my bed mate & fellow worker in hospital, died today of blackwater fever. Long a chronic malaria victim, nevertheless he continued working in the clinic. Thursday he suddenly began passing blood & was taken into hospital. Yesterday he lapsed into a coma. His death is the first real shock I've had here.

~ March 26 Monday

Allen [was] buried this afternoon in double grave with S. A. Moutain, 62, British Malaya planter who died this a.m. H. G. Hammett, British Civil Service, conducted services 1 p.m. beside hospital, then to graveside where longer & complete Church [of] England burial prayers [were] read. 27 men at funeral including Sung, Oosten, de Bruyn, Everatien Napier, Bakker & Nagel of Tokyo, Joseph Rottiere, D. C. Thompson, Sangers, Hilling, Hollweg. Less British than Dutch because Allen alienated himself from British community & Moutain's few friends sick or indifferent. Working party carried coffins, lifting over barbed wire fence, to small clearing in rubber trees about 200 meters north of camp. Allen lies on south side of grave. Allen had only some 27 guilders left (he borrowed 90 from Hollweg); his few clothes, a knapsack & blanket were sold by lottery among British community. Kramer took all medicines Allen had (which Allen reportedly had been selling).

~ March 27 Tuesday

Kramer severely ill—dysentery & malaria. I gave Bishop 5 hydrochloride quinine pills (only kind usable for injections) for Kramer, because hospital knew Bishop had 5 I'd previously given him for Fr. [ ] & not used. No one knows origin of pills except Bishop, when ill in hosp. with dysentery. Previously I gave Bishop 6 doses Yatrine I'd saved since July '42 against dysentery attack. Told him the price was that he pray I don't catch it.

Am feeding Harold Lawson, who [is] recovering from blackwater fever (febris nalmogerbinurica) of which Allen died. Blood transfusion (which I volunteered for Allen but offer not used) is best way [of] saving blackwater cases. Dr. Lentze said only 10% chance recovery without transfusion.

⁓ MARCH 28 WED.

Koot gave us 2 kilos idjau & ½ of maize for priests shorts he traded in black market expedition Monday night.

⁓ MARCH 29 THURS

Capt. Seki addressed camp, warning of black marketers, persons caught outside fence would be shot & if not hit or killed would be taken away & never return [to] this camp. Persons caught outside camp or convicted of going outside would be severely punished & goods confiscated. Also, he promised that husbands & wives would be united & live together at some vague future time. Told us not [to] have dealings with Hihos (native guards). Altho threats sound harsh on paper, his speech more pleading & conciliatory than threatening. Speech followed story from black marketers who outside Tuesday night said natives said that day Kampon Chief (Kapala Kampong) summoned natives, told them Jap ordered him [to] announce "War will end this year no matter what happens" (win or lose?).

Also learned 2 white Germans of Benkoelen interned here in special barracks outside fence for new internees—all Indos—who [were] picked up past two weeks & some of whom said Germany surrendered March 6; wherefore believe German internment confirms it.

On heels of Seki's appeal black market boomed as never before. Hihos completely disregarded it, were letting men thru fence at $5 per head & cut of barang when returned. Many went out, brought in rice, maize, beans, salt fish. (But so far Germann & I [have not] succeeded [in] get[ting] any, our deals still hanging fire. We're holding out for fair prices.)

Today resumed working [in] Jap office on death certificates. Glad of it, for [I] may be able [to] do business.

Natives outside reportedly state semi-revolt, refusing [to] sell [to] Japs, demanding goods. Money nearly valueless.

⟶ March 30 Friday

Camp office officials put me on Jap job as daily corvee. [Later note: keeping record of our sick & dead & stealing Jap newspapers.]

⟶ April 1 Easter Sun

Happy day—2 letters from Mother, of 1/14/44 & 2/26/44; one from Lily Hawkes, 3/6/44 & card from Mary Bell 4/9/44 from Berkeley, Cal., where she is. Must have been exchanged or otherwise repatriated—to my utter astonishment. Her address—3130 Eton Ave., Berkeley, Cal. "Family thriving. Chrismike remained behind. Met folks Ogden. Overjoyed hearing news your safety. Living for our reunion. Praying daily. Love you always. Your Mary."

Lily B. Hawkes, Margarita Club, 1566 Oak Ave. Evanston, Ill.

Mother's 1/13 "Your privilege of Mass cheers me, dear boy. Mary is in California. We love her dearly. We are working for you. Be patient & courageous." 2/25: "Everyone well. Nice letter from Mary. She likes Calif. Gertrude has a 10 months baby boy. God bless & bring you home to me. With dearest love, Mother."

⟶ April 3 Tues

Wrote letter to Allen's wife. [Later note: For delivery after war.]

⟶ April 8 Sund.

Yesterday for first time since internment Japs gave us entertainment—23 piece military band gave concert within camp, on hilltop, playing about 1 hr.—10 pieces—all but 2 Western music, mostly Italian. Japs seem anxious [to] conciliate us now, but apparently can't do much. Although this region [is] rich [in] maize, rice, vegetables, fruit, tobacco, coffee—we get only maize, rice & spoiled vegetables—much so rotten [as to be] uneatable. Japs complain lack [of] transportation, but native non-cooperation plus Jap indifference also must be responsible. Got meat yesterday for 2nd time over [ ]—8 kilos. One man figured it at 18 pounds meat in 14, 700 meals—or average 1 pound per day for entire camp.

L. Pessy [?] gave me 2 of 2½ kilos rice for an old shirt of priests. He was caught coming in—first time ever caught & 53 kilos taken.

⮞ April 10 Tues

Yesterday camp received telegraphic *Christmas* greetings from American Red Cross (signed Basil O'Connor, Australian Gov. & Aust. Red +).

Japs with coolie labor building hospital isolation ward & a structure outside camp believed for chapel.

⮞ April 15 Sun.

Have read recently Rhinehart's "State vs. Elinore Norton," Jackson Gregory's "Desert Thoroughbred," ? "The Open Sky" & ? "The Round Trip."

Japs sentenced 4 men caught outside blackmarketing to 4 weeks each Loeboek Singgen—1st week no food, 2nd & 3rd week half jail rations, 4th week full jail rations. Later they modified sentence to 4 weeks full rations. One man, Boller, who was caught 3rd time tied [to a] tree [for] 10 hours, kicked & struck by several Hihos, in full view of camp.

On account of Hihos running away & continued black marketing, Japs now have native police, remnants of old Dutch police, guarding camp in circle between Hiho outside guards & Kampongs [villages] (or Ladonsas called here), making black marketing very difficult.

Food situation still bad. No maize (Djagong) for 2 weeks.

First group [of] 240 women arrived Thursday at the new camp 2½ kilometers from here, from Muntok. No contact yet.

Our hospital situation worsening so much, many patients discharged to shift for themselves in Blocks because of the shortage of attendants. Men won't volunteer anymore on account of abominable conditions, food (calories) extra rations & danger of infection 4 attendants now dysentery—George Bryant serious. I helped obtain [for] him some doyatrene for which [ ] had [to] pay 50 guilders plus his only good shirt. I gave him a few OP Bis tablets. Drs. K & K both ill—Kramer dysentery & Kampschuur tropical malaria.

⮞ April 20 Frid

Memorable book—Warwick Deeping's "Ropers Rowe."

⮞ April 21 Sat.

622 women now [in] women's camp. 4 more men died Muntok—totalling 255 there thus far & 30 here. Total since April '42—300.

APRIL 28 SAT.

E. E. de Bruyn's (B.P.M. Refinery Chief) philosophy of mankind & organization: 4 kinds men:—1. Bright & active. 2. Bright & lazy; 3. Dumb & active; 4. Dumb & lazy. No. 1 must be fired because they [are] too bright & too active to fit harmoniously with organization which consists of categories 2–4; No. 2 [are the] best men because [the] little they do they do well & [they] don't interfere or inject themselves elsewhere. No. 3 also must [be] fired because they do too much damage. No. 4 [one should] keep because [they are] not dangerous & will do only what told. Nos. 1 & 3 are unhappy men because 1 is frustrated by world's inertia & essential mediocrity & No. 3 always in hot water. Happy men are 2 & 4—No. 2 because they usually have a sense of humor & no desire to reform or build too passionately; No. 4 because he knows no better & "ignorance is bliss."

Jap office work keeping me busy all day. They now want daily records of all sick & names of those too sick to work. I compile info in camp & enter classifications in Jap characters—tedious work.

— MAY 4

Read Readers Digest reprint, "The Rock," June '39 "good and bad" Catholic Popes: canonized saints, 79; excellent to passable, 164; some blotches but not very bad, 13; accused of immorality with solid proof, 5; very bad, 2. Total 263, of whom 243 "good men." "Nothing comparable in any government that has ruled men."

Messenger Sacred Heart, Nov. '39, church marriage annulments Sacred Roman Rota in 1938 judged 73 appeals for declaration of nullity of marriage. Of these cases, 40 too poor to hire a lawyer so lawyer was provided gratis. 46 of the 73 cases decided against pleaders (Rota refused [to] nullify). Of 46 rejected cases 25 hired own lawyers & 21 poor got lawyers gratis. 27 cases decided *for* pleaders as null & void marriages, of which 19 were of poor persons who got lawyer gratis. "Evidently Rota's decisions not influenced by financial consideration."

2 more men died Muntok—Stephenson & Vroland.

— MAY 26

Events recently: Kramer's operation V. D. Vossen; Japanese and Malayan papers revealing European armistice 4/27; I sold J's 2 watches—one for Bishop at $130; one for Treverow at F. 350; & 3 shirts for 12 kilos brown beans, over 3½ soup; sold pen & pencil Chinese [ ] 440 cc oil & F 30;

Tani gave me Vitamin B & cod liver oil; J's gave me regular meals until 5/25 when [they] apologized—no rice; their attitude re black market [ ].

⇀ JUNE 4, MOND.

Fr. Elling's 36th birthday. We'll celebrate it after my next successful trip, scheduled tonight but postponed account [of] Monday's septic legs. Yesterday Germann cooked up whacking feed beans (patchand merah); ladang rice from my 16 kilogram haul; bread roasted oebi kagoe & boiled open papayas. We eat 200 grams each daily [of] spring rice & are rapidly improving physically as a result. Black market trip netted us 16 kilos ladang (red) rice nite [of] May 25. Remainder [of] sick & hospital workers arrived from Muntok nite [of] 25th. 5 sick survived of original 14. Workers all fat & fit—said plenty bulk & sugar, all put on many kilos. Our own food situation here again worsening—only rice from Japs today but camp managed [to] pick some vegetables outside.

10 men caught coming in from night raid on Ladang Sunday morning kept foodless in guard house since. 4 men returned from Loeboek Lingang & 50 days [in] jail there for black marketing. Jap sergeant told Asbeck today men caught yesterday [were] only amateurs & if experts only go out they wouldn't be caught. Neither Japs nor Hihos, he said, want to catch us, but each [are] afraid of [the] other. Hypocritically, though, guard increased around camp.

Hihos & men from Linggau say Terahau [?], Brelikpapeng & Macassar captured. Persistent rumors fighting Atche (North Sumatra) & Loeraboya captured. Russia progressing into Manchukuo. Hitler died about April 4. Roosevelt between 4/7 & 4/24; Churchill resigned, succeeded by Eden.

⇀ JUNE 16 SAT.

Recapitulating diary gaps:-
Black Market trip 6/12 with Max Breuer, black-skinned Indo-European policeman, Sierriere, van Noorden & Maitimo—(all Indos) to Ladand homes of Ali & Carman on main road L.L.-Padang. Max traded them out of all rice & maize they had (similar to previous time at Barto's with Manotang) & I returned empty handed. However I'm scheduled to go with Mandang tonight & hope for better luck. Tuesday night's trip tough & pitch darkness—walking single file each man holding on to man in front— Breuer feeling his way with bare toes. He knows the trail so well—and it's a mere dim twisting line through rubber trees & heavy undergrowth—he

successfully strikes the numerous narrow foot bridges & logs which serve as such purely by sense of touch. Once he missed a bridge—or rather stepped through a hole in it—& suffered [a] nasty fall, with [a] load of some 20 kilos. I carried back about 12 kilos maize for him. We used bark torches after passing womens camp & until reaching main road, which is another danger point.

We left camp barefooted about 7 p.m., crawled thru barbed wire fence, inched our way through undergrowth around barrier of felled trees which rings camp, donned shoes when out [of] earshot [of] camp. At that spot my knapsack spilled & I lost—not discovering until later, however—a heavy red silk ribbon & sack of Bishop's, which were found next day by bullock herder & given to Japs, who consequently tightened guard around that particular exit & hampered black market operations for new nights.

Greatest danger of such trips—aside from capture—is in breaking a leg or suffering some other serious injury which would necessitate lying outside until discovered by Japs.

Black marketers earn every penny of the commissions they take. I prefer working with Mandang, who is a thoroughly reliable & canny Minadonese. I got 16 kilos of ladang rice on my trip with him last month. Tonite there will be a new moon the first half of the night. Because of the ribbon trouble he has fixed a Hiho.

Have had strenuous week. Last Sunday nite (6/10) Germann & I left camp about midnight, trying for a new route to the Jap ladang near camp where we steal ubi papaya & cooking bananas. We failed to find ladang & about 4 a.m. came out of rubber to west end of camp & thought we had stumbled onto womens camp. While debating, along came Stegeman with load of rice. We scared him violently. He [was] so scared he refused [to] tell us where we were for fear we'd follow him. Finally we learned our location & sneaked back in about 5 a.m. Monday night we tried again—choosing a light rain to screen the sounds of crawling thru the barrier. Chose the well used route which Germann took once before successfully—& returned with about 50 kilos of ubi, 2 green papayas & six green bananas. Ubi must be pulled up like potatoes. Ladang is a huge cultivated area now going to seed. Japs station a guard there but he is easily avoided. Dr. Kampschuur also shoots pigs there who come to root out ubi. Being shot for a pig is greatest danger.

Japs let off lightly men caught returning from Ladang, but severely punish those trading with natives, such as I am doing. Of 10 men caught two months ago, 6 served 50 days in Loeboek Linggau put on 150 grams food daily—3 are still there & one—Boller—died in jail of starvation & weakness. Japs gave cause of death as beri-beri & malaria.

While at Ali's I bandaged up sore on his wife's leg, after having given her a silver guilder in hopes of trade. She gave me two eggs (chicken) for 1 silver guilder. Rice, Ali said, now is 400 guilders a kaling (kerosene tin holding 15 to 16 kilos). Sugar impossible to obtain. Tobacco 5 guilders lampeng—more expensive than camp price, a chicken 40 guilders.

(More anon on black market)

Camp events:—Today's market price for one rat—1 guilder (sold by Bish to unnamed man [Later note: Drysdale]) Today died Postma, who entered hospital several weeks ago after eating a rat. But many other men have eaten them safely, including J. Drysdale, Brit Representative.

Drysdale is too ill—chronic malaria—to work, but he refuses to resign & allow another man to replace him on committee which is running camp just as high-handedly as Oosten ever did. I'm more than ever convinced all Dutchmen are alike—fundamentally they are egotistical bullies, ill mannered, their gods being their bellies & pocketbooks. They lack breeding, courage &, except for the priests, spiritual courage.

Hospital being moved to new shed at east end of camp & to buildings now occupied by British—36 of whom signed a petition saying only physical violence could move them, but, like the sheep they are, are moving meekly. We must move into building being vacated by hospital. Chances of infection are great.

Operation:—Kramer operated V. D. Vassen in open air, removing intestinal obstruction: used a table knife, fork & spoon in process. Operation completely successful.

→ JUNE 22 FRID

Tuesday night, 19–20, made 3rd black market trip. With Mandang, Tempelers, Hages[ ] & Sitanala to "Pecanaan" Landang where traded clothes, silver money & thread for 19 kilos maize, 2.2 kilos rice, 2 bottles oil, & 1 chicken. Total cost 3 pairs shorts, 1 singlet, 1 ball black yarn, 2 rolls white thread unravelled from pair white stockings; 2 silver guilders, 2 pieces white muslin cloth 1 ft. wide & 18 foot total long (bandage cloth). Paid 2 guilders for present & meal for 5 persons consisting [of] rice, few small river fish (minnows) & shite (jaberawit).

Received 5 card letters this week; 1 from Mary, 1 Jean, 1 Gertrude,

1 Tommy Shields & 1 letter from Mary—the first she'd written, dated June 7, 1944. Letters varied thru May & June. Sat. 23rd received card from Joe Jones, UP, New York, Aug. 10, '44 (220 E 42 St) & one from Malayan Research Bureau, Sidney, Aust, signed Roger Dolbey, saying family & Mary Bell received my card of March, 1943, but were anxious [for] my welfare, dated 5/1/44.

Petanoon, a Javanese colonization settlement of 70 men & their families. Mandoer, or head man, named Mangoen. Japs take all their crops at very low figure—confiscation—so they hide as much as possible. Rice harvest finished & we could get only a small amount. Peanuts harvested all confiscated. Make their own palm oil & tobacco. Eat only rice, vegetables & few fish—but look well nourished. No skin troubles but much malaria & no quinine. They appear [to be] poor people living day to day—but then appearances can be deceiving.

Took new route which [was] easier walking but longer—about 3 hours returning loaded, 2½ going. Left 6 p.m., returned 5:30 a.m. with fixed Hiho (1 new towel costing 4 kilos of rice & 1 bar toilet soap [culebri]). I can bargain with natives now but need more experience.

Black marketing hard, risky work. Anton Breet caught at fence yesterday 5 p.m. by Hiho who took his barang & let him go. Hihos, finding great difficulty themselves trading, are taking it out on us.

Guarding camp increasing vigilance. Barrier of felled trees grows daily, Hihos stationed [at] strategic points & also patrolling inside.

Last 3 men in Loeboek Linggau jail returned Thursday, thin, weak from starvation diet.

Capt. Seki's favorite hen stolen. Camp members suspected.

⁓ JUNE 24 SUN.

Drysdale resigned this week. Elections due. Have much barang for trip tonight. Will attempt [to] bring back [at] least 6 chickens alive.

[At] least 6 men caught yesterday & last night but paid off Hihos & released. Treuerow & Breet paid 200 guilders; Wilmans paid 1 shirt & 1 short—he returned having sold nothing. Crawford & V. D. Zuesan paid jewelry, including necklace I had been trying to trade. I finally agreed with J. for 200 guilders.

⁓ JUNE 27 WED.

Wrote 50 word card to Roger Dolbey, Malayan Research Bureau,

90 Pitt St., Sidney, Australia asking him to inform family "my health good, living conditions atrocious," & specifying letters received.

Because of dry spell creek low—little more than ankle deep. Men fishing with nets catch minnows—one man got 1 1/2 kilos yesterday. One group used a mosquito net this morning, but caught fewest.

Today died L. K. Rethmeier, 22, of "intestines." An abnormally large youth—6'3" he entered camp at 18 yrs. A voracious eater, he could not get food enough & began to steal—turning into a kleptomaniac. He broke [out of] camp repeatedly in Muntok only to get food, was disciplined by camp jail cell, taken into hospital, escaped hospital & caught outside near road gate. Despite his abnormal health & mind he was not given extra food for sufficiently long time. Doctors did their best but camp frowned on it & so he died—a black mark against this camp.

⟶ JUNE 29 FRIDAY

Feast of Sts. Peter & Paul, received letter from Getrude dated March 20, '44 enclosing picture of Jeannie, 3 1/2 years & Peter Paul, 11 months. Jeannie looks exactly as Gertrude did at same age & also reminds me much of Aunt Carr. Peter bears some resemblance to my own baby pictures. Can't see any of Carrico in either.

Today I bought 15 guilders in silver for 55 paper from Tempelers. 2 1/2 guilder pieces at 5 to 1 & single guilder pieces at 3 to 1—for future investment or to use outside to buy rice at 1 guilder per catty, which with rice at 30 per kilo in here works out at about 6 to 1. A catty = 600 grams, 2 catties = 1.2 kilos. 1 kilo = 2.2 pounds.

⟶ JULY 8 SUNDAY

Eventful week. Last Sunday night to Petanshan with Mandang, Sitanda, Persign. But they had nothing there except maize & little of that. I bought 1 bottle oil for 5.50 silver guilders & traded thread for 2 more bottles (one of which he did not give me, but promised for next trip which we arranged for Wednesday night). Bought a chicken for 4.50 silver & had to kill it because it made so much noise. Picked about 3 kilos oebi. Mandang managed to get a kuling of maize—12 kilos. Unable to collect 2 kilos rice Radi owed me from Barti's trip. Javanese living in fear [of] police, who are continually inspecting ladang houses. Friday previously police arrested 15 Javanese in whose homes European clothing [was] found. Trouble started when a Javanese sold [a] pair [of] shorts [in] Loeboek Linggau with a number in it from here. We were late in getting started back & came straight through without stopping. I left a singlet with Samat & white toweling polo shirt with Mangoen.

Wednesday night we started again with the addition of Max Breuer & V. Noorden. Hiho Hadje Basai [was] fixed, but he counted us through fence & made us return—said [we were] too many. So we [were] unable [to] keep appointment. Thursday night we fixed another Hiho—2 guilders per man—but because of trouble at fence—Smit & Stegenam nearly caught—& a bloody towel found near sentry box followed by Jap inspection of block with flashlites, we were late in starting. Night pitch dark & had to feel our way past womens camp, whereafter we used palm oil lamp. While approaching edge of rubber trees near Petanshan saw auto lights & heard motor racing as though stuck. Waited ½ hour until it drove away, whereupon we entered ladang & discovered car was Jap police which had arrested 5 or 6 Javanese for trading. Rest of men were in hiding. Unable [to] get anything but oebi. Reached camp 5:20 a.m. exhausted—again missing our fixed Hiho who [was] on duty 3 to 4 a.m. But we had to pay anyway.

July 4 Germann & I feasted—killed the chicken I got June 19. Fried legs & wings, stewed remainder. Baked maize cake which we ate with "tape" fermented oebi. Had Fr. Elling in for 11 a.m. nayi goreng. Ate tiffin meal with fried chicken & cake at night. Gave Mandang big piece of cake with American flag stuck in it. Best meal I ever ate in my life—that chicken—first in 3½ years.

Moved Wednesday from Block 7 quarters to old hospital block which now houses only British. A bamboo barracks with grass roof, dirt floor, cooler but far from creek & long haul for water.

Sold watch through Murao for 250 guilders, 50 guilders profit, but had to split with Woodford. The 25 went for Hiho fixing.

Surprise roll call today 11 a.m., but all people accounted for. Unknown reason. We had Bishop down for nayi goreng at time & took us two hours to eat it because had 2 successive roll calls.

Brought back about 12 kilos oebi—split with Perijn & sold 3 kilos for 4 guilders a kilo.

➞ JULY 13 FRIDAY

Lying up today because of swollen gland—lymphangitis from Pal Bottom spots & black marketing muscular strain.

Selling rice, tob[acco] & oil for Hilling & Thompson on 10% commission basis. Previously sold F 160 worth oil & tob[acco] for them. Cash getting scarce in camp. People have goods but no money. Therefore harder & harder [to] sell for cash. Bought 2 springits (silver 2½ guilder pieces) yesterday for paper F 2—4 to 1, as invested for black marketing. Leaves 40 in belt & 10 in pocket.

⌐ July 21 Sat

Smit, Palembang Hotel prop. & Stegeman, Eurasian policeman, missing since Thursday nite—presumably caught on main road while traveling to Tahanan on black market trip. Same night Eurasian Vink caught near Ladang. Vink was in party of 4, others escaped. Vink now with Crawford locked in room behind Seki's office. Smit & Stegeman presumably taken directly [to] Loeboek Linggau jail.

Night of Wed-Thurs. German to Landang with Johnny Close & 2 Dutchmen—He brought back 35 kilos ubi from which we made 49 guilders selling at 3.50 per kilo.

Black market most difficult now, dangerous. Kampons guarded, no rice except thru Hihos.

Germann paid 10 guilders to get out to Ladang. I paid 20 for Tahana & 25 previously—both trips fruitless, so lost 45.

⌐ July 24 Tues.

Successful day yesterday—net profit F 102.50, bottle oil, 10 grams tobacco, small quantity Vitamin B powder. Sold 1 pair shorts & 1 pair long trousers to Sone (Jap) for F 375—making 62.50; also 2 jars hair grease I made myself from vaseline & Eau de Cologne & Brilliantine for F 40—clear profit. Thompson gave me the oil for helping them sell tobacco & Hilling gave tobacco for efforts [to] sell 5 kilos rice, which they suddenly decided against selling. I'm in the black market deeply now. Have much Barang—some of it highest quality—including real silk kimono jacket & a piece of black silk 5½ square meters. Trying to get F 1400 for the two.

Serg-Tani gave me the B[arang].

Germann & Elder Boswell got into knock down fight yesterday. When separated, Germann had Boswell down & [was] sitting on him. Later, when Germann [was] returning from bathing, with his hands full, Boswell slugged him in [the] face, but spectators saved Boswell from retaliation. Began from Boswell cutting limb from tree, Sedo [?] warned limb would fall on our fireplaces & clothes lines, Boswell persisted. Limb fell, Germann bawled out Elder, who called Germann "Bloody Sod," & fight started.

⤙ JULY 30 MON

Busy all week black marketing but sold little. Night of Wed-Thurs Germann & I [went] to Ladang, getting big load ubi kajoe. Cost F 30 for fixing Hiho. We sold enough to pay the fix & make about F 20 extra, plus buying an old pen for 4½ kilos from Crocker. Pair tennis shoes for 5 kilos. 250 grams maize 1¼ kilos & gave some away for good will. Eric made a scale for weighing up to a kilo.

Mandang, Templlers Flores Sitanala & his brother, Eric & I went out together. First three continued to Oeloenese Kampong & we waited for them in old Ladang, where we filled three sacks, getting about 35 kilos between us. Eric then went alone to Jap ladang—sneaking into their garden within 50 feet of Jap house & in full view of anyone within because of brilliant moon, took some katchang pandjang—long beans—which made good stew [the] next day. Mandang, Temp., & Sitanala joined us about 2:15 a.m. & we all came in together at 3, just before change of watch. Hiho—I think Aki—tried to increase payoff to 20 each but Mandang refused. We then waded the creek behind hospital & came into camp. Eric & I roasted some ubi on return, then went to bed about 4:30 a.m., & so it goes.

Eric & I are getting reputations in camp as big black marketers & ubi kings. Various totally untrue & fantastic things are attributed to us. Actually, we are small fry in the black market circles. Probably our association with Mandang & [the] fact we also sell ubi & tobacco gives rise to them.

Mugs (Mandang) had better luck in trading, but made date for Friday nite to pick up load of maize for barang & furnished him—a sheet, black shorts, black cloth & old sarong—total 29 kilos. Friday night we couldn't get out in time, so at midnight Eric & I went to bed. But Mugs got out at 1:30 a.m. & returned with a small load at 5:30 a.m. I got only 10 kilos to pay my owners. Mugs has another date for Wednesday night to get balance.

I have spent last days bargaining with Hihos without success. Relations with them are distasteful & definitely not in my line. My Malay is too poor & I haven't the Oriental temperament. I enjoy going outside, but trafficking inside is pure drudgery & deceit. From now on I'll confine my efforts to outside & the Japs.

⌐ Aug 2 Thurs

Sold 2 more jars hair grease to Sone yesterday for F 70, making F 40 profit. Previous day sold Hiho pair [of] sunglasses for F 25, which Eric paid 50 cents for in Palembang.

⌐ Aug 5 Sund.

Last night devoted to oebi gathering & black marketing. Party comprising Mandang, Tempelers, Flores Sitanala, Haggeman, Germann, Johnny Close & me left camp with fixed Hiho between 8 & 9 p.m. In Ladang Close & I remained to pick oebi while others continued to Oeloenese Talang for trading, which [was] successful. Eric carried back 2 kalings of maize (2 kerosene tins holding 13–14 kilos maize each), which enabled us [to] pay our owners. I got enough oebi—20 kilos—to pay oebi debts. Re-entered camp 5:30 a.m. Journey details:—Hiho Aki on duty behind Hill Blocks, on far side of camp from Ladang, necessitating circuitous route through rubber & across two creeks. Japs patrolling Ladang trail. We lay quiet until their lights disappeared, then crossed road & into Ladang. After others continued to Tolang, Close & I heard loud voices, speaking Malay, near us on trail thru Ladang. We lay quiet [for a] long time, thinking perhaps [they were] Hihos. Began uprooting bushes again when flashlight approached us, coming from direction Jap Ladang. Again we lay quiet for leastly 30 minutes. Was midnight before we began digging in earnest. Oebis scattered, most of the area having been picked clean & took us until 3:30 to get a load. Others met us at a banana tree rendezvous at 4:30 a.m. & we retraced out steps, heavily loaded.

Germann described [the] trail to Talang as most difficult. The way lies thru jungle & up a steep hillside, crosses 3 large streams, & cross two dry culverts on precarious logs. Previous day one Oeloener had been arrested, so others fearful. Trading done outside on a platform which collapsed under them. No food cooked for fear [of] search, although past midnight. Some prices—Kangkong 10 guilders, onions F 5 a pound, tobacco F 5 per lempeng of 40 grams.

⌐ Aug 7 Tues

Mugs to Oeloenese Talang last nite but obtained nothing. Japs had arrested 3 more men, terrorizing natives. He was leading a party of 8 men to Ladang for oebi, when just as passing through gate in barricade (left open by fixed Hiho), Jap guard commander appeared, flashed light on them. Ric & another man were already through gate & jumped into rubber, others scattered but being between the barricade & fence, were trapped. Three— Pel, Rijnders & V. D. Meulen [were] caught immediately. Germann circled camp & came in safely behind Hill blocks. Sneuwijuct came in later with another party. V. Aselt, victim of night blindness, waited until dawn, but was caught coming thru fence. Nietler also safe.

Two Hihos, Aman Musan & Djinal beat up Pel, Rijnders & Meulen. While at Jap office this morning Rijnder managed [to] tell me Japs [have] been trying [to] obtain names of others who escaped, but he refused to tell. A Hiho, Genap, told Doeve, the fixer, that captured men did tell, but so far there is no sign they did, & I think nothing more will come of it. But [it was] tough on those captured. Meulen served 50 days L. Linggau jail after being caught once before.

⤙ Aug 19 Sund.

They did "squeal"—revealing names to Japs of Germann, Bret, Sneuw- jacht & Nieteler—who were summoned to office, questioned by Seki, then released.

Wednesday night Peter de Groat & I to Ladang for oebi, Germann stayed home because of fever. We worked from midnight to 4:15 p.m. get- ting load—I 24 kilos, Peter about 30—of lovely bin oebi. I was leading & lost trail returning. Spent much exhausting time finding trail again—with time factor perilous. We had to get in between 5 & 6 a.m. with fixed Hiho. Roll call at 6. I finally found trail again. Load so big I could not lift it un- aided & every fall [was] time consuming. Suddenly, a flashlight shone in front of us on trail. "Caught!" I thought. I moved off trail, still carrying load—intending to drop it behind some bush & lie low until Japs left— with Peter, who I knew had no chance, he having banged into trap. But, thank goodness, it was not Jap but Mandang & his party enroute home from Talang. We continued—I fell twice & second time decided to dump part of load for [I was] too exhausted to carry it. But Mandang picked it up on top of his own knapsack & carried it in. Good, stout fellow! I never could have made it otherwise. It taught me a lesson: don't attempt a load you cannot lift alone & unaided.

Thursday night disastrous for oebi raiders. Christie, Bagby, & Martin caught at fence coming in, dropped loads & ran. Hiho fired, but they es- caped & got inside safely. Shortly after 5 more men coming in on a fix ran into Jap who got them all. They were badly beaten up by Hihos. Gilbrook, Attenborough, Van Geyzel, Wennings, Kenwood escaped. Gillbrook kicked in stomach & now reported very sick. All held in small room at Seki's office, sleep on concrete floor. No covering. No food for 2 days. Vink released after 29 days.

We are theorizing possible betrayal by camp member—Indo-Dutch—who quarreled with 3 British whites.

Sold pair long khaki trousers & 2 singlets to Sone for 320 guilders. He also took Bish's black silk cloth to Linggau for sale.

Today for first time fathers scheduled [to] see their children in women's camp, meeting slated for place between 2 camps.

Jap paper July 13 comments U.S. & Brit intend [to] strip Japan after war & Americans now "cruelly bloodily" attacking them.

Mugs to Talang in worst storm of season, nearly drowned in flooded stream.

Fathers returned from meeting children, with conflicting stories: children sufficiently fed & children starved. Most agreed that children there thinner than here. Women's deaths since arriving here about same rate as ours—90 thus far.

⌐ AUG 20 MOND.

Smit & Stegeman returned last night after 31 days imprisoned for being caught on main road enroute to Petanaan. They were caught on edge of road as leaving rubber. They walked into two Japs and a "Je Ho." Some small buildings near the road, site of an abandoned rubber factory, now house 50 "Je Hos," a band of conscripted men, similar to Hihos, who do police work. Hihos are enlisted as military soldiers for two years. "Je Hos" are conscripted in Kampongs & given choice of working as coolies in Palembang or serving as "Je Ho" police. They carry spears & now are patrolling the road & this estate, including rounds of this camp.

⌐ AUG. 23 THURS

20 new Japanese military arrived last night & this morning, took over guarding camp from Hihos. Seki & his men are leaving. They returned barang to owners & paid their debts. Sone sent back the silk cloth. New arrivals evidently [a] complete surprise to Seki. This morning old guard busy packing & burning papers.

Children whose mothers [are] dead & fathers here, were brought from women's camp to here this morning to live.

Japs yesterday sent to headquarters a list of camp authorities in their order of precedence: No. 1 Oranje; 2 Bishop Mekkleholt; 3 Hammett, together with Christian names. Something certainly is in the air. 4 motored bombers have flown over camp several times recently—impossible to distinguish insignia.

— AUG 24 FRID

Camp alive with rumors—all attributed to various Japs—war is over. An official announcement of some sort scheduled for 2 p.m. roll call. Suzuki is said to have told Tussenbrook, Hartog & Kampschuur war [is] ended [in] Dutch East Indies.

Last night Japs announced phenomenal ration increase—560 grams rice, 420 grams oebi, 180 fish or meat (if available), 600 grams vegetable, 20 grams salt, 35 cc palm oil, 20 grams sugar per man per day! We cheered, but skeptically await fulfillment.

However, now—12:30 p.m.—I'm sure war is ended at least in these parts. Now to collect a chicken from Dr. Lentze, with whom I made a bet in June, we would be free—or at least war over here—by Aug. 31.

Suzuki gave Koot brand new shirt & shorts; camp commandant gave him new breeches. This morning Suzuki gave Kampschuur a raincoat, telling him war over & [he had] no further use for it.

— AUG. 25 SAT

Captain Seki yesterday 2 p.m. announced war ended in Pacific. To camp members assembled outside barbed wire fence between Block 7 & Seki's office he said through Jap interpreter speaking Malay & Camp Committeeman Vorstman translating into Dutch, peace signed [in] Manila, noon Tokyo time. American military will take over Sumatra & British soldiers might also come. Japanese troops will return home. Did not know when Allies would arrive. Recalled he [was] in charge of camp since April, '44. That he had done his best for us, although he knew it was not enough & that food [was] insufficient, but [he was] powerless to do more. Men & women permitted [to] visit respective camps beginning Saturday morning. Camp members permitted outside camp to Ladang under escorted parties, not individually. No more roll calls. No more details of peace & armistice.

Interpreter for first time since he had relations with us, addressed gathering as "Orang kepala Tuan-Tuan dan anak-anak," using the polite formal instead of the familiar & rude "Kamoe orang."

Partly because we had been expecting the announcement & partly because it seemed unreal & distant from us, men took it quietly, calmly—little emotion displayed. Faces surrounding Seki mostly expressionless. No Jap guards in evidence, except routine fence patrol. A Jap Major stood behind & to side of Seki. Interpreter (with face swollen from extracted tooth) beside him & Medical Sergeant Tani in background. Seki was every inch a soldier. Took courage to do that, & to chance unpleasant, for him, demonstration. But he was master of the situation. Finishing, he saluted, we bowed, & he retired, leaving us to an orgy of handshaking, congratulations, & general misty-eyedness. Some hospital patients danced in the ward—others lay & sang, others lay & cried. British Andrew Carruthers, swollen & dying of beri-beri, with tears streaming down his face, said he was crying from happiness & pain. Elder Boswell, who fought with Germann, came, offered his hand. They called it "even & quits." I won a bet of a chicken with Dr. Lentze, but so far haven't collected.

Neither Germann nor I felt any particular sense of exhilaration—that probably will not come until we see Allied troops—American, we hope. We know no details of capitulation, nor how far Allies reached. Rumored that Singapore fell after bitterest fighting. Far East & Java occupied from Batavia to middle Java.

Few men slept last night. Germann & I not until 1 or 2 a.m. & when I arose at 5 a.m. so many people [were] up & around fires it looked as though they had not gone to bed at all.

Camp program included High Mass 6:15 a.m.; breakfast; Dutch Protestant & English church services; camp assembly with speeches by Resident Oranje & Brit. Rep. Hammett. Hammett briefly reviewed events past 4 years & told listeners although peace signed now, the war [was] really won in 1940 by [a] handful of RAF boys in Battle of Britain. (How I hope *American* troops occupy Sumatra & arrive here.)

About 11 a.m. women came here. Except for [a] few Javanese women in Petanaan they are first I've seen since Sept. '42. Camp immediately served them coffee.

My own particular curse right now is that I'm wearing rags because of mild case of itch which doctor says might be scabies. So I must keep out of sight as much as possible.

Jap sentinels allowing anyone who asks to leave camp for Ladang, but Camp Committee says private parties [are] not allowed & anything brought back must be turned over to hospital or kitchen. Breet came in with papayas & pisang & V. Asbeck took his load. Germann is still out. Starken, fishing at creek, is posted to warn him against bringing in load.

Mandang & Tempelers have gone to Petanaan to arrange for collection (in ducks & chickens) of what's owed us.

‒ AUG. 29 WED

Busy days. Despite Camp Committee, men visit Oeloenese & Javanese Ladangs in search of chicken, fish, fruit. Germann & I have been to former black market haunts. Interesting—& instructive—to travel freely & easily over trails [on which] we used to inch our way apprehensively at night. At Oeloenese place we traded in old sheet & 1 kilo of salt for 2 big chickens, 30 fish, & 2½ kilos peanuts. At Radi's house in Petanohan Baroe, traded 2 singlets & 2 toetoep jackets & 300 grams salt for 6 chickens. Seven Javanese, including Mangoen, the Ladang head, & Loebroto, a Catechist, had returned 3 days previously from Loeboek Linggau jail & beatings by Jap Kempai (military police) after their arrest for trading with us. They were all happy at war's end & greeted us with smiles. Mangoen too sick, however, to talk business. They fed us a meal of rice, vegetable, & chicken—but small portions because so many of us. The trail behind women's camp we formerly used we found cleared of fallen trees & all bridges repaired—presumably to facilitate patrolling the estate in order to stop us black marketing.

I also visited women's camp, which appalled me. But more of that later after I can thoroughly inspect it & talk with various women.

Mrs. G. B. Hinch, an American by birth (Milwaukee) but married to a Britisher, Headmaster of Anglo-Chinese School Singapore, is leader of British in women's camp. She is a thoroughbred, patrician, dynamic, & from what we heard, took nothing from Japs, but rather kept them on defensive. Once, for demanding certain concessions, Japs locked her up for 3 hours.

‒ AUG. 31 FRID

Day opened with Oranje raising Dutch flag, speeching patriotically that flag now flying over all [the] world, & singing national anthem. Mother Laurentia, leader [of] Dutch women, & Mrs. Hinch, paid official visit [to] Oranje. Various natives also came to meet Civil Service men. Natives are coming to camp to trade. Yesterday Germann & I had Mrs. Hinch & her assistant Mrs. McCallum to dinner.

― SEPT. 2 SUNDAY

Busy nearly every day going somewhere to trade. Yesterday to Petana-han where got 4 big chickens & 1 small [one] for Bishop's red Palembang cloth & a towel, plus 8 [?] chickens for balance of our barang—an old torn sheet, [ ] hat, threadbare trousers, bandages, various small jars & bottles ointments & 2 tubes quinine. Radi took me to Oeloenese Kanpong but trading poor—three coconuts for few jars ointment.

Last night Dr. Lentze left for Palembang, accompanied by Bavink, a kitchen man. Whether for camp or treatment for his cancer I don't yet know.

Brought Radi, his wife, & malaria-ridden 10 month baby to camp for doctor to examine. We traveled through heavy downpour. Kampschuur examined child, said chronic malaria & gave pills. Brought them thru gate, passing Jap guard who remonstrated feebly. After inside I shouted they [are] going to [the] doctor & he said nothing more.

Japs have given us soap, cigarettes, pair socks each, 1 tin butter each, 2 cookies.

So much food in camp now I can't eat full regular meals. Stomachs unused to such quantities—really less than normally eat but still too much suddenly. So camp members plagued with stomach troubles. Eric & I have had our share [the] past few days.

Japs informed Oranje & Hammett that Allied Command in Macassar had instructed all internees [in] Sumatra [to be] concentrated [in] three places—north at Medau, central Pekau Broe, south, Palembang. Oranje & Hammett refused [to] allow this camp [to be] moved until 1st receiving direct order from Allied Command, 2nd, inspecting facilities to receive us at Palembang. Later, Jap doctor who [was] evidently in charge [of] these two camps said he quite understood our refusal [to] move without assurance [of] proper medical facilities, in view [of] our past experiences. He also allegedly said conditions here [were] bad. Japs have flooded us with medicines now—all from Jap army stores. The butter & milk for sick is Australian & American repectively, either from Red Cross stocks Japs kept back or old stocks obtained when N.E.I. [was] captured.

6,000 guilders from *Vatican* received for our two camps.

⁓ Sept. 4 Tues.

Sunday afternoon I walked alone to Petanahan to collect 5 chickens which had not been delivered to me as promised Sunday morning. Barto & Rasi greeted me warmly, invited me to stay the night & promised [a] good meal, probably a combination of bad conscience & natural hospitality. Their excuse for not delivering was that the big chicken escaped. Had excellent meal—biggest yet from natives. 1st two dishes—a gappleck, dry spongy pudding with shredded coconut; then stewed chicken & rice. It was a big meal, coming on top of camp dinner with chicken. My second chicken of day & after the long, fast walk—made Petanahan in one hour flat—I feared consequences. (24 hours later—now—they come) After eating I was taken to Mangoen's house by Chokas, who stopped en route at his own house & asked me to examine his baby, which I did & decided it has worms. (Whenever I visit Penahan people crowd around asking for medicine or wanting me [to] examine sick persons.) Saturday on returning from Pet. brought Radi, his wife & chronic malarial 10 months child to camp for doctor to examine. Kampschuur gave Radi quinine for infants. Jap guards at gate objected (feebly) to Radi entering camp—but we didn't stop to talk & shouted child was sick & must get to doctor. We had come back through pouring rain, soaked to [the] skin. Mrs. Radi a busy, betelnut chewing woman, was seized with malarial chill & left for return journey shivering & shaking.

But resuming at Petanahan, at Mangoen's house were a dozen Javanese gambling with Chinese cards, & a dozen more squatting about talking. Among gamblers was Soebrota, who engaged me in political discussion. He was in deadly earnestness & others listened carefully to our words. Soebota wanted to know if now Indonesians were equal with Dutch, Americans & British; also, if Indonesians would be permitted to enter universities. Before war Indonesians were not allowed to enter higher schools, he said. He said that if Indonesians were treated after war [the] same as before, "there will be trouble."

He probably reflects [the] thoughts of [an] educated Indonesian nationalist. I have not yet been able to decide in my own mind whether the average illiterate farmer or Kampong dweller cares about anything which does not directly affect his living.

I stayed at Mangoen's until 11 p.m. eating oebi kajoe chips, bananas, & drinking coffee. Mangoen is Petanahan chief & also police head, but he runs the gambling concession.

Everyone wanted "soerats," or certificates of character, which they can show later when applying for work. They especially want soerats from me, an American. Rasi took me back in the rain, by torchlite. We slept, coverless in our wet clothing, on shelf-like place under eves of Barti's house. I was very cold but managed to get a little sleep. Rained all night. At daybreak we breakfasted on boiled oebi manis (sweet potato) in the jacket—which apparently is their normal breakfast. Javanese are light eaters, at least at their established 2 meals a day. They may be all day nibblers, however.

Barto accompanied me to camp. He used to work on this estate. As soon as he saw the tins of butter here he wanted one.

Japs have distributed boots, wash basins, tinned meat, sugar, tobacco (mildewed & useless), butter, cloth (also lipstick & silk stockings to women), soap, cigarettes, blanket material. All the stuff looks like having been stored in godowns for years. They could have and should have given it to us long ago. Now they evidently are trying to put on a good show of generosity for benefit of incoming Allies.

Also received [in] camp—3 metal cylinders dropped from Allied plane containing matches, soap, towels & cigarettes (not yet distributed).

Whole camp is plagued with stomach disorders [as a] result [of] excessive food.

Bishop gave Eric & me each [a] pair of shoes.

⟶ Sept. 6 Thurs.

3 Dutch & 1 Chinese paratroop cadets arrived here after being dropped over Benkoelen this morning. Said 4 men dropped also [over] Palembang, Padang & Medan, with radio sets to report condition [of] all internees. Said possibly 2 months before we [will be] able [to] leave here. Whole world in chaos. They treated Japs in very offhand manner, hope their manners don't complicate things with Japs, who [are] now most courteous & unobstructive. Seems all Sumatra occupied by about 20 Dutch paratroops from Colombo.

Hotel Smit left for Palembang 3 days ago after a Madurese told him American ships [were] there, which paratroops prove false.

Paratroops are members [of] "Korps Insolinde." Their names: Regimental Sergeant Major Hakkenberg, commander; Corps Officer Wilhelm; Sergeant van Hasselt; Chinese Officer Suet. All are members [of the] Royal Netherlands East Indies Army. Hasselt estimated 150,000 to 200,000 Jap troops Sumatra & same number war prisoners & internees. Added, "They say three things won the war: 1, Douglas twin engined planes, 2, the Jeep, and 3, medicine which powerful antiseptic (Penninsulfide?)." Several paratroops visited Sumatra secretly during war on espionage work, Hakkenberg 5 times. Submarines brought them. Sumatra & Malaya under SEAC—South East Asia Command, Lord Mountbatten in Colombo. Java, Borneo, Celebes, etc. Southwest Pacific Command under MacArthur.

— SEPT. 10 MOND.

Officially announced Dr. Peter Tekelemberg died—when, where, or how, unknown. He was among those sentenced 10 years. Sent to Bangka with similarly imprisoned Ambonese. This news a blow to entire camp. We knew him as one [of the] best doctors [of] our lives, sterling character. He helped us immeasurably in Charitas Hospital.

Saturday Eric & I [went] to Petanahan, where we gave presents to Barto, Rasi, Mrs. Radi—whose child died—& few others. Barto gave us chicken & rice lunch. Sat. was Moslem New Year "Tahoen Baroe" so all natives had open house. We had various cakes & sweets at several other places, then walked 12 kilometers to Loeboek Linggau, arriving after dark. At home of Mok A Oen, a Chinese mechanic, we met Mandang & Tempelers & Koolymans-Bynen, had [an] excellent meal, drank [a] bottle [of] cheap brandy which cost 60 guilders & spent [the] night. Sunday morning Eric & I [went] to [the] house of Controleur de Mey, where [we] breakfasted with paratroopers & Bemkolen civil servants who [had been] released from jail to which [they were] sentenced 10 years. Benkoelen resident was beheaded. They said native friends supplied them secretly with food. Otherwise [they] might [have] died [of] starvation. Also said Kempei had planned another drive on both European internees & cetain natives outside for this "poeasa" period. Kempei Tandjong Karong "proceeded with arrests despite end of war, but [in] other places dropped plans" [for] Kempei drives during war staged during "peoasa" or fast period preceding Tahoen Baroe. 1st poeasa against Dutch civil servants & Ambonese, 2nd against Chinese, 3rd (present) scheduled more Dutch.

Oen's wife prepared excellent Chinese midday meal for us, but I felt sick & ate nothing. Later returned [to] Controleur's houses, procured ride back to camp.

This morning I entered hospital—my own request—for "rest sure" & soft food diet.

⟶ Sept. 11 Tuesday

British Marine Major Jacobs inspected British portion camp & sick. Seemed [to] pay little or no attention [to] Dutch. Said he [was] going elsewhere but leaving party of four in Loeboek Linggau. Said [there are] 10 camps, civilian & military, in Sumatra. This one [is in the] most favorable condition [of] them all. Grimmest [is] a military camp where prisoners [were] building new Jap railway.

Jacobs had not heard of Dr. West at any camps wherefore we fear for him unless he was transferred from Sumatra. I've feeling Kempei might have gotten him for some obscure reason, although he [was the] last man in camp who could be suspected [of] anything anti-Jap.

Bruitenhaus says native chief, a Pasira, released [from] Palembang jail reported Dr. Ziesel & Lublin Weddig [were] beheaded Nov. 9, 1943 same date 9 other civil servants similarly executed. Pasira said entire native population shabbily treated by Japs, any suspected of prewar Dutch friendliness imprisoned, tortured, many killed. Indeed an incomprehensible attitude toward population with whom Jap propaganda advertised friendship, equality, independence, "Sama Warna, Sama Bangsa."

Jap CINC Sumatra suicided as Jacobs landed [by] parachute [at] Medan airdrome. Jap remained [in] his home instead [of going to the] airport & when [he] saw chutists hara karied.

Pangkal Panangers recognized Jap officer wearing large Red Cross armband & accompanying Jacobs as high Kempei official. We may not get some Kempei men yet.

6,000 Brit parachutists landed Malaya & two shiploads internees sent Madras. Allied shipping here impossible [on] account [of] mines which Japs must sweep up. Large Allied planes unable [to] land [in] Sumatra [on account of] great fuel loads and unable [to] refuel here because Jap gasoline unsuitable. Jacobs inspecting Sumatra via Jap plane.

Our names will not be sent by radio, must wait until planes arrive, all radio traffic military.

⟶ Sept. 12 Wed.

Mandang said 15 men left camp yesterday for Palembang.

⟶ Sept. 13 Thursday

Two British Liberators dropped 38 packages in our camp, mostly by parachute, some sacks [of] bread or papers loose. Letter explained crews part of large air scheme designed to relieve us "shortly." These two based Cocos Islands. Parcels contained bread, papers, medicine, cigarettes, food stuffs. Some parcels still missing. We had no planned organization spot & picked packages. In fact this camp now has less planned organization than ever, Oranje is a complete, total loss as a leader. Pompous ass.

Sone & Aoki brought me 5 eggs, also brought piece [of] pink cloth for 20 packs cigarettes.

On published Cocos crewmen's letter was postscripted, "What do you think of a Labour government?"

⤳ SEPT 16 SUND.

Yesterday two Liberators dropped 38 more parcels. Last night 60 Australian women, including all nurses, left for Palembang & home.

⤳ SEPT. 17 MOND.

Sick British men, group [of] women, left last night [for] Singapore.
Palembang war prisoners 908 (Dutch 371) 270 hospital.
Panginen, near Padang, 3207 Indian prison.
Rantau Brapat, near Medan 6910 (1,000 died past 3 months)
Pakan Baroe, 4307 (possible internees)

⤳ SEPT. 20 THURSDAY

Yester night journeyed [to] Lahat where boarded Dakota (with 35 internees) for Singapore.

⤳ SEPT. 29 SAT

Moving every minute since left camp. Now aboard C-54 to Calcutta which took off 5:15 p.m. from Singapore. Yesterday flew [to] Palembang Mitchell [ ] bomber, dug up notes buried Boekit Besar camp August '43—perfectly preserved. Met Bishop Mekkelholt, Mother Alacoque, Father van Gisbergen in Charitas hospital [ ] Jap military hospital during war. Inspected Palembang Jail where Native prisoners now held, found English speaking Chinese, pitiful state, skeleton-like from starvation & dysentery. Begged me to help him, tears streamed down face [as he] described his plight (refer notes). Correspondents aerial touring Far East fixed up trip so I could recover notes. Among correspondents were AP Vern Hoagland, American Broadcasting Fred B. Oper of Shanghai days, INS Clark Lee, former AP Tokyo & Shanghai, Allen Darius, former UP London to whom I dictated Bandoeng stories, *NY Herald* Homer Biggart, *Time* & *Life* Wm Howland, UP Jim McGlincy. Col. C. A. Coltharp, 27, Newport, Arkansas, Operations Chief 5th Bomber Command & Lt. V. W. Pennonen, Rochester, Mich., W. H. Oosten & G. T. Schorel of NKPM went with me when [I] dug up notes as several bewildered Japs looked on but didn't interfere. Boekit Besar camp after we left became women's camp, then Jap truck depot. It's now shambles & old hospital under floor where [I] buried notes 27-30-33 feet from corner has only roof on it. In Hotel Buys, Palembang, found Oosten, V. Hilton, Tussenbroek, De Bruyn, James Schoorel, also some Dutch & British officials, few enlisted men. While I dug up notes, other correspondents & Lt. Edward E. Muhs, USNR, who will be stationed in Palembang, looked after oil interests.

In Singapore I stayed 1st night in Public Relations Office quarters, where someone stole my 1st aid kit bag containing notes, passport, etc. Bag found later in ashcan, but belt with passport & notes missing. [This mysterious theft is not easily explained, because McDougall either recovered his passport or had another one made, and he also recovered the notes, transcriptions of which constitute this book. Perhaps he neglected to record the restoration of the documents, or perhaps the notes in question were something other than his diaries.]

Then into office walked four U.S. officers—Major S. C. Munroe, San Francisco, Col. K. K. Kennedy, Oaksdale, Wash, Capt. R. M. Williams, Indianopolis, Ind, Capt. Gunnar Larson (Press Censor), Dorcester, Mass. They took me to their mess, which was also the headquarters [of] Brig. Gen. Robin Pape, Liaison Officer U.S. forces Singapore, where I stayed until I left for Calcutta.

⌐ Sept. 30 Sund.

Arrived Barak Poge airdrome about 2 a.m., ate & slept [in] tent billet, then to PRO office Hindustan Bldg. where met UP Ernest Dharma, a Senegalese & damn fine fellow, Lt. Jack Slone of PRO & former United Presser who took us to his room (61) in Great Eastern Hotel, where also met Don Huth, P.P. & Charlotte Ebener, INS & later Frank Yao, formerly China Central News Agency & now OWI. Monday night Jack & Charlotte took me to Brit-Am. Club for my first dancing since 1941. Dancing is like riding a bicycle, you never forget, although you might get rusty.

⸺ Oct. 5 Friday

Wednesday admitted [to] 142nd base hospital for medical clearance, where am now getting thorough physical exams including X-rays of chest & spine, cholera & smallpox shots, etc.

Last night saw first movie: Hedy Lamarr & Robert Walker in *Princess & the Bellboy.*

[List of names of people in Singapore]

⸺ Oct. 7 Sunday

Yesterday gave Bishop Mekkleholt's telegram to Father John F. O'Reilly, M.S. Mission La Salette.

⸺ Oct. 11 Thursday

Today discharged from 142nd base hospital & 2nd Convalescent Camp. Wrote letters for Msgr. Mekkelholt to Father Gouaart, Viale Mazzini 32, Rome, & Missieprocure, Walenbergerweg, Rotterdam. Mailed 5 large envelopes to Jean, containing buried notes.

⸺ Oct 14 Sunday

Aboard C-54E enroute China, Japan, and home. One of the luckiest breaks yet is getting me home. Left 142nd base hospital Wednesday, returned [to] Great Eastern Hotel Room 61 with Capt. Kiesle of Pro & Don Huth of AP. Despite messages to UP for money, nothing materialized except New York saying War Dept. called Randy asking I be accredited in order to get Army plane transportation home.

During Calcutta stay I did no sightseeing & only most essential shopping, visiting Neumarket where I bought canvas handbag. Dined twice Karnanie Estates & Brit-Am. Club (run by Cranwell? of Fatty Arbuckle case). Karnanie (check spelling) is a large residence apartment converted to officers mess. Two dining rooms & two bars—one each, of which requires Bush Jacket or Officers blouse & formal gowns for women. Met Major McIver, Press Censor, Southerner, pleasant, likeable.

[More names of people met.]

Huth & I met Lt. Col. Benjamin C. Bowker, Public Relations Officer who introduced us to [Assistant Secretary of War John J.] McCloy, who allowed us to interrupt his dinner for chat & insisted I stay & tell of internment camp. Later Bowker, Huth, Kiesle & I to Brit Am Club for dinner where Bowker suggested [the] possibility [of] my returning with McCloy's party to States.

Saturday McCloy issued me invitational travel orders & this morning took off about 9:30.

[Touring war sites with McCloy's party made McDougall's homeward journey slow and circuitous, but fascinating to the journalist who had missed out on covering one of the greatest stories of the twentieth century. Their itinerary included prolonged stops in Shanghai, Peking, and Tokyo before flying to Iwo Jima, Hawaii, and San Francisco.]

— Nov 1 Thurs.

Slept till noon in bunk [on airplane] but awakened just in time to sight the U.S.A. Its rugged coastline came out of the mist & reached for me. A tiny green patch became Golden Gate Park & the pillars of Golden Gate Bridge framed hazy section of S.F. Bay, the Oakland Span & dark mountains. Then the Golden Gate span materialized & we dropped lower, passed over city, Telegraph Hill, Market & out to Mills Field where Gen. ———————— & string of Command Cars waited. State Dept. men boarded plane & took up our passports (mine No. 184 issued in Calcutta). A Marine officer informed me I'd have to check in at Marine Hospital.

Then Paul Carrico came aboard as I wrestled over luggage & said Mary was waiting. She was unchanged in any way & wearing the brown otter coat I remembered in Shanghai. Drove to Carrico home, Gertrude & three kids, Jean, Peter & Timothy—handsome, husky youngsters. "Jean & Peter have been praying for Uncle Bill." Visited Bill Flynn, his wife & mother & dad who were in S.F. Then to Press Club & saw UP Bureau Chief Ron Wagener. Spent nite at Carrico's. (AP Carroll Cross & photographer interviewed me at airport.)

— Nov. 2 Friday

Germann's mother & sister-in-law & Fr. Dick Meagher visited me. Cashed Travelers draft & gave $250 to Paul for Mrs. Breese, to pay for coats. Talked it out with Mary, whose attitude is splendid. Paul & Mary accompanied me to hotel where I left them & drove to Mills Field with McCloy. Took off at dusk for N.Y. Up to 13,000 ft. for trip across mountains, over Salt Lake & Cheyenne.

— EPILOGUE —

During his desperate hours drifting in the ocean after the sinking of the *Poelau Bras*, McDougall's Catholic faith came to the fore as he prayed for rescue. It was during that time that he resolved vaguely to "do something for Christ" if he were rescued. Just what that would be became the topic of a quest that lasted during his incarceration and for some time afterward. As the diaries show, he attended daily Mass as long as it was available, and he struggled with inconsistent success to maintain vows he had made to give up smoking and drinking. And he engaged in frequent novenas—nine-day cycles of systematic prayer for a specific purpose—and other devotional exercises. All of that marked a significant change from the more routine Catholic observance of the ambitious young reporter of the prewar years.

After liberation, McDougall worked as Washington, D.C., bureau chief for United Press. In 1946 he was accepted as a Nieman Fellow in Journalism at Harvard University. It is one of the most prestigious awards available to journalists, allowing them to read and study independently or in classes for an entire year with no obligations or restrictions beyond an agreement to return to their journalistic post for at least a year following the fellowship. Although McDougall had been at least informally engaged to Mary Bell, an American woman he had met in Shanghai before his capture, while at Harvard he began to pursue a vocation to the priesthood which he apparently felt as far back as his POW years. He entered seminary at Catholic University of America in 1948, graduating in the same class as the later Joseph Cardinal Bernardin of Chicago. It was during those seminary years that McDougall published his two books, *Six Bells Off Java* (1948) and *By Eastern Windows* (1949).

Ordained in 1952 at Salt Lake City's Cathedral of the Madeleine by Bishop Duane G. Hunt, McDougall became assistant pastor and eventually rector of the cathedral. Among his first acts as priest were to baptize his father and to conduct the funeral of his sister Gertrude, who had died of cancer. He was named Monsignor in 1963. During his years as priest he also taught at Judge Memorial Catholic High School and edited the *Inter-mountain Catholic*. Despite open heart surgery and the frail health that carried over from his prison years, McDougall was known for the tireless work ethic developed during his journalism career and for his compassionate advocacy for the disadvantaged and the unborn.

McDougall retired in 1981 to live with his sister Jean at the family home in Salt Lake City, in La Jolla, California, and eventually at St. Joseph Villa in Salt Lake City, where he died December 8, 1988, the Feast of the Immaculate Conception of Mary, to whom he had a special devotion. He was preceded in death by his parents as well as his older sister.